TRANSITIONAL JUSTICE

A distinguished group of authors critically prise open images of transitional justice, with rich insights on mediated memory, music and theatre. Some brilliant re-framings of rituals of transition are in store for the reader.

John Braithwaite, Australian National University, Australia

This book is about justice with a difference; justice which transcends legal procedures and is sensitive to memories, rituals and artistic expression. Beautifully written and with a deep understanding of its subject, it is not only a source of knowledge, but also of wisdom. I would warmly recommend it.

Katja Franko Aas, University of Oslo, Norway

AF695575

Advances in Criminology

Series Editor: David Nelken

Recent titles in the series

The Arts of Imprisonment
Control, Resistance and Empowerment
Edited by Leonidas K. Cheliotis

The Hidden Order of Corruption
An Institutional Approach
Donatella della Porta and Alberto Vannucci

Comparative Criminal Justice and Globalization
Edited by David Nelken

Racial Criminalization of Migrants in the 21st Century
Edited by Salvatore Palidda

Pervasive Prevention
A Feminist Reading of the Rise of the Security Society
Tamar Pitch

Children's Rights and the Minimum Age of Criminal Responsibility
A Global Perspective
Don Cipriani

Hate on the Net
Extremist Sites, Neo-fascism On-line, Electronic Jihad
Antonio Roversi

Decisions to Imprison:
Court Decision-Making Inside and Outside the Law
Rasmus H. Wandall

The Policing of Transnational Protest
Edited by Donatella della Porta, Abby Peterson and Herbert Reiter

Migration, Culture Conflict, Crime and Terrorism
Edited by Joshua D. Freilich and Rob T. Guerette

Re-Thinking the Political Economy of Punishment:
Perspectives on Post-Fordism and Penal Politics
Alessandro De Giorgi

The full list of series titles can be found at the back of the book.

Transitional Justice
Images and Memories

Edited by

CHRISJE BRANTS
ANTOINE HOL
DINA SIEGEL
Utrecht University, The Netherlands

Routledge
Taylor & Francis Group
LONDON AND NEW YORK

First published 2013 by Ashgate Publishing

2 Park Square, Milton Park, Abingdon, Oxon OX14 4RN
711 Third Avenue, New York, NY 10017, USA

Routledge is an imprint of the Taylor & Francis Group, an informa business

First issued in paperback 2016

Copyright © 2013 Chrisje Brants, Antoine Hol, Dina Siegel and the contributors

Chrisje Brants, Antoine Hol and Dina Siegel have asserted their right under the Copyright, Designs and Patents Act, 1988, to be identified as the editors of this work.

All rights reserved. No part of this book may be reprinted or reproduced or utilised in any form or by any electronic, mechanical, or other means, now known or hereafter invented, including photocopying and recording, or in any information storage or retrieval system, without permission in writing from the publishers.

Notice:
Product or corporate names may be trademarks or registered trademarks, and are used only for identification and explanation without intent to infringe.

British Library Cataloguing in Publication Data
Transitional justice : images and memories. – (Advances in criminology)
1. Transitional justice. 2. Transitional justice in art.
I. Series II. Brants, C. H. (Chrisje H.) III. Hol, A. M.
IV. Siegel, Dina.
340.1'15–dc23

The Library of Congress has cataloged the printed edition as follows:
Transitional justice : images and memories / by Chrisje Brants, Ton Hol and Dina Siegel.
pages cm.—(Advances in criminology)
Includes bibliographical references and index.
ISBN 978-1-4094-3885-4 (hardback)
1. Transitional justice. 2. Reparations for historical injustices I. Brants, C. H. (Chrisje H.) II.Hol, A. M. III. Siegel, Dina.

K5250.T733 2013
340'.115—dc23

2012047609

ISBN 978-1-4094-3885-4 (hbk)
ISBN 978-1-138-25696-5 (pbk)

Contents

List of Tables

Notes on Contributors

Chrisje Brants is Professor of Criminal Law and Criminal Process at the Willem Pompe Institute for Criminal Law and Criminology, University of Utrecht. She is a member of the Académie Internationale de Droit Comparé and the Association for International Criminal Justice. Her main interests, on which she has published widely and in which she combines a multidisciplinary background in law and criminology, are international criminal justice, comparative studies on different aspects of criminal procedure, and crime, criminal justice and the media. She is also an amateur First World War historian. Her most recent book is *Issues of Convergence: Inquisitorial Prosecution in England and Wales?* (Wolf Legal, 2011).

Kees Brants is Honorary Professor at the University of Amsterdam's School of Communication Research and Emeritus Professor of Political Communication at Leiden University. He specializes in journalism studies, media and politics, published in 2011 *Political Communication in Postmodern Democracy: Challenging the Primacy of Politics* (Palgrave Macmillan, edited with Katrin Voltmer).

Lodewijk Brunt is Emeritus Professor of Urban Studies at the University of Amsterdam. From the early 1990s onwards he conducted anthropological field research in India, mainly in Bombay. Apart from writing books and articles for scholarly journals he has been involved in the making of documentary films (for example *Blessed by the Plague*, 1999) and translating poems, songs and short stories from Hindi into Dutch (*Ik zag de stad*; *Mijn lippen vroegen om een lied*; 'Laghukatha', *De Gids*, 1 (2012), in collaboration with Dick Plukker).

Danielle Celermajer is an Associate Professor in Sociology and Social Policy at the University of Sydney and Director of the Faculty's Human Rights Program. She was awarded and is the director of two European Union funded programmes, one developing postgraduate education for rights advocates across the Asia Pacific region and the other exploring more effective approaches to torture prevention, focusing on the military and police in Sri Lanka and Nepal. Her book *Sins of the Nation and the Ritual of Apology* (Cambridge University Press, 2009) forms part of her longstanding interest in how societies can be turned from patterns of violation to forms of politics and sociality that respect human rights.

Gülhan Demirci studied political science at the University of Leiden. She obtained a master's degree with a thesis on the role of the Battle of Gallipoli during the First World War, its significance in the formation of Turkish identity and the nation state, and its memoralization in monuments and history books. She is currently a researcher and journalist with a Dutch broadcasting company.

Lauren Gould is a PhD and Lecturer at the Centre for Conflict Studies, Utrecht University. Her research focuses on how identity boundaries are drawn and become increasingly antagonistic due to violent conflict and how this impacts day-to-day relationships and policies in the aftermath of civil war. Her research takes a grounded theory approach to understanding how transitional justice instruments are assumed to address these boundaries towards facilitating reconciliation and how this is evolving in practice in the case of Uganda. Here, she critically analyses the nexus between local, national and international actions aimed at the (re)negotiation of (collective) identities and changing discourses.

John Hagan is John D. MacArthur Professor of Sociology and Law at Northwestern University and Co-Director of the Center on Law & Globalization at the American Bar Foundation in Chicago. He received the Stockholm Prize in Criminology in 2009 and was elected in 2010 to the American Academy of Arts and Sciences. Hagan is the Editor of the *Annual Review of Law & Social Science*. His research with a network of scholars spans topics from war crimes and human rights to the legal profession. He is the co-author with Wenona Rymond-Richmond of *Darfur and the Crime of Genocide* (Cambridge University Press 2009), which received the American Sociological Association Crime, Law and Deviance Section's Albert J. Reiss Distinguished Publication Award and the American Society of Criminology's Michael J. Hindelang Book Award. He is the co-author with Sanja Kutnjak Ivkvoić of *Reclaiming Justice* (Oxford University Press 2011).

Antoine Hol is Professor of Jurisprudence at Utrecht University, the Netherlands and director of the Montaigne Centre for Adjudication and Conflict Resolution. He also has been appointed as a Deputy Justice at the Court of Appeal of Amsterdam, and as Judge at the Court of Haarlem. His research is in the field of the theory of adjudication and conflict resolution in adjudication in modern democracies. Related to the topic of his chapter in this volume is 'Adjudication and the Public Realm: An Analysis Based on the Work of Hannah Arendt', *Utrecht Law Review*, 1(2) (2005), 40-45; available at http://www.utrechtlawreview.org/index.php/ulr/article/viewFile/7/7.

Susanne Karstedt is a Professor of Criminology and Criminal Justice at the University of Leeds, UK, and Adjunct Professor at the School of Justice, Queensland University of Technology, Australia. She has widely researched and published on international and transitional criminal justice with a focus on post-war Germany. Her present research addresses prevention and intervention in mass atrocities and genocide. Her most recent publications in this field include *Legal Institutions and Collective Memories* (Hart, 2009).

Bernadette Kester PhD is Assistant Professor in the Department of Media & Communication at the Erasmus University Rotterdam. Her teaching and research activities lie in the fields of journalism studies, media and representation, and film history. Her current research examines the representation of foreign news in Dutch and European media and the position and role of foreign correspondents. She holds an MA degree in History and received her PhD from Erasmus University Rotterdam in 1998. Her dissertation concerned the representation of the First World War in German films during the Weimar period. From 2000 to 2004, she worked as a research fellow for the Dutch Royal Institute for Military History. Kester is a former board member of the Dutch Association for Audiovisual History (GBG) and she presently serves as chair of the editorial board of a Dutch journal on Media History.

Katrien Klep (LLM and MA Arts) is a PhD student and junior lecturer at the Cultural Anthropology Department of Utrecht University. Her research explores the production of collective memory of the military dictatorship (1973-1990) in the public space of Santiago de Chile through the analysis of transitional justice mechanisms and commemoration practices. She is involved in research on truth- and history-telling in international criminal justice and transitional justice in the project 'Imageries of Transitional Justice' at the Faculty of Law (UU). She has contributed an article on 'Transitional Justice: History Telling, Collective Memory and the Victim-Witness' (with Chrisje Brants) to the forthcoming *International Journal of Violence and Conflict*, Special Issue on 'Transitions from Violence: The Impact of Transitional Justice'.

Sanja Kutnjak Ivković is Professor at the School of Criminal Justice, Michigan State University. She holds a doctorate in criminology (PhD, University of Delaware) and a doctorate in law (SJD, Harvard University). Her research focuses on comparative and international criminology, criminal justice and law. Professor Kutnjak Ivković's most recent book, co-authored with John Hagan, is *Reclaiming Justice: The International Tribunal for the Former Yugoslavia and Local Courts* (Oxford University Press, 2011). She is also the author of *The Fallen Blue Knights: Controlling Police Corruption* (Oxford University Press, 2005) and *Lay Participation in Criminal Trials* (Austin & Winfield, 1999), co-author with Carl Klockars and Maria R. Haberfeld of *Enhancing Police Integrity* (Springer, 2006) and co-editor with Carl Klockars and Maria Haberfeld of *Contours of Police integrity* (Sage, 2004), which received the American Society of Criminology International Division Honorable Mention. Professor Kutnjak Ivković's work has appeared in leading academic and law journals, such as the *Law and Society Review*, *Journal of Criminal Law and Criminology*, *Criminology and Public Policy*, *Law and Policy*, *Stanford Journal of International Law*, *Cornell International Law*

Journal, *Policing and Society* and *Policing: An International Journal of Police Strategies and Management*.

Ton Liefaard is UNICEF Professor of Children's Rights at Leiden University, Law School. His research focuses primarily on the interpretation and implementation of international human rights law, in particular the UN Convention on the Rights of the Child, affecting children and the law at the domestic level. He has published various academic articles and a number of books and research reports. One of his key publications is *Deprivation of Liberty of Children in Light of International Human Rights Law and Standards* (Intersentia, 2008). He teaches child law, juvenile justice and children's rights courses for bachelor and master students and professionals. He supervises a number of PhD students on various children's rights issues, including children's participation in youth courts and children in alternative care.

Srdjan Radović, M. Phil and PhD candidate in socio-cultural anthropology and research associate of the Institute of Ethnography of the Serbian Academy of Sciences and Arts (SANU), was born in 1976 in Titograd (present Podgorica), Montenegro. He graduated from the Faculty of Philosophy in Belgrade (Department of Ethnology and Anthropology) in 2002 and became M. Phil. at the same department in 2007. He is currently a final year PhD candidate in socio-cultural anthropology at the Belgrade University (Faculty of Philosophy). He has been a research fellow of the Serbian Ministry of Science since 2005, and in 2008 he became a research associate of the Institute of Ethnography of the SASA. He took part in three basic research projects of his home institution, and in three international projects pursued in collaboration with the Institute of Ethnography and partner institutes from Slovenia and Bulgaria. He has published one book, several papers, reviews and translations, and has participated in a dozen scientific conferences. He is a member of anthropological associations InASEA and EADS.

Dina Siegel PhD is a professor of Criminology at Utrecht University in the Netherlands. She received her PhD in Cultural Anthropology from the VU University, Amsterdam. She is a president of IASOC and a member of the scientific board of CIROC. She has published on the Russian mafia, human trafficking, crime in the diamond sector, the XTC industry, underground banking and the role of women in criminal organizations. Her most recent publications include *The Mazzel Ritual: Customs, Culture and Crime in the Diamond Trade* (Springer, 2009) and *Organized Crime: Culture, Markets and Politics* (with H. Nelen) (Springer, 2008).

Jay Winter, Charles J. Stille Professor of History at Yale, is a historian of twentieth-century Europe, focusing in particular on the First World War. He taught at the University of Cambridge from 1979 to 2001. He won an Emmy award as co-producer of the BBC/PBS eight-hour television series *The Great War and the*

Shaping of the Twentieth Century (1996). He is the author of *Sites of Memory, Sites of Mourning* (Cambridge University Press, 1995) and *Dreams of Peace and Freedom: Utopian Moments in the Twentieth Century* (Yale University Press, 2006). His biography of René Cassin appeared in French, published by Fayard, in 2011 and will be published by Cambridge University Press in an English version in 2013. He is editor-in-chief of the *Cambridge History of the First World War*, to be published in 2014.

Acknowledgements

The editors would like to thank Utrecht University for the financial support that made this volume possible, and the directors of the *Focus and Massa* research cooperation on human rights for their encouragement throughout the project.

Introduction

Chrisje Brants[1]

There is a park in southern Lithuania where one can literally visit the imagery of that country's unfortunate history. Grūto Parkas near Druskininkai houses the socialist-realist statuary that occupied important positions in the parks and squares of Lithuanian towns until the demise of communism in Eastern Europe. It represents twentieth-century communist heroes, men and women whose fortunes waxed and waned as one regime followed another. Persecuted for their opposition to Imperial Russia, which regarded Lithuania as a Russian province until 1917, then imprisoned by the authoritarian Lithuanian government that ruled until 1940, they briefly became ideological and political leaders after the Soviet invasion of that year, only to be hunted down by the Nazi invaders as they took to the forests in partisan units. After the war, they rose to power under Stalinist rule.

Each statue bears a name, and a little notice outlining the owner's deeds – not so much in terms of political opposition, but of atrocity and oppression. If their communist sympathies never wavered, the political and social definition of their actions as heroism has certainly changed. The 'idols' have been taken 'off the pedestal', as the park's website puts it,[2] and the change of location and status has 'substantially altered the ideological content of the monumental sculptures'. Although its aim is deadly serious: to unmask 'the naked Soviet ideology which suppressed and hurt the spirit of our nation', the park also has a zoo and an old-fashioned funfair where visitors can stick their heads through cardboard cut-outs of little girls in the communist pioneers uniform – all of which give it a bizarre Disneyland feel. Marking the transition from ideological tyranny and repression to democracy, the once great and good of Lithuania now live in a fun park as a visitor attraction. It is a very particular form of justice.

Grūto Parkas has an important symbolic function for Lithuanian society, but as a specific memorialization of (in)justice and transition, it is also symbolic of the subject of this volume: transitional justice as a theatre of imagery and memory. Transitional justice is concerned with both settling accounts after violent conflict and/or repression, and coming to terms with the traumatic damage inflicted on individuals and society; with the definition of heroes and villains, victims and perpetrators; with the delineation of the morality and immorality of past events and actions. It is inextricably bound up with history-telling and attempts to

1 With thanks to Katrien Klep for her helpful comments and suggestions.

2 http://www.grutoparkas.lt/istorija-en.htm.

develop shared collective memories, for it looks towards a viable future by making a certain specific sense of past events. Inevitably, the ideological content of those events will change and the 'idols' will fall from their pedestals, although their fate may be worse than becoming figures of fun.

This book represents the culmination of a multidisciplinary project on transitional justice in which the original focus was on principles of human rights and transparency in the context of international criminal justice. But, although the book originated in the faculty of law at Utrecht University and despite the connotation of the word 'justice', as Grūto Parkas so eloquently demonstrates, transitional justice is not only a matter for the law.

International criminal justice is the international community's reaction to mass atrocity and for the time being its development during the twentieth century has culminated in the International Criminal Court (ICC) established at The Hague. Yet, dealing with atrocity within the (narrow) limits of legal discourse implies a reduction of the human experience that can never fully address the multitude and complexity of issues involved in justice – the very meaning and significance of which depend on the historical, social and political conditions in which it functions. Likewise, 'transparency', generally regarded as a pre-condition of legitimate justice, is not an unambiguous concept, a quality that attaches to justice automatically if certain (legal) conditions are met. Rather, what people see of and in justice depends to a large extent on perceptions and images of what it can achieve and thus contribute to healing in the aftermath of conflict. At the same time, its legitimacy in the community concerned depends on perceptions of the conflict itself and the way it is remembered.

On justice

Despite the multifaceted nature of 'justice', 'international criminal justice' has become practically synonymous with the ICC. Consequently the topic has been more or less hijacked by specialized legal scholars, to the detriment of other disciplines equally well equipped to study its many aspects and variations. The ICC, however, is only one of the manifestations, albeit the most recent, of international criminal justice, and in its turn international criminal justice is only one of the many different ways in which individuals and societies struggle to come to terms with gross violations of human rights committed in the course of armed conflict and political repression.

Murder, rape, deportation, persecution, collaboration, resistance or simply turning a blind eye – all are phenomena as old and inevitable as conflict itself. Equally inevitable is the reckoning afterwards that has many guises: from lynch mob to truth or reconciliation commission and national or international trial. These, however, are the exceptions. Even discounting lynching and other forms of spontaneous 'justice', such procedures are not the end of the process of dealing with the past, despite their claims to legitimately establishing the truth about who did what to whom and why. They bring truth and justice in the narrow procedural sense. As such they may be part of coming to terms with a history of atrocity, and they represent particular forms of transitional justice. Their ultimate aim is the transition from a society divided by the chaos, illegality and injustices of the past to one in which democracy and the rule of law are the leading and binding principles of stability.

Employing the term 'transition' in this sense, however, implies a 'before' and an 'after' which one could perhaps argue do not exist or, in any event, may not necessarily be felt or lived as such. Procedures of transitional justice mark a particular point in time and establish a particular socially, politically, culturally and legally determined version of events, in a particular prescribed manner. Their results are not necessarily perceived as either just or true by those who lived through the traumatic past: the winners and losers, perpetrators and victims and the great majority of bystanders. How they remember and continue together in future, and whether they can accept specific forms of procedural justice as legitimate, depends on their memories, experiences, perceptions and expectations – of the past, and of the procedural settling of accounts. For that very reason, international criminal justice has been criticized for its inability to do justice to the past in the wider meaning of enabling a society to make sense of what has happened and to impute a shared significance to past events that recognizes the reality of individual and collective suffering and makes a shared future possible.

That is particularly true of the ICC, whose remit is both universally neutral and highly political, and whose legal discourse is embedded in western legal culture while the countries in which it actively intervenes are almost all in Africa. At the same time, we cannot discount the discursive power of law and its highly publicized procedures to change and perhaps universalize perceptions of what is morally (un) acceptable, even in the extraordinary conditions of armed conflict. International humanitarian and criminal law provide some particularly salient examples of once acceptable actions to which global opprobrium now attaches (which is not to say, of course, that slavery or rape by conquering armies, for example, no longer occur). The quarrel is probably not so much with the substantive norms of international criminal law as with the universal pretensions ascribed to its procedures.

It is certainly true that dealing with atrocity within the limits of (international) criminal law by definition reduces the human experience to what is legally relevant to the primary aim of a criminal procedure: determining the guilt of those who happen to be standing trial. Although determining guilt involves 'truth-finding', only a specific, truncated truth emerges from a criminal trial. The other major aims of prosecution and conviction by a criminal court are establishing and recognizing the wrongs suffered by victims, and providing, through punishment, just and proportional retribution. But, nothing can ever be proportional to an event such as genocide. And, if we want to know the 'truth' about Auschwitz, we would do better to read Primo Levi than a transcript from the trial of a single camp guard.

Although truth commissions probably leave more room for national culture and victims' concerns, they too function within a specific political and legal remit that determines how and to what extent they establish which truth. All transitional justice in the narrow, procedural sense leaves unaddressed a multitude of the complex issues that surround the transition from chaos and hopelessly divided society to stability, from conflict to peace. Justice is much more than legally established procedure: it is a process, involving different imageries and histories, and many different rituals, ways of remembering and of coming to terms. The process of transitional justice is more than official truth-finding, more than 'bringing to justice' although these may be part of it. It is also about 'doing justice to', and about perceptions of what is just. Too much law, it has been said, skews the truth and brings too little justice.

But what is justice in the context of conflict and atrocity; and for whom? The answer that justice is for the victims or the victims' families is reflected in the heightened awareness of the needs of victims – a paradigm shift even – in (international) criminal procedure and in debates on the presumed greater suitability of forms of transitional justice like truth commissions to meet such needs (whatever they may be, a debated question in itself). That, however, would imply that justice is somehow impaired if the victim is not around to receive it, even that where no victims are left, no survivors (as in genocide), there can be no justice.

A wider perspective acknowledges that the many forms that justice takes reveal different though interrelated functions for different people and for different societies. The ICC statute speaks in the Preamble of 'ending impunity', although in the limited meaning of bringing perpetrators to trial: not allowing them to 'escape justice' by avoiding deserved punishment. A broader approach might say that, by their very nature, first the crimes and then the impunity harm and degrade not only the victims but all of the individuals, groups and societies concerned. That includes not only perpetrators, bystanders and those who resisted in the society where the crimes took place, but also the wider international community. Impunity implies not only that perpetrators have avoided punishment for their crimes, but that the shared responsibility of recognizing and rectifying the harm they caused has also been avoided at a national and international level.

Justice, then, is about recognizing the broad scope of the harm and degradation, the need for rectification and the different ways in which that need may find expression. Although ending impunity forms the justification of the specific type of international criminal justice dispensed by the ICC, justice is not necessarily a top-down endeavour instituted by nation states or the community of states, but a gradual and ever-shifting process of definition and counter-definition, image and counter-image, history and counter-history. During that process, and at the local level, people attempt to come to terms with their past in ways that are rooted in their own local histories and experiences, even though they may be informed by what happens in the legal (inter)national context.

This might seem to suggest that the quest for justice is somehow a consensual undertaking, but in the context of conflict and atrocity that is very unlikely. Crimes are rarely committed by one side only. And despite the universality of genocide and crimes against humanity, definitions of what were justified or, on the contrary, criminal actions, and who were victims and who perpetrators, are interchangeable. This is not to deny the gross immorality of such crimes. It is merely to point out that, like all crime, they are social constructions that depend on time, place and perception, and are fuelled by the imagery that is produced. Transitional justice is a process of negotiation between competing imagery that has many internal and external dimensions.

Official procedures of transitional justice are one source of such imagery, but the legal competes with the political and military when actors have a stake in what goes down as history and their part in it; and with the individual and social – those who seek to remember and record their own version of the past in memorials, in rituals, in books, films and other forms of art. This dimension of source is closely linked to the power associated with the discursive field where images are produced, but power alone does not create an everlasting imagery. Power relations change (although the staying power of law and legal principles is considerable), perceptions and memories fluctuate, images alter with the passage of time, so that there is also a temporal dimension to transitional justice – not as a matter of 'before and after', but of a permanent process.

About this book

Many studies provide a legal analysis of procedural transitional justice or an evaluation of its effectiveness. This volume presents a wider perspective on justice than the purely legal, attempting a critical appraisal of the different dimensions of the *process* of transitional justice that affect conflicting images and constructions of the past and contribute to discrepancies between experience, perceptions and expectations. In transcending the legal, although by no means denying the significance of law for the imagery of transitional justice, the book also attempts a multidisciplinary, holistic approach and has chapters by criminal and international lawyers, cultural anthropologists, criminologists, political scientists and historians.

Part I, **Hidden Histories**, looks at the tensions inherent in the imagery of past atrocities and attempts to resolve them, and at the development of both collective memories and collective amnesia. However permanent specific images might seem, history is a never-ending process and what is remembered, and how, is dependent on the reality of power relations in politics and society. If, or rather when, these change, so the ideology behind the imagery is called into question and it too becomes openly contested and gradually takes on new forms. Nevertheless, this new imagery and its physical manifestations in memorials, historiography and social and political debate remain temporary social constructions of the past. Grūto Parkas is a case in point, where the imagery of Lithuania's past is turned on its head – at least, a part of it is. It is difficult to find such well-advertised memorialization of another dark side of that country's history – the role of Lithuanian society in the destruction of its Jewish component, which, for whatever reason, is relatively unacknowledged. Many histories remain hidden behind the self-evidence of specific constructions and not only in Lithuania.

In a contribution on Turkey and the so-called Armenian question, Gülhan Demirci examines how memories of the destruction of the Armenian community are reflected in Turkish historiography and Turkish identity and why this is now becoming a political and social issue in Turkey. The very term 'Armenian question' is indicative of contestation. It contains a denial of the genocide that the outside world, and in particular the European Union, insists took place during the First World War and demands that Turkey should acknowledge. While the official Turkish history admits that many Armenians died, it continues to maintain that Turkey – then the Ottoman Empire – was a victim of external and internal elements (the First World War Allies, and Armenians and other ethnic groups respectively) whose purpose was to divide and destroy the Turkish nation. It is a version of events that served for decades to bolster an ideological vision of Turkey as a united, homogeneous and secular state.

As this history has been increasingly contested, another history of the same period has been memorialized on the battlefield of Gallipoli. Yet, the commemoration of what is presented as a glorious period has been unable to prevent the continuous negotiation of and change in imageries of Turkish identity and Turkey's role in destroying the Armenian community. Recognition of what the 'Armenian question' implies may mean that the gradual emergence of this hidden history in Turkey – what Demirci calls 'collective amnesia' – will bring a measure of justice to those who still live in the Armenian diaspora; such justice in itself may not heal, but injustice will always fester. It will also 'rehabilitate' Turkey in the eyes of the outside world, recognition of 'genocide' being a condition, if not an official one, for Turkey's desired membership of the European Union.

Germany is usually seen as having been successful in coming to terms with its exceedingly troubled past and part of that success is attributed to the international criminal justice dispensed by the Allies after the Second World War. The Nuremberg trials demonstrated that ending the impunity of the leaders and instigators of war crimes and crimes against humanity through an international criminal trial was no longer impossible. They were also specifically aimed at 'educating' the German people. As such they are regarded as the precursors of international criminal justice as it exists today, the specific aims of which are ending impunity and promoting democracy and the rule of law. It is impossible to say to what extent the trials were a necessary factor in Germany's remarkable transition from Nazi tyranny to democracy, but it cannot be denied that they did bring a sense of justice and they were, moreover, generally accepted as just and legitimate in Germany.

In the next chapter, however, Susanne Karstedt uses cases of Nazis sentenced at Nuremberg and their return to German society to show how they enjoyed a particular sort of impunity that law is helpless to counter. In an abstract sense Germany may have accepted the Nuremberg trials as necessary and just, but that did not mean that all who were sentenced were regarded as criminal. On the contrary, depending on the images they were able to disseminate of themselves, many reoccupied their former or similar high status positions as if nothing had happened: a 'social construction of silence' that involved German society in general and a number of social institutions such as the army and the church in particular. This was especially the case if former war criminals were able to portray themselves as having been no more than 'soldiers doing their duty'; an image perfectly in tune with that of the German *Wehrmacht* as a disciplined fighting force concerned only with winning battles and far removed from the 'criminal rabble' of the SS who were responsible for the atrocities and genocides of the Second World War. Then generally accepted, this is now increasingly contested imagery in Germany. Ending a culture of impunity, Karstedt contends, takes more than sentencing obvious perpetrators and must include re-educating perpetrator groups and re-establishing moral standards of society. It is part of the process of transitional justice that is as much about defining perpetrators as recognizing victims, about determining the immoral elements of the past and the moral requirements of the future.

While transitional justice after the Second World War is usually associated with Germany and Japan, it is often forgotten that Europe itself was in transition during that period, seeking new forms of law and justice that would ensure that such horrors could never happen again. Transitional justice would be unimaginable without individual human rights, while to enforce it internationally requires limitations to the sovereignty of the nation state that were unthinkable even in 1945. Nuremberg, after all, was a form of victor's justice (not necessarily a derogatory term, it all depends who the victors are). In the historical order of things, universal human rights and international courts empowered to enforce conventions and/or to penalize the perpetrators of gross violations are very recent phenomena. In the final chapter of this section, Jay Winter traces the development of the paradigm shift that made them possible. He does so through the lifework of René Cassin, who stands for the group of people who promoted ideas that emerged in new and striking ways in the 1940s. These people and ideas are part of a little recognized history of international criminal justice that did not simply 'start' with Nuremberg but is a culmination of intellectual efforts after the First World War.

The second part of the book is concerned with **Processes and Rituals**. A criminal trial (international or otherwise) may be a legal process, but it also has ritual elements that determine perceptions of justice in the aftermath of conflict and atrocity. Antoine Hol sees these ritual elements as the seat of the potential educational value of the trial for the general public. Using the trial of Adolf Eichmann as an example, he compares the ritual of the public trial and involvement of the public in it to Greek tragedy. Given the great difference between theatre, which can educate through moralization and/or promoting historical understanding, and a criminal trial, where establishing the guilt of an individual is the central goal, Hol concludes that it is doubtful whether the trial and its rules as we know it are adequately equipped to 'perform justice'. This was also the conclusion drawn by Hannah Arendt and by other observers of the Eichmann trial: it was legal process and tragedy rolled into one, not least because of decisions by the prosecutor to include masses of historical documentation that was not, strictly speaking, relevant to the establishment of individual guilt. For that reason, many doubts have been voiced as to whether the trial was a 'success', even if Eichmann was found guilty and hanged.

The Eichmann trial was perhaps exceptional in its emotional impact and its political significance for the state of Israel. Nevertheless, international criminal trials also have a tendency to spill over into moralization and history-telling – the latter being, according to some, a specific goal of such justice. Consequently, prosecutors are inclined to overemphasize the historical background of conflicts and/or the extreme immorality of atrocities, among other things, through the excessive use of victim testimony that is not necessarily relevant to the question of guilt. While this both serves to give the victims rather than the perpetrators their 'day in court' and provides powerful imagery, it creates tensions with principles of fair trial and legal procedural requirements of justice.

The limitations of a criminal trial are compounded because it is a form of top-down justice that need not coincide with the expectations and needs of the society concerned. Other types of ritual that develop within such societies are bottom-up. They develop over many years, may reinforce or compete with legal procedures such as trials and truth commissions and are usually politically contested manifestations of local imageries of justice, memory politics and memorialization. They can be particularly potent if concentrated on public spaces that constitute *lieux de mémoire*, places where particular memories of particular past events can be sited. The next two chapters examine the totally different paths that such bottom-up initiatives have taken in Serbia and Chile respectively.

Srdjan Radović looks at attempts to memorialize Sajmište, a former Second World War concentration camp in Belgrade,. He notes that the national and local politics of memory ignore rather than discuss controversial, violent episodes from the nation's past and that for a long time the site of the camp was denied any special significance. This was exacerbated by the fact that powerful local elites are more interested in Sajmište's potentially lucrative location in the centre of the city than in its meaning as a space of memory. As a result, economic exploitation of the site prevented attempts at memorialization, an example of how powerful internal sources can suppress competing imageries. However, following an international outcry, the external dimension of the international imagery of (in)justice has saved the site from becoming simply a nightclub and shopping mall and made possible its future re-commemoration and revitalization.

In Chile, the memorialization of former sites of torture under the Pinochet regime is of a different order. In the story of the house at Londres 38, Katrien Klep shows how 'official' transitional justice (two truth commissions) and grassroots memory initiatives took place independently, simultaneously and in different directions, but also converged and enhanced one another. This social process, a search for justice in transitional Chile, was a grassroots contestation of the official narrative produced in the reports of the two truth commissions which, in the eyes of the victims, failed to do justice to their experience of political repression and atrocity. That this was the case was due in no small part to the legal remit and official goal of the commissions to tell a particular truth about Chile's history in order to pave the way for reconciliation and democracy. While the reports were an official acknowledgement of the repression and human rights violations that took place, they did not satisfy the desire of the family members of those who had disappeared to know what had happened to their loved ones and did not name the perpetrators of the crimes, while survivors of political imprisonment and torture were not officially recognized as victims. As a result, family members, survivors, human rights organizations and others pressed on for justice and more truth. Consequently, Londres 38 has become an active, participative, social space of commemoration, with demands for more truth and justice, and engagement in present-day social issues.

The final chapter in this part is by Danielle Celermajer. She looks at a very specific (and increasingly popular) type of ritual as a means of providing justice for past wrongs: the political apology. This has been used for such divergent historical events as slavery, the forced removal of aboriginal children in Australia, specific colonial atrocities (grudgingly admitted by the Dutch government, for example) and, more famously, the Holocaust. Like Hol, Celermajer questions whether current practice, in particular that of legal procedure, provides the most efficacious rituals of transition. She asks whether a ritual frame can be broadly applicable to the field of transitional justice, considering its task of so altering the normative framework of the society concerned that it will come to respect human rights and the rule of law. Drawing on classical debates in Judaism concerning ritual efficacy and intentionality, and social anthropological work on ritual theory, she concludes that there is a case for the potentially transformative effects of rituals.

Interestingly, where political apology is often criticized as being no more than an expedient and thus insincere form of gesture politics, Celermajer emphasizes the significance of the symbolic nature, the potential of the ritual itself – the fact of apologizing, regardless of whether the apologizer carries any blame or is even sincere, can itself serve to create potent images of justice. With regard to the Holocaust, the political (although also, perhaps even primarily, individual and certainly sincere) apology by Chancellor Willy Brandt of Germany, who fell to his knees at the site of the Warsaw ghetto, proved so powerful that his gesture is remembered in a separate memorial to the apology itself. It is a small replica of the official Jewish memorial to the ghetto, near to which it stands, and is a wonderful example of the continuous defining and redefining of the imagery of transitional justice and the different forms it can take.

Part III, **Contradictory Perceptions of Conflict and Justice**, deals specifically with concrete and conflicting images of conflicts, victims, perpetrators and international criminal justice. Contradictions in presentation and interpretation of the same events are inherent in how perpetrators and victims define each other and are defined by outsiders, including international criminal courts. But there are also contradictions in how the role of international criminal justice is perceived by international courts themselves and in the post-conflict societies where they operate. This is partly a result of the fact that international criminal justice is both an idealistic and a political undertaking, and is therefore potentially problematic. Discrepancies between the ideals and practices of international criminal justice undermine its legitimacy and its efficacy as a form of transitional justice.

Chrisje Brants, Kees Brants and Lauren Gould look at the ongoing conflict in Uganda and at how the ICC intervention there is presented and perceived by the different actors involved and by the media. Their findings indicate that the legitimacy of the ICC is affected not only by the competing imagery of parties to the conflict, but also by its own attempts to disseminate images of its core identity. These of necessity portray Court and Prosecutor as embodying the ideals of impartiality and the rule of law. Images and narratives in Uganda itself, however, are the social construction of a lived reality that includes the ICC, but reflects its inherently political nature, often to the detriment of the ideal image it wishes to communicate.

In the next chapter Ton Liefaard examines the conflicting imagery of child soldiers as either 'victims' or 'perpetrators'. Such portrayals emphasize the extremes of the phenomenon, but deny that they may simply be different sides of the same coin. International law and policy primarily portray child soldiers as passive and innocent victims, forced into combat and subjected to extreme violence and abuse by adults. Liefaard recognizes the child soldier as vulnerable, but argues that the primary focus of international discourse on child soldiers as victims is problematic and potentially contra productive: children *are* perpetrators, sometimes particularly savage ones, and to ignore this by perpetuating the imagery of the child soldier victim is to deny the lived reality of the conflicts of which they are a very real part, and to make their rehabilitation all the more difficult. In light of the complex reality of armed conflict and local perceptions, but also of the imagery of the child under international human rights law as an autonomous human being capable of decision-making, he sees the interests of child soldiers as best served by a rights-based imagery that takes both vulnerability and autonomy into account.

Next, Sanja Kutnjak Ivković and John Hagan explore what the victims of war crimes and crimes against humanity think about who the appropriate decision-makers in the aftermath of a violent conflict should be, and why. The results of their empirical study in the former Yugoslavia emphasize that respondents' ethnicity remains the most critical demographic characteristic for their choice in the matter. But the findings also suggest that ethnicity is an approximation of different sets of values, potentially influenced by the political climate in the country, what they term 'cognitive landscapes': 'defeated' ethnic groups – such as Serbs – generate more negative views of justice delivered by the International Tribunal for the Former Yugoslavia (ICTY) than 'defended' ethnic groups – such as Bosnians/Muslims. However, *the* key in explaining the respondents' choice of primary decision-maker is the perceived fairness of the ICTY. This suggests that there is a paradoxical element to transitional justice when it takes the form of international trials: criminal law with its procedural principles has a powerful discursive dimension of international proportions that cuts through national and local imagery; but, although the justice may be international, its interpretation remains highly contextual and local.

Finally, Part IV takes as its point of departure **Discourse and Artistic Expression**. The history-telling that is part of the process of transitional justice is not only a matter for historians or the by-product of an international trial or the meetings of truth and reconciliation commissions. Artistic expression in literature, theatre, film and so forth also reflects and influences images of justice and perceptions of events past and present. Art produces especially powerful imagery that is unencumbered by procedural considerations, but for that very reason it is also open to political manipulation. The chapter by Dina Siegel is an example of the political use of imagery generated by artistic expression to perpetuate a particular 'truth' about both the past and the present. She asks why playing Wagner is still forbidden in Israel and what this says about conflicting social and political discourse on the Holocaust and its meaning for contemporary Israeli society. Concerned with the so-called 'Wagner myth', she analyses the expression of Wagner's anti-Semitism in his operas and other music, and discusses the political reasons for preserving the 'myth' in Israel as part of the collective memory of the Holocaust. That memory, or rather the political use to which it is often put, is now increasingly contested in an ongoing political and public debate on the nature of the state of Israel as a state in transition, where efforts to make sense of the past coincide with conflicting images of justice and injustice in the present.

Bernadette Kester follows with a chapter on how the genocide in Rwanda has been represented in cinematic terms. An important criticism of the international community's reaction to the genocide has always been that it was after the fact, setting up a tribunal to judge the perpetrators while ignoring what was happening at the time. 'Where were you then?' has always been part of the imagery of the western type of transitional justice dispensed by the International Criminal Tribunal for Rwanda (ICTR) and has played an important part in undermining the legitimacy of the tribunal among the Rwandan population.

Kester argues that, unsurprisingly, the 'global mediated memory' of events in Rwanda includes the imagery of the West ignoring and thus exacerbating the genocide. She closely examines the dialogue in two famous films that appear to condemn the West for its passivity while at the same time rationalizing it. These rationalizations, pronounced by western characters, conceal an attitude of cynicism, a 'seeing through' of the western ideal of humanitarianism and, at the same time, a portrayal of most of the Rwandan characters as naïve. The third film, however, also presents a narrative from a predominantly Rwandan perspective, which includes a human uncertainty, a not-knowing, that may well be based, Kester suggests, on the principles of Rwandan legal culture. Here, justice is more geared to reconciliation and rehabilitation than to producing a one-dimensional image of truth that is expressed in terms of guilt or innocence.

The final chapter of the book is concerned with the way images are expressed in words that attempt to make a specific sense of past conflict. Lodewijk Brunt describes the partition of India, the atrocities that accompanied it and the way writers have dealt with the trauma of division that was its lasting legacy. He notes the great variety of images that have been used to describe the violence and the difference between internal and external sources of those images, between terms used by insiders (eyewitnesses, novelists and short story writers) and those used by outsiders (students of Partition looking back from a greater distance in time). The imagery of the novelist is emotional – 'fury', 'catastrophe', 'massacres', 'slaughter' – and depicts direct, personal and confrontational violence which closely corresponds to what actually took place. Outsiders employ words like 'holocaust' and 'genocide', analytical concepts that both describe the indescribable and impute to the violence of Partition the same significance for humanity as what the 'civilized' West has been shown to be capable of. The discursive power of this external imagery, which draws on specific, globally recognized images of other atrocities, lends particular potency to interpretations of the conflict surrounding Partition in terms of criminal events that demand a particular sort of justice. This was, and remains, highly unlikely to happen, perpetrator and victim groups being separated by the very fact of the geopolitics of Partition itself. Consequently, the atrocities that were one of its main characteristics live on in the imagery of literary expression in India, keeping the wound of the injustice of Partition open.

This final contribution on a conflict often ignored in western discourse about transitional justice completes what, we hope, has been a project on transitional justice with a difference. It has attempted to acknowledge and capture the kaleidoscopic quality of the phenomenon in contributions on the very different ways that (transitional) justice is imagined. At the same time, it offers a critique of the legal view on transitional justice and turns some of its basic presumptions upside down (the victim–perpetrator dichotomy; images of victimhood; the necessary predominance of professionals and procedure). In short, it is our construction of what transitional justice and the imagery involved can mean for a better understanding of processes of justice, truth and reconciliation, and as such it is open to contestation.

PART I
Hidden Histories

Chapter 1

The Question of Turkey: Contested, Forgotten and Remembered Memories

Gülhan Demirci

On 24 April 1915, a large number of Armenian intellectuals were arrested in the capital of the Ottoman Empire, Istanbul. The date is still commemorated as the symbolic trigger of collective violence and genocide against the Armenians. Within a year and a half, the majority of Armenians had been deported and whole communities wiped out from the places they had known as their homeland. One day after the arrests in Istanbul, on 25 April, the Gallipoli landings took place. The Ottoman Empire had entered the First World War on the side of the Central Powers, and French and British troops attacked the Gallipoli peninsula in an attempt to reopen and (re)gain entrance to the Black Sea in order to supply their Russian ally. The Dardanelles campaigns were won by the Ottoman Empire, and have been commemorated in Turkey since the 1990s with increasing fervour. While the Turks celebrate 25 April 1915 as the victory of their great leader (and first president of the Turkish Republic) Mustafa Kemal Atatürk and as the first steps towards modern Turkey, the Armenians remember 24 April 1915 as the beginning of the end.

Although the Armenian genocide, referred to in Turkey with great consistency as the 'question of Armenia', is still a very sensitive and disputed issue, there are those who publicly oppose the homogeneous national discourse that follows the official account of what happened to the Armenians, and why, in 1915. The official Turkish view denies there was genocide but, increasingly, does accept that Armenians were killed and deported. However, the Turkish interpretation of how these 'events of 1915' happened differs from the Armenian. This chapter is concerned with how these contested memories are reflected in Turkish historiography and Turkish identity and why these different narratives are now becoming an issue in Turkey. It deals first with events in 1915 and the two competing versions of them, one confirming and one denying that they amount to genocide. This is followed by the contested memories in Turkey and how the official Turkish version is closely connected to the development and identity of the nation state in the wake of the collapse of the Ottoman Empire.

This in its turn is related to the question of who was the perpetrator and who the victim in that situation, which is much more than a matter of academic definition but is, in practice, about recognizing suffering. In recent decades, the official state ideology and historiography have come under pressure as alternative discourses have been put forward. A case in point is the Battle of Gallipoli, in the narrative of which imageries of Turkish identity are continuously negotiated as different actors use the commemoration of the battle for different purposes. The question remains whether the ongoing contestation of official Turkish historiography will slowly undermine its homogeneity.

The road to a 'solution' of the so-called 'Armenian question'

Views on what happened to the Armenians towards the end of the Ottoman Empire are highly politicized. The Turkish interpretation is dominated by the predominant Republican narrative and promoted by the modern Turkish nation state and its institutions. Turkish scholars working for state universities funded by the government disseminate a view that denies the massacre, and even argue that Turks themselves were the victims. The dominant view from the Armenian disapora takes a completely opposite position, implying or even stating that there was an inherently violent, destructive streak in all Turks that caused the tragedies at the beginning of the twentieth century and, by implication, would bring about their occurrence even today unless a constant and vigilant guard is kept. Both historiographies are biased. The last decade has seen a lively debate among scholars, both Turkish and Armenian, and there is a growing consensus that genocide was committed.

Things were already problematic for Armenians in the Ottoman Empire before 1915. There had been pogroms and widespread killings in 1896 and 1909, although the systematic deportation and massacre of the Armenian population that is the 'Armenian question' took place in the period between 1915 and 1919. At present, many, including Turkish academics, maintain that these events constituted genocide.[1] It arose in a dynamic combination of three mutually related and reinforcing processes: the deep political crisis that had engulfed the Ottoman Empire, the CUP revolution by the 'Young Turks' (see, for example, Karpat 2000; Zürcher 1984; Zürcher 2005) and the First World War. The CUP (Ittihat ve Terakki Cemiyeti, IT – Committee of Union and Progress) was officially founded in 1895 in opposition to Sultan Abdülhamit (1842-1918). Originally comprising several groups, it united in 1907 and consisted for the most part of young officers and civil servants; they took power in 1908 and were a powerful force to be reckoned with for years to come.

The Balkan Wars of 1912-1913 had dramatic consequences for the Ottoman army and for the population. Many Muslims fell victim to war crimes, and important territory, lives and possessions were lost. Muslims fled in huge numbers towards Istanbul and Anatolia. Many Young Turks, including future leaders, were

1 For extensive literature in which the genocide is considered proven beyond doubt, see Akçam (2006), Bloxham (2005), Dündar (2001), Kevorkian (2011) and Üngör (2011). For an opposing view, see, among others, Lewy (2005a, 2005b) and McCarthy (1989).

among the refugees, or heard the traumatic stories from family members. With the Balkan provinces, the Ottomans lost what had been the core of the empire, its richest and most developed part, for 500 years. These events were to have a decisive impact on the development of Ottoman society, culture and identity, and on the development of a nation state.

The Young Turks were determined that such a defeat should never again occur in the remaining territories. But it had also demonstrated the weaknesses of the once so powerful Ottoman Empire, which had become known as 'the sick man of Europe', both economically and militarily subordinate to the rest of the continent in a semi-colonial relationship of dependency. France, Russia and Britain, all interested in the Ottoman Empire, each feared that the others would gain more territory and disturb the balance of power. None of them wanted, therefore, to destroy the empire, though secretly they agreed on how to divide it up. The big powers already had a great deal of influence on the position of Christian minorities in the country because of the Capitulations and Treaties that had been agreed over the years, on the basis of which they intervened regularly in internal affairs (something the Ottomans regarded as a breach of their autonomy); such 'humanitarian interventions' as the western powers called them, allowed them to disguise any desire for carving up the empire, while protecting Christian minorities and supporting their aspirations of independence.

Meanwhile, the loss of the Balkan territories fed the myth of being 'stabbed in the back' by the Christians living within the empire's borders, reinforcing deep distrust of their loyalty and inflaming Turkish-nationalist feeling.

In January 1913, the Young Turks, united in the CUP, staged a coup that gave them complete power. Within the CUP itself, a small group, the Central Committee, took the most important decisions. This is thought to be the group that made the decision both to take part in the First World War and to deport the Armenians.

The outbreak of the First World War, little over a year after the Balkan Wars, took all parties by surprise and was eventually to prove fatal for the Ottoman Empire, and certainly also for the Christian minorities within its borders.

The Young Turks had already discovered how diplomatically isolated the empire could become and were determined to find allies to prevent its demise. The only major power prepared to enter into an alliance with the Ottomans on the basis of equality was the German Empire. While the hope was that victory would liberate the country from its semi-colonial status, at the same time the radical nationalistic branch of the CUP saw the war as a drastic solution for the many problems facing the empire (Akçam 2001; Üngör 2009). The Young Turks also hoped to reclaim lost territory – that loss being a permanent trauma of both late Ottoman and Turkish political culture.

The Armenian question

Relations between the Armenians, the Kurds and the Muslims in the east were already strained and there were regular clashes. The Balkan Wars, increasing distrust towards the non-Muslim population and rising Turkish nationalism exacerbated the situation. The outbreak of the First World War encouraged further distrust, reinforcing the more radical elements in the CUP and creating an atmosphere in which they seemed to be working towards the destruction of non-Turkish and non-Muslim groups within the empire.

In December 1914, the Ottoman army suffered a disastrous defeat by the Russians near Sarıkamış under the leadership of Enver Pasha, general, minister of war and CUP leader. Due to poor preparation, cold and exhaustion, only 12,000 of the 90,000 men with whom he set out on this venture survived (Erickson 2001). After this huge blow to to the Ottoman army, nationalist Armenians saw their chance to create their own state and, encouraged by Russian propaganda, many rose against the Ottomans. This led to harsh repercussions and a further tightening of a policy to keep the Armenians in check. Fearing a Russian invasion led by Armenian 'traitors', the Central Committee of the CUP found in the rebellion in the provincial capital of Van (1915) an extra reason for pushing on with plans for deportation; consensus was growing that what was called the 'Armenian question' should be definitively solved. Once the decision was made, the deportations and persecutions were processes relatively separate from the ebb and flow of the war, the policy remained to get rid of the Armenians. The Armenian society whose home was Anatolia was destroyed to the extent of never recovering. Exact numbers are unknown, but the latest figures stand at between 800,000 and 1,500,000 dead. The wider context of this massacre was 'ethnic cleansing' with a view to creating a homogeneous nation state.

An untouchable history

Interest in the 'Armenian question' is not new and this is a piece of hidden history that has re-emerged in Turkey. There were already reports of mass murder and deportations of Armenians in the east of the Ottoman Empire during the First World War. American ambassador Morgenthau wrote:

> On April 15th, about 500 young Armenian men of Akantz were mustered to hear an order of the Sultan; at sunset they were marched outside the town and every man shot in cold blood. This procedure was repeated in about eighty Armenian villages in the district north of Lake Van, and in three days 24,000 Armenians were murdered in this atrocious fashion. (1918: 111)

In his report, Morgenthau even mentions massacres that took place in 1895. He gives numerous examples and describes the deportations, concluding that what the CUP was doing amounted to 'merely the preparatory steps in the destruction of the race' (1918: 115).

In 1916, the British government published a document known as the 'Bleu Book' (Bryce and Toynbee [1916] 2000), detailing the treatment of the Armenians and the mass murders. It was intended as propaganda against the Ottoman

Empire, and it shows that the desperate Armenian situation was known to foreign governments at an early stage. Historians such as Arnold Toynbee (Bryce and Toynbee [1916] 2000) and Herbert Gibbons (1917) were among the first to claim that this was a systematic destruction of the Armenians. Turkey's ally Germany, with its wide network of consuls and other diplomats in Turkey, also learnt about the dramatic events as early as 1915 (Gust 2005).

After the First World War, and under pressure from Britain and France especially, several tribunals were established to try the perpetrators of the Armenian massacres (the term 'genocide' did not become generally known until 1948). The most important case began in Istanbul on 28 April 1919. Twelve men, including members of the CUP and ex-ministers, stood trial. Key figures such as Talât Pasha, minister of the interior, Enver Pasha, minister of war, and Cemal Pasha, governor of Aleppo, had fled and were sentenced to death in absentia (Adrian 1991, 1997).

The fact that crimes had happened that could not bear the light of day was not completely unknown among Turks either (mostly the elite) and was discussed in parliament after the war. Motions were even tabled asking for punishment for the persecution of both 'the Armenian nation' and 'the noble Arab people' (Akçam 2006). But then, too, there were those who maintained that the Turkish people had also suffered in the course of history and had been victims of mass murder. Originally the Turks were not averse to the idea of tribunals to try war criminals, partly because they expected this would have a favourable influence on the Peace Conference in Paris. The Allies, however, also had ulterior motives in wishing to punish the Turks, given that they had already decided before the war to divide up the Ottoman territories (Helmreich 1974, in Akçam 2006). When the Turks became aware of this, their original willingness disappeared. One of the treaties following the Conference, the Treaty of Sèvres of August 1920, imposed such severe terms that it not only carved up most of the Ottoman territory but also meant a de facto loss of autonomy for the government. To the Armenians it promised a political entity, an autonomous homeland.

The new nation state and its leader, Mustafa Kemal, dismissed any connection to the CUP, which was held not only responsible for losing the empire but also for the massacres. Any counter-interpretation of the official nationalist narrative was rendered subversive by the subsequent promulgation of the laws of treason against the Turkish state and Mustafa Kemal. The series of social reforms enacted by the young Republic also made it difficult if not impossible do deal with the traumatic past.

Contested memories

Today, the events of 1915 are still not recognized as genocide in Turkey and the very term occasions fierce emotions. As far as this part of history is concerned, Turkey appears to suffer from collective amnesia. This is closely related to the development of Turkish historiography and national identity. The modern nation state exists partly thanks to remembering. In 1882, Ernst Renan asked: 'What is a nation?' only to answer: 'The possession in common of a rich legacy of memories'. But he also maintained:

> Forgetting, I would even go so far as to say historical error is a crucial factor in the creation of a nation. Indeed, historical enquiry brings to light deeds of violence which took place at the origin of all political formation, even those whose consequences have been altogether beneficial. Unity is always been affected by means of brutality. (Renan 1882)

Remembering – and especially forgetting – forms the collective memories of a country. What is selected to be remembered is confirmed in a number of ways. Zerubavel speaks of 'a master commemorative memory' that is fed by collective days of celebration, stories, monuments and schoolbooks (1995: 6). The most important stories of commemoration are directed towards the specific group identity and its historical development. Describing this identity as the collective movement of a people through time and events contributes to the forming of a nation. Silhouetted by selective forgetting, these memories help form and maintain 'imagined communities' (Anderson 2006). And so the nation state will go to great, not to say any, lengths to keep remembrance under control. After the foundation of the Republic of Turkey, those in power monopolized channels of socialization, schools, the army and the media in order to impress their ideology on society. Their success also helped keep the official version of history uncontested for decades.

In search of Turkish identity

Turkish historiography developed in antagonism to the Ottoman Empire and its fall and is, moreover, teleological in nature. The political, the military and the biographical form the elements through which the thread of state formation is developed, so that Turkish history seems to write itself towards the foundation of the nation state in 1923. Dominant ideology still has it that modern Turkish culture was formed within the nation state post-1923. It is presented as a homogeneous culture, not multi-ethnic, and the Turkish state as having only found its true identity after 1923 (and some primitive experimenting in the final Ottoman period). From this same point of view, the First World War – the direct reason for the struggle for independence and the foundation of the Republic – is interesting only as the transition from multi-ethnic state to homogeneous nation state.

The three most important schools of unifying ideology at the beginning of the twentieth century were Ottomanism, Islamism and Turkism (see, for example, Özkırımlı and Sofos 2008), and their central question was what would be the future foundation of the loyalty of citizens to their state. Externally dictated conditions were such that the ideology of Turkism eventually proved most viable. The loss of Balkan territory reduced the ethnic diversity of the empire. The flight of hundreds of thousands of Muslims towards the Turkish capital was repeated as the Russians advanced during the First World War. The Armenians were virtually annihilated by deportations and massacres. The conflicts, the famines and the treaties after the war caused the displacement of other population groups too, and drastically changed the demographic situation in Anatolia, the last remains of the once so powerful Ottoman Empire. Ethnically and religiously it grew more homogeneous; the characteristic ethnic diversity of the empire was gone.

The ideologues of the 1920s saw homogeneity of national identity as the basic condition for survival of the state. There was no place for divergent ethnic or religious elements. This was the message borne by the Education Ideology (Deren and Bora 2003; Kaplan 2005), the Turkish Historiography, the History Thesis (Ersanlı Behar 1996) and the synthesis of the three – Kemalism. With the founding of the Republic of Turkey, education became the main carrier of the nation state project, the principle purpose of the Turkish educational system being to train 'loyal citizens' in the official ideology. Since Mustafa Kemal thought that 'writing history is as important as making history' (Çambel 1939: 272), new textbooks ensured that the new regime directly mirrored its ideologically motivated assertions in educational content. The 'Turkish History Thesis' gave shape to new historical claims about the greatness of Turkishness. Especially with regard to identity creation, this depiction of history determined the ideological pillars of Turkishness during the 1930s and for years to come.

Historiography and nation-building

History and historiography provide those in power with tools for building a new nation with a view to realizing a new identity. The construction of national memory is an aspect of the creation of a new national culture. An embryonic nation needs a collective self-image in which to educate its citizens. Honouring heroes and leaders from the past, establishing days of national commemoration, building monuments and nationalizing history create consensus with regard to a cultural heritage, a commemorative narrative. A central part of this is the continuous emphasis on ties with the past, not with what happens to be a people's history, but with what are presented as natural, almost organic ties, so that the national identity seems to have sprung from natural roots. A common narrative creates the imagined community to which people belong, and in this new identity a new memory comes into being.

Collective, identity-affirming memory also requires a symbolic turning point – the myth of origin. Since the foundation of Turkey in 1923, the 1919/1922 struggle for independence has been designated as the turning point. This notion, predominantly determined by Atatürk's *Nutuk* (Speech) in 1927, sees the Turkish Republic as rising like a phoenix from the ashes of the Ottoman Empire. Since then, the republic has carefully distanced itself in its historiography from the empire and brushed it aside as degenerate and corrupt. The Ottoman state was identified with decline, while the republic presents itself as a modern and progressive nation. 'The contradiction of myth of origin requires a twofold strategy of emphasizing a new beginning as well as discontinuity with an earlier past' (Zerubavel 1995: 43).

Atatürk saw 1923 as the year zero, rejecting all history, culture and tradition that came before. A new Turkey was born by imposing a collective amnesia that allows little scope for defeat, recognition of intentional massacres, deportations and other 'cleansing' of ethnic minorities.

Atatürk and his followers needed many reforms to create this new Turkey. Some were symbolic and lasting, such as getting rid of the customary headwear, the fez, and other regulations of dress. Others had much greater consequences. Replacing Arabic script with the Latin alphabet in 1928, for example, made anything written before inaccessible to the younger generation, thereby erasing part of a collective past. History was now determined by specially appointed academics; participation in the First World War, the 'Armenian question' and the Ottoman past in general were to remain a closed chapter for many years to come. Until recently, this periodization of nationalism has formed a major obstacle in contemporary Turkey, for it dismisses the significance of prior historical events and therefore leaves very little room for debate and other views on these issues.

Contested identity

After the proclamation of the Republic of Turkey on 29 October 1923, Mustafa Kemal became the first president and head of the Republican Peoples's Party (RPP), which was the only party allowed. After Atatürk's death in 1938, parliamentary government and a multi-party system gradually took root in Turkey and after the elections of 1950 the Democrat Party (DP) won the majority of votes. It would take at least until the 1960s before this two-party format was transformed into a real multi-party system. Rapid socio-economic transformation brought substantial differentiation to social and political life and more parties and interest groups entered the political field. Yet, the dominant ideological environment of the period meant that it would not be until the 1980s that important developments and real transformations could take place. A third military coup in 1980 (there were two previous coups in 1960 and 1971) was headed by the Chief of the General Staff Kenan Evren under the pretext of ending the social conflicts and parliamentary instability of the 1970s.

The military claimed (and still claim) to protect Kemalist ideology, but the turmoil of the 1970s had shown that it no longer sufficed to hold the country together, and the question of homogeneous identity and culture was increasingly raised. 'A major characteristic of this period under the pressure of the liberal environment of the time was the creation of room for a civil life within the public realm, brought about by the lessening of the political authority's sovereign domain' (Çaha 2005: 20). Increasingly, politicians and intellectuals debated privatization, minimum and neutral government, a constitutional state and in general the position of the state in public life. The ideology of the political system itself began to be questioned. Kurdish separatists led by the Partie Kerkeran Kurdistan (PKK) and

Alevi[2] demanded recognition, the latter challenging the spread of Sunni Islam. The Islamists, however, also felt unrecognized in the official politics of secularism. While Turkey was and still is nominally 99 per cent Muslim, officially it has been a secular state since 1937 (this was one of the Atatürk's reforms). Strict separation of religion and the state in effect meant that politics and political parties based on religion were banned and wearing Islamic-style head scarves in government offices and schools forbidden.

At the same time, liberal reforms from the 1980s onwards led to a growth in commercial media that undermined the monopoly of the TRT (Turkish Radio and Television Broadcasting) and thus also the monopoly on the dissemination of official history. Private broadcasters brought many hitherto taboo subjects and scrutiny of government policy into the public debate. There seemed to be a real need for this since some of these programmes became immensely popular. Television had a big impact in Turkey, given the low literacy rate, especially in rural areas.

Besides these internal changes, there was another important and even bigger external factor. The Turkish desire to become a member of the European Union forced reforms that allowed the Islamists and Kurds more scope. The ban on Islamist parties was made more difficult and religious freedom recognized. Turkey abolished the death penalty in support of its bid to be admitted to membership of the European Union and the oppression of the Kurds in general became less severe (Kurds are now allowed to speak their own language and give Kurdish names to their children). From the middle of the 1980s, such events both in and outside Turkey led several groups to cast doubt on homogeneous Turkish identity and history. Many issues, until then successfully repressed by Kemalist culture (religion, ethnic diversity and the Ottoman heritage), were brought into the open and into a contest for the reconstruction of current collective memories.

Europe's continuing dismissive attitude to Turkey's attempts to join the EU has brought old resentments to the fore and revived old traumas. For many Turks it is proof of the old adage 'Türk'ün Türk'ten başka dostu yoktur' (The Turk has no friends but the Turk). It was remembered how, in the Treaty of Sèvres in 1920, the European powers had divided the vestiges of the Ottoman Empire among themselves and their Armenian and Greek 'clients'. A 2005 survey of Turkish attitudes to the European Union revealed that 78 per cent of respondents agreed that 'The West wants to divide and dissolve Turkey as it did with the Ottoman Empire' (Göçek 2011). This fear of being divided and disappearing as a political

2 The PKK was a neo-marxist political movement founded in 1978 with a view to establishing an independent and socialist Kurdish state in south-eastern Turkey that has become a paramilitary group fighting a guerilla war against the Turkish state since 1984. The Alevi are a religious and cultural offshoot of Shia Islam and have always formed a persecuted minority, for which reason they were staunch supporters of Atatürk, hoping that his secular ideology would put an end to discrimination. To this day, they are not officially recognized in Turkey.

entity goes back to the Ottoman period and its aftermath and, still present in Turkey, is known as the Sèvres syndrome.

Gallipoli: a heroic epic

One of the most significant end results of the persistence of the foundation myth up to the present is the permanent disconnection of the Turkish people from the origin of their traumas. Education of the history of the nation through national myths instead of actual historical events is laden with emotions of incessant dread, anxiety and fear of annihilation by the West. *Yeni Sevr* or the 'Sèvres syndrome' is a buzzword in Turkey and stands for the whole complex of individual, group and institutional distrust of all internal and foreign interaction seen from a perspective of fear of potential destruction, division and betrayal of the Turkish state by the West. In the 1920s, only the determined resistance of the people and their leader Mustafa Kemal Atatürk is said to have swept this treaty under the table and allowed the Turks to maintain their dignity and autonomy. Such sentiments have also mythologized the Battle of Gallipoli into a panacea for the dented morale and identity crisis of the Turkish people. Did they not defeat the British and French, considered invincible, at Çanakkale? The slogan *Çanakkale geçilmez* (Çanakkale cannot be taken) that adorns the hills in huge white letters not only represents the heroism of the Turkish soldier and the sacrifice of the people, but is also a warning to the outside world that Turkey does not give up.

Gallipoli is also an example of a renewed struggle for the ownership of collective memory and commemorative narrative. The Gallipoli campaign in 1915, better known in Turkey as *Çanakkale Savaşları*, is the only major First World War battle – or rather series of engagements – won by the Ottomans, but it was to prove a pyrrhic victory at the cost of enormous casualties while the war itself would be lost.[3] Nevertheless, history books portray Gallipoli as a tremendous loss for the Allies (which it was not, although it was a defeat) and as an unprecedented victory for the Turkish people. The imagery of this war and Gallipoli in particular combines several unsolved issues, such as national identity, Turkish historiography and who and what is remembered, with fundamental changes in contemporary Turkey.

The scarred hills of Gallipoli have become a new battlefield on which contending political movements in Turkey, from ultra-nationalists to Islamists, occupy entrenched positions in the current political debate. Gallipoli has become what Mosse calls 'a myth of war' (1990: 7), transforming memories of war into a sacred event with sacred places that can be visited and rendering cemeteries and memorials, the permanent proof of national pride, significant locations in

3 In Gallipoli, of 310,000 Turkish soldiers, 57,263 died in battle and 21,000 died as a result of disease, while 10,000 remained missing. Including the wounded and prisoners of war, the casualties stand at around 250,000, proportionately a much greater loss than that suffered by the Allies.

the process of nation-building. Such *lieux de mémoire* (Nora 1994) become sites where people connect with a perceived collective past, and live and re-live national identity. For the Turks, Gallipoli has become such a sacred site. The question is what national past they are connecting with.

The Battle of Gallipoli was almost simultaneous with the initiation of the genocide of the Armenians. In Turkey, however, the two are never linked and are seen as two separate events. One of the few who makes a link is Taner Akçam (2006). He states that because of the disaster in Sarıkamış and the fear that Istanbul would soon be captured the nation felt on the verge of destruction. In this line of reasoning, the empire felt threatened in its very existence and would not hesitate to destroy another group it held responsible for its situation – in this case, the Armenians. Already at the outbreak of war in August 1914, the German ambassador Wangenheim had warned Henry Morgenthau (the US ambassador) that the Turks would massacre the Armenians in Anatolia. To which he replied: 'So long as England does not attack Çanakkale [the Turkish fortress at the Dardanelles] … there is nothing to fear. Otherwise, nothing can be guaranteed' (Akçam 2007: 137). Çanakkale was attacked the day after Armenian intellectuals were arrested in Istanbul. There is no direct proof that the decision to attack the Armenians had a direct link with Gallipoli. The genocide was a constellation of events although Gallipoli may have sped up the process.

The importance of Gallipoli is that it has been instrumentalized into a cult of another, perhaps more heterogeneous national identity – an identity that also contains Islam and depicts the First World War, and Gallipoli in particular, as a war fought by common people. Preceding the commemorations of Gallipoli in 2012, posters in Turkish and Kurdish were disseminated in the eastern parts of Turkey (were most Kurds live) containing messages such as 'Our unity would make them [martyrs and veterans of the war] happy' and 'Çanakkale victory gained by the alliance of hearts'. Increasingly, Gallipoli is depicted as an epic struggle in which people of various ethnicities fought together to win the war, as an example of unity and togetherness between people of different ethnic backgrounds.

Of victims and perpetrators

In the 'myth of war' the dead do not die for nothing and the living remember their sacrifice for the nation. Because they died, we can exist. A much heard Turkish variation of this is *Şehitler ölmez, vatan bölünmez* (Martyrs do not die, the Fatherland remains undivided), a sentence that reveals the omnipresent fear of division. The present government has stimulated Gallipoli commemorations and invested more than 40 million YTL (about €20 million) in numerous projects, including the restoration of many monuments, announcing proudly during the annual commemoration on 18 March 2008 that visitor numbers to Gallipoli now exceed three million (Erdoğan 2008). Representing Gallipoli as a site of remembrance for ordinary soldiers, the sons of the people, encourages a national symbol as an alternative to the Mausoleum for Atatürk, a secular sanctuary, the ordinary soldier and not Atatürk as the saviour of the nation. It also provides a convenient lightning conductor and counter-narrative about the First World War. For as the cult of remembrance at Gallipoli has taken hold, so too the fate of minorities in the last days of the Ottoman Empire, and that of the Armenians in particular, has gathered more attention and become the subject of fierce debate. Not only external and internal (geo)political pressure, but also the activities of Armenians themselves (especially in the diaspora) have brought the genocide to international attention. And in general, the enormous rise in memory studies has bolstered interest in the subject of collective memory.[4]

Yet there is a huge difference between the Turkish and western views of the First World War and what happened to the Armenians, as is reflected in political speeches but also in schoolbooks, especially since 2005. In that same year the 'Bleu Book' was reissued, occasioning an official protest from the Turkish government to the British government, and even a demand for an apology for ordering the crimes against the Armenians to be recorded at the time. According to the Turkish government, the book had been no more than propaganda, and was therefore based on lies. The letter of protest was signed by both the prime minister and the then leader of the opposition, and was read out in parliament. As a reaction, Taner Akçam (2005) published an article in which he argued that the 'Bleu Book' was certainly based on facts and that it is totally out of order to demand an apology. The official Turkish point of view on the 'Armenian question' is that simultaneous acts of terror by the Armenians led to great losses on the Turkish side, a reciprocity that makes loss and suffering mutual. As both sides hold fast to their own version of history, these contested memories make a solution, or even the beginning of mourning a traumatic past, impossible. In Turkish eyes, Turkey might have perpetrated this cruelty, but was certainly also a victim.

According to Olick (2007), the public recognition of atrocities perpetrated in the name of a nation can lead to significant problems of legitimacy for national institutions. Neil Smelser (2004) maintains that if such collective memories are transformed into eradicable facts, they may be experienced as threatening to the group as such. While the trauma of the Armenians is immense, the Turkish state has its own collective trauma in the (increasing) fear that recognition of the events of 1915 will eventually lead to the destruction of the Turkish state: 'The fundamental fear that shapes the contours of citizenship politics in Turkey is fear of the disintegration of the state' (Kadıoğlu 2011: 43). And so, the principles of official state ideology dictate that the past must be left in peace and that all effort must be concentrated on the here and now and on safeguarding the future. This makes it exceedingly difficult to debate events that occurred at the very foundation of the state. But at the same time, external and internal factors have made that very same state ideology itself a topic of debate, while ever more historians and other

4 See, for a small selection from the pile of more recent studies, Confino (2008). On Turkish collective memory, see, for example, Özyürek (2001, 2007).

intellectuals stress the importance of past events and their continued influence on the present.

Conclusions

Turkey must be seen as still embroiled in a process of transition from the Ottoman Empire to the Republic of Turkey and its corresponding identity. This has left little to no scope for any narrative other than the official one. Preoccupations with national security and the international context in which the new nation state found itself (such as the Second World War and the Cold War) relieved the Turks of the necessity of facing up to their own history, but also of acknowledging their own suffering and loss. By now, however, the passage of time has complicated confrontation with collective violence committed by the state and its subjects. As soon as historical atrocities are mentioned, the reaction is to highlight Turkish suffering and compare it to that of others; one's own always appears far greater. Against this background it becomes difficult to recognize the other as a victim.

At the same time, Turkey was founded to counter both internal and external attempts to dismantle and divide the Ottoman Empire. The founding narrative emphasizes that it is the army that managed to maintain the sovereignty of the new republic against all odds. To admit that the elimination of the Armenians was intentional would undermine the legitimacy of the idea of Turkish victimhood, national trauma and, eventually, national redemption. It would also damage the legitimacy of the army, according to the official ideology the saviour of the nation and the most trustworthy (political) institution in the land. The nationalistic narrative is promoted and sustained by the modern Turkish nation state and its various institutions. It considers the Turkish state and Turkish society as one and the same and to criticize or even to call this imagery and narrative into question is considered to undermine Turkey, or even to commit an act of treason. Since the reforms and liberalization of the 1980s, political organizations have been established and a civil society has emerged. Minorities like Greeks, Kurds, Alevis and even Armenians have demanded a voice and while they might still not be fully seen as equal citizens, they are recognized and accepted as part of Turkey.

Increasingly, Islamists have been an important factor and they have formed the ruling party since the elections of 2002. They have begun to challenge the dominant, secular nationalistic history-writing and to highlight the agency of religion in Turkey. Gallipoli has become the subject of intense commemoration since the 1990s and commemoration, ceremonies and monument-building have been ongoing ever since. In Gallipoli we can see the continuation of negotiation of identities but also the paradox of the question of Turkish identity. It comprises both the great self-assurance and feelings of not being recognized that make Turkey quick to assume the role of victim. The Sèvres syndrome then rears its head, as it did during the commemorations at Gallipoli in 2010 when the prime minister berated the international community and foreign parliaments who talk of genocide against the Armenians for besmirching the memory of the fallen at Gallipoli, and called on them to first learn what Gallipoli meant and still means (Çanakkaleden Soykırım Dersi 2010). Elsewhere, Turkey in the First World War is a black page in history; in Turkey itself, the talk is of glorious deeds and hard-won freedom.

Turkey is now at a turning point, and the republic itself is being contested. In an interview with a Swiss newspaper (Teuwsen 2005), the Turkish writer and Nobel prizewinner Orhan Pamuk said 'A million Armenians and 30,000 Kurds were murdered in Turkey. Nobody talks about it, and they hate me because I talk about it.' This statement led to hate campaigns in the Turkish press and to Pamuk being charged with treason. Just how deeply and violently entrenched nationalism in Turkey still is, was also demonstrated by the brutal murder of the Armenian-Turkish human rights activist and journalist Hrant Dink in January 2007 (Freely 2007). This time, however, the press reacted with horror, and the prime minister was quick to denounce what he called 'a shot aimed at Turkey' (Kurşun Dink'e değil Türkiye'ye sıkılmıştır 2007). Thousands of Turks took part in demonstrations to honour Dink and to express their anger at his cowardly assassination. Many carried placards with texts (in Turkish, Armenian and Kurdish) such as 'We are all Hrant Dink', 'We are all Armenians'. The reaction was swift. During a demonstration in February organized by left-wing Turkish movements and referring to the founder of the Republic of Turkey, Mustafa Kemal Atatürk, the slogan was 'We are all Mustafa Kemal, we are all Turkish'.

The year 2015 will see the commemoration of the 100th anniversary of the Battle of Gallipoli and of the Armenian genocide. It remains to be seen how developments might affect the official Turkish position on the Armenian deaths in 1915, and the country's own traumas. As yet it is a moot question whether the shameful facts of the Armenian genocide can still be repressed by the glorious deeds of Gallipoli. Or will internal and external pressures make it impossible to disguise the 'Armenian question' any longer, thereby making collective amnesia into collective, if probably still contested, memory?

References

Adrian, M.N. 1991. The Documentation of the World War I Armenian Massacres in the Proceedings of the Turkish Military Tribunal. *International Journal of Middle East Studies*, 23, 549-576.

Adrian, M.N. 1997. The Turkish Military Tribunal's Prosecution of the Authors of the Armenian Genocide: Four Major Court-Martial Series. *Holocaust and Genocide Studies*, 11(1), 28-59.

Akçam, T. 2001. *Insan Haklari ve Ermeni Sorunu: Ittihat ve Terakkiden Kurtuluş Savaşına* [Human Rights and the Armenian Question: From Ittihat ve Terakki to the War of Liberation]. Istanbul: Image.

Akçam, T. 2005. Bir Skandal: Türkiye Büyük Millet Meclisi'nin Mektubu ya da Şükrü Elekdağ ve Justin McCarthy bu Ülkeyi Nereye Sürüklüyorlar?

[A Scandal: The Letter of the Turkish Grand National Assembly, or, What Are Şükrü Elekdağ and Justin McCarthy Dragging This Country Into?] *Birikim*, May, no. 1934.

Akçam, T. 2006. *A Shameful Act: The Armenian Genocide and the Question of Turkish Responsibility*. New York: Metropolitan Books.

Akçam, T. 2007. *De Armeense genocide: een reconstructive*. Amsterdam: Nieuw Amsterdam.

Anderson, B. 2006. *Imagined Communities: Reflections on the Origin and Spread of Nationalism*. London: Verso.

Bloxham, D. 2005. *The Great Game of Genocide: Imperialism, Nationalism, and the Destruction of the Ottoman Armenians*. Oxford: Oxford University Press.

Bryce, T. and Toynbee, A. [1916] 2000. *The Treatment of the Armenians in the Ottoman Empire, 1915-1916. Documents presented to Viscount Grey of Falloden by Viscount Bryce*. Reading: Taderon Press.

Çaha, Ö. 2005. The Ideological Transformation of the Public Sphere: The Case of Turkey. *Turkish Journal of International Relations*, 4(1-2). Available at http://www.alternativesjournal.net/volume4/number1/caha3.pdf (accessed October 2012).

Çambel, Hasan Cemil. 1939. Atatürk ve Tarih. *TTK Belleten*, 3(10) (April).

Çanakkaleden Soykırım Dersi [Lesson on Genocide from Çanakkale]. 2010. *Yeni Şafak*, March. Available at http://yenisafak.com.tr/Politika/?i=247567 (accessed February 2012).

Confino, A. 2008. Memory and the History of Mentalities. In *Cultural Memory Studies: An Interdisciplinary Handbook*, edited by A. Erll and A. Nünning, 85-97. Berlin: Walter de Gruyter.

Deren, S. and Bora, T. 2003. Milli eğitim üzerine muhafezakar görüşler. In *Modern Türkiye'de Siyasi Düşünce: Muhafazarlık*, edited by A. Çiğdem. Istanbul: İletişim Yayınları.

Dündar, F. 2001. *Ittihat ve Terakki'nin Müslümanları İskan Politikası* [The Muslims' Resettlement Policy of the Committee of Union and Progress (1913-1918)]. Istanbul: İletişim Yayınları.

Erdoğan: Tarihe yeni bir altın sayfa yazmak istiyoruz [We Want to Add a New Golden Page to History]. 2008. *Sabah gazetesi*, March. Available at http://arsiv.sabah.com.tr/2008/03/18/haber,E57C7DA31B2B4B94AF1ADEC461B6A020.html (accessed January 2012).

Erickson, E.J. 2001. *Ordered to Die: A History of the Ottoman Army in the First World War*. Westport, CT: Greenwood Press.

Ersanlı Behar, B. 1996. *Iktidar ve Tarih. Türkiye'de "Resmi Tarih" Tezinin oluşumu (1929-1937)*. Istanbul: AFA Yayınları.

Freely, M. 2007. Why They Killed Hrant Dink. Available at http://www.eurozine.com/articles/2007-06-06-freely-en.html (accessed December 2011).

Gibbons, H.A. 1917. *The Blackest Page of Modern History Armenian Events of 1915 – the Facts and Responsibilities*. New York and London: Putnam's Sons.

Göçek, F.M. 2011. *The Transformation of Turkey: Redefining State and Society from the Ottoman Empire to the Modern Era.* London: I.B.Tauris.
Gust. W. ed. 2005. *Der Völkermord an den Armeniern 1915/1916. Dokumente aus dem Politischen Archiv des deutschen Auswärtigen Amts. Zeitschrift für Geschichtswissenschaft*, 53(1-6). Berlin: Deutscher Verlag der Wissenschaften.
Helmreich, P.C. 1974. *From Paris to Sevres: The Partition of the Ottoman Empire at the Peace Conference of 1919-1920.* Columbus: Ohio State University Press.
Kadıoğlu, A. 2011. The Twin Motives of Turkish Nationalism. In *Symbiotic Antagonisms: Competing Nationalisms in Turkey*, edited by A. Kadıoğlu and E.F. Keyman. Salt Lake City: University of Utah Press.
Kaplan, I. 2005. *Türkiyede Milli Eğitim İdeolojisi.* Istanbul: İletişim yayınları.
Karpat, K. ed. 2000, *Ottoman Past and Todays Turkey.* Leiden: E.J. Brill.
Kevorkian, R. 2011. *The Armenian Genocide: A Complete History.* London: I.B. Taurus.
Kurşun Dink'e değil Türkiye'ye sıkılmıştır [The Bullet Didn't Hit Dink, But Turkey]. 2007. *Zaman*, January. Available at http://www.zaman.com.tr/haber.do?haberno=490064&title=kursun-dinke-degil-turkiyeye-sikilmistir&haber Sayfa=3 (accessed January 2012).
Lewy, G. 2005a. *The Armenian Massacres in Ottoman Turkey: A Disputed Genocide.* Salt Lake City: University of Utah Press.
Lewy, G. 2005b. Revisiting the Armenian Genocide. *Middle East Quarterly*, 12(4), 3-12.
McCarthy, J. 1989. *Turks and Armenians: A Manual on the Armenian Question.* Washington, DC: Committee on Education, Assembly of Turkish American Associations.
Morgenthau. H. 1918. *Ambassador Morgenthau's Story.* Available at http:/www.blackmask.com (accessed December 2011).
Mosse, G.L. 1990. *Fallen Soldiers: Reshaping the Memory of the World Wars.* Oxford: Oxford University Press.
Nora, P. 1996. *Realms of Memory*, vol. I: *Conflicts and Divisions: Rethinking the French Past.* New York: Colombia University Press.
Olick, J.K. 2007. From Usable Pasts to the Return of the Repressed. *Hedgehog Review*, 9(2), 19-31.
Özkırımlı, U. and Sofos, S.A. 2008. *Tormented by History: Nationalism in Greece and Turkey.* New York: Colombia University Press.
Özyürek, E. ed. 2001. *Hatırladıklarıyla ve unuttuklarıyla. Türkiyenin toplumsal hafizası.* Istanbul: İletişim Yayınları.
Özyürek, E. ed. 2007. *The Politics of Public Memory in Turkey.* Syracuse, NY: Syracuse University Press.
Renan, E. 1882. *What is a Nation* [Qu'est-ce qu'une nation?]. Lecture delivered at the Sorbonne on 11 March 1882. Available at http://ig.cs.tu berlin.de/oldstatic/w2001/eu1/dokumente/Basistexte/Renan1882EN-Nation.pdf (accessed January 2011).

Smelser, N.J. 2004. Psyological Trauma and Cultural Trauma. In *Cultural Trauma and Collective Identity*, edited by J.A. Alexander, R. Eyerman, B. Giesen, N.J. Smelser and P. Sztompka, pp. 31-59. Berkeley: University of California Press.

Üngor, U.U. 2009. Young Turc Social Engineering: Mass Violence and the Nation State in Eastern Turkey, 1913-1950. Dissertation UvA, Amsterdam.

Üngör, U.U. 2011. *The Making of Modern Turkey: Nation and State in Eastern Anatolia, 1913-1950*. Oxford: Oxford University Press.

Zerubavel, J. 1995. *Recovered Roots, Collective Memory and the Making of Israeli National Tradition*. London and Chicago: University of Chicago Press.

Zürcher, E.J. 1984. *The Unionist Factor: The Role of the Committee of Union and Progres in the Turkish National Movement 1905-1926*. Leiden: E.J. Brill.

Zürcher, E.J. 2005. *Turkey: A Modern History*. London: I.B. Taurus.

Chapter 2

The Lives and Times of Sentenced Nazi War Criminals: Re-negotiating Guilt and Innocence in Post-Nuremberg Germany 1950-1975[1]

Susanne Karstedt

The end of impunity?

'Ending impunity' is perhaps the most compelling image and vision behind the extraordinary development of international criminal justice that has taken place over the last decades. As a battle cry it has also driven the global development of transitional justice procedures in post-conflict and post-authoritarian societies. Without doubt there has been an unprecedented, and unexpected, proliferation of international and national procedures across the globe that deal with atrocities of past regimes and conflicts and aim to bring perpetrators to justice. Since 1990, there has been a steady increase in such procedures at the national and international level, and at least two have been active each year since 1990 (Karstedt 2012a). This process has coincided with a decisive shift away from the perpetrators to the victims of mass atrocities and grave human rights violations (Karstedt 2010a). While punishment and deterrence, or 'staying the hand of vengeance' were defining objectives in the Nuremberg trials after the Second World War, and deterrence was explicitly included as a major objective in the United Nations Convention on the Prevention and Punishment of the Crime of Genocide in 1948, contemporary transitional justice procedures decisively aim at doing justice to and for victims. Ending impunity for perpetrators simultaneously implies that the dignity of victims is restored and their needs are addressed. It is in this context that questions arise as to what actually constitutes an 'end to impunity' for horrendous crimes and often numerous perpetrators that will equally satisfy the thirst for justice of domestic victims, citizens and finally the international community.

As much as the proliferation of these procedures, which I will call collectively 'transitional', indeed signals an end to impunity for perpetrators, this development is increasingly accompanied by voices of criticism (for example Koskenniemi

1 I am grateful to Matthias Koch, MA Sociology, University of Bielefeld for research and data collection. This chapter is partially based on Karstedt (2010a, 2012b).

2002). These question the role of international and national procedures in actually ending impunity, the success of courts and truth commissions in doing justice to and for victims, and the potential bias on whose impunity is ended (and who goes unpunished). International efforts to end a culture of impunity are intricately linked to the politics of punishment and/or impunity, to international as well as domestic power relations, and as such inevitably incur the blame of being 'victor's justice'. Ending a 'culture of impunity' implies more than meting out sentences for perpetrators; it includes efforts at re-educating perpetrator groups about these crimes and at re-establishing moral standards of society, both objectives that pose immensurable challenges to societies emerging from long-term conflicts.

In its quest for the end of impunity, the international community has considerably raised the thresholds for impunity. The attempt to universalize an 'end of impunity' is confronted with transitional justice institutions and procedures in the domestic sphere and on the ground, where these – often established as truth commissions – provide an 'extra-legal' space and mechanisms that can ensure de facto impunity (Holtermann 2010).

Contemporary perspectives on the end of impunity are focused on procedures, courts and sentencing, and neglect the actual execution of sentences, such as, for example, length and conditions of imprisonment. However, ending impunity also implies executing sentences and actually subjecting perpetrators to punishment. As Hannah Arendt pointed out during the Nuremberg trials, any sentence (even the death penalty) is inadequate in the light of horrendous and incommensurable crimes that simply defy justice (cited in Koskenniemi 2002). When the International Criminal Tribunal for the former Yugoslavia (ICTY) was established in the 1990s nearly half a century after the International Military Tribunal in Nuremberg, the attention of the international community was naturally focused on bringing the perpetrators to trial for genocide, war crimes and severe human rights abuses (Hagan 2003). Consequently the drafters of the respective treaties and agreements that established the ICTY, the Rwandan Tribunal and later the International Criminal Court, almost entirely neglected questions regarding the execution of sentences, where these should be served and which national laws should apply to those subsequently incarcerated in various prisons scattered across Western Europe. This also implied questions of rehabilitation of these perpetrators, their early release and parole, in sum how the execution of sentences was in line with general and human rights based principles of sentencing (see Schabas 1997, 2000). As Van Zyl Smit (2002a, 2002b, 2005) points out, sentencing guidelines did not exist, and it was equally left undecided which (national) laws and regulations should apply. In fact, the contrast between meticulous regulation of the prosecution and the trial and the nearly total neglect of regulation for the execution of sentences speaks to a myopic court – and procedure-centred approach to the 'end of impunity'.

This chapter addresses these contemporary problems of impunity and punishment in international criminal justice through the lens of the post-war history of (West) Germany, where, between 1950 and 1975, hundreds of sentenced war criminals returned from prison, including the 'celebrity' defendants of the

Nuremberg trials who had served their sentences in Spandau Prison (Goda 2007). They had stood trial for war crimes and crimes against humanity (genocide), and had received the death penalty (which had been commuted) or (life)long prison sentences. In Germany, this group of (mostly) men comprised a considerable number; more than half of the 6,500 perpetrators who stood trial in (West) Germany were sentenced in the immediate post-war period (Karstedt 2008; Rückerl 1984). This group included numerous high-ranking members of the military, political and administrative elites (Karstedt 1998, 2010a) and those from lower ranks who had been directly involved in mass atrocities.

This study explores guilt and impunity at the interface between individual lives and reputations and the moral climate in post-war German society. These perpetrators in many ways represented the overall collective experience of the post-war population of Germany. Their experiences of their trials, imprisonment and final release, as well as their life afterwards exemplify the ways in which guilt and innocence were (re)constructed, managed and shared by offenders, their social circles, the media, politicians and the government, and the wider public. As many of them had been well-known figures during the Nazi regime, they also shaped the ways in which other and minor, less implicated members of their groups and organizations re-defined their reputations. Thus, they had a role in the development of collective amnesia in post-war Germany and the general climate of impunity that pervaded German society during the first decade after the war.

Ending impunity and the transitional context: history and theory

Ending impunity of leaders, generals and bureaucrats was the rationale behind the first successful attempt at international criminal justice in the Nuremberg trials, the International Military Tribunal (IMT) and its follow-up trials. However, the history of bringing perpetrators to justice after the Second World War and the respective record has often been perceived as one of impunity writ large, and a failure of justice. This applies particularly to (West) Germany itself, which has a long and tormented history in which impunity, silence, amnesty and missed opportunities have alternated with recognition, prosecution and major trials up to the present day. After the efforts of the Allies had terminated in the foundation of the Federal Republic of Germany in 1949, its first decade until the early 1960s was dominated by collective amnesia and a thorough absence of credible efforts at prosecuting genocide and crimes against humanity. This did not differ decisively from the situation in other European countries, and as the historian Tony Judt argued, 'without … collective amnesia Europe's astonishing post-war recovery would not have been possible' (2005: 61). In sum, since 1945, about 6,500 perpetrators have been punished in the area/jurisdiction of West Germany (respectively the zones of the three Western Allies), out of about 90,000 investigations. In more than 80,000 cases no sentences were obtained because the perpetrators had not survived the war, their individual responsibility could not be proven, they had already been sentenced in other countries or had fled the country (Rückerl 1984). Many of the perpetrators received a pardon or were released before they had served their sentences. Nonetheless, in hindsight, the prosecution of the perpetrators of war crimes and the Holocaust cannot be rated as a total failure, and it has been vigorously – though not without glaring omissions and mistakes – resumed since the 1960s, the last major trial being that of John Demjanjuk (2010/2011).

If sentences are incapable of reflecting the enormity of crimes, as Hannah Arendt argued, what is their significance within the context of ending impunity? Punishment of offenders, as Durkheim famously claimed, has its main function for the community not in the control of crime but in enhancing social solidarity. This implies solidarity with the victim – though as such not explicitly mentioned by Durkheim – and strengthening the common and shared values and norms of the community. The ceremonial procedures of courts and tribunals are important in addressing and eliciting collective sentiments, but of equal importance is the social context where moral judgements are made, and where impunity and punishment are lived and experienced. While contemporary international courts and national procedures aim first and foremost at reaching out to the communities of the victims of such crimes, their audience actually represents a community of victims *and* of perpetrators (and bystanders). While the penal functions of affirming values and norms of the community, of confirming the justice system and its legitimacy, and of reinforcing group solidarity (including the victim) will work in established communities, this will hardly be possible in transitional and post-conflict societies. These are divided societies, without a common core of values or even common interests defined. Consequently, solidarity is limited and confined, in particular in societies with entrenched conflicts where victims were and still are 'enemies'.

In sum, in transitional societies, decisive structural and normative requirements are not in place for punishment to actually function as reinforcement and affirmation of norms within communities, as a mechanism to establish solidarity with victims, censure perpetrators and 'outlaw' impunity. Reactions of communities might therefore amount to actual impunity for perpetrators: they are exonerated in the eyes of the public, they receive support that is normally not granted to criminal offenders and they emerge from court procedures and imprisonment with their reputations unscathed (Karstedt 2010a, 2012b). These reactions in turn will confirm and (re-)establish the offender's own perceptions of his or her actions, of the crimes committed, of the legitimacy of the court and judgment, and in particular will allow the offender to neutralize the sentence, renegotiate guilt and re-establish innocence. In this context, the community of perpetrators is as important as the community of victims in bringing impunity to an end, as they are powerful actors in thwarting the message of 'ending impunity'.

Communities provide the moral environment in which punishment and impunity are juxtaposed, where memories and amnesia conflict, where offenders return and are received back, and where they are confronted by victims. Individual and collective morality, guilt and perceptions of responsibility are intricately linked in these encounters and processes. According to Fine, reputations, and perceptions of guilt and innocence are 'embedded in social relations, and as a consequence, reputation is connected to the forms of communication embedded within a community' (2001: 3). Reputations are managed and shaped by individuals, but this cannot be done without the sounding board and mirror of public opinion, and acceptance or rejection of the (proposed) image by the community; they provide the space where damaged reputations are re-established and repaired, and for re-negotiating guilt and innocence after sentences and punishment.

Legal procedures, moral assessment and public opinion in post-war German society

The Nuremberg trials: message and legacy

It is widely accepted that the German population perceived the Nuremberg trials as 'victor's justice', thus thwarting the tribunal's aims of uncovering the 'truth' and educating the public about the horrendous crimes committed in its name, and paving the way towards impunity for the many perpetrators (for example Koskenniemi 2002). However, contemporary public opinion was much more supportive than this common imagery of rejection suggests, and ambivalent rather than unequivocal. On several occasions in the following decades, the Nuremberg trials were evoked as a model transitional justice; the continuous appeal of an international tribunal like Nuremberg is evidenced by a considerable proportion of Germans who suggested it in the case of Eichmann and after German re-unification for the crimes of the former GDR elites (Karstedt 1998, 2008).

The Nuremberg Tribunal was only one of the numerous trials that were conducted elsewhere in Europe, where the crimes had actually taken place. It was without doubt the most outstanding and visible amongst the trials, and the one that defined the whole process. The defendants represented a carefully selected group from party, military and administrative elites in order to demonstrate the implication of the state, party and military machinery. The Nuremberg Tribunal was designed to achieve *symbolic justice for all victims* by punishing a small number of members of the highest leadership echelon. Public opinion on and support for the Tribunal was situated in the more complex post-conflict situation, which contributed in itself to how Nuremberg and other proceedings were perceived by the Germans and shaped their perceptions of justice and punishment. Contemporary surveys show that the majority – between 80 and 75 per cent – of Germans rated the trial as fair from the beginning and did not significantly change their minds. Already at the start of the IMT, 70 per cent agreed that all the defendants were guilty. The majority (60 per cent) rated none of the final verdicts as 'too harsh' and 55 per cent found them 'just'. The German public obviously found 'victors' justice' just and fair, and supported the way it was accomplished as well as the final outcomes. Though never for a majority, the Nuremberg trials instilled a sense of collective moral guilt in the Germans. When the IMT had come to an end in December 1946, after the final verdicts and the execution of the death sentences, 30 per cent of Germans were willing to accept such a collective moral responsibility for the atrocities (for a detailed account, see Karstedt 1998, 2008).

The moral message of the Nuremberg Tribunal was by no means unambiguous, and several of its characteristics made it easy for Germans to perceive themselves as victims and claim impunity. First, only representatives from the highest echelons were on trial, thus leading the public to put all blame for the crimes on the Nazi leadership. Second, the Tribunal itself had revealed the plans of the Nazi government to implement scorched earth policies in Germany at the end of the war, thus confirming the belief that the Germans had been held victim by their own leadership. Third, nearly all voices of the actual victims were silenced and excluded (Karstedt 2010b). Consequently, the Nuremberg Tribunal was a trial that gave voice only to the perpetrators, and addressed a public nearly exclusively composed of the people of the perpetrators. In the 'audience' of the trial the Germans were 'among themselves' as perpetrators and they could also avoid any confrontations with victims in their everyday lives. Finally, the foundations of the Tribunal prioritized the charges of state aggression and conspiracy, rather than war crimes and crimes against humanity. Among the latter, charges of war crimes defined the public perception of the trial rather than the crimes of the Holocaust. This turned out to be important in later facilitating the renegotiation of guilt for perpetrators who returned from prison.

It is exactly this ambiguity of the message of the Nuremberg Tribunal that might have contributed to its widespread support. In a much less straightforward way than would have been desirable from the perspective of ending impunity, the Tribunal instigated a public re-evaluation of the Hitler dictatorship and the Nazi regime, allowing the German public to put all blame for the disaster on this small group, and feel themselves exonerated. Further to this, as the people of perpetrators were among themselves they could easily adopt the role of victims who had been misled by their leadership. Thus, in a paradoxical way the Nuremberg Tribunal provided the opportunity for the Germans to revenge themselves on their leadership through the victorious Allies.

Impunity and collective amnesia 1949-1960

The IMT itself, the series of simultaneous and follow-up trials, as well as the de-Nazification procedures in Germany demonstrated that the criminal justice model had emerged as the main instrument of the Allies to end impunity for the perpetrators of crimes against humanity and those who had orchestrated the Holocaust. However, amnesties were an integral, though unplanned part of the model, and sweeping amnesties had already started under the auspices of the Allies. The mixture of criminal justice and ad-hoc amnesties shaped public opinion and assessment of the Nuremberg trials and de-Nazification for the decade to come and gave rise to a climate and politics of impunity.

After the foundation of the Federal Republic of Germany in 1949, the mood of the public turned to closing the books and putting the past to rest, though this never included the former Nazi leadership (Karstedt 2008). First, Chancellor Konrad Adenauer expressed this mood when publicly asking for a halt to further scrutinizing of the past of high-ranking officials and civil servants. This encouraged networks of former high-ranking Nazi officials and SS officers to promote blanket amnesties and a general pardon, which did not materialize because of the adamant opposition of the Americans and Adenauer himself (Herbert 1996: 501). Nonetheless, those who had been ousted from office by de-Nazification were allowed to resume their offices (with the exception of high-ranking SS officers) or claim their pensions by a bill passed in parliament in the early 1950s. Other amnesties ensured indemnity for violence and killings at the very end of the war if the acts had been committed in the belief that they had been ordered as a duty, which amounted to a blanket amnesty for atrocities and war crimes (Perels 1999: 207). In 1953, when acceding to the European Convention of Human Rights, the German government decided to do so with a proviso concerning Article 7, 2; this section had been introduced against the background of the Nuremberg trials, and allowed for retrospective punishment of 'any act or omission which, at the time when it was committed, was criminal according to the general principles of law recognized by civilized nations'. This would have facilitated the prosecution of atrocities that had been deemed legal during the Nazi regime, and in particular it established the legality of the Nuremberg trials; debates in the German parliament demonstrate that the government and politicians were well aware of this background and prospect (Lippott and Turzer 2009). When ratifying the International Covenant on Civil and Political Rights in 1968, which included an identical clause, the then German government did not express any reservations, and thus quietly opened the door for further prosecution (Lippott and Turzer 2009).[2] Until the 1960s, legal provisions amounting to a stealthy amnesty for atrocities were slipped in under the cover of other laws (Perels 1999: 211). Not surprisingly, German politicians and criminal justice officials were reluctant to resume the prosecution of war criminals and those who had been involved in the Holocaust.

Polls from the late 1940s and throughout the 1950s give evidence of this thorough swing in public opinion with regard to the trials and the lessons to be drawn from them. In September 1952, those who thought that it was unjust to keep the Nuremberg defendants (Dönitz, Schirach, Hess, Speer) in prison, were outnumbering those who thought it justified in all cases (Noelle and Neumann 1956: 202). In 1951, in hindsight about a quarter of the population disapproved of the trials and the de-Nazification procedures, however the overwhelming majority did not count them among the major flaws of occupational policies (Noelle and Neumann 1956: 140). In 1953, the majority (55 per cent) were of

2 This discrepancy went largely unnoticed, and was finally removed in 2001 by a declaration to the Secretary General of the Council of Europe (see, for details, Lippott and Turzer 2009).

the view that German soldiers could not be reproached for any wrongdoing in the war (Noelle and Neumann 1956: 137). Nonetheless, in a 1958 poll, which asked if war criminals should still be prosecuted and punished, a bare majority of 54 per cent of the public opted for punishment in contrast to 34 per cent who were in favour of closing the books on the past (Noelle and Neumann 1965: 221). It is important to note that, even during the period of collective amnesia, the better educated and those in higher positions or in the professions were generally more supportive of prosecution (Emnid 1949: 8-10; Emnid 1954: 6). In sum, public opinion was ambivalent and divided on the question of impunity, notwithstanding a strong tendency towards an 'end to punishment'. This ambiguity is mirrored by the policies of the government, which took a cautious stance towards amnesties, commuting of sentences and release of prisoners.

Changing the climate of impunity: the impact of major trials

Preparations for resuming the prosecution of war criminals and those involved in mass killings had started with the inauguration of the Central Office for the Investigation of National Socialist Crimes (Zentrale Stelle der Landesjustizverwaltungen zur Aufklärung nationalsozialistischer Verbrechen) in 1958, which still owed very much to the relentless efforts of a handful of individuals. Due to increasing pressure from abroad and international organizations like the Jewish Documentation Centre founded by Simon Wiesenthal in Austria after the war, it had become clear that many of the most atrocious crimes had not been brought to justice, and that a concerted effort was necessary. From the beginning of the 1960s, three important trials thoroughly and forever changed the way Germans could look back at their past: the Eichmann trial in 1961 in Jerusalem, the Auschwitz trial of 1963-1965 and the Majdanek trial from 1975 to 1981, both in Germany.

The significance of these trials was mostly due to the fact that they made the victims visible and their voices heard. In the first of these, the Eichmann trial, the Germans found the final confrontation with the victims' voices hard to bear: 51 per cent feared that Eichmann would symbolize Germany in the future and hurt its reputation – which was certainly justified. Nonetheless, a majority (72 per cent) were in favour of prosecution and punishment, and also of severe sentences, either the death penalty or life imprisonment (Noelle and Neumann 1965: 227, 228, 225). The Auschwitz trial in Frankfurt from 1963 to 1965 was *the* 'key event' (Ein Prozess 2005) for German society. Even if it could muster less attention among the German public than the Eichmann trial, Pendas (2006) rightly terms it a 'cultural watershed' which mainly became visible in media coverage. The trial illuminated the horror of the death camps and the Holocaust in graphic detail, the victims had a real presence in Germany for the first time, and media coverage was extensive. This time mass murderers of a very low rank were on trial, though only 20 of the more than a thousand guards and officials who had served in Auschwitz. As one of the victim witnesses ironically put it, 'the rest has dissolved into the population' (Ein Prozess 2005).

Contemporary polls do not fully support the significance later attributed to the trial (for example Silbermann and Stoffers 2000). While a slight majority (53 per cent) supported the trial and found it 'right', among these one-third named the recovery of truth as their main reason and two-thirds supported the trial because 'those responsible for the mass murder in Auschwitz should be adjudicated and punished' (DIVO 1964: 6). However, nearly 40 per cent were against the trial because 'after so many years these things should not be brought up again' (DIVO 1964: 8). Importantly, business and industry leaders were mostly opposed to the Auschwitz trial, since for the first time it revealed the full extent of their involvement in the genocide of the European Jews. For both the Eichmann and Auschwitz trials, the impact on the new generation was strongest. Both trials paved the way for the abolishment of the statute of limitation for murder, which allows for the prosecution of perpetrators up to the present day.

Former Nazi war criminals and their lives after punishment: redefining guilt and innocence

The patterns of exoneration, impunity and renegotiation of guilt in post-war (West) Germany are explored here through exemplary cases of sentenced Nazi war criminals from a more comprehensive database (34 cases). These perpetrators of genocide and war crimes were sentenced in the various trials conducted by the Allies (mainly the US) at Nuremberg between 1945 and 1949, and later in the Federal Republic of Germany (until the 1980s). Cases were collected from secondary sources for different groups, each representing a specific group in the hierarchy of the Nazi regime and the military. Perpetrators who were sentenced in the occupied countries or in later trials in these countries are not included, and the sample of cases is built exclusively on perpetrators of German nationality. The selection was mainly guided by the availability of information about their lives after punishment. The sample, from which exemplary cases are presented here, includes the following groups: (a) members of the Nazi elite, who were tried at the International Military Tribunal in Nuremberg between 1945 and 1946, and in the follow-up trials in Nuremberg between 1946 and 1949; (b) high-ranking members of the armed forces who were charged with war crimes and tried in one of the follow-up trials in Nuremberg (Trial of the High Command of the Army) and by the Allies in their respective theatres of war; (c) members of the SS mostly directly involved in genocidal action; these were mainly sentenced in the 'Task Force Trials' conducted between 1947 and 1948 in Nuremberg, but also in the Federal Republic of Germany in the 1950s (for the full sample, see Karstedt 2010a, 2012b).

The full sample represents all hierarchical levels of the machinery of killing in the Nazi state, while the cases included here were mainly from its upper echelons.

As they stood trial in the immediate post-war situation, they could take advantage of the overall climate of impunity. Their trials and later imprisonment took place in a historical period and within a collective that was still fully over-shadowed by the Nazi regime, the experience of war, defeat and the post-war years. Numerous cases in the sample typically started with death sentences, which were later commuted to life by US High Commissioner McCloy; most of the perpetrators served a fraction of their sentences, and with the exception of the Nuremberg defendants, none served the full sentence. Those sentenced in the immediate post-war period usually did not spend more than 10 years in prison, and most less than five years (Karstedt 2010a). In sum the overall sample is characterized by a pattern of 'post-sentence amnesty' or 'retroactive impunity' that was symptomatic of the first decades after the war.

Karl Dönitz: 'prisoner of war' in the community of the defeated

It had been the deliberate policy of the Allies to put the core leadership of the Nazi state on trial first, including the leadership of the armed forces, the economy, the Nazi bureaucracy and the media. Thus 24 men of highest status, rank and reputation stood trial, representing their institutions and organizations, as well as their members of lower ranks. Most were sentenced to death, three were acquitted, and of those who had received prison sentences four had a more public life after punishment.

Among these was Admiral Karl Dönitz, who had been the commander of the Navy since 1943 and succeeded Hitler as chancellor during the last days of the Nazi regime in 1945. He was sentenced in Nuremberg to 10 years imprisonment on charges of planning aggressive warfare and war crimes. His sentence was contested from the very first, and he saw it as a miscarriage of justice as he indicated in an interview in the 1970s (Dönitz 1972). After his release in 1956, he wrote his memoirs, *My Ever-Changing Life* (Dönitz 1968), which were modestly successful, and travelled the country first as speaker at meetings of veterans, and soon as speaker to the newly established Federal Army, respectively the Navy. As such, he led a semi-public life restricted to the smaller and professional, however never sub-cultural, social circles of the previous and new army. His case demonstrates the importance of organizations and networks for high-ranking members of the Nazi regime, and simultaneously the marginal role that they could assume even in such an environment and within a public that was overall receptive to claims of innocence and demands for impunity and forgetting.

In contrast to other defendants at the IMT (such as Speer) his sentence was based on charges of war crimes committed in the course of warfare and not against civilians. This allowed him to cast himself as a dutiful soldier and his prison sentence as time served as a prisoner of war of the Allies, a fate that many veterans shared and could identify with. Serving time as a prisoner of war was a duty that had to be accepted for losing the war, and this interpretation cleared him from the stigma of a penal sentence and imprisonment. His own accounts shed light on the mechanisms within these networks where his reputation was established and retained. In an interview in the 1970s (Dönitz 1972), he described how when travelling he was often approached by veterans and asked whether they might join his table, a wish willingly granted. As they shared memories, they conjured a sense of common fate and 'sameness', as former prisoners of war and more generally as soldiers, which put common soldiers and the former commander on a (nearly) equal footing. Karl Dönitz still embodied the values and norms of the military community; that he had been sentenced for war crimes was ignored. However, he never returned to politics or was granted an influential role in the establishment of the new army, as he had imagined he would do when in Spandau Prison (Speer 1975). When rearmament started and the new Federal Army was finally established in 1955, difficult questions arose around the highly sensitive issues of integrating the commanders and experts of the previous army, and of incorporating the military 'traditions' of its predecessor, the army of the Nazi state (*Wehrmacht*), which had been involved in the most heinous crimes and mass murder. It was not until the late 1970s that the Federal Army stopped naming barracks and other sites after high-ranking commanders in Hitler's army, and started renaming some of those linked to the names of war criminals. Unlike other former generals and high-ranking military leaders, such as Albert Kesselring (see below), Dönitz was well aware of his essentially fragile position and reputation and did not transgress the (invisible) boundaries set by the German government and international opinion and pressure. Like Speer, he was cautious in his hindsight evaluation of the Nazi regime, the war and his own actions.

Albert Speer: navigating legal and moral guilt

Already as a defendant at the IMT Albert Speer had attracted international media attention. He had established his reputation as 'Hitler's architect' and had been part of his inner circle. He was sentenced to 20 years imprisonment for his responsibility as minister of armament for organizing forced labour, including prisoners of war. From the start of the trial, he had accepted 'responsibility' as a member of the Nazi elite and government, though he always denied guilt in legal terms of the charges against him. In his memoirs and 'Spandau Diaries' (Speer 1969, 1975), which were international bestsellers, he presented himself as a technocrat who had been charmed by Hitler, and who was unaware of the atrocities and genocide planned and executed by the regime. He certainly had been decisive in orchestrating forced labour during the last years of the war, and it is also probable that he knew about the Holocaust, notwithstanding his denial (Sereny 1996). After having served the full term of 20 years and been released in 1966, his hugely successful memoirs and books provided him with a comfortable life, socially as well as financially. His intimate knowledge of Hitler made him a sought-after interview partner, and attracted the attention of leading international journalists and authors (Sereny 1996). His reputation as an 'innocent technocrat' not only triggered a public debate on the links between the neutrality of technology and its inherent necessities, totalitarian regimes and atrocities (Reif 1978), but also provided him with a relatively untarnished reputation that paved his way into the conservative elites of the emerging democracy. All this made him a kind of celebrity of his time.

However, his reputation was not uncontested, as in the mid-1960s public opinion and in particular attitudes in the younger generation had changed. The Holocaust was acknowledged as a crime sui generis, and the perpetrators indeed seen as criminals. The climate of impunity came to an end, even if slowly. Former members of the Nazi regime were deemed unacceptable when they returned to high positions at a similar level in the federal and state governments. In particular the nascent German student movement named, shamed and even attacked numerous individuals who were seen to be implicated in the Nazi regime and its atrocities. Speer himself admitted to his biographer Sereny that on his release he had not been aware of the extent to which public opinion had changed and condemnation of Hitler and his regime had come to dominate the public realm (Sereny 1996: 157). His reputation within high-level social circles was contested publicly and in leading print media (Reif 1978). He never revised his increasingly implausible claim that he had been fully unaware of the atrocities and the Holocaust (Sereny 1996). Like Dönitz, Speer could offer a backdrop for personal identification and thus both their reputations could rub off on the many others; for Speer, these were the high-level technocrats who had served the Nazi regime and orchestrated the Holocaust.[3]

Albert Kesselring: the realpolitik of retro-active impunity

According to agreements between the Allies, military leaders were extradited to the countries where they had committed their crimes, or were tried by court martial by the Allies, mostly in the countries of their respective theatres of war. Like Dönitz, former General Albert Kesselring had been a well-known commander during the war. He was tried by a British court martial in Venice as the commander responsible for shooting 335 Italian citizens who had been taken hostage in retaliation for the murder of German police officers by the Italian resistance army. His initial death sentence was first commuted to life imprisonment and later to 21 years by the British government. Having been diagnosed with cancer, he was released in an act of clemency by the Queen in 1952 (von Lingen 2009). During his detention and imprisonment, Kesselring had become a relentless reputational entrepreneur, who from his prison cell directed the support and activities of lawyers, university professors and politicians. Surprisingly, a campaign for his release sprang up in Britain, led by Lord Hankey and military historian Basil Liddell Hart (von Lingen 2009) and supported by high-ranking politicians, including Churchill, as well as

3 The image of the 'neutral technocrat' was useful and widely used; thus Speer's close collaborator Hans Kehrl, sentenced to 15 years of which he served two, published a book in 1973 with the title 'Crisis Manager in the Third Reich' (Kehrl 1973).

military leaders. The campaign was based on his reputation as an 'honest enemy', and certainly also driven by the prospect of integrating Germany into the new western alliance of NATO. As long as its former military leaders were imprisoned, the German public could hardly be persuaded to support the distinctly contentious issue of rearmament.

When still in prison, Kesselring had accepted the offer to become president of the largest association of veterans. After his release he embarked on public activities and issued statements that not only would clear him from any involvement in war crimes and exonerate him from any guilt, but also attempted to make his acts as commander in the Italian theatre appear as particularly honourable. This was not in line with the cautious diplomacy of the German government, and certainly transgressed what was acceptable to the British government and Italian citizens. In the ensuing diplomatic upheaval, he was summoned by the German government and ordered to refrain from further public statements, and was never involved in the planning for the new army. He did not become the public figure he had envisioned for himself. In his books, published during the 1950s, he never distanced himself from his crimes, nor did he dissociate himself from his loyalty to Hitler.

Even in the push towards retroactive impunity by the overt realpolitik of the Western Allies, Kesselring not only misjudged the normative and political climate when he tried to re-establish his reputation, he also overrated the support and backing that the German government could afford in this situation. Claiming total innocence was a step too far. He further underestimated the necessity to dissociate himself from the Nazi regime, which was essential for both his supporters outside Germany and the diplomacy of the German government. Kesselring's public statements and the ensuing diplomatic fall-out were brought to light and critically discussed in the emerging liberal press, which for the first time asserted its seminal role in shaping and changing the climate of impunity.

SS Task Force members and Protestant churchmen: campaigners, apologists and supporters

The SS Task Forces executed the Holocaust behind the front lines of the German Army. The men who were sentenced at the Task Force trials in Nuremberg had been deeply implicated: many of them were literally mass murderers; they had overseen the men who shot hundreds of thousands of Jewish men, women and children or, like Martin Sandberger, had orchestrated the genocide for large regions (Browning 1992). At the Nuremberg Task Force Trial, where mainly the commanders of SS Task Forces had been tried, many had received death sentences for the mass killings; these were often subsequently converted into life sentences, of which they eventually only served a fraction (Karstedt 2010a). The three cases included here are therefore representative of numerous others. Importantly, they also shed light on the dubious role of the Protestant Church and churchmen in campaigning against the death sentences, securing early release and positions afterwards for men who had been deeply involved in the most atrocious crimes.

Eugen Steimle received the death penalty for mass murder of the Jewish population in the Soviet Union, one of his most atrocious crimes being the mass killing of 50 disabled children. The sentence was commuted to 20 years imprisonment in 1951, of which he had served only three when he was released in 1954. After his release, the Protestant Church secured him a position as a teacher (for which he had trained) of history and civic studies at a Protestant gymnasium (grammar school), one of the faith-based schools run by the church. Ernst Biberstein had been a Protestant pastor before he joined the Nazi party and the SS. Because of his direct involvement in mass killings of more than 3,000 men, women and children he was sentenced to death at Nuremberg, which was commuted to a life sentence in 1951. The Protestant Church of North Germany was decisive in a campaign to turn the death sentence into life imprisonment. It continued to campaign for his final release in 1958, and he was offered a position in the administration of the church. As the Protestant Church revised its own position at the beginning of the 1960s (Conway 1992), he was soon dismissed.

Martin Sandberger had been one of the leading figures in orchestrating the genocide in the Baltic States and was responsible for the deaths of hundreds of thousands of victims there and later in Italy. At the Task Force Trial, he and more than 20 other defendants were found guilty of murdering over a million men, women and children, and 14 death sentences were imposed, more than at the IMT. Sandberg's sentence was commuted to life imprisonment by US High Commissioner McCloy in 1951, and he was released seven years later. He came from a family with strong and traditional connections to church leaders and a network of affiliated politicians. The Protestant Church of South-West Germany, represented by its bishop, and high-ranking politicians, including leading members of parliament, campaigned in Germany and the US for his release. Other supporters of the campaign included a highly renowned Social Democrat with impeccable anti-Nazi credentials, the prime minister of the state and the Federal President. These regional and church-affiliated networks secured him a position as a legal adviser in a major company, from where he rose to become a member of the management board. Attempts to resume prosecution all failed, as his lawyer was successful in arguing that he had been summarily sentenced for all crimes by the US in the Nuremberg Task Force Trial.

Both major churches in Germany were involved in shielding perpetrators from justice after the war. In particular most of the Protestant Church had been assimilated into the Nazi regime and had endorsed Nazi ideologies of war, racism and anti-Semitism. After the war, the Catholic Church supported fugitive war criminals en route to Latin American countries rather than engaging with sentenced war criminals. In contrast, The Protestant Church as an institution as well as a number of high-ranking churchmen committed themselves to pastoral as well as more encompassing care for prisoners of war and those who had been sentenced to death or imprisonment as war criminals. They attended to these men first mostly outside of Germany but increasingly in Germany itself, which shifted their concern from prisoners of war to perpetrators of mass atrocities. Whether deliberately or not, the boundaries between sentenced war criminals and prisoners of war became blurred, as the church and its representatives saw it as their duty to alleviate the plight of both groups. The controversial background of a number of churchmen made them more receptive to claims of unfair 'victor's justice', rejection of guilt and protesting the innocence of their charges. They campaigned for the release of the IMT defendants who were serving their sentences in Spandau Prison (Goda 2007), as well as for war criminals sentenced in France, the Netherlands and Belgium. In these endeavours they could enlist support from both church leaders untainted by involvement in the Nazi regime and government officials (Webster 2001). Consequently, the Protestant Church raised its voice for sentenced perpetrators of genocide, and added its moral weight to a broader consensus across the ideological and institutional spectrum that mirrored the climate of impunity and the general mood of the public.

When does impunity, when does punishment end?

When a 50-year sentence was given to 65-year-old Charles Taylor for numerous charges of international crimes, William Schabas invoked the clauses of the International Covenant on Civil and Political Rights that state the human rights of prisoners. He also recalled the 'haunting precedent' of Rudolf Hess, the last Nuremberg defendant, who was never released from Spandau Prison. He argues that 'there is no reason why Charles Taylor cannot be reformed and rehabilitated. This must not be forgotten as the Court attempts to find a sentence that adequately reflects the horror of the crimes that he committed' (Schabas 2012). This resonates with arguments that Federal President Theodor Heuss made on behalf of Martin Sandberger, when writing in support of his release from prison to US ambassador James Conant: 'Deprivation of liberty might – and I explicitly stress: might – have a purgatory (cathartic) impact' (quoted in Halbgott in Feldgrau 2010), expressing, like Schabas, the possibility of rehabilitation for this perpetrator of genocide.

As at its incipient moment when it first aimed at ending impunity, international criminal justice today is confronted with the vexed question of how to end punishment, if at all. They are intricately linked. In contrast to the Nuremberg trials, capital punishment was excluded when international criminal justice was resumed at the end of the twentieth century (Schabas 2000). However, as this research demonstrates, due to realpolitik and a climate of impunity that took hold in post-war Germany, many death sentences were commuted to life sentences, of which only a fraction were served even by the worst perpetrators.

Perhaps the most disturbing and shocking result of this research is that the climate of impunity, of 'post-sentence' amnesties and 'retroactive impunity', prevented any sense of shame or guilt – legally and morally – in the perpetrators, any expression of remorse, regret or sympathy for their victims. With the exception of Albert Speer, no such statement is known from any of the perpetrators in the overall sample. When Martin Sandberger was interviewed by journalists in 2010 (he died in 2011), he downplayed his involvement and refused any such statement. As his post-war career and that of many others shows, there was no vital need to reassess their atrocious actions or to signal any moral change as is usually expected from released and rehabilitated prisoners; even as the climate of impunity changed, they were largely forgotten and could slip under the radar of criminal justice.

The historical evidence of Germany provides several lessons. It demonstrates that international criminal justice needs support within the group of perpetrators, and needs to address these as audience; otherwise impunity is extended, and not ended. It suggests that truth and reconciliation commissions like the one in South Africa, even when related to amnesties, can be powerful instruments in changing the climate of impunity, as they force perpetrators out in the open and solicit public expressions of guilt and remorse rather than leaving the perpetrators within their own networks. It further shows that the voice of victims is decisive in ending impunity and changing the normative climate in society, and that major trials can achieve this. These changes need to penetrate, and be endorsed by, the major institutions of society, in particular those implicated in crimes against humanity and genocide. Ending impunity solely in the courtroom is not enough, and neither is harsh punishment. As it can never reflect the crimes, punishment needs to reflect the values and human rights that were violated in the first instance. Only in this way can international criminal justice forge the collective sentiments and solidarity that endorse moral change and end impunity.

References

Browning, C. 1992. *Ordinary Men: Police Battalion 101 and the Final Solution in Poland.* New York: HarperCollins.

Conway, J. 1992. The Political Role of German Protestantism 1870-1990. *Journal of Church and State*, 34, 819-842.

DIVO. 1964. *DIVO-Pressedienst*, July (I/II), Frankfurt: DIVO.

Dönitz, K. 1968. *Mein wechselvolles Leben* [My Ever-Changing Life]. Göttingen: Musterschmidt.

Dönitz, K. 1972. *Deutsche Strategie zur See im Zweiten Weltkrieg: Die Antworten des Grossadmirals auf 40 Fragen.* Frankfurt/Main: Bernardt & Graefe.

Ein Prozess, der die Republik veränderte. 2005. *Die Zeit*, 34, 19 August.

Emnid Institut für Marktforschung und Marktbeobachtung. 1949. *Sind wir Demokraten?* Bielefeld.

Emnid Institut für Marktforschung und Marktbeobachtung. 1954. *Zum Problem des Antisemitismus in der Bunderepublik: September/Oktober 1954.* Bielefeld.

Fine, G.A. 2001. *Difficult Reputations: Collective Memories of the Evil, Inept and Controversial.* Chicago and London: University of Chicago Press.

Goda, N. 2007. *Tales from Spandau: Nazi Criminals and the Cold War.* Cambridge: Cambridge University Press.

Hagan, J. 2003. *Justice in the Balkans: Prosecuting War Crimes in the Hague Tribunal*. Chicago: University of Chicago Press.

Halbgott in Feldgrau. 2010. *Der Spiegel*, 14, 5 April, 38-41.

Herbert, U. 1996. *Best: Biographische Studien über Radikalismus, Weltanschauung und Vernunft 1903-1989*. Bonn: Dietz Nachfolger.

v. Holtermann, J. 2010. The End of 'the End of Impunity'? The International Criminal Court and the Challenge from Truth Commissions. *Res Publica*, 16, 209-225.

Judt, T. 2005. *Postwar: A History of Europe since 1945*. London: William Heinemann.

Karstedt, S. 1998. Coming to Terms with the Past in Germany after 1945 and 1989: Public Judgments on Procedures and Justice. *Law and Policy*, 20, 15-56.

Karstedt, S. 2008. The Nuremberg Tribunal and German Society: International Justice and Local Judgment in Post-Conflict Reconstruction. In *The Legacy of Nuremberg: Civilising Influence or Institutionalised Vengeance?*, edited by D.A. Blumenthal and T. McCormack, International Humanitarian Law Series, 20, 13-35. Leiden: Koninklijke Brill.

Karstedt, S. 2010a. Life after Punishment for Nazi War Criminals: Reputation, Careers and Normative Climate in Post-War Germany. In *Escape Routes: Contemporary Perspectives on Life after Punishment*, edited by S. Farrall, R. Sparks, S. Maruna and M. Hough, 240-275. Abingdon: Routledge.

Karstedt, S. 2010b. From Absence to Presence, from Silence to Voice: Victims in Transitional Justice since the Nuremberg Trials. *International Review of Victimology*, 17(1), 9-30.

Karstedt, S. 2012a. Globalisation, Mass Atrocities and Genocide. In *Globalisation and the Challenge to Criminology*, edited by F. Pakes, Abingdon: Routledge.

Karstedt, S. 2012b. Contested Reputations and the Construction of Collective Memories: Sentenced Nazi War Criminals in Post-War Germany. In *Transitional Justice and the Rule of Law*, edited by S. Parmentier and A. Czarnota. Antwerp: Intersentia.

Kehrl, H. 1973. *Krisenmanager im Dritten Reich* [Crisis Manager in the Third Reich]. Düsseldorf: Droste.

Koskenniemi, M. 2002. Between Impunity and Show Trials. In *Max Planck Yearbook of United Nations Law*, vol. 6, edited by J.A. Frowein and R. Wolfram, 1-35. Amsterdam: Kluwer Law International.

Lippott, J and Turzer, I. 2009. Verspätet und versteckt, aber konsequent: Die Rücknahme des deutschen Vorbehalts zu Art. 7 Abs. 2 EMRK. In *Kompetenz und Verantwortung in der Bundesverwaltung: 30 Jahre Fachhochschule des Bundes für öffentliche Verwaltung*, edited by T. Bönders, 507-526. Munich: C.H. Beck.

Noelle, E. and Neumann, P. eds. 1956. *Jahrbuch der öffentlichen Meinung 1947-1955*. Allensbach: Verlag für Demoskopie.

Noelle, E. and Neumann, P. eds. 1965. *Jahrbuch der öffentlichen Meinung 1958-1964*. Allensbach and Bonn: Verlag für Demoskopie.

Pendas, D. 2006. *The Frankfurt Auschwitz Trial, 1963-1965: Genocide, History and the Limits of Law*. Cambridge: Cambridge University Press.

Perels, J. 1999. *Das juristische Erbe des 'Dritten Reiches'*. Frankfurt and New York: Campus.

Reif, A. ed. 1978. *Albert Speer: Kontroversen um ein deutsches Phaenomen*. Munich: Bernard & Graefe.

Rückerl, A. 1984. *NS-Verbrechen vor Gericht*. Heidelberg: C.F. Mueller.

Schabas, W. 1997. Sentencing by International Tribunals: A Human Rights Approach. *Duke Journal of Comparative and International Law*, 7, 461-517.

Schabas, W. 2000. Life, Death and the Crime of Crimes: Supreme Penalties and the ICC Statute. *Punishment & Society*, 2(3), 263-285.

Schabas, W. 2012. On 50-year Sentences for Tyrants. PhD Studies in Human Rights. Available at http://humanrightsdoctorate.blogspot.co.uk/2012/05/on-50-year-sentences-for-tyrants.html (accessed 31 May 2012).

Sereny, G. 1996. *Albert Speer: His Battle with Truth*. New York: Vintage.

Silbermann, A. and Stoffers, M. 2000. *Auschwitz: Nie davon gehört?* Berlin: Rowohlt. Speer, A. 1969. *Erinnerungen*. Berlin: Ullstein (published as *Inside the Third Reich*, London: Weidenfeld & Nicolson, 1970; page numbers refer to the German edition).

Speer, A. 1975. *Spandauer Tagebücher*. Berlin: Propyläen (published as *Spandau: The Secret Diaries*, London: Collins, 1976).

Van Zyl Smit, D. 2002a. Punishment and Human Rights in International Criminal Justice. *Human Rights Law Review*, 2, 1-17.

Van Zyl Smit, D. 2002b. Sentencing and the International Criminal Court. *Sentencing Observer*, 1, June, 1-2.

Van Zyl Smit, D. 2005. International Imprisonment. *International and Comparative Law Quarterly*, 54, 357-384.

Von Lingen, K. 2009. *Kesselring's Last Battle: War Crimes Trials and Cold War Politics, 1945-1960*. Kansas City: University Press of Kansas.

Webster, R. 2001. Opposing 'Victor's Justice': German Protestant Churchmen and Convicted War Criminals in Western Europe after 1945. *Journal of Holocaust and Genocide Studies*, 15(1), 47-69.

Chapter 3
René Cassin, State Sovereignty and Transitional Justice in the Period of the Second World War

Jay Winter

Transitional justice would be unimaginable without recognition of rights that inherently and inalienably belong to each individual human being. International transitional justice, that is, justice enforced by the community of states, is impossible without limitations to the sovereignty of the nation state to act at will against the rights of individual human beings and even, if it sees fit, to put aside the rule of law. And yet, the legal state of affairs in the world today, with its concept of universal human rights, limited state sovereignty and courts empowered to enforce conventions that confirm individual human rights and even to penalize those who commit gross violations of them, is, in the historical order of things, very recent.

This chapter traces the development of the paradigm shift that made possible the UN Declaration of Human Rights in 1948, the European Court of Human Rights and Fundamental Freedoms in 1959, and eventually the International Criminal Court in 2002. It does so through the lifework of one remarkable French, but what is perhaps more relevant, global, citizen, René Cassin. He stands for the group of (legal) scholars and others who, from the end of the First World War onwards, promoted ideas which, in the 1940s, emerged in new and striking ways. These people, and these ideas, are part of the hidden history of transitional justice in an era in which Europe itself was in transition, struggling to cope with the aftermath of the Second World War but, more importantly, to ensure that it would never happen again.

Rethinking state sovereignty: Geneva and The Hague

On 9 December 1948, René Cassin presented to a plenary session of the General Assembly of the United Nations the Universal Declaration of Human Rights. The road to the Palais de Chaillot was a long one, passing through many places during and after the Second World War, and finally reaching Oslo and the Nobel Peace Prize. But to appreciate fully the thinking that went into Cassin's contribution to the Universal Declaration, we must go to interwar Geneva and the League of

Nations. There, he and a group of distinguished international jurists had thought through the premises on which absolute state sovereignty rested.

These explorations in legal theory antedated the Nazi seizure of power, when the contours of what Cassin termed the Leviathan State became visible to all. Then, in 1933, a petition for redress presented to the League of Nations brought to the fore the importance of giving the individual human being standing in international law. Together these lines of thinking – truncating the sovereignty of the state and advancing the right of individual petition against violations of rights in the state in which he or she lived – provided the core of Cassin's approach to human rights in the post-war decade. In addition, in the 1920s Cassin had also worked for the International Labour Organization (ILO) in Geneva on behalf of disabled veterans, where he became familiar with another strand of human rights thinking and established the principle that disabled men, for whichever army they fought, had rights, not to charity, but to justice.

René Cassin entered the League of Nations in 1924 and found there a community of jurists engaged in a far-reaching and fundamental critique of the concept of state sovereignty. Many were either French-trained or had taught in French universities, among them the Greek jurist Nikolas Politis, a naturalized French citizen who taught law at the University of Paris at the turn of the century (Holsti 1942). He was a delegate to the Paris Peace Conference and one of the central figures in the first decade of the League of Nations, where he was closely involved in framing the 1924 Geneva protocol for the peaceful resolution of international disputes. Politis later became Vice-President of the League's Commission on disarmament, and in this capacity, as in others, earned the admiration and respect of Cassin.

In both Geneva and The Hague, new institutions opened in the interwar years to provide a home for such scholars struggling with difficult questions of war and peace, and the role of the League of Nations in curtailing state sovereignty. In 1927, the University Institute of Advanced International Studies opened in Geneva. The great legal theorist Hans Kelsen taught international law there from 1934 to 1940. Cassin gave annual lectures at the Institute during his stay as French delegate every autumn. A second pole of intellectual activity was The Hague Academy of International Law, which opened in 1923, providing a venue for lectures and publications by leading jurists. Here was another forcing house of new ideas in the field of international law.

This was no more evident than in the series of lectures Politis gave, and published, 'On the problem of limiting sovereignty and the theory of the abuse of rights in international affairs' (Politis 1925). He announced unabashedly that international law was at a turning point. It used to be the case that it was essentially and exclusively the law of states; individual people were ignored. It also used to be the case that states acted as if they were 'sovereign moral persons, who were not subject to the authority of the rule of law, save when through their free and independent assent, they accepted its compulsory force'. Both premises were no longer valid. 'The dominant feature of our times is the intertwining of human relations both within and across borders.' The magical aura of the state had given way to the view that it was 'an administrator of a federation of public services' (Politis 1925: 5).

In the international realm, Politis argued, a host of developments since the nineteenth century pointed towards transnational legal authority. The Versailles settlement had established mixed arbitration tribunals, a regime for the protection of minorities, alongside those features of positive law requiring states to act in cases of piracy, the slave trade or the attack on commercial shipping ruled illegal by the Washington Naval convention of 1922. In every one of these instances, individuals were defended under international law (Politis 1925: 8-9) and no state stood outside of its reach. 'What will assure the final triumph of this new conception of international law is the ruin into which the alternate principle of classical theory – that of sovereignty – will fall irreversibly' (Politis 1925: 10). Only if a new idea were to penetrate the fog of legal and political inertia could an international organization like the League of Nations survive and another war be averted. That idea was limited sovereignty or sovereignty limited by international law, sovereignty that 'cannot be ascribed solely to the state' (Politis 1925: 10/18-19) – a critical shift.[1] The search for new concepts of limited sovereignty was the most important challenge for legal theory and international peace (Politis 1925: 115-116).

This spirited intellectual challenge appeared just as Cassin took up his task as a member of the French delegation to the League and he began to develop an original approach to the problem of sovereignty. Though he shared much of the critique offered by Politis in his 1925 Hague lectures, when it was his turn to speak to these weighty issues, his approach took some of Politis's ideas in new directions. His 1930 Hague Academy lectures were entitled 'The new conception of domicile in the resolution of conflicts of laws' (Cassin 1930). His aim in this extended argument was to 'desacralize' claims of state sovereignty to create an environment in which the all-powerful state could not by its own fiat and with impunity trample on the rights of the individual.

The original intellectual move Cassin offered in these lectures was to juxtapose the right of domicile to the right of citizenship as a basis of political rights:

> The tie of nationality is not a primary or a unique bond among the members of a nation: there are other more elementary ones … the district, the region, the province, and so on. Precisely because the right of domicile rests on a universal and permanent fact, the concreteness of a place where one lives, a place where families reside, it has been taken into consideration everywhere to determine the point of juridical attachment of persons and to order more or less completely the status of the individual. (Cassin 1930: 740)

Regimes change, but (with luck) domiciles remain. People remain attached to their homes whatever happens at the political level. The right of alien residence

1 Politis cites Kelsen here, among other authorities.

(while obeying the laws of a land) in a host nation is therefore based on the prior and superior force of domicile over nationality. Cassin cites explicitly the plight of over one million Russian and Armenian refugees whose personal status was thrown into doubt by war and revolution. Their standing, he claims, must be based on a right of domicile independent of nationality.

The implications of Cassin's argument are far-reaching. Domicile over nationality describes the bonds of the veterans of different countries who came together to work with Cassin in his international veterans' organization. Domicile over nationality is the principle defence of vulnerable minorities stalked by powerful nationalist movements in states worried about their ethnic composition. Domicile over nationality helps correct the imbalance in the then current international law 'which confers to the sovereign nation a competence which is too exclusive, simplistic, and ill adapted to satisfy the complex needs of international life' (Cassin 1930: 771). What is worse, 'the principle of nationality has exhausted its beneficial effects and has become a germ of doctrines destructive to the international community and oppressive to the individual' (Cassin 1930: 801). And finally, by privileging the concept of domicile over nationality, Cassin points the way to establishing the standing of the individual within international law itself.[2] Note the date: three years before the Nazis came to power and used sovereign law to destroy every single trace of natural justice, Cassin constructed a powerful argument against the extremes of state sovereignty then still unrealized. How much more powerful then, his argument against the all-powerful state once that state under Hitler had made war first on millions of his own citizens, and then on the rest of Europe.

As the descent towards war, and the eclipse of the League of Nations, progressed, Cassin became more focused on 'The Leviathan State'. In April 1940, just on the edge of a disaster he had foreseen, he wrote an essay on the subject for *Les nouveaux cahiers*. He started by linking Nazi aggression and the Soviet war in Finland to the appearance in the twentieth century of monster states, whose power, matched by 'an ideology of violence and terrorist methods applied on a huge scale', enabled them to reduce millions of men and women to mere instruments of their will (Cassin 1972b: 63). Cassin traces the deformation of the idea of the state as a reflection of popular sovereignty to German romanticism with its 'irrational and mystical aspirations' about language and race, mixed with a remarkable martial prowess. It was Hegel, after all, Cassin offered as an aside, who said that in a true state 'individuals do not exist' (Cassin 1972b: 66). Instead of the rationalism of Kant, the humanism of Goethe, the liberalism of Schiller, the heart of German nationalists beat to another, more militant, drum.

After the First World War, the new order of the League of Nations established modalities for the protection of the rights of minorities and other oppressed

2 The Institute of International Law adopted this same line of argument in 1929, when it drafted a 'Declaration of the international rights of man', which Cassin cites directly (1930: 770).

peoples. But the conditions of the Great War reinforced the power of the state. Consequently, the League rested on the conscious solidarities of separate sovereign states, still jealous of their sovereignty. The new organization was still international, not transnational, not a representative of the masses across borders but of the states behind them. Impotent, the League could do little to stop the descent into another war. The concentrated and disciplined power of the German state swept all before it. The risk was that the future would be dominated by a few Leviathan states, bent on war and expansion. The only alternative, Cassin pleaded, was if the Allies made the war one for the defence of human rights. They had to create a new 'Universal declaration of the rights of the human person, bolstered by specific guarantees', requiring no less than 'the curtailment of the *absolute* sovereignty of states' (Cassin 1972b: 71).

Towards UNESCO

After the outbreak of the Second World War, the centre of gravity of international thinking on war and peace moved, of necessity, from Geneva and The Hague to London, New York and Montreal, cities that, at the same time, became havens of free French thought. At the core of many of these wartime networks was René Cassin. He joined a remarkable group of jurists-in-exile, who shaped what emerged as Allied policy on trying those guilty of war crimes.

Through this work, he made a direct contribution to the preparation of what became the Nuremberg trials. But at the same time, his work in 'Free France' enabled him to braid together transitional justice with a commitment to construct a universal declaration of human rights.

One of the men who made it possible for him to do so was Henri Laugier, a polymath and a man of seemingly limitless energy with truly catholic interests (*Biologie et développement* 1968). During the war he settled in Montreal, and one of his most successful projects was the association France Forever (Amyot 1999: 258), which sponsored a successful publication series on science and world affairs. Here is his preface to one of these volumes:

> At the very time when a shadow covers the path of French destiny, a small light will continue to glow, showing the way, linking, in the darkness to which we have sunk, the luminous past of French science and its future which, one day will shine again, reminding everyone, if they have forgotten, that French scientific thought is still alive despite its misfortunes; that it still occupies its place in the life of international exchange; and that one day, as soon as France recovers from her humiliation, through the victory of the United Nations, her human and universal mind will regain its radiance and its greatness.
>
> As André Breton put it: the Flame, stronger than the Ashes. (in Pecker 1995: 3)

These words were music to Cassin's ears. On 1 September 1942, he wrote to Laugier to tell him about the work of the commissions he had set up within Free France to examine the reforms that would be needed after the war (Prost and Winter 2011: ch. 6). Cassin asked for his help with respect to international juridical questions:

> For your part, I would very much like you to collaborate actively with us on the following points: a) human rights. You have retaken the direction of the International League of Human Rights, and I have spoken about this on radio broadcasts to France. However would you please send me a review of the state of the movement in America, towards an International Declaration of Human Rights? … Our role as Frenchmen must be to produce something important by the end of the war.[3]

Cassin confided to Laugier that in London they had to fight against the view in some Anglo-American quarters that given their weakness, the Free French had to be 'supple and docile', and 'on the international level … remain in the "frigidaire" until the end of the war'. Instead, Cassin concluded: 'My present task, *while here*, is to renew France's role as intellectual leader, which the fine French team in America usefully occupies there.'[4]

Here is the point of departure for one of the most creative partnerships in the history of the Universal Declaration in 1948. As National Commissioner for Justice and Public Instruction, Cassin found a way to assert France's voice in the planning of a just peace to follow a just war. Laugier's friendship and influence were essential in that effort from 1942 onwards. Having Laugier as a close ally was the equivalent of the support of dozens of lesser men. This pivotal friendship was but one element in the revival of pre-war Republican and internationalist networks on both sides of the Atlantic whose attention increasingly turned to educational reconstruction and human rights.

From November 1942 on, Cassin served as Free France delegate to the inter-Allied committee on education, chaired by Rab Butler, President of the Board of Education in England, their task to prepare for the repair of the staggering damage done to libraries, schools, museums, newspapers, journals and universities during the conflict. The plan Cassin and Laugier formed and carried out to create UNESCO, and to ensure that it was based in Paris, originated here. The final part of the international project Cassin and Laugier had planned was realized when Laugier was named as deputy secretary at the United Nations, with responsibility for social affairs, including population, scientific research, drugs and, above all,

3 National Archives, Paris 382AP63, Cassin to Laugier, 1 September 1942. On its own, this letter makes it very difficult to accept Samuel Moyn's statement (2011) that no one had discussed human rights during the war, aside from Hersch Lauterpacht.

4 National Archives, Paris 382AP63, Cassin to Laugier, 1 September 1942.

human rights. The heads of UNESCO and the nascent Commission on Human Rights reported to him (Morelle and Cremieux-Brilhac 1998).

The Commission on Human Rights

At the founding meeting of UNESCO in London on 16 November 1945, Cassin addressed the delegates:

> Our duty will be more completely defined when our charter has been adopted by all the United Nations, and when, on what I hope may not be a far distant day, we have the great Soviet Republic in our midst … We shall never lose sight of the fact, so adequately expressed at the opening of our deliberations, that it is not the sum of knowledge that is to be the distinguishing mark of the activities of our future organization, but the development of culture. One of our great authors has said: 'Science without conscience is but the ruin of the soul'. We can say: 'Knowledge without morality can only result in barbarism', we who know that there can be no democracy without culture, will direct our efforts towards adding something else to knowledge: a great ideal, a clear vision of the great problems to be solved in the cause of international peace and, lastly, and perhaps most important of all, the mastery of self.[5]

Here Cassin laid out the path that he and the delegates had to follow. First, to bring on board the Soviet Union, for without the Soviet bloc, none of their ventures would command universal authority. And second, to address problems of a moral order, to ensure that the peace so dearly won could be protected against the perversion not only of science, but of state power trampling on human rights. That required action not only in the educational sphere, though that dimension was critical to Cassin, but in the realm of international law.

Cassin and Laugier were both committed to turning a just war into a just peace. But they could not construct such a peace by a return to status quo ante bellum, nor, indeed, by returning to the state of affairs before 1914. It was the problem of sovereignty itself which lay at the heart of the failures of the League of Nations in the 1930s, and it was to address that problem and create constraints for state power within a new kind of international moral order, and, if possible, a new international legal order, that Cassin, Laugier and a host of other men and women turned in the later 1940s.

If UNESCO was one facet of the successful partnership of Laugier and Cassin, the creation of the Commission on Human Rights (CHR) within the orbit of the Economic and Social Council of the UN (ECOSOC) was another. Article 68 of the UN Charter explicitly charged ECOSOC with setting up a commission for the promotion of human rights. One of Laugier's first acts was to construct such

5 The Birth of an Ideal. *The Courier: Unesco* (Oct. 1985), 8. The reference is to Rabelais, in chapter 8 of *Pantagruel* (1532).

a commission in February 1946, its brief to prepare a document for ECOSOC enumerating precisely what were the rights signatories of the UN Charter had agreed to defend.

Laugier asked John Humphrey, an international lawyer in Montreal, to head the new commission's secretariat. Drawing on their wartime friendship, Laurier and Humphrey worked well together. Humphrey was a formidable lawyer whose socialist views – to the left of the New Deal without a trace of Communist sympathies – gave him an affinity with many of the Latin American delegates with whom he was to work. He did not have the temperament of a diplomat. He was an acerbic, outspoken, straight-talking scholar perfectly suited to complement Laugier's chain-smoking, elegant, yet driven Gallic romanticism. Humphrey provided the prose and precision needed to turn Laugier's poetry into the language of international law. And Humphrey's mastery of both French and English prose gave him a distinct advantage over both Laugier and Cassin. In short, he was the perfect international civil servant to guide the work of the CHR in the preparation of an international bill of rights (Hobbins 1994).

The Universal Declaration: a collective manifesto

The Universal Declaration of Human Rights is a house of many mansions. The question as to who was its principal architect is still contested. Mary Ann Glendon (2001) has emphasized the crucial role of the chair of the Human Rights Commission, Eleanor Roosevelt. She also pointed to the intellectual authority of Charles Malik of Lebanon and P.-C. Chang of China, in orienting the commission's thinking on matters of principle and providing it with a profile not restricted to European ideas. Others have emphasized the work of John Humphrey and his secretariat (Hobbins 1989: 7-26, 1998: 323-42, 1999: 24-41). Still others have called René Cassin the father of the Universal Declaration (Agi 1998), and it was in that capacity that he was honoured with the Nobel Peace Prize in 1968. All of these statements are true, and all are incomplete. The Universal Declaration was the product of a process in which dozens of individuals made their voices heard and through which a consensus emerged enabling the document to receive the assent of the General Assembly of the United Nations in Paris on 10 December 1948 without a single dissenting vote.

What is most surprising about the Declaration is that it happened at all. The climate was, to say the least, inclement. The year 1948 was not a good one for human rights. Czech democracy had come to an end in February. The Arab-Israeli war had ended, leaving one million Palestinians in refugee camps. The Berlin blockade opened in June and continued for 11 months. The Chinese Communists came within striking distance of Beijing, which they took in January 1949, completing their seizure of power. In April 1949, the North Atlantic Treaty Organization was founded. Four months later, the Soviet Union tested its first atomic bomb. The Cold War was well and truly on.

Yet, the Universal Declaration was in no sense a Cold War document. We need to understand it from the standpoint of those who lived in the moment, in order to see what it meant to its creators. Then we can see the error of those who say the document was a failure, a backward step away from enforceable human rights, a cover for imperial designs, an insignificant, rhetorical flourish, full of sound and fury but, in essence, signifying nothing of importance in international history. This view has emerged forcefully in recent years, and requires re-examination (Mazower 2009; Moyn, 2010; Normand and Zaidi 2008).

A focus on René Cassin and his role in the drafting of the document is particularly useful here. In engaging with efforts to repair the damage of war, and to help construct the foundations of a just peace, he was fully aware of the opposition he would face in trying to constrain the power of the sovereign state. Yet the horrors of the Nazi regime had created a consensus around the need to shift the balance of power away from the state and towards civil society and the individual. No state, no party, no individual was above the law. The Nuremberg trials and the Universal Declaration of Human Rights came out of that belief. In effect, the Universal Declaration was Janus-faced. It looked to the past and to the future at one and the same time. Its vision of the future was, perforce, unclear. But its indictment of the doctrine of unbridled state sovereignty was unmistakable.

Throughout his life, Cassin dealt in the art of the possible. He was not blind to the storm clouds, not on the horizon but rather straight overhead. He believed that a document, a statement of principles concerning rights, a manifesto securing the support of all those who had brought down the Nazi regime, was all that could be accomplished at that time. That was no mean achievement. A legally binding covenant on human rights was simply an unreachable destination. Was it better to wait until such a covenant would be acceptable? Not in his view; the time was ripe for creating a foundational document, one on which a later generation could build. Indeed, since 1975, a new human rights movement has emerged on the foundations of the old, and it is both unnecessary and unwise to separate the two as if they are unconnected.[6]

The Universal Declaration of Human Rights was the final political and moral act agreed to by the alliance that won the Second World War, a cruel and gruelling struggle against a Leviathan state that had nearly brought all Europe to its knees. In that war, Soviet losses were greater than those of any other ally. They were part of the alliance, however repugnant the regime. A United Nations without them, a Universal Declaration without at least their tacit approval, made no sense.

It is critical to understand the terms imbedded in the Universal Declaration. What it does not say is as striking as what it affirms. It is not an international treaty, rather a moral and educational manifesto, affirming the need to restrict the sovereignty of the nation state. The term 'the state' is used only three times. Instead its focus is on the inherent rights we all share and which we all express in our families and in civil society. It is not a statement of unbridled individualism,

6 For the opposite view, see Moyn (2010).

but of the moral force of associative life, without which human development is impossible.

It is a position entirely consistent with everything Cassin did. He had worked tirelessly for the injured, the disabled, the disadvantaged in the veterans' movement first in France and then throughout Europe. In the Alliance Israélite Universelle, the leadership of which he assumed in 1943, he affirmed the dignity of the Jewish people in the face of indignity, the magnitude of which was both evident and difficult to fathom at the end of the Second World War (Prost and Winter 2011: ch. 11). He saw his mission as helping to remedy the damage war inflicted, on individuals, on social groups and on the rule of law itself. In the Juridical Committee his aim was the restoration of Republican order at home; in the UN, the restoration of the very notion that there was a rule of law, embodying principles, the violation of which had created the circumstances out of which war had emerged and would emerge again.

This mission was shared for different reasons and in different ways by his colleagues on the Commission on Human Rights. Each contributed an element to the task at hand, but no one was responsible primarily and singly for the outcome (although certainly without the work of the Secretariat, the Universal Declaration would never have been written). It is futile to isolate one individual and to say he or she wrote the Universal Declaration of Human Rights. A collective – and that includes the member states of the United Nations – wrote it.

In this collection of equals, some were more equal than others. Cassin was the draftsman par excellence, the international jurist trained to write the law and to give it the precision and clarity it required. In all the minutes of the drafting committees, Cassin is always called 'Professor'; he had the authority of the academy behind him, and used both it and his considerable negotiating experience to redraft and present article after article of the Universal Declaration in a form that would win the widest possible support of delegates and delegations from all parts of the world. At his side was Laugier, ready to add his support and above all working hard to ensure that the Declaration made it to the General Assembly. Without him, there would never have been a vote on the Universal Declaration of Human Rights.

In May 1948, the delegates took the decision not to move towards a Covenant. Cassin played an important role in these discussions. On 15 June 1948 he faced the matter directly.[7] The Declaration, he said, would be a recommendation, not a legal obligation. This might sound like a return to the impotence of the League of Nations, but it was nothing of the kind.

7 Quotes from League of Nations archive, Geneva, E/CN.4/147, 'Exposé de M. René Cassin, représentant de la France, sur la mise en œuvre des droits de l'homme', 16 June 1948: 1, 2, 7.

> The events preceding the Second World War, in which millions of men lost their lives, have proved that the organization of peace may require some limitation, on the basis of reciprocity, of the traditional sovereignty of States in this respect.
>
> I was personally present at the dramatic debates which took place at Geneva between March and October 1933. At that time the only way in which the criminal actions of Hitler Germany towards her own nationals could be brought to the notice of the Council of the League of Nations was to resort to the indirect procedure of invoking the Polish-German treaty on the protection of minorities concluded in 1922. On the day on which the Assembly dared to refer to the general principles authorizing the legally-organized international community to protect human rights, even in a sphere not covered by some special minority treaty, Hitler took advantage of the Third Reich's absolute sovereignty over its citizens and denied the League of Nations any right of inspection; and on 11 October 1933, Germany left the League.

Now, in June 1948, that position had been rendered untenable. 'The legal competence of the United Nations is, therefore, in principle, incontestable under the Charter.' Now that the individual was an active subject of international law, 'any programme for the international implementation of human rights must, at the present stage of the law of nations, be in a form acceptable to States'.

In essence, this document represents Cassin's thinking on the Declaration. Although some argued vehemently that Cassin and the HRC betrayed the principle of human rights by choosing an unenforceable declaration instead of a convention (Lauterpacht 1948), it was a first but by no means final step towards the construction of a new international legal order. That would take time. To stand on the ground of principle and demand a convention and nothing but a convention in 1948 was to ask for the impossible. That kind of high-mindedness was not the kind of gesture Cassin wished to offer to the world.

What the Declaration offered was a way towards national and transnational action in defence of human rights,

> when it calls on States Members gradually to bring their legislation into conformity with the principles formulated in it, and to set up, within the sphere of their Jurisdiction, systems of appeal to judicial and administrative bodies, in order to prevent and, if necessary correct or suppress such violations of human rights as may have been committed within their territory.[8]

Cassin was responsible for many other features of the final document as adopted. One in particular stands out: the substitution of the word 'universal' for 'international'. It appears in a list of amendments agreed on 15 November 1948. Following a Haitian recommendation, Cassin on behalf of the French delegation

8 E/CN.4/147, 'Exposé de Cassin', pp. 1-2.

framed this amendment, which was agreed by 17 votes to 11, with 10 abstentions.[9] This change in terminology was not trivial. The document now represented a statement of human rights as something not limited to relations among states, but as a matter defining the relationships of individuals to each other and to the groups they formed for their benefit and well-being. A universal declaration not only places the dignity of the human person above the writ of any individual state, truncating state sovereignty, but also gives notice that the struggle for human rights entails vigilance by non-governmental organizations too. Universal human rights are everybody's business.

On 9-10 December 1948, with intense lobbying continuing behind the scenes, the Universal Declaration was put to the vote after nearly three years of work (Morsink 1999: 33). The General Assembly was seated in the Palais de Chaillot, just a few steps from the spot where, in 1940, Hitler had surveyed his new dominions. Eight years later, Cassin rose to speak. 'I have the honour', he began, 'to report the firm support of France' for the Declaration, which, '100 years after the Revolution of 1848 and the abolition of slavery on all French territory, constitutes a global step in the long struggle for the rights of man'. At a staggering cost in human lives and effort, a just war had been won. Now, the delegates were asked to vote on a document which aimed to form the basis of a just peace: 48 countries voted yes, eight abstained, and there were no 'no' votes. The wartime Alliance had held, if only for this one, very last time.

Cassin could rightly take some pride in the outcome. He was not the sole or even the primary author of this triumph, but one of the leaders of a remarkable collection of people from all over the world. The success of this project depended on the work and support of many others, especially in the Latin American delegations. Even getting the Soviet delegates to abstain was a triumph, enabling Cassin to say that the document represented world opinion as a whole.

The European turn

René Cassin was elected Vice-President of the CHR in 1949, under the Presidency of Eleanor Roosevelt. He continued to serve as a delegate to the Commission, and in 1955-1956, presided over it. These years were increasingly difficult for him, both as a leader in the effort to turn the Universal Declaration into enforceable international treaties, and as a spokesman for France. It took 17 years for the CHR to formulate, and the UN to adopt, two separate Covenants, one on economic, social and cultural rights, which came into force on 3 January 1976, and another on civil and political rights, which came into force on 23 March 1976, just four weeks after Cassin died.

It was not only the slow and painful progress on drafting the Covenants that troubled Cassin. It was also the attitude of France towards them and the European

9 League of Nations archive, Geneva, A/C.3/339, 'Projet de la Déclaration Internationale des Droits de l'Homme : France : Amendements': 1.

Convention of Human Rights, signed by France in 1950, but not ratified until 1974. The French government withheld its ratification of the UN Covenants until October 1980.

Clearly Cassin's commitments were not shared by a series of French governments, including those formed during the Presidency of Charles de Gaulle. Right from the start, the problem of colonial power complicated discussion of French compliance with any future United Nations covenants respecting human rights. Cassin urged his colleagues to recognize it was impossible to separate the rights of those in Metropolitan France from the rights of those in territories under French administration. The principle was applicable to 'everyone or to no one' (Soutou 2008: 80). The breaking point came over considering the right of individual petition, to which Cassin was firmly wedded. Not so his colleagues in the French Foreign Office, who saw it as a potentially useful device for those protesting against human rights abuses in France's colonies.

Already in January 1949, British and Belgian diplomats had asked their French colleagues to act in concert to block the right of individual petition, which they saw as a danger to all three colonial powers (Soutou 2008: 71). Cassin was sensitive to these objections: 'if France had to move forward' on the question of individual petition, 'she should not become a target' (Soutou 2008: 72). He tried to incorporate safeguards against the use of the right of petition for purely political ends, but these were not enough for his colleagues at the Quai d'Orsay. They objected forcefully when Cassin went ahead anyway and tabled at the CHR in 1949 a draft including the right of individual petition. He tried to find middle ground, leaving the right of petition to governments and opening the door to individual petition later on, also agreeing to argue that the Covenant would come into force only when two members of the Security Council agreed to ratify it. Seeing that the USSR and the US were against the right of petition, for very different reasons, France would be in a favourable position to protect its interests. In June 1949, Cassin presented this compromise to the Foreign Office. The Secretariat of Conferences rejected it, instructing France's delegation to ECOSOC to vote to defer or abandon the right of petition. Cassin was dismayed. On 10 December 1949, precisely a year to the day since the UN had accepted the Universal Declaration, he wrote to the Quai d'Orsay:

> The future pact on human rights will remain less than the law of the League of Nations, and the only debate which, with reference to the Jews of Upper Silesia, through the complaint among others of the Counsel of the League in Geneva managed to put Hitler in a difficult position, in 1935 [sic], would be impossible today, if the French position following from the lessons of the Second World War were rejected or abandoned.[10]

10 'Note du Président Cassin concernant la mise en application des Droits de l'Homme, 10 décembre 1949', as cited in and reproduced facsimile in Soutou (2008: 79 and 81).

They were unmoved and once again issued instructions for the French delegation to block any move in the direction of individual petition.[11]

Consider Cassin's dilemma: his nomination as French delegate to the CHR was renewed for three years in 1950, but he was at loggerheads with the civil servants who were his masters. He was there to speak for France, but he could not be assured of the vote of the French delegation on issues he believed were of major importance. Worse still, the Cold War was turning the UN into a site of confrontation and paralysis. American politicians fled from contact with human rights activists, frequently tarred by the brush of crypto-communism. The Soviet Union used blocking procedures to delay and frustrate efforts it felt were not in its interests or were covers for American plots. Both great powers were determined to stop any progress on reaching agreement on the Covenants or on ways to enforce them.[12]

Throughout this difficult period, Cassin soldiered on alongside Humphrey, keeping to the key assignment of drafting Covenants on human rights, treaties with binding legal force. This was a huge task, overseen by Humphrey. He said he would have preferred to develop particular conventions on particular rights than to create a huge basket of rights, but that was not to be.[13] He served as Director of the Human Rights Division, and had cordial relations with Cassin, until 1966, when the drafting marathon was done. It was clear, though, that the momentum, the urgency of human rights work at the UN had been lost. Decolonization came first. The CHR seemed to lose direction. It certainly faded from the headlines. During Cassin's tenure as president in 1956, he tried to get the UN Secretary-General, Dag Hammerskjöld, to attend the opening of that year's session, in order to celebrate the tenth anniversary of the setting up of the 'core committee' which had framed the CHR. His hope, he said, was to end the Commission's evident 'eclipse'; the invitation was declined.[14]

It is hardly surprising that Cassin began to think of other ways to serve the cause of human rights. In May 1948, before the adoption by the UN of the Universal Declaration, a group of centre-right political groups had met at The Hague determined to create a Council of Europe.[15] The following year that body was formed, and in turn drafted the European Convention on Human Rights,[16]

---

11 UN archives, Geneva, SOA 317/1/02, Schwelb to Humphrey, on French opposition to right of petition, 17 March 1954.

12 National Archives, Paris, 382AP129, 2nd Report of HRC, 17 May 1949, and 3rd Report, 5 June 1949.

13 UN archives, Geneva, SOA 317/1/01 B, Humphrey to Guillaume Georges-Picot, 14 Jan. 1953.

14 UN archives, Geneva, SOA 317/2/01, Cassin to Humphrey, 14 Feb. 1956.

15 Council of Europe, Historical archives, CE (MIN) P.8 Final 4th May 1949, Conference for the establishment of a Council of Europe. Communiqué.

16 Council of Europe, Historical archives, Dossier 12124, vol. 1. European court of human rights.

which established a Commission on Human Rights to examine petitions and a European Court of Human Rights in Strasbourg with the right to hear and judge them.

The ideological tilt of many of the founders was further to the right than that of Cassin, Humphrey and others in the HRC. Winston Churchill was the key figure in the European movement, assisted by David Maxwell-Fyfe, former Nuremberg prosecutor and Conservative jurist. This was primarily a Cold War initiative to protect the rights of Europeans against any Soviet encroachment. Yet, in their championing of the cause of human rights and in creating the court, these Conservatives and their allies set up a system that reached a much wider constituency. What they had to offer was a trade-off: states would cede some sovereignty for greater political stability (Moravcsik 2000). This was an essential step in the judicial construction of Europe.

The European Convention of 1950 set in motion the creation of the European Court of Human Rights (Costa 2004; Duranti 2012; Marguénaud 1996; Tietjen 2000). After eight ratifications, the Court was constituted and began its deliberations in 1959. Cassin was nominated as a judge by France and elected on the first ballot (Robertson 1959). He served as vice-president from 1959 to 1965, then as President from 1965 to 1968. In Cassin's years at the Court, he played an important part in establishing its rules, procedures and competence.[17]

Cassin's time in Strasbourg completed what he had begun in Paris in 1948. Both in his work on the CHR and in the European Court, Cassin had established the institutional foundation for developing the European approach to human rights. He left sites on which others would build in the future. That is what pioneers do – provide a point from which to move on.

Conclusions

Not long after he stepped down from the presidency of the European Court of Human Rights, in 1968 Cassin was awarded the Nobel Peace Prize: recognition of a lifetime of work, as a soldier, as a veteran, as a spokesman for the men and women damaged and disfigured by war. It was given to the ILO collectively the following year. Together these two awards recognized the long, hard struggle undertaken since the First World War by many people of Cassin's generation, people born in the 1880s, who came of age before the Great War and bore arms during it; people who took up the cause of the disabled and the cause of peace precisely because they knew what war was; people who suffered the dark years of Nazi ascendency and still retained their faith in human dignity; people who came to the United Nations determined to find a way to secure the peace. Their limitations are evident. They were not a generation of saints but of strivers: men

17 On his work as a judge, see the abundant documentation in 382AP137 (n. 12 above). See also Pettiti (1985).

and women too stubborn to be reduced to silence and cynicism. René Cassin won the Nobel Peace Prize for the generation of the two world wars.

In the same year, 1968, Cassin captured this truth in some words he offered in honour of Henri Laugier, born a year after him, in 1888. 'The men of our generation', he began, 'those who have forgotten neither 1789 nor 1848, those who lived through 1914-1918, 1940-1944, and 1948, they will have fulfilled their mission if, in their lifetime, the tribunal of the human conscience, so necessary today, will be able to flourish, and, following the words of Henri Laugier, if, "the cries of the victims will finally be heard"' (Cassin 1968: 36-37).

Cassin was an imperturbable optimist. He believed that human rights would advance in world affairs, but only at glacial speed, primarily through education. The key was to set norms of behaviour to which states could be held to account. That normative project would carry on whatever the political setbacks human rights activists faced.

And those reverses have been many and painful. It is clear that since 1976, when Cassin died, human rights movements have emerged as a popular global force. It is also clear that states have clawed back their autonomy from documents that cannot be enforced. The existence of the legal black hole of the Guantanamo Bay detention camp is but one instance of the failure of statesmen, and not only American statesmen, to respect the norms the Universal Declaration set forth more than 60 years ago.

Yet, the universalization of rights, beginning with those of disabled men, then extending to minorities under threat and finally reaching every citizen of every state in the United Nations was a significant achievement. It amounted to the establishment of a distinction between *loi* and *droit*, between statute and what Cassin termed the 'general principles of law' which made transitional justice thinkable, and at times even attainable.

References

Agi, M. 1998. *René Cassin: Prix Nobel de la paix, 1887-1976: Père de la Déclaration universelle des droits de l'homme*. Paris: Perrin.

Amyot, É. 1999. *Le Québec entre Pétain et de Gaulle: Vichy, la France Libre et les Canadiens*. Saint-Laurent, Quebec: Fides.

Biologie et développement: Hommage à Henri Laugier à l'occasion de Xe anniversaire de l'E.D.I.E.S, présenté par F. Perroux. 1968. Paris: PUF.

Cassin, R. 1930. La nouvelle conception du domicile dans le règlement des conflits de lois. In Académie de droit international, *Recueil des Cours*, vol. 34, 658-809. The Hague.

Cassin, R. 1968. Préface. In *Biologie et développement*, edited by F. Perroux, 36-37. Paris: Presses Universitaires de France.

Cassin, R. 1972a. Historique de la Déclaration Universelle de 1948. In *La Pensée et l'action*. Paris: F. Lalou.

Cassin, R. 1972b. L'Etat-Leviathan. In *La Pensée et l'action*. Paris: F. Lalou.

Costa, J. 2004. La Cour européenne des droits de l'homme: un juge qui gouverne? In *Etudes en l'honneur de Gérard Timsit*, edited by G. Lyon-Caen, 67-88. Bruxelles: Bruylant.

Duranti, M. 2012. *Human Rights and Conservative Politics: The History of the European Convention on Human Rights, 1945-50*. New York: Oxford University Press.

Glendon, M.A. 2001. *A World Made New: Eleanor Roosevelt and the Universal Declaration of Human Rights*. New York: Random House.

Hobbins, A.J. 1989. René Cassin and the Daughter of Time: The First Draft of the Universal Declaration of Human Rights. *Fontanus*, II, 7-26.

Hobbins A.J. ed. 1994. *On the Edge of Greatness: The Diaries of John Humphrey, First Director of the United Nations Division of Human Rights*, vol. 1: *1948-49*. Montreal: McGill University Press.

Hobbins, A.J. 1998. Eleanor Roosevelt, John Humphrey, and Canadian Opposition to the Universal Declaration of Human Rights: Looking Back on the 50th Anniversary of UNDHR. *International Journal*, Liii(2), 325-342.

Hobbins, A.J. 1999. John Peters Humphrey and the Genesis of the Universal Declaration of Human Rights. *Journal of Oriental Studies*, IX, 24-41.

Holsti, R. 1942. In Memoriam: Nicolas Politis: 1872-1942. *American Journal of International Law*, xxxvi(3), 475-479.

Lauterpacht, H. 1948. The Universal Declaration of Human Rights. *British Yearbook of International Law*, xxv, 354-381.

Mantoux, P. Le rôle de la SDN dans la vie international, 19 mai 1923. *League of Nations Archives*, *Mantoux papers*, Geneva.

Marguénaud, J. 1996. *La Cour européenne des droits de l'homme*. Paris: Dalloz.

Mazower, M. 2002. The Strange Triumph of Human Rights. *New Statesman*, 4 February.

Mazower, M. 2009. *No Enchanted Palace: The End of Empire and the Ideological Origins of the United Nations*. Princeton: Princeton University Press.

Moravcsik, A. 2000. The Origins of Human Rights Regimes: Democratic Delegation in Postwar Europe. *International Organisation*, Liv(2), 217-252.

Morelle, C. and Cremieux-Brilhac, J. 1998. *Henri Laugier 1888-1973: Un citoyen au service de la science et des droits de l'homme*. Paris: La Documentation Française.

Morsink, J. 1999. *The Universal Declaration of Human Rights: Origins, Drafting and Intent*. Philadelphia: University of Pennsylvania Press.

Moyn, S. 2010. Human Rights in History, *Nation*, 11 August.

Moyn, S. 2011. *The Last Utopia: Human Rights in History*. Cambridge, MA: Harvard University Press.

Normand, R. and Zaidi, S. 2008. *Human Rights at the UN: The Political History of Universal Justice*. Bloomington: Indiana University Press.

Pecker, J. 1995. Henri Laugier, l'édition scientifique, la documentation scientifique et l'audiovisuel. In *Henri Laugier en son siècle*. Cahiers pour l'histoire de la recherché, 3. Paris: CNRS Editions.

Pettiti, L. 1985. René Cassin, juge à la Cour européenne des droits de l'homme. *Revue des droits de l'homme*, December, 106-117.

Politis, N. 1925. Sur le problème des limitations de la souveraineté et la théorie de l'abus des droits dans les rapports internationaux. In Académie de Droit International, *Recueil des Cours*, vol. 6, 1-122. Paris: Sirey.

Prost, A. and Winter, J. 2011. *René Cassin et les droits de l'homme: le projet d'une generation*. Paris: Fayard.

Robertson, A.H. 1959. The European Court of Human Rights. *International and Comparative Law Quarterly*, viii(2), 396-403.

Soutou, G.-H. 2008. *La France et la Déclaration universelle des droits de l'homme du 10 décembre 1948*. Paris: Les Editions du Diplomate.

Tietjen, P. 2000. *Aux sources de la Cour et de la Convention européenne de droits de l'homme*. Bordeaux: Ed. Confluences.

PART II
Processes and Rituals

Chapter 4

The Theatre of Justice: On the Educational Meaning of Criminal Trials

Antoine Hol

The trial of Adolf Eichmann in 1961 provides an important case for analysing the imagery of international criminal justice, in that it may help us address the question of how to present trials for serious crimes such as genocide or mass murder. My specific concern is with the potential educational role that trials such as that of Eichmann can fulfil. Following the Second World War, the cry has often been: *nie wieder*! (never again!). But we can only learn and perhaps prevent what happened in the past repeating itself by understanding. To understand, we must study the political, cultural, economic and historical context that teaches us what went 'wrong' in that past.

First and foremost, it is important that those who will have to take political responsibility in the future understand and learn. But, looking back at what happened reveals that not only politicians, captains of industry and bankers were complicit in what we now regard as horrendous crimes. Like other cases, Nazi Germany teaches us that many people are usually involved, including 'ordinary' citizens; not perhaps because they actively supported the criminal system, but because they did not resist when they should have done. So, my question can be narrowed down to: how can 'ordinary' people learn from the past? I believe that trials like that of Adolf Eichmann do have educational value for the general public, but only if they are held in a specific way.

Criminal trials are about the law, but they are also about what we think is morally abject. Morality and law are interrelated in criminal law. Under a rule of law system, the law allows us to punish a person for acts that we also regard as immoral. Some trials lay too much emphasis on the legal side of the case, others moralize the issues to the extreme. Either way the possible educational effect of criminal trials will be nullified.

To understand how a trial like that of Eichmann could have educational benefits, it is helpful to make a comparison between theatre and legal trials. I will focus here on Greek tragedy, and in particular on the description of this form of theatre given by Aristotle. This will allow me to analyse part of the academic debate on the Eichmann trial, and to answer my question of whether criminal trials can have educational benefits for 'ordinary' people, and if so, under what conditions. Hannah Arendt's report on the Eichmann trial will be an important guide.

Trials and tragedies

Trials are open to the public. Lawyers understand this openness as a requisite of the rule of law. Indeed, transparency is a necessary condition for the control of judicial power. But openness to the public has another function too. As we shall see, the public are essential to a trial, because their presence and involvement in the courtroom allows them to take part in proceedings, even if they do not participate as a party. In some ways, the role of the public during a court session is not very different from that of spectators at a sporting event or the audience at a stage play. The question is, however, in what way the public are involved.

The sort of theatre Bertolt Brecht developed has been called the epic theatre – or *Lehrtheater* in German. It was Brecht's intention that people should learn from watching his plays, or by playing roles in them. Theatre is not for entertainment only, but has an educational function. The same applies to the tragedies that were performed in the city states of Classical Greece. These tragedies were an important part of the Dionysian festivals. All citizens were more or less obliged to attend the performances. Why was this, and why were these tragedies regarded as so important that citizens were expected to attend them?

All people desire some diversion and relaxation every now and then. Why make this obligatory? The reason lies in the political constitution of the Greek city states. It has been emphasized that the tragedies 'served to construct and reinforce a strong sense of the Athenians as a religious and political community' (Easterling 1997: 17; Meier 1988: 54-61). There is, however, another important aspect. In the city states, the citizens themselves had to take turns in fulfilling governmental roles, including deciding on legal cases. Of course, not all Greek citizens were well-educated academics. Most were skilled craftsman and lacked special training in intellectual matters. Against this background, it becomes clear why it was regarded as important that the citizens attended performances of tragedies. These tragedies must be seen as a sort of *Lehrtheater*, a theatre from which the spectators could learn. What they learned is how to make good decisions.

Tragedies have a great advantage over philosophical and theoretical treatises. While general and abstract principles are central to philosophy and theory, tragedies can be regarded as a kind of exemplum, cases that teach about aspects of life in a concrete or particularistic way. This means that tragedies are easier to understand than philosophical or theoretical treatises. If one wants to teach the average citizen, tragedies therefore provide a better educational instrument than philosophy.[1] This also applies to trials, which, like tragedies, are down to earth and about the particular. They present us with cases not on the law in general, but on how it works in practice. Interestingly enough, for the Greeks a comparison between theatre and trials seems to have been quite obvious. Tragedy writers were often also the writers of legal speeches. It therefore comes as no surprise that several tragedies refer to law suits, or even make these trials a central part of the

1 Reading novels could have a similar function (Nussbaum 1995).

play.[2] It is also no coincidence that the Greek word *hupocratēs* means both an 'actor' and a respondent in a trial (Hall 2010: 62). So, given the correspondence with theatre, it might be justifiable to assume that trials too can have an educational function.

Characterization of tragedies and trials

If we want to learn something of the characteristics and function of tragedies, Aristotle's *Poetics* is an important source. In this text, Aristotle distinguishes six components in his description of the tragedy's form (*Poetics*, VI), a number of which are particularly interesting for our comparison.

The first and most important component of a tragedy is actions. As Aristotle explains, tragedies are about happiness and misfortune, and only through actions can we become happy or unhappy. The representation of these actions is called the 'plot'. Related to actions is the component of character, the function of which is more or less derivative. The players' characters are important in so far as they are needed to render the choices they make comprehensible. In a similar way, we can discover both components in legal trials. As in tragedies, in a trial, too, the plot is the central component. Trials are not primarily about the character of a person, but about his or her actions and whether these were or were not against the law. People cannot be punished for what they think, or who they are, but for what they have done, or have not done.

This does not mean that character is not important at all. It is common in criminal law that the character of a defendant can also play a role, but only in relation to his or her actions or failure to act. Insight into the specific character traits of the defendant can make the actions more understandable for the judge and others. Insight into the character can also be relevant when estimating the sorts of punishment and measures that are required and justified. As we shall see, the character component became a focal point in the Eichmann trial.

Aristotle refers to another important component of a tragedy: 'thought'. Thought means that the *dramatis personae* of a tragedy are able to analyse their case and to plead for their standing and interests. Again, in law suits it is not otherwise. Central to a law suit is that parties, or the defendant, are able to plead and make their case as strong as possible.

The last component is that of spectacle. It is interesting to note what Aristotle writes in this regard: 'Spectacle, while highly effective, is yet quite foreign to the art and has nothing to do with poetry. Indeed the effect of tragedy does not depend on its performance by actors, and, moreover, for achieving the spectacular effects the art of the costumier is more authoritative than that of the poet' (*Poetics*, VI, 27). So, the foremost role of a tragedy is not, apparently, to touch the spectators. And again, it is not very different in the case of a trial. Although the spectacle

2 Aeschylus' tragedies on Orestes are perhaps the most well-known example.

might be 'highly effective', it is still foreign to the law, assuming that law is about right and wrong, and not about what touches people.

All of this brings us to our central question: if the aim of theatre (and trial) is not primarily to touch us, then what is its most important function?

To Aristotle, tragedies are important for a democratic society because they teach citizens how to make decisions (Salkever 1986). How can tragedies fulfil such an educational function? Two things are important. First of all, the tragedy itself must present a complex situation in which actors get involved and have to make decisions. Second, the plot of the tragedy must be constructed in such a way as to arouse certain passions, especially those of pity and fear. 'Tragedy', says Aristotle, 'is a representation of an action that is heroic and complete, and of a certain magnitude … it represents men in acting … and through pity and fear it effects relief to these and similar emotions' (*Poetics*, 1449b (VI, 2)). But, why pity and fear, and why relief? To understand the meaning of pity and fear, it is helpful to distinguish these passions from others such as anger, 'the painful desire for revenge' (Aristotle, *Rhetoric*, 1387a). The problem of the very angry – Aristotle also speaks of the 'manly' – is that they cannot feel fear or pity. This is because they are not capable of anxiety about evils to come. Other 'manly' passions such as confidence and disgust have a similar effect. But why is it important that human beings are capable of anxiety about evils to come? The answer is simple. It is only because of this that we start to deliberate. Those who can feel only disgust, revenge or anger will not be stimulated to deliberate and ask themselves how future evil can be prevented. 'Fear and pity are humanizing emotions insofar as they develop the deliberative life, the sort of life that constitutes human virtue within the realm of human actions' (Salkever 1986: 296).

An example may illustrate what is meant here. Take Sophocles' tragedy of Antigone. This tragedy represents a complex situation. Antigone wants to bury her brother Polynices who has been killed, which is an absolute familial duty. However, Creon, head of state and future father-in-law of Antigone, forbids her to do so. Polynices must be regarded as a traitor since he had served in the enemy army, and therefore the law of the state forbids his burial. How to choose? Two sorts of duty collide, one according to the law of the family, the other according to the law of the state. The fault of both Antigone and Creon is that they are stubborn and simply continue to hold a one-sided view of the situation. The effect of this obstinacy is disastrous. Creon punishes Antigone when he learns that she has neglected to obey the law of the state, and has indeed buried her brother. When locked up in a cave, separated from her fiancé Haemon, Antigone hangs herself. Confronted with her terrible death, Haemon throws himself on his sword and kills himself. On receiving news of the drama, Haemon's mother, cannot bear it, and also kills herself. The complexity of the situation is enhanced by Creon's change of attitude. At a certain point, he was persuaded to set Antigone free. However, because of powers beyond him, call it fate, he was too late and events took their course as described.

Will there be even one spectator who is not be overwhelmed by emotions on seeing such a spectacle? One of these emotions will definitely be fear, aroused by seeing the effects of the stubborn attitude of both Antigone and Creon. Fear will also be aroused when experiencing how difficult, if not impossible, it is to get a grip on events. Spectators will also be touched by the feeling of pity. How could they not be, seeing the failed attempts of Creon to save Antigone, his self-reproach because of his faults, his distress over the loss of his wife and son? This is what we hear Creon saying at the end, or is he screaming: 'O the curse of my stubborn will! … I know not where I should turn, where to look for help. My hands have done amiss; my head is bowed with a fate too heavy for me' (Sophocles 1974: 160-162).

So, according to Aristotle, we can regard tragedies as a learning school for deliberation and decision-making. Citizens learn about the whimsical nature of existence and thus how difficult it is to make the right decisions. In this way, tragedies helped to prepare the citizens for their tasks as governors and judges in the democratic city states in Classical Greece. Fear and compassion were indispensable 'passions' for the fulfilment of these tasks. To be able to make prudent decisions we must avoid overconfidence and mercilessness and let fear and compassion counterbalance these faults.

The Eichmann trial as theatre

Aristotle's description provides us with an interesting framework within which to analyse the Eichmann trial. Could the trial be understood as a kind of theatre or be read as a tragedy? Is it possible to understand the function of such a trial as a school for decision-making? As we shall see, the Eichmann case is somewhat ambivalent in this regard. Although it can easily be understood as a theatre of justice, and be read as a tragedy, the trial reveals a tension between two different approaches. The one approach reads the case from the perspective of the victims of the Nazi regime and regards its most important function as an act of so-called historic justice. It is history itself that is put on trial.

This reading of the trial was also expounded by the then prime minister of Israel Ben Gurion.

> It is not the penalty to be inflicted on the criminal that is the main thing … but the full exposure of the Nazi regime's infamous crimes against our people. Eichmann's acts alone are not the main point in this trial. Historic justice and the honor of the Jewish people demand this trial. (cited by Felman 2002: 113)

Several commentators on the trial have developed an interesting theoretical framework that allows such a reading in a positive sense. Felman, for example, emphasizes the monumental historical meaning of the trial.[3]

3 See also Osiel (1997) and Horsman (2011: chs 1 and 2). Martha Minow has not analysed the Eichmann trial, but her remarks on what we call historic justice are also interesting. See Minow (1998).

> What makes of a case a monumental historical case is the dramatic, totalizing way in which the legal institutions undertake to put on trial history itself, thereby setting the whole world as the stage and as the audience of the trial ... Whereas the Nuremberg trials view murderous political regimes and their aggressive warfare as the center of the trial ... the Eichmann trial views the victims as the center of what gives history its monumental significance as an act of historic justice. (Felman 2002: 112)

The other approach, which is that of Hannah Arendt, emphasizes the importance of legal justice and therefore insists on the centrality of the perpetrator and the delivery of a verdict. 'Justice demands', she says, 'that the accused be prosecuted, defended, and judged ... On trial are his deeds, not the sufferings of the Jews ... not even anti-Semitism or racism' (Arendt 1994: 5).

Although they emphasize different functions, both approaches bring forward important insights for understanding the functions of trials in the case of mass murder and other horrendous crimes. In so far as they are one-sided, it might be a matter of how to balance both. The point I want to discuss here is how to evaluate the two approaches from the point of view of the educational function of the trial.

Arendt's criticism of the prosecutor's strategy

Hannah Arendt gives an interesting description of the auditorium for the trial in the introductory chapter to her book on Eichmann. 'Whoever planned this auditorium in the newly built Beth Ha'am, the House of the people', Arendt writes, 'had a theatre in mind, complete with orchestra and gallery, with proscenium and stage, and with side doors for the actors' entrance' (1994: 4).

She found this courtroom not a bad place for 'a show trial' with, as she wrote, Prime Minister Ben-Gurion as 'the stage manager' (Arendt 1994: 4-5). Arendt feared not only that the trial would become a show trial, put on for purely political reasons, but also that it would become merely an instrument for the writing of history: 'It is not an individual that is in the dock at this historic trial, and not the Nazi regime alone, but anti-Semitism throughout history' (Arendt 1994: 19). A trial has to be set up to do justice, which 'demands that the accused be prosecuted, defended, and judged, and that all the other questions of seemingly greater import – of "How could it happen?" and "Why did it happen?" of "Why the Jews?" and "Why the Germans?," of "What role of other nations?" and "What was the extent of co-responsibility on the side of the Allies?," [and so forth] – be left in abeyance' (Arendt 1994: 10).

What struck Arendt most was the theatrical performance of the advocate general. As a modern public man, he gave press conferences and interviews for television during the trial. He permitted himself 'spontaneous' outbursts to reporters in the court building – 'he is sick of cross-examining Eichmann, who answers all questions with lies'. His rule 'permits frequent side glances into the audience, and the *theatrics* characteristic of a more than ordinary vanity' (Arendt

1994: 5-6; italics in the original). Arendt seems to be describing here what Aristotle meant when he referred to the 'highly effective'. And does not the same apply to the manner in which Hausner started his opening address.

> As I stand here before you, Judges of Israel ... I do not stand alone. With me stand six million accusers. But they cannot rise to their feet and point an accusing finger toward the man who sits in the glass dock and cry: 'I accuse'. For their ashes are piled up on the hills of Auschwitz, and in the fields of Treblinka, and are strewn in the forests of Poland ... Their blood cries out, but their voices are not heard. (*Attorney General* v. *Eichmann* (Proceedings of the District Court of Jerusalem, 1962), quoted in Hausner 1966: 323-324)

How much Hausner was focused on the theatrical effects of his performance is also apparent from what he wrote in his memoirs. On one of the documents that were prepared for him by Bureau 06[4] he notes the following. 'Very good brief from a police point of view', but it failed to tell the whole story of the Nazi persecution and mass murder of the Jews and would hardly arouse the public worldwide. 'This was the course adopted at the Nuremberg Tribunals', Hausner recalled, 'a few witnesses and films of the concentration camps, interspersed with piles of documents. It was all efficient and simple. But it was also one of the reasons why the proceedings there failed to reach the hearts of men.' In the final event, Hausner was not content to find Eichmann guilty on the basis of incriminating documents: 'I knew we needed more than a conviction; we needed a living record of a gigantic human and national disaster' (Ceserani 2004: 250; Hausner 1966: 267).

Arendt found that the judges had a completely different attitude, writing that Judge Landau did 'his very best, to prevent this trial from becoming a show trial under the influence of the prosecutor's showmanship'. Contrary to Hausner's attempts to sensationalize the trial, the judges showed great restraint. 'At no time is there anything theatrical in the conduct of the judges. Their walk is unstudied, their sober and intense attention, visibly stiffening under the impact of grief as they listen to the tales of suffering, is natural' (Arendt 1994: 4). To them it was not a 'forum for clarification of questions of great import'. It was their responsibility to focus on the defendant's actions and to 'entirely eliminate' anything foreign to this process (Lipstadt 2011: 141). The trial should not 'degenerate into a spectacular history lesson' (Ceserani 2004: 255). For this reason, Arendt was critical of the role of the witnesses in the trial. Part of the testimony was devoted to what she calls 'background witnesses' (Arendt 1994: 207). These witnesses helped to 'paint a picture' of the Holocaust in general, but had often no relation to Eichmann's case. The problem for Arendt with such a historic approach is that it diverts attention from the accused and his acts.

4 Bureau 06 investigated the Eichmann case before the trial.

The educational role of the Eichmann trial

Was Arendt right? Or is the story of the 'destruction' of the Jewish people so affecting that reacting to it detachedly would constitute a kind of insult? And are there serious objections against ascribing to a trial the function of facing history? Perhaps Arendt's approach is too rigid, but from the perspective of education, much can be said for the opposite. Let us look again at the components Aristotle distinguished in his description of the tragedy and apply these to the trial of Adolf Eichmann. In the first place, the Eichmann trial could be regarded as a strong educational instrument because it presents us the exemplum, the specific case of Eichmann: 'Justice insists on the importance of Adolf Eichmann, son of Karl Adolf Eichmann' (Arendt 1994: 5). 'Ordinary' people learn more easily from concrete examples than from the general and abstract. This means that the lessons we can learn from a trial that focuses on the writing of history will become more general, more abstract. Of course, in history writing the exemplary can have its place, but behind it the historian is looking for patterns he or she wants to explain.

Second, if we look at trials from the perspective of education, the plot will be central, not the spectacle. Although it is possible that a trial will touch or affect the public, that is not its primary aim. Maybe Arendt's remark (1994: 5) that it was Eichmann's deeds that were on trial, 'not sufferings of Jews' could be understood in this way. In any event, if the spectacle were to become dominant over the plot, the trial could become moving, but not educational. Hausner struggled with the fact that the trial was often not moving at all, but instead rather boring.

Character

This brings us to the component of the character. Although the character is not unimportant, as in tragedy, it is not, or should not be, the focal point in a trial. The character of the actors has to be understood as explanatory to the acts that are at the forefront. It is not because of his character that a defendant is on trial, but because of certain acts. And if we look to the other actors in a trial, judges, prosecutors and defending lawyers, it is obvious that their character is or should not be important at all. The very gowns they wear are perfect symbols of depersonalization. They are the costumes for when they are on stage. In so far as one can ascribe a character to these actors, it is, or should be, related only to the role they play in a trial.

Things are different in the Eichmann case. Here we see a great deal of emphasis laid on the character of the defendant. This is understandable considering the outrageous kinds of crimes this criminal had been involved in. How could one ever get a grip on crimes that caused such inconceivable suffering? Surely it is reasonable to find the explanation for the inconceivable in the inconceivable – to regard the criminals who are responsible for mass murder and genocide as 'inconceivable', beings of an 'abnormal' nature, with an 'abnormal' character? Some sort of 'monster' with evil instincts, from which one can but turn away in disgust. The assumption of 'abnormality' or even 'monstrousness' seems indeed to have been part of Hausner's strategy of proving the defendant's guilt; like others, Hausner was looking for the abnormal in Eichmann.[5] His book on the trial opens with a chapter on 'The Mask and the Man', suggesting that he wanted to unmask Eichmann, who presented himself as a dull, calm, polite person who always acted in a well-considered way. Under this mask, Hausner and others suggest, you will find a fanatic, with a genuine hatred for Jewish people.

> Hausner dwelled on Eichmann's character and cited Wisliceny, Höss and Kurt Becher on the extent of his zeal, ruthlessness and hatred of Jews. None of this had changed since the fall of the Nazis, Hausner insisted. 'He did not repent. He still believes that he did what was right and proper in destroying millions.' (Cesarani 2004: 261)

Spectators also tried to unmask Eichmann over and over again. Although he presented himself as an impassive man, when he became impatient Eichmann let his mask slip. Then 'Eichmann's voice sharpened: the cold snarl, the bark that many of the witnesses remembered was there' (Martha Gellhorn, cited by Cesarani 2004: 272).

The component of character has become a much debated subject in discussions of the Eichmann trial, although not so much because of the way Hausner or others depicted it. It was Hannah Arendt in particular who made people wonder about Eichmann's character. Arendt painted an image of Eichmann that could be regarded as the opposite of the picture painted by others. Not a 'monster', not an 'abnormal' being. What was shocking to her was to discover Eichmann's 'normality'. To begin with, the way he appeared in court must have been confusing to many. When he entered the small dock in which he was locked during the court sessions, he started to dust off his little desk with his handkerchief. He was well-dressed, ordered the files, stood up when the judges and others addressed him. Eichmann did not have the appearance of a monster. Rather, he gave the impression of a dull official who no one would mind having as a neighbour. Indeed, Arendt emphasized this side of Eichmann's character. She found in him the example of the criminal as a product of modern totalitarianism. Not the fanatic killer, but the willing bureaucrat prepared to play his role as a cog in the machine. This does not mean that Arendt excused Eichmann. At the end of her report on the trial she leaves no doubt about this.

> Let us assume, for the sake of argument, that it was nothing more than misfortune that made you a willing instrument in the organization of mass murder; there still remains the fact that you have carried out, and therefore actively supported, a policy of mass murder. For in politics it is not like a nursery; in politics obedience

5 He attempted to prove, for example, that Eichmann had ordered a Jewish boy who had stolen some fruit from a garden tree to be killed, although there appeared to be no evidence.

> and support are the same. And just as you supported and carried out a policy of not wanting to share the earth with the Jewish people and the people of a number of other nations – as though you and your superiors had any right to determine who should and who should not inhabit the world – we find that no one, that is, no member of the human race, can be expected to want to share the earth with you. This is the reason, and the only reason, you must hang. (Arendt 1994: 279)

Thought

When Arendt introduced the notion of 'the banality of evil', it was not because she thought that little or no responsibility could be ascribed to Eichmann. It was because she discovered what many saw as an unprecedented kind of evil, or wrongdoing. What Arendt tried to explain was that ordinary people too, people with whom we could easily identify, can do wrong and become willing supporters of murderous systems. What was wrong with Eichmann? What made him collaborate with others to destroy the Jewish people? It is interesting what Arendt says about the ever-returning defence strategy, in which he tried to present himself as a dedicated servant, acting according to the rules and commands of others. What was wrong with Eichmann was that he neutralized his ability to be critical towards these rules and commands. Eichmann was not able to 'think'. This inability to 'think' has to do with 'a more decisive flaw in his character', Arendt writes, 'his almost total inability to look at anything from the other fellow's point of view'. Eichmann was not able 'to think from the standpoint of somebody else. No communication was possible with him, not because he lied but because he was surrounded by the most reliable of all safeguards against the words and the presence of others, and hence against reality as such' (Arendt 1994: 47-49).

Eichmann was not a fanatic motivated by hatred against the Jewish people. According to Arendt, he had no motives at all. 'He merely … never realized what he was doing' (Arendt 1994: 286), because he was not able to imagine what he was doing. He lacked the ability to imagine. Here Arendt refers to Kant's notion of reflective judgement.[6] This kind of judgement is needed when we cannot simply apply a general rule to a concrete case, such as having to judge a piece of art. However, in such cases we do not stand alone. We can start with our own estimation, but test it on others' estimations. What do you think of it? How do you judge? It is by sharing my viewpoint with the viewpoint of others that I will enlarge my imagination. As Arendt (1988: 43) writes '[t]o think with enlarged mentality means that one trains one's imagination to go visiting'. And to 'go visiting' is important: it will improve my judgement, because it will be more general. It will not only be 'my opinion', but a more generalized judgement that is shared with and by others.

---

6 See also on this notion in the context of the Eichmann trial the interesting article by Bilsky (2001).

> The more people's standpoints I have present in my mind while I am pondering a given issue, and the better I can imagine how I would feel and think if I were in their place, the stronger will be my capacity for reflective thinking and the more valid my final conclusion, my opinion. (Arendt 1993: 241)

However, this capacity for reflective thinking was what Eichmann lacked. 'He was not stupid', Arendt writes.

> It was sheer thoughtlessness – something by no means identical with stupidity – that predisposed him to become one of the greatest criminals of that period. And if this is 'banal' and even funny, if with the best will in the world one cannot extract any diabolical or demonic profundity from Eichmann, that is still far from calling it commonplace. (Arendt 1994: 287-288)

Lessons to be learned

It was exactly all this that Arendt thought we could learn from the Eichmann trial.

> That such remoteness from reality and such thoughtlessness can wreak more havoc than all the evil instincts taken together which, perhaps, are inherent in man – that was, in fact, the lesson one could learn from Jerusalem. (Arendt 1994: 288)

This lesson clearly differs from the lessons Hausner wanted to teach. What are the main differences and how can we estimate these different approaches when it comes to learning? Our short analysis of the tragedies and what people can learn from them will direct us here.

To start with, the main difference between the approaches to the case appears to be that Arendt wants us to give an interpretation of the trial in which the spectator is strongly involved, while in Hausner's lessons that spectator remains a bystander. Hausner's strategy is primarily to concentrate on the history of the genocide. Most of the witnesses he wanted to hear had no (direct) relationship with Eichmann or his part in all of the crimes. Their stories were important to allow a depiction of the history of the genocide. But the question remains whether or not these stories were part of the plot. Did they teach us about the actions, the decisions of the accused? These stories did, of course, move the spectators. But, as we have seen, moving the spectators was not the foremost aim of a tragedy. Perhaps it is not the function of legal trials either.

Although one can still say that we can learn from the history as presented in the trial, the other part of Hausner's strategy seems to annul the capacity of the trial to teach us a lesson. By demonizing Eichmann, this criminal is radically estranged, and for that reason spectators will not identify themselves with him. This man comes from another world.

In terms of the components of a tragedy this all means that instead of putting the plot, the actions of Eichmann, at the centre of the trial, the emphasis is on the character component and the spectacle component. The component of the plot is important to give the spectators an exemplum. Because of its more general description of what happened, the historical picture could not function as such an exemplum. And because the actors are not at the centre of the trial, the spectators will also miss the component of thought.

After what we have seen from her report on the Eichmann trial, it is clear that Arendt's approach better resembles the tragedy as an educational instrument. She gives less weight to the component of spectacle, while emphasizing the strong restraint of the judges. Although she did concentrate on Eichmann's character, her fascination with it was bound up with her search for an explanation of his actions and thought, or rather: for his inaction and thoughtlessness.

The main difference between these two approaches is that of the spectator's role: merely spectator in Hausner's approach, a participant too in Arendt's. This difference in approach is well described by the modern thinker Martha Nussbaum. She asks herself why there has been such tremendous enthusiasm for Daniel Goldhagen's *Hitler's Willing Executioners* (1996).[7] Her explanation for this is that many people wish 'to believe that the culture that gave birth to the horrors of Nazism was a monstrosity, an aberration' (Nussbaum 2001: 450). And those who committed the awful crimes were 'unique, disgusting monsters'. Such a picture is comforting. This is so, because evil is represented as something that is 'outside, alien, has nothing to do with us'. And, 'by allowing ourselves to see evil people as disgusting, we conveniently distance them from ourselves' (Nussbaum 2001: 451). This implies that it might be quite uncomfortable if we do not demonize, and feel disgust for, criminals like Eichmann. Seeing Nazis depicted without disgust

> is alarming, because it requires self-scrutiny, warning us that we might well have done the same thing under comparable circumstances. It alerts us to the presence of evil … in ourselves, and requires us to ask how we might prevent similar phenomena from materializing in our society. We have to confront the fact that we might become them; but this means that in a significant sense we already are them – with the fearfulness, weakness, and moral blindness that go to produce such evils. (Nussbaum 2001: 451-452)

This last observation of Nussbaum could easily be read as an explanation for the educational function of tragedies, but also of trials. If they are performed in the right way we, as spectators, can learn from both tragedies and trials. We learn from these 'performances' because they arouse fear and perhaps also compassion. As Nussbaum explains, they arouse fear when we discover that, like them, we too could suffer from 'weakness and moral blindness'. And Arendt could add that it is 'thinking' that could perhaps prevent us from doing evil.

---

7 On this question, see also Ceserani (2004: ch. 9).

But then, what about compassion? Approaching criminals like Eichmann as 'ordinary' human beings, that is to say, not as a monster coming from elsewhere, but as 'one of us', implies that we have to take him seriously. In our culture, taking a person seriously implies that one holds him responsible for his acts, something which Eichmann did not understand the meaning of. This was well illustrated at the point at which Eichmann summarized Kant's ethical principles. Eichmann gave a nearly correct description of Kant's principle. 'I meant by my remark about Kant that the principle of my will must always be such that it can become the principle of general laws.' However, what Eichmann did not understand was that this implies that one has to ask oneself if one could ever will a certain principle to be law. As Arendt says, Eichmann had distorted Kant's principle to read: 'Act as if the principle of your actions were the same as that of the legislator or of the law of the land' (1994: 136). But, although one can hold a person fully responsible for what he does or has done, the case remains that there are always circumstances that influence one's perception of the world, or perhaps distort that perception. We feel compassion for the actors in a tragedy because they are the victims of short-sightedness or even mere fate, but still take full responsibility for their faults. Oedipus, for example, having discovered that he had killed his own father and slept with his own mother, felt enormous guilt, although it was merely fate that led him astray. He cut out his own eyes and banned himself from his kingdom. Of course, with criminals like Eichmann it is completely different. But still, although we hold him responsible for his faults, as an involved spectator we will understand that it is also a kind of 'fate' that made him become one of the most outrageous criminals of the twentieth century (Nussbaum 2001: 341-391).

Catharsis

Above, I suggested that Arendt's approach is one-sided. That is so because she scarcely has an eye for the possible historical function of a trial and the position of victims in it. One might especially wonder why she overlooks the meaning of the trial for the victims. Against the background of her political theory one can easily plead for arranging ample space for victims to also raise their voice in a trial. A trial, like political institutions, can easily be understood as a public realm that arranges an open communication between citizens (Hol 2005). Given that in the past all rights of the Jews and the Jewish people, including the right to speak for themselves in public, had been erased, the Eichmann trial could be seen as a historic event to restore this injustice by giving the victims voice. This has been noticed by Felman, who says that a 'victim has no language of his own ... is *robbed of a language* with which to articulate his or her victimization'. And because they had the opportunity to speak in the trial 'victims were thus for the first time gaining what as victims they precisely could not have: authority – historical authority, that is to say, *semantic authority* over themselves and over others. Ultimately, the acquisition of semantic authority by victims is what the trial was about' (Felman 2002: 125-127; italics in the originals). In line with this argument, others have ascribed a kind of therapeutic function to the trial. In a tragic reading of the Eichmann trial, Susan Sontag emphasizes its function of giving relief, or healing:

> The truth is that the Eichmann trial did not, and could not have conformed to legal standards only ... Masses of facts about the extermination of the Jews were piled into the record; a great outcry of historical agony was set down. There was, needless to say, no strictly legal way of justifying this. The function of the trial was rather that of the tragic drama: above and beyond judgment and punishment, catharsis. (cited by Horsman 2011: 23)

This tragic reading is interesting, and indeed neatly fits what Aristotle indicated as the ultimate effect of a tragedy: catharsis. Perhaps unexpected, this notion of catharsis brings us back to the matter of the educational function of tragedies and trials. As Salkever puts it, this notion has several meanings. Besides healing or relief – Salkever speaks of purgation or purification – there is another important meaning. He sees the way a tragedy has been set up as having the effect of arousing both fear and compassion, and causes the spectators to start to deliberate, or to 'think'. This effect can also be understood as a kind of catharsis. As Salkever says, it is 'part of the process of transforming a potentially good democracy ... into one that is actually such ... The suggestion here is not that tragedy has the power to move its audience immediately and decisively to a better course of action, but that it can make its audience more inclined to act well, or at least not to act badly' (Salkever 1986: 300). As reasoned above, the same function can be ascribed to trials.

What does this all mean? It is not easy to answer this question. But, if one wants to do justice to the complexity of the meaning of catharsis, it will be clear that one has to strike a certain balance between the position of victims and the position of perpetrator, or between historic justice on the one hand and legal justice on the other hand.

To conclude

A trial is like a theatre, or should one say 'is theatre'? And like theatre it can educate the people. However, there remains an unbridgeable gap between theatre and trials. Although one could hold that the ultimate aim of theatre or tragedies is to educate the people, the ultimate aim of a legal trial is different. As Arendt emphasized, the Eichmann trial had to take place in the interest of justice. This implies that historical understanding or moralization must not be at the centre of the trial for that means 'the defendant is taken as a symbol and the trial as a pretext to bring up matters which are apparently more interesting than the guilt or innocence of one person' (Arendt 1994: 286). So it is the function of a trial to concentrate on the defendant, and his guilt or innocence. Again, this means his actions, the plot, must be brought to the fore; all other components are but a function of this. One could ask if the trial and its rules as we know them are adequately equipped to perform justice in such a way. In any event only then will we be educated. Educated to decide, educated to do justice.

References

Arendt, H. 1988. *Lectures on Kant's Political Philosophy*. Chicago: University of Chicago Press.

Arendt, H. 1993. *Between Past and Future*. New York: Penguin.

Arendt, H. 1994. *Eichmann in Jerusalem: A Report on the Banality of Evil*. New York: Penguin.

Aristotle, 1991. *The Art of Rhetoric*. Translated with an Introduction and Notes by H.C. Lawson-Tancred. Harmondsworth: Penguin.

Aristotle, 1999. *Poetics*. Cambridge, MA and London: Harvard University Press.

Bilsky, L.Y. 2001. When Actor and Spectator meet in the Courtroom: Reflections on Hannah Arendt's Concept of Judgment. In *Judgment, Imagination, and Politics: Themes from Kant and Arendt*, edited by R. Beiner and J. Nedelsky, 257-286. Lanham, MD: Rowman & Littlefield.

Cesarani, D. 2004. *Eichmann: His Life and Crimes*. London: William Heinemann.

Easterling, P.E. 1997. *The Cambridge Companion to Greek Tragedy*. Cambridge: Cambridge University Press.

Felman, S. 2002. *The Juridical Unconscious: Trials and Traumas in the Twentieth Century*. Cambridge, MA and London: Harvard University Press.

Goldhagen, D. 1996. *Hitler's Willing Executioners: Ordinary Germans and the Holocaust*. London: Little, Brown.

Hall, E. 2010. *Greek Tragedy: Suffering under the Sun*. Oxford: Oxford University Press.

Hol, A., 2005. Adjudication and the Public Realm: An Analysis Based on the Work of Hannah Arendt. *Utrecht Law Review*, 1(2), 40-45. Available at http://www.utrechtlawreview.org/index.php/ulr/article/viewFile/7/7 (accessed 1 May 2012).

Hausner, G. 1966. *Justice in Jerusalem*. New York: Harper & Row.

Horsman, Y. 2011. *Theaters of Justice: Judging, Staging, and Working Through in Arendt, Brecht, and Delbo*. Stanford, CA: Stanford University Press.

Lipstadt, D.E. 2011. *The Eichmann Trial*. New York: Nextbook Schocken.

Meier, C. 1988. *Die politische Kunst der grichischen Tragödie*. Munich: C.H. Beck.

Minow, M. 1998. *Between Vengeance and Forgiveness: Facing History after Genocide and Mass Violence*. Boston: Beacon Press.

Nussbaum, M. 1995. *Poetic Justice: The Literary Imagination and the Public Life*. Boston: Beacon Press.

Nussbaum, M. 2001. *Upheavals of Thought: The Intelligence of Emotions*. Cambridge: Cambridge University Press.

Osiel, M. 2000. *Mass Atrocity, Collective Memory, and the Law*. New Brunswick, NJ and London: Transaction.

Salkever, S.G. 1986. Tragedy and the Education of the Dēmos: Aristotle's Response to Plato. In *Greek Tragedy and Political Theory*, edited by J.P. Euben, 273-303. Berkeley: University of California Press.

Sophocles. N.D. 1974. *The Theban Plays*. Translated by E.F. Watling. Harmondsworth: Penguin.

Chapter 5
Memory Culture and Urban Reconstruction: The Case of Staro Sajmište in Belgrade[1]

Srdjan Radović

It could be argued that political power is expressed through control of both landscape and history, with the goal, among other things, of contributing to the establishment of a desirable political and/or national consciousness among the population (Light *et al.* 2002: 136). Ideologically encoded space, with its communicational power and discursive potential, becomes an active participant in the construction and perception of social reality, therefore transforming history into an element of 'the natural order of things', hiding at the same time its induced and artificial character (Azaryahu 1997: 481). Politics of space (and place) usually tend to transform undefined space into place, a space that occurs at the level of identity (Tuan 1977). Such politics of space/place, combined with continuously defining a culture of remembrance in Europe's periphery, show the gradual formation of a cultural management of place(s) and socio-cultural engineering of national identity in transitional Serbia, which is especially noticeable in respect of the reconfiguration of Serbia's historical heritage of the twentieth century. Already by the 1990s, the gradual European shift from 'patriotic memory' to the 'memory of genocide' (the Holocaust in particular) in public remembrance of the Second World War (Francois 2006: 228), had found its equivalent in Serbia with the focus of memory being relocated from resistance mythology to the evocation of ethnic Serb victims of that war. At the same time, a new East European culture of remembering communism (especially Stalinism, gulags and the Soviet occupation) found its counterpart, notably in the first decade of this century, in the public narratives of perceived Serb suffering under communism (Leggewie 2009). These politics of memory in Serbia sometimes legitimize themselves with growing transnational memorial culture, while at the same time they extensively alter and mystify such politics in the local context and for local (political) use. Wrapped in the web of multifaceted national and global politics of memory and space/place, Serbian elites generally try to ignore the recent past (wars in the former Yugoslavia), focusing instead on narratives and images of previous historical eras and thus pursuing a discursive politics which could be designated as the 'simulation of

1 This contribution is a result of research pursued within the project Cultural Heritage and Identity (No. 177026) financed by the Ministry of Education and Science of the Republic of Serbia.

continuity' (Maleševic 2008: 17). A combination of memory politics and politics of space leads to the creation and management of particular ideological spaces, notably monuments, memorials and memorial places. All such significant places usually undergo significant symbolic and ideological alterations with the passing of time, with new meanings and values being attributed to them, especially at times of significant societal change (which has been ongoing in Serbia since the late 1980s). A memorial, or any ideologically encoded place, can go through substantial symbolic and factual transformations which are determined by various social actors. Thus, memories, surrounding narratives and physical structure can change dramatically. In the following pages one such *lieu de memoire* will be examined and the reasons for the site's transformation and its effects discussed.

Sajmište in the public spotlight

Within the frame sketched above, numerous ethnographies of transitional time/space reconfiguration emerge in Serbia, but a few years ago one of them received special attention. The British pop band Kosheen scheduled a concert in Belgrade for 3 November 2007. The concert venue was the Poseydon club in the city's Staro Sajmište area (Staro Sajmište meaning Old Fairgrounds in Serbian, as to be distinguishable from the modern fairground venues built in the 1950s). The concert eventually never took place: there was a combined domestic and foreign red alert, since the internationally acclaimed musical group was to hold a gig in a building which, although now occupied by the Poseydon club, had in the 1940s been mostly frequented by Nazi guards and concentration camp inmates. The first major concert by an international band planned at this site triggered public acknowledgment of a more or less acknowledged fact, namely that the particular venue used to be a pavilion of the German-run Second World War concentration camp locally known as Staro Sajmište or Sajmište, internationally known as Sajmiste, Sajmiste (Semlin) or Semlin Lager (Semlin being the German name for the once separate town of Zemun, now a major Belgrade borough). After several years during which the public had ignored the fact that the former house of terror was being used as an entertainment facility, the story was out, and there was no going back. It should be noted that the cancelled concert represented the culmination of long-lasting inadequate concepts of (mis)use of this particular site. How this specific public location with historical importance (the so-called Spasić pavilion which functioned as the camp's hospital during the occupation) ended up in the hands of private owners is unclear to this day (there is an ongoing legal dispute between several municipal agencies and alleged owners). In any event, the lack of scruples when commercial interests are involved was more than evident from the public statement made by the agents organizing the ill-fated concert, who tried to calm public fury by saying that 'during Nazism the Spasić pavilion was merely a hospital where the deaths of camp inmates were officially declared'.[2]

The entire affair in late 2007 exposed numerous contradictions. City officials deplored the matter and appealed for the concert to be relocated, but systematically avoided explanations on how such a location could be leased or sold to private entrepreneurs. Additional resentment was triggered by the fact that only the arrival of an internationally popular band had prompted any official reaction on the matter, while previous uses of the former camp building for parties and concerts of somewhat lesser prominence had left most of the officials silent and uninterested. Who the actual whistleblowers in the affair were remains unclear: while some city officials claim that they are the ones who 'finally' pointed out the misuses of the site, other sources allege that the question was launched into the public arena by the members of the British group who were appalled upon realizing the history of the proposed venue, or by members of the Serbian and foreign civil sector interested in the Holocaust. With public condemnations mounting significant pressure, local organizers of the concert eventually cancelled the entire event and Kosheen did not perform in Belgrade at that time.[3] The general lack of interest in the matter among most city officials before the autumn of 2007 is demonstrated by a statement by the private owners/renters of the pavilion that they had 'asked the City and the Municipality for guidelines on managing the site on several occasions, but no reply ever came'.[4] Several city and municipal authorities renounced responsibility for the current uses of the location, while at the same time most of them promised to settle the matter in an ethical and appropriate way (without mentioning any deadlines). That such public reactions were more or less 'extorted' from otherwise indifferent officials is apparent from the statement by the acting mayor of Belgrade, who said he hoped 'that this entire affair, which, of course, we didn't need, and which doesn't represent us in a good way, will end in such a way that this area becomes a memorial centre'.[5] Unease related to the public surfacing of the problem of inadequate memorialization and general lack of interest regarding this site, and concerns about the capital city's public image were actually the only genuinely honest reactions in the entire affair; public pledges by officials mostly represented ad-hoc damage control. Confirmation of the latter came just one month after the beginning of the 'Kosheen affair': once the case had been removed from the public spotlight, a boxing match was scheduled at the former camp building. Entrepreneurs managing the Spasić pavilion alleged that no one, besides the media, had contacted them since the inception of the affair, while

2 As reported by several Serbian media outlets.

3 As reported by the news site www.b92.net, text 'Otkazan koncert na Starom Sajmištu' (news archive for 3 November 2007).

4 As stated in the article 'Juče logor, danas koncerti', published on the news portal www.b92.net (news archive for 26 October 2007).

5 From 'Alimpić: Grad traži rešenje za Staro sajmište', published in Belgrade daily *Danas*, 7 November 2007.

municipal and city officials found out about the planned event from journalists still inquiring into the Sajmište question.[6]

Staro Sajmište, and its wartime heritage, is simply forgotten – by most of the public and almost all of the local elites. The context of the location and persons connected with it (both the victims and the perpetrators) are far removed from public interest in the 2000s, and the temporary focus on the matter in 2007 and early 2008 turned out to be no more than a fleeting issue (as is apparent from the silence and oblivion in the years that followed, which will be discussed later). While Staro Sajmište never represented a central landmark on the symbolic map of Second World War history in Belgrade, with other sites gaining more prominence in public discourses and representations, its association with events in the Nazi camp gradually faded over the years, culminating in almost complete neglect after 2000. Transformations of this location over the period of more than 70 years, and a discussion of meanings and uses of its heritage, and corresponding memory and urban planning policies, are the focus of this chapter.

Functional and symbolic metamorphosis of the site

The Staro Sajmište complex was opened as a modern fairground area in 1937 (the year of the great World Exposition in Paris) and it represented (as was the case with many other grounds where mass exhibitions were held) an architectural showcase of the nation's progress and identity. Exhibition grounds, and representative fairs in general (especially the historic World Fairs, and to some degree contemporary Expos), had an important role in national promotion, where nation states had the opportunity to represent themselves through new technological and economic achievements and specific displays of arts, culture and especially architecture. It could be argued that organized marketing and branding of nation states were present from at least the time of the establishment of Great World Expositions (Bolin 2006: 193). The importance of architectural and symbolic spatial design could be observed clearly at the Parisian World Expo of 1937, given the architectural, sculptural and ideological competition that took place during the planning, building and enhancing of the national pavilions of the Third Reich and Soviet Union, which directly faced each other on the Seine river bank (Adam 1992: 244). Competition of this kind was also characteristic of less important 'players' in the international market of national and political identities of the inter-bellum era – international exhibitions also saw young and ambitious post-First World War states lavishly represent themselves in the period of global political alignments. Thus, the Kingdom of Yugoslavia sought to express the external firmness of the state and internal cohesion of the nation at the 1937 Paris Expo – the Yugoslav pavilion followed the prevailing architectural trend of that time in

6 As reported in the article 'Koncert ne može, a boks meč može', in Belgrade daily *Blic*, 12 December 2007.

Yugoslavia, one of 'monumental robust classicism as a symbolic expression of authoritarian politics'. The entire architecture – and, partly, the exposition – of the Yugoslav pavilion conveniently testified to the gradual symbolic and ideological realignment of Yugoslavia from the camp of Little Entente and its western allies towards the European Axis powers (Ignjatović 2004: 67-68).

It could be argued that exposition sites represented, in terms of both architecture and the exhibitions themselves, important spatial agents of ideological and national didactics. Such sites of massive fluctuation of people (who often visited them as organized groups) served political purposes, both at international expositions and particular national exhibition sites (for example VDNKh, former permanent Exhibition of Achievements of the National Economy of the USSR in Moscow, which represented a locale par excellence for cultural and ideological instruction of Soviet citizens).[7] A venue serving such functions in the Kingdom of Yugoslavia was the Sajmište complex, opened in 1937 – its monumentality and modernism with classicist premises also represented an 'ideological screen' (Leach 2002: 88) aimed primarily at Yugoslav nationals and Belgrade's inhabitants, and partly at the outside world. It was also the architectural centrepiece of Belgrade's urban expansion, since it was the first urban quarter built on the other bank of the river Sava (which also bore significant symbolic power given that it was located on the territory of former Austria-Hungary before 1918). The fairgrounds encompassed a dozen pavilions, many of which were the national exhibition halls of several European countries. During the 1930s, the Kingdom started aligning itself more with totalitarian nations, and its foreign policy was clearly displayed in the parallel presence of exhibition halls of both the traditional Yugoslav allies (Czechoslovakia and Romania) and novel partners (monumental pavilions of the Third Reich and Fascist Italy). Together with the neighbouring bridge named after the late King Alexander, Sajmište represented the most prominent modernist urban area of the capital and an important urban landmark. This location was clearly visible from most places in central Belgrade and easily accessible by the new tram line, and it rapidly became integrated with the city's core, both physically and symbolically.

Shortly after the beginning of the so-called April war in 1941, Axis powers and their allies occupied Yugoslavia. The territory of the former Belgrade municipality was occupied by the *Wehrmacht* and divided between a Nazi-ruled Serbia led by a quisling government and a Nazi-controlled puppet 'Independent State of Croatia'. The Sajmište area was part of the latter, but in the zone directly controlled by German military authorities and still closely connected with central Belgrade on the other side of the river; the former fairground pavilions were turned into a Nazi

7 Synergy of architectural and structural monumentality, and massive flux of people, also found its adequate scenery between the two world wars in huge parade venues, where mass political rituals took place, be it under totalitarian (for example the Nuremberg complex for rallies of the National Socialist party – *Reichsparteitagsgelände*) or democratic regimes (for example the monumental Strahov stadium in Prague, *Velký strahovský stadion*, where mass gymnastic rallies of the *Sokol* were held).

concentration and transit camp. From the autumn of 1941 until mid-1942, the Sajmiste camp was a concentration site for Jewish women and children (*Judenlager Semlin*), mostly from Belgrade (the majority of male Jews in Serbia had already been annihilated by firing squads in the autumn of 1941). They were killed on-site or, more often, in moving gas vans (transport wagons turned into mobile gas chambers where victims were suffocated to death with carbon monoxide while the van was still moving). Approximately 6,500 mostly Serbian Jews lost their lives in this way and occupied Serbia was proclaimed to be the first *Judenfrei* European territory. The entire fairground area served the camp purposes, with the largest pavilion (former Yugoslav pavilion no. 3) being a building where inmates were housed, while the above-mentioned Spasić pavilion served as the camp hospital. Some Holocaust researchers see the Sajmiste case as a significant landmark in the escalation of Nazi policy towards Jews from then onwards – the utilization of gas vans and swift extermination of Serbian Jews 'presaged the efficiency and routinized detachment of the death camps' (Browning 1985: 84).

Once the Serbian Jews were annihilated, the site became a transit camp for antifascist resistance fighters, partisan sympathizers and civilians from Yugoslavia and neighbouring countries (*Anhaltelager Semlin*). It is estimated that some 30,000 men and women passed through the *Anhaltelager* during this period (most of them were transferred further to forced labour camps and death camps), of whom more than 10,000 died from exhaustion, dysentery and beatings in the camp (Byford 2009). At that time, Allied bombing campaigns started to be deployed in the Balkan area and, since a strategic bridge and Belgrade's river port and railway station were in the close vicinity of the camp, albeit on the other side of the river, many of the camp's buildings were destroyed from the air. Less than five years after its lavish opening, the Sajmište complex was transformed from the space of official representation into a place of fear and public silence. This dubious position of the camp, located less than a kilometre from the city centre and on the other side of the Axis drawn border, where thousands of people suffered and whence they were transported to their deaths through the Belgrade streets (either in gas vans or in trucks heading for Jajinci and other grave sites around Belgrade), was, moreover, enhanced by the almost complete panoramic visibility of the camp from the city. As David Albahari, a prominent Serbian author, wrote, 'the camp wasn't humiliating only because of its inhumane nature, but also because it was entirely on display to Belgrade's gaze, to the city that silently watched it'.[8] The firm grip of the occupying and quisling forces on the city prevented any substantial public outcry or action regarding the atrocities happening in the camp. Sajmiste was finally shut down in September 1944, merely a month and a half before the city's liberation; only a few camp pavilions had survived the Allied bombardments.

Following the end of the war, the former camp facilities still standing after the Allied bombings deteriorated further. Some badly damaged pavilions were

8 From Albahari's novel *Gec i Majer*, as quoted in Manojlović Pintar and Ignjatović (2008).

demolished, while those that remained temporarily housed voluntary labour brigade members, artists' studios, people with no adequate housing and so forth. Up to the present day, this area has only been altered minimally in terms of urban construction, and it was gradually becoming less prominent in the urban tissue despite being centrally positioned. In the construction boom that occurred in the socialist era, Novi Beograd (New Belgrade) emerged to the west of the Staro Sajmište area – a showcase of socialist architecture and urbanism, a new urban borough with up to 500,000 people currently resident there. In contrast to this, the buildings of the former camp and adjacent areas were slowly becoming a specific 'grey zone' located between the city centre and the modern quarters of Novi Beograd – a paradox of parallel urban and spatial centrality – and almost total symbolic marginality within the 'city text' emerged. Indeed, both the space and those few inhabitants of the Sajmište area still represent the internal 'Other' of the developing capital, visible only to those who intentionally explore or visit this quarter (Vučinić 1995). While several urban plans during the Yugoslav period proposed a complete reconstruction of this location (which usually meant demolishing the last remnants of the former camp), none of them actually materialized, and until now most of the physical structures have remained more or less unchanged (and badly managed), with some being leased or sold to private establishments in the late 1990s and early 2000s. As for memorialization of the site, it was as insignificant as the reconstruction effort in the area – the first memorial plaque commemorating the camp was not placed until 1974; the second plaque was installed in 1984, both by a Second World War veterans organization and local political groups. The former camp area found its way into the spotlight only in the 1980s: once a year remembrance rituals and commemorations were held, the remaining camp pavilions were officially designated as memorial sites, the area was declared a protected urban zone and, in 1995, a larger monument commemorating camp inmates was unveiled nearby (Byford 2009). What led to the most significant terror site of the Second World War in the Belgrade area, and probably in all of Serbia, receiving so little attention during almost the entire socialist period and most of the 1990s and 2000s? Several determinants might have contributed to such a situation.

Suppressing and moulding memory

There are manifold reasons for the stagnation of this urban area during socialism and they range from lack of interest in urbanization of the wider area of Sajmište (because of private ownership of land parcels surrounding it) to Yugoslav politics of remembrance of the Second World War. The construction of Novi Beograd (the borough where Sajmište is located), one of the most prominent building projects of the socialist era in Yugoslavia, also meant that 'the *erection* of the new city determines the *demolition* of the past and *construction* of the specific ideology of oblivion'; particular plans for the Sajmište area in the period of the state monopoly in the field of construction and urban planning were never definite and they never materialized, thus transforming this location into 'a kind of *terra incognita*, an empty space without meaning or memory' (Manojlović Pintar and Ignjatović 2008: 107). However, the matter of limited memorialization of the site is somewhat more complex. Focal loci of remembrance of the Second World War in Belgrade during the socialist period were the sites of Jajinci (the major execution ground where inmates from most Belgrade prisons were killed and buried) and Banjica camp (a prison camp heavily populated with political prisoners and resistance fighters during the entire war), with Sajmište significantly put aside. It could be argued that this was the case because Sajmište was mostly the site of transit and imprisonment of civilians not usually subjected to police interrogations. Namely, in the initial phases of the creation of memory of the war in Yugoslavia, ideological 'priority' was given to sites and events of 'resistance' rather than those of 'terror' – authorities regularly commemorated places of the Partisan battles and urban guerrilla activities, while the reign of terror against civilians was usually relegated to second place. One might argue that the socialist nation-building of multi-ethnic Yugoslavia preferred the image of the victorious Partisan cult, depicting popular resistance, to the martyr cult of the victimized and tortured population (Radović 2009: 152). Accordingly, camps where prominent Partisan fighters or political prisoners were incarcerated fared somewhat better in the overall memorialization endeavour than those that represented sites where the civilian population was tortured.

However, with time, military and political victims of the war lost their central position in the processes of social integration and civilian victims gradually became the basis for the construction of the community of 'non-questioning belief' (Manojlović Pintar and Ignjatović 2008: 97). Therefore, non-military sites also gained prominent memorialization. However, no significant evocation or monumentalization of the Sajmište area took place until the mid-1980s despite these changing attitudes. Some authors (like Jovan Byford) argue that the Yugoslav perception of the Holocaust also played a significant role in the memorial neglect of this site, since official narratives did not emphasize the unique and specific character of the genocide against the Jews in the Second World War (a discourse that was wholly absent in other socialist countries and acquired prominence in the West only after the 1960s). In Yugoslav official discourses and historiography, all civilian victims of actions pursued by different occupying, quisling or collaborationist forces (generally designated as 'fascist terror') were labelled with the general term 'victims of fascism', and the Holocaust was usually perceived as one of many reflexes of general racist and fascist policies of occupying forces in Yugoslavia. Bearing in mind that, in the first phase of its existence, Sajmiste camp served exclusively as a Jewish extermination camp, complete and overall memorialization of the site would pose a possible contradiction to the then prevailing politics of Second World War remembrance, which placed genocide against Yugoslav Jews aside in the mainstream representations of the war (Manojlović Pintar and Ignjatović 2008). Thus, the Sajmište site was officially labelled, as were many other similar locations throughout the country, as the 'site of torture of the peoples of Yugoslavia' (in Serbo-Croatian: *mučilište naroda Jugoslavije*). The erection of memorials to civilian victims of the war in this period primarily served to establish a record of tragic, yet glorious, history, demonstrating respect to the victims and acknowledging the violent past, and to much lesser, if any, extent to provide restitution or symbolical compensation for the civilian victims. With the strong antifascist premise of the Yugoslav socialist state, and the basic continuity of the wartime resistance political movement in the new state structures, the guilt for war crimes and the restitution of victims were consequently transferred to the 'other' side: Axis countries and their forces, and their quisling allies. The possible role of Yugoslav nationals in genocidal policies during the Second World War (either as part of organized collaborationist movements or as individuals) was steadily overlooked in that it was depicted as automatically and overwhelmingly determined by the occupying forces' policies; thus the possible accountability of the new state for its citizens' misdeeds was readily dismissed.

Not only had identity politics pursued by the hegemonic elites of socialist Yugoslavia contributed to the limited memorialization of Sajmište and some other sites, but the same could be argued for politics of identity and discourses and concepts stemming more independently or autonomously from wider strata of the population (Hill and Wilson 2003: 3). As demonstrated by West Germany until the mid-1960s, when German ruling elites' lack of interest in dealing with the country's national-socialist past determined the spontaneous creation of a 'memory wall' (as defined by Paul Connerton, 2004), there is a general inclination of the masses to put aside or avoid evocation or commemoration of the dark past, especially when no targeted public communication on the matter is present (very paradigmatic of this could be the case of memorialization of the Dachau camp – see Koonz 2006: 296). A certain unease about dwelling or commuting in locations heavily associated with tragic historic occurrences could exist within the general population; elopement from history (especially dark history), which does not necessarily have to be perceived as one's own, might be a natural impulse of the masses. (Of course, there is no organized society without historical narratives and memory culture, the only question is what kinds of narratives and culture are being publicly promulgated.) What used to be unease because of the overt visual display of the concentration camp to citizens during wartime might find its equivalent in potential 'overt representation' of remembrance of the camp's history during peacetime in the, now centrally positioned, urban area with its massive fluctuation of citizens. Indeed, not only in this specific case but in general, a trend of eviction of representations of death (especially tragic deaths) from evident public displays in urban areas could be assumed (Pavićević 2009). Additionally, already during the 1950s and 1960s parts of the public were unaffected and uninterested in the official evocation of the Second World War as defined by the then ruling circles – *lieux de mémoire* commemorating the People's Liberation War, fallen soldiers and victims of fascism were sometimes ignored, neglected and even hostilely received by some 'consumers of memory' (Bergholc 2007). Therefore, the sight of the non-commemorated or partially commemorated and neglected Staro Sajmište area was not the only or isolated case of politics of either organized or spontaneous oblivion in Belgrade and former Yugoslavia. This state of memorial ambivalence towards and neglect of this site was to last until the mid-1980s.

In the 1980s, a temporary commemorative 'revival' of the Sajmište site occurred with the erection of a monument dedicated to Second World War camp prisoners and annual evocation rituals on the former camp premises. This revival was determined by efforts to consolidate the crumbling socialist ideology and, even more, by the eruptive restitution of Serb nationalism which emphasized the Serb civilian martyr cult (Manojlovic Pintar and Ignjatović 2008: 108). With the onset of the Yugoslav wars, the site was additionally exploited by the Serb nationalist regime led by Slobodan Milošević, which (mis)used the historical heritage of the camp to promote ideas about the establishment of a Serb Yad Vashem in the remaining camp pavilions (which would mostly commemorate ethnic Serb victims of the Second World War in the former Yugoslavia); it also emphasized Serb victims of fascism (not only of the Sajmiste camp but of other terror sites in the former Yugoslavia) while publicly neglecting victims of most other ethnicities (Byford 2009). This transition from socialist and Yugoslav concepts of remembrance of war victims, previously ethnically and otherwise undifferentiated 'victims of fascism', is evident from the dropping of previously dominant categories in official public discourse: instead of evocation of 'patriots' and 'fallen heroes', the 1990s saw the omnipresent recalling of 'innocent Serb victims', and in a matter of a few years, former 'victims of fascism' (of Staro Sajmište and other sites) became simply 'Serb victims (of fascism)' (Radović 2009: 154). This transformation was in complete accordance with lateral public discourses of the era, which depicted the Yugoslav wars of the 1990s as a continuation of the Second World War (itself very often perceived more as a civil war than a war of liberation against occupying forces), which 'ethnicized' official narratives on Second World War resistance and such like (Erdei 1994: 131). While physical intervention at the Sajmište site was minimal, the ritual and propaganda effort politically exploited the camp's public image, which distorted historical facts even more than was previously the case, and sometimes even forged them. While the (limited) concept of memorialization of Sajmiste in the previous period was not aimed at symbolic compensation of the camp's victims (since the Yugoslav state acknowledged zero responsibility for the inmates' sufferings), narratives and memorialization proposals from the nationalist era called for justice for the camp victims. But in very selective and limited ways, since victimhood was solely or primarily attributed to ethnic Serbs, and to some lesser extent to the Jews, while victims from other backgrounds were clearly downgraded. Such highlighting of the Serb and Jewish victims of the camp actually served the purpose of enhancing the myth of the Serb 'martyr nation' and of comparison, identification and even competition with other perceived 'martyr nations' in history, primarily Jews (Manojlović Pintar and Ignjatović 2008: 108). Given that, the novel views and discourses of the Sajmiste camp represented a substantially distorted and politically instrumented, belated form of justice for (selected) victims and basically ran parallel to the prevailing public narratives of Serb martyrdom in the wars of the 1990s in the former Yugoslavia. However, following the downfall of Serb nationalist projects in the second half of the 1990s, Staro Sajmište sank into complete public oblivion – being of no further political use to the ruling elites.

Following the fall of the authoritarian regime in 2000, the former camp area no longer represented the place of 'reduced' history (which was the case in socialist times) or the place of 'fabricated' history (as in the Milošević era), but empty space 'cleansed' of any history (Radović 2009: 155). The newly established ideological hegemonic coalition continued to consign the Second World War, its results, context and heritage to further (public) oblivion. Three key pillars of contemporary memory politics of the Second World War (and of recent Yugoslav wars too) are gradual amnesia, partial amnesty and substantial official revisionism with a cluster of discourses comprising revisionist historiography, banal anticommunism, selection of memory and 'anti-antifascism' (Kuljić 2002: 405, 441). Given such ideological circumstances, the most appropriate concept of the camp's memorialization was no memorialization whatsoever – that is, further marginalization of the site. Thus, several buildings of the historic site have been sold or leased over the last ten years, and used for different activities, including entertainment (Radović 2009: 155). Seventy years after its initial erection, this location has returned to its original use, commerce and amusement, but this time lacking pre-war grandeur and representation, and presenting itself in the normalized context of small-scale amusement entrepreneurship instead.

Memory politics vs. politics of urban planning

Yet, a question arises: why was the Sajmište issue brought to public attention in 2007 amid overall oblivion and revision of the Second World War in Serbia? A possible answer might originate from the global, rather than local context: the 'Kosheen affair' was at least partially initiated abroad rather than in Serbia. Special sensitivity and attention towards the treatment of Holocaust sites across Europe is facilitated by the network of transnational organizations and groups who nurture genocide memorial culture while enabling intensive reinterpretation of Second World War remembrance across Europe (Francoise 2006: 232). Such increased focus allowed the embarrassing commercial activities taking place in the remaining camp facilities in Serbia to be spotted. Subsequently, there was a responsive echo in Serbia, given that the frontrunners in the 2007 campaign included organizations dealing with the Holocaust such as the Simon Wiesenthal Centre and others. Rather than being a grassroots response, the issue might have been brought to public attention from abroad. Such a situation also testified to the political potentials of particular associations: while the attention initiated by Shoah researchers and organizations resulted in an immediate, albeit temporary, official and media outcry, previous initiatives regarding the state of the former camp by groups of Second World War veterans and antifascists from former Yugoslavia left the public discourse unchanged and silent. With new groups exercising dominant influence on majority elites in this matter, public perception of the Sajmiste camp in Serbia is gradually shifting towards the image of Staro Sajmište as primarily a Holocaust site (a perception already dominant in foreign academic and cultural circles) rather than a 'fascist terror site' as it was usually perceived in previous decades. This shift does not originate in a special sensibility regarding the Holocaust or an acceptance of a newly defining global European Second World War memorial culture, but rather in systematic denial and rejection of local, Yugoslav and Serbian, memorial culture and the heritage of the war in former Yugoslavia. Advocates of the victims of *Judenlager Semlin* have therefore encountered a somewhat better reception recently, unlike the organizations that cherish the memory of the victims of the *Anhaltelager*. The reason may well be that unequivocal memorialization of the latter would publicly resurrect the heritage of Partisan resistance (resistance fighters represented the bulk of the inmates of the *Anhaltelager*) which has been systematically downgraded in recent years.

Embracing the newly raised issue, Belgrade officials and elites promptly and loudly announced the future establishment of a memorial and museum complex in Staro Sajmište and overall regulation of the area. But, the silence that occurred just several months after the Kosheen incident indicated that adoption of the camp issue might have been prompted by other motives than those publicly acknowledged. Rather than being based on principles of just commemoration of the terror site, it seems that the responsiveness of local elites was determined by the need for definite urban regulation of a previously neglected area. Staro Sajmište, with surrounding urban parcels of land, remains one of the last unbuilt spaces in central Belgrade, conveniently placed on the Sava river bank less than one kilometre from the historic city centre. The construction boom, which was at its height in the mid-2000s, is guided by the profit-oriented goals of private financiers, who put large amounts of capital into those construction projects in Belgrade that seem to be the most profitable. Unlike in previous decades, in the last few years state-sponsored public investments in the construction industry have almost come to a standstill. Private financial interests cannot ignore or indefinitely delay the issue of urban and infrastructural renovation and the construction of one of the most attractive Belgrade areas on the river bank (furthermore, this interest entirely overlaps with the goals of the city officials). Given that Staro Sajmište is located in the midst of this unbuilt or sparsely built urban area, it could be argued that, besides political and cultural elites, financial circles represent equally influential players in this potential urban planning and memorialization project. At the same time, the ruling political elites effectively pursue the politics of revision of results and values of the antifascist struggle – with Second World War victims and their commemoration as collateral damage. Thus, to maximize either political or financial gains (or both), the most powerful social players of both physical and symbolic city-building tend to ideologically destruct certain historic localities (Staro Sajmište included) and try to transform what once represented, or still represents, (anthropological) place, a space congested with meanings and values shared by many people, into a 'non-place', a locality not connected with collective identities and cultural significance (Ože 2005: 52). Such parameters of definition and reconstruction of an urban area, even when it holds 'added historical value', are more or less unavoidable under present circumstances: like many other transitional post-socialist cities, contemporary Belgrade lacks both funds and regulation with regard to large-scale urban projects. Contemporary urban policies, not only in Belgrade, no longer aspire to lead or regulate the direction of urban economic and social development, but merely try, either directly or indirectly through taxation, to adjust the framework already defined by market forces guided by profit-oriented goals (Smith 2008: 77). Post-socialist cities have thus already moved far away from concepts of urban policies implemented during socialism. They are now characterized by, at best, lukewarm enthusiasm for political, economic and institutional reforms in the area of urban policies, while absolute priority is given to strategies aimed at attracting private investment: post-socialist urban circumstances are typically postmodern given the obvious diversification of policy-making actors (Petrović 2009: 55). Naturally oriented towards maximizing gains, commercial interests involved in urban (re)construction realize that the less history per square metre of a construction plot, the bigger the profits.

Such ambitions with regard to the urban planning of Staro Sajmište can be located by reading the subtext of several suggestions for memorialization of the site. In contrast to the time that immediately followed the intensive debate in 2007 (when the sole and unanimous option was a memorial museum dedicated to victims of the camp or of fascism in general), 2008 saw somewhat novel concepts being proposed. The favoured option ceased to be a public memorial or a museum and, instead, a concept of what was sometimes described as a 'multifunctional centre' emerged. The media reported on a proposal for a museum centre that would include a number of institutions besides the Sajmište Museum, such as a 'Tolerance Museum' and a range of other museums, including a museum of fine arts. Other options suggested adding additional facilities to the historic site such as cafés and concert halls, and some went so far as to opt for the complete demolition of the remaining Sajmište pavilions. The common denominator of all such proposals was bluntly delivered aloud at the 2008 'Belgrade Salon of Architecture', a thematic exposition of Staro Sajmište reconstruction plans that exhibited projects by several designers to whom a specific approach was suggested. As the Belgrade daily *Blic* reported in its issue of 22 April 2008, the designers were advised to bear in mind that 'the memory of those who lost their lives there should be present, but it should not be dominant'. A discourse of 'suppressed memory' in recycled and interpolated space opportunely blurs and marginalizes particular historic memory and, at the same time, introduces commercial interests into the planning and exploitation of urban space (Radović 2009: 158). Although opposing opinions can be heard on this issue, such voices lack social power, while economic interests are gaining momentum. When dealing with certain public spaces, financial circles accommodate, to use Connerton's expression again, a 'memory wall' to detach potential consumers from cultural meanings associated with particular places that could negatively affect attendance or consumption in certain commercial (non) places/spaces. Just as building a place from space is sometimes deemed necessary, the opposite process, destruction of a particular place, serves a similar function. Amid a slowly emerging global memorial culture of the Second World War and the presently oppositional memory of the Second World War in the former Yugoslavia (mostly defined during socialism) on the one hand, and the prevailing and politically opportune culture of Second World War revision and oblivion in contemporary Serbia on the other, it seems that possible memorial construction of the Staro Sajmište area in the near future would, at best, send out an additionally reduced and commercially restrained message to the public. In that case, instead of a memorial place one could expect to visit a memorial 'non-place'. The prospect of an only limited future commemoration of the camp, and the corresponding lack of interest in raising public awareness about the camp's history and its victims, indicates a strong possibility that such a commemorative framework could serve as an alternative to justice and genuine confrontation with the past. As James Young writes, 'once we assign monumental form to memory, we have to some degree divested ourselves of the obligation to remember – in shouldering the memory-work, monuments may relieve viewers of their memory burden' (1993: 5). The incomplete and isolated memorialization plans for Staro Sajmište might follow just such a pattern: by erecting (or planning to erect) a memorial centre without sincerely reaching out to the victims and observing the complete historic truth about the camp, it seems as if contemporary society and its leading circles are trying to close the historic chapter without thoroughly discussing it. And thus, the future memorial site would not serve one of the common goals of modern memorials – that of doing justice to victims and providing them with symbolic restitution. One could argue that such a memorial would facilitate not memory, but oblivion.

Gloomy prospects for this site's future memorialization are also partly determined by the logic of the 'political economy' of real estate with historical importance. As Jennifer Jordan argues, finances, land use and ownership play a very important part in determining what memorials get to be built, and what sites end up being (un)commemorated. This is not only about memory politics, but also about 'how to treat real estate with a difficult past'. Besides 'memorial entrepreneurs', who push forward certain memory agendas, important factors for the emergence of a memorial site are the absence of competing land uses and public ownership of the location (Jordan 2006: 2-3). The creation of a Staro Sajmište memorial centre does not fare too well if we take this into account: ownership of most of the former camp buildings is disputed or unclear; interested memorial entrepreneurs are few and are mostly not part of the powerful cultural or political elite; and, finally, actors interested in exploiting this site are plenty. Had Belgrade's *Juden-* and *Anhaltelager* been located at a different, less central location, proposals for the memorialization and urban design of such a site might have been different. Bearing in mind Sajmište's potentially lucrative location, commercial interests seem to be an important factor in this issue, not only regarding the physical creation of the area, but also when it comes to the symbolic: the less explicit the connotation of the area with the tragic heritage of the site, the better the chances for large attendance and consumption in establishments whose marketing would prefer to avoid association with the memory of the camp. If partial memorialization and urban neglect of the Sajmište area during socialism were determined by socialist urban management which facilitated the building of Novi Beograd as a symbol of a new beginning, the contemporary standstill in urban regulation and sporadic announcements of only limited commemoration of the camp are the result of commercial politics of urban construction and hegemonic identity politics.

Since 2009, however, even modest proposals promoting partial and limited commemoration and regulation of the wider Sajmište area have been rarely heard. The Sajmište question has once again sunk back into darkness. Not surprisingly, this sudden lack of interest in Sajmište coincided with economic crisis, in which the real estate business and construction industry in Serbia were most severely hit. Probably the most influential actors in Belgrade's politics of urban planning are currently having a hard time – thus the (temporary) sidelining of potential plans for reconstruction of this area. Nowadays, few mention the potential memorial, while occasional gatherings at the Poseydon club show that everything is, more or less, business as usual. The only noticeable novelty is the mammoth shopping mall built 100 metres away from the former camp pavilions in early 2009 – the transitional consumerist city is inevitably approaching the historic site. The public astonishment caused by efforts to build a shopping mall opposite the entrance to the Auschwitz memorial site in the 1990s (which eventually wasn't undertaken) repeated itself in Belgrade in 2007 and 2008, once current uses of former camp facilities were publicly acknowledged, and the question from the Polish case was occasionally raised: 'Is it appropriate to place a mall in the vicinity of a former concentration camp?' However, it seems that in this particular Serbian case local elites are now haunted by a somewhat different dilemma: Is it appropriate to erect a memorial to a former concentration camp in the vicinity of a mall?' – genocide and dark past simply don't make for a good business opportunity. At the same time, a general lack of will for overt and complete memorialization of the area, determined also by contemporary politics of memory regarding the Second World War in Serbia, demonstrates quite weak public awareness of the fact that public commemoration also represents a means of recompensing victims and doing justice. The recent rejection by Belgrade's city monuments committee to consider the erection of a memorial dedicated to the victims of the 1995 Srebrenica massacre testifies to the fact that this might be the case. That official circles feel no need to symbolically acknowledge the victims of the most recent war directly waged by Serbia, or forces backed by Serbia, demonstrates a poor commitment to pursuing transitional justice, at least in the area of public memorialization. If this applies to the most recent military conflict in the Balkans, the sense of acknowledging the wrongdoings or victims of earlier historical epochs, including the Second World War, is even less developed, especially when guilt for the civilian death toll is almost entirely transferred away from one's own side. Very likely, the entire resurfacing of the Sajmište issue was determined by actions pursued by social actors based outside of Serbia, since the poor state of many other memorials from that war is not discussed or challenged at all, given that they usually don't attract much attention beyond Serbia's borders. The newly arisen prospects for possible future re-commemoration and revitalization of the Sajmište site emerged not thanks to, but in spite of the current public mindset regarding the Second World War and its civilian victims: general politics of memory of past violent conflicts prefer to ignore rather than discuss more or less controversial historical episodes from a nation's past, be it from recent or not so recent history.

References

Adam, P. 1992. *Kunst im Dritten Reich*. Hamburg: Rogner und Bernhard.

Azaryahu, M. 1997. German Reunification and the Politics of Street Names: The Case of East Berlin. *Political Geography*, 16(6), 479-493.

Bergholc, M. 2007. Među rodoljubima, svinjama, kupusom i varvarima – spomenici i grobovi NOR 1947-1965. *Godišnjak za društvenu istoriju*, 2007(1-3), 61-81.

Bolin, G. 2006. Visions of Europe: Cultural Technologies of Nation-States. *International Journal of Cultural Studies*, 9, 189-206.

Browning, C. 1985. *Fateful Months: Essays on the Emergence of the Final Solution*. London: Holms & Meier.

Byford, J. 2009. Semlin Judenlager in Serbian Public Memory. Available at www.open.ac.uk/socialsciences/semlin (accessed 30 May 2009).

Connerton, P. 2004. *Kako se društva sjećaju*. Zagreb: Izdanja Antibarbarus.

Erdei, I. 1994. Medijska konstrukcija realnosti korišćenjem različitih vremenskih modela i perspektiva. In *Kulture u tranziciji*, edited by M. Prošić Dvornić, 129-136. Beograd: Plato.

Francois, E. 2006. Velike pripovijesti i lomovi brana sjecanja: Sjecanje na Drugi svjetski rat izmedu nacionalizacije i univerzalizacije. In *Kultura pamcenja i historija*, edited by M. Brkljacic and S. Prlenda, 219-238. Zagreb: Golden Marketing – Tehnicka knjiga.

Hill, J. and Wilson, T. 2003. Identity Politics and the Politics of Identities. *Identities*, 10, 1-8.

Ignjatović, A. 2004. Politika predstavljanja jugoslovenstva: jugoslovenski paviljon na svetskoj izložbi u Parizu 1937. godine. *Godišnjak za društvenu istoriju*, 11(2-3), 65-83.

Jordan, J. 2006. *Structures of Memory: Understanding Urban Change in Berlin and Beyond*. Stanford, CA: Stanford University Press.

Koonz, C. 2006. Između pamćenja i zaborava. Koncentracijski logori u njemačkom sjećanju. In *Kultura pamcenja i historija*, edited by M. Brkljacic and S. Prlenda, 285-312.Zagreb: Golden Marketing – Tehnicka knjiga.

Kuljić, T. 2002. *Prevladavanje prošlosti: uzroci pravci promene slike istorije krajem XX veka*. Beograd: Helsinški odbor za ljudska prava u Srbiji.

Leach, N. 2002. Erasing the Traces: The 'Denazification' of Post Revolutionary Berlin and Bucharest. In *The Hieroglyphics of Space: Reading and Experiencing the Modern Metropolis*, edited by N. Leach, 80-91. London: Routledge.

Leggewie, C. 2009. Schlachtfeld Europa: Transnationale Erinnerung und europäische Identität. *Blätter für deutsche und internationale Politik*, 2, 81-93.

Light, D., Nicolae, I. and Suditu, B. 2002. Toponymy and the Communist City: Street Names in Bucharest, 1948-1965. *GeoJournal*, 56, 135-144.

Malešević, M. 2008. Nasilje identiteta. In *Kulturne paralele: svakodnevna kultura u postsocijalističkom periodu*, edited by Z. Divac, 11-32. Beograd: Etnografski institute SANU.

Manojlović Pintar, O. and Ignjatović, A. 2008. Prostori selektovanih memorija: Staro Sajmište u Beogradu i sećanje na Drugi svestki rat. In *Kultura sjećanja: 1941. Povijesni lomovi i svladavanje prošlosti*, edited by S. Bosto, T. Cipek and O. Milosavljević, 95-113. Zagreb: Disput.

Ože, M. 2005. *Nemesta: Uvod u antropologiju nadmodernosti*. Beograd: XX vek.

Pavićević A. 2009. Spomenici i/ili grobovi – sećanje na smrt i/ili dekoracija. In *Spomen mesta – istorija – sećanja*, edited by A. Pavićević, 47-62. Beograd: Etnografski institut SANU.

Petrović, M. 2009. *Transformacija gradova: ka depolitizaciji urbanog pitanja*. Beograd: Institut za sociološka istraživanja Filozofskog fakulteta.

Radović S. 2009. Gradski prostori od mesta do nemesta, i vice versa: slučaj beogradskog Starog Sajmšta. In *Spomen mesta – istorija – sećanja*, edited by A. Pavićević, 145-160. Beograd: Etnografski institut SANU.

Smith, N. 2008. Novi globalizam, novi urbanizam: gentrifikacija kao globalna urbana strategija. In *Operacija: Grad*, edited by L. Kovačević *et al.*, 60-85. Zagreb: Savez za centar za nezavisnu kulturu i mlade etc.

Tuan, Y. 1977. *Space and Place: The Perspective of Experience*. Minneapolis: University of Minnesota Press.

Vučinić V. 1995. Antropologija u divljim naseljima: pogled na Staro Sajmište u Beogradu. *Glasnik Etnografskog instituta SANU*, 44, 168-184.

Young, J. 1993. *The Texture of Memory: Holocaust Memorials and Meaning*. New Haven: Yale University Press.

Chapter 6

Transitional Justice and Local Memory: Commemoration and Social Action in Londres 38, Espacio de Memorias

Katrien Klep

In the centre of Santiago de Chile, in a street called Londres, passers-by may notice black and white tiles in the pavement, alternated with 96 cast iron tiles each carrying the name of a person, their age and the abbreviation of their political party or movement. This is the Memorial Londres 38; it commemorates 96 persons who were disappeared or died under the Chilean military dictatorship (1973-1990) in the house at Londres 38. The memorial is a reminder of the black and white tiled floor inside, which the prisoners could see just below their blindfolds. The tiles will lead you to large plaque in front of the great wooden door of the house, which reads:

LONDRES 38

SECRET DETENTION, TORTURE, DISAPPEARENCE AND EXECUTION CENTRE

11 SEPTEMBER 1973–SEPTEMBER 1974

96 PERSONS OF THE MANY THAT WERE DETAINED HERE, TWO OF THEM PREGNANT, ARE DISAPPEARED, WERE EXECUTED OR DIED AS A CONSEQUENCE OF TORTURE.

TO HIDE THESE FACTS DURING THE DICTATORSHIP THE NUMBER 38 WAS REPLACED BY 40.

IN 2005 IT WAS DECLARED A HISTORICAL MONUMENT BY THE COUNCIL OF NATIONAL MONUMENTS.

In this chapter I will take a closer look at the relationship between transitional justice initiatives and grassroots memory initiatives.[1] Often caught in seemingly

1 This chapter is based on the author's doctorate research which explores the processes of memorialization of the Pinochet dictatorship (1973-1990) in the public space

clear-cut terms like 'official truth-telling' and 'unofficial truth-telling' efforts, what is actually referred to is an intricate constellation of narratives, networks and actors. Ashplant *et al.* (2000: 7-9) have pointed out that war memory and commemoration have been looked at either from a political perspective 'as a practice bound up with rituals of national identification' shaped by the state or as an expression of mourning performed by civil society. They have argued, however, that the two are interrelated and constitutive of each other.

I will argue that transitional justice initiatives and grassroots memory initiatives are part of the same process in society but develop from different sets of concerns and needs. They take place independently, simultaneously, take different directions and contest each other, but can also converge and enhance one another. Truth-telling or memory initiatives at the grassroots level generally have a long history rooted in mourning and resistance, more often than not preceding transitional justice initiatives. These local initiatives then are both independent of and interrelated with other truth-telling events such as truth commissions; their dynamics, however, are determined by their own local force field.

My endeavour requires me to delve into the Chilean process of transitional justice and memorialization, starting with the Chilean truth commission that dealt with the aftermath of the Chilean military dictatorship. In 1991, the National Truth and Reconciliation Commission (CNVR 1991) documented the fate of 2,025 persons who were either disappeared or had died at the hands of state agents or people in its service. Thirteen years later, the National Commission on Political Imprisonment and Torture (CNPPT 2004) looked into the fate of tens of thousands of political prisoners, and recorded the use of torture and imprisonment during the dictatorship throughout Chile, thus broadening the official, publicly recognized narrative of the dictatorship.

Memory initiatives from grassroots organizations in Chile were and are profoundly related to the disappearance and death of the victims. Commemorative plaques, memorials with names and other tokens have appeared at cemeteries, at mass graves and also at places where detained-disappeared persons lived and worked, for example streets, plazas, hospitals, schools and universities. Over time, memory initiatives have surged to include the living memory of the

---

of Santiago de Chile through the analysis of the interplay between transitional justice mechanisms and commemoration practices. The author has done fieldwork (two periods of eight months between 2005 and 2008, and short visits in 2009, 2010 and 2011) in Santiago. In the case of Londres 38, she interviewed several members of the grassroots organizations involved with the house, one of the architects of the Memorial Londres 38, and spoke to visitors, volunteers and others to whom she is very grateful. The author visited Londres 38 regularly, attending meetings, activities and commemorations, and traced material in private and public archives. I would like to thank my interviewees in Chile for sharing their time and thoughts with me and the reviewers whose comments have improved my arguments. I would also like to thank Gloria Elgueta and my co-supervisor Dr Fabiola Jara for the many inspiring conversations.

victim-survivors who have brought the dimension of social and political agency into commemoration practices and have built new spaces for social action in the present. These memory initiatives include reclaiming former detention and torture centres for commemoration and social action. Londres 38, Espacio de Memorias is such a new active space. The imageries of justice of the grassroots organizations at Londres 38 are not only related to the truth about the fate of the detained-disappeared and to demands that justice be done, but also encourage an open and participative debate about social and political power relations in Chilean society in the past and today and engagement in present-day social struggles.

Transitional justice and local memory initiatives

Deeply entwined with the political transition process, truth commissions are highly political instruments negotiated between many actors. In the last few decades, many countries have attempted to confront the aftermath of violent conflict and atrocity through the creation of truth commissions.[2] In the wake of the authoritarian regimes of the 1970s and 1980s, the debate on transitional justice in Latin America was driven by intertwined demands for justice and truth, and the need to legitimize the new governments that had come to power. 'Truth' in this context was understood as the obligation of the successor state to investigate and establish the facts about past violations. Questions about whether there was a duty to punish human rights violators lingered.[3] Truth-telling efforts were seen as a minimum requirement of justice (Arthur 2009: 353-356).

In truth commissions, the victim is central and the focus is on truth-telling for the sake of the healing of both (individual) victims and the nation. The importance of a truth commission lies in providing an official arena and a report which both acknowledges victims' voices and endows them with official authority vis-à-vis the nation and the world. At the same time a master narrative is constructed (Phelps 2004: 79) to underpin the legitimacy of the new regime and its efforts at nation-building.

Some authors suggest that the assumption that truth-telling before a truth commission is healing or cathartic may be overstated (Hayner 2011: 5). Others take issue with the constraints of the truth commission's arena. Greg Grandin (2005: 48), for example, emphasizes how truth commissions in Latin America have framed the past as a 'dark backdrop on which to contrast the light of tolerance and self-restraint' of the present, thus avoiding any questions about the roots of

2 Worldwide, there have been 40 truth commissions, from 1974 (Uganda) to the beginning of 2010 (Kenya) (Hayner 2011: 256).

3 Cath Collins signals that 'the transitional school of thought, which grew out of the Latin American experiences of transition in the 1980s, underestimated the extent to which questions of criminal and civil responsibility for state crimes of torture, disappearance, and genocide would persist and eventually resurface in postconflict societies' (2008: 20).

the conflict, its historical and political context, the parties and groups involved, the socio-economic differences and power relations in a country at a given time. The discourse of individual human rights violations and the focus on the legal category of the individual victim may obscure stories of social and political agency and the collective dimension of the repression. This may lead to what Hackett and Rolston (2009: 364) have called 'scripted' testimonies that are focused on the human rights violations per se, endowing the testimony giver with the singular identity of the victim, leaving out stories of agency.

Inevitably there will be disjunctions between the narratives of those who testify before a truth commission and the master narrative that the commission eventually relates in its report. This narrative may very well be contested, as was the case in Chile, by different groups in society that push on for justice, reparations and more truth.

One of the expressions of truth-telling and memory at the local level is the creation of memorials by grassroots organizations. Memorialization efforts at the grassroots level arise spontaneously from local needs and local social and political concerns such as mourning and resistance, and engage with other projects of memorialization. Political elites may use memorialization as part of a nation-building project. Monuments and memorials then can be understood as both part of and expressions of processes of interaction, contestation and negotiation.

James Young (1993: 14) contends that it is crucial to study the coming into being of a monument in order to make visible the 'activity of memory' in monuments. A study of the 'inner life of monuments', so he argues, will show us the 'tempestuous social, political and aesthetic forces' at play and broaden our understanding of memory as relational, dynamic and related to the present. Rachel Ibreck (2010: 331), writing about memorialization in Rwanda, has argued that 'survivors and relatives of the dead in Rwanda resist state appropriations of their experiences and losses through contributions to the construction of genocide memory', by creating their own memorials and trying to influence the public memory of genocide. Referring to the work of Ashplant *et al.* (2000) and her fieldwork, she underlines that the need of people to mourn and to honour the dead is imperative to remembrance and the struggles over memory. 'But importantly, public remembrance is also a focus for civic activism and political critique' (Ibreck 2010: 332).

Monuments and memorials then are shaped by the various networks which run through the local and (inter)national level, at a certain historical moment. They are dynamic and relational; their meaning and use changes over time. A monument or memorial must be understood in relation to its place, its 'time' (the historical moment) and the actors that surround it and in relation to other manifestations of memory.[4] In Chile places of memory are profoundly related to the tireless search for the disappeared. The disappearance of people, the search by family members

4 This approach draws on a research workshop given by the Argentinian anthropologist Ludmila da Silva Catela on 6 April 2009 organized by Programa Domeyko

and others to find them, and the testimonies that put a certain person at a certain place where he or she was seen for the last time have marked places in public space. Many are not publicly designated as places of memory; others have become active spaces of commemoration, denunciation, memory, education, protest and debate.

In the introduction to the book *The Art of Truth-Telling about Authoritarian Rule* (Bilbija *et al.* 2005: 2-4) the authors point to what they call 'alternative truth-telling' or 'unofficial truth-telling' to distinguish between truth-telling in the context of transitional justice instruments, especially truth commissions, and other forms of truth-telling. They emphasize that unofficial truths are informed by official truths but independent of them. 'Tensions develop between official and unofficial accounts. Official truths appeal to the need to move forwards quickly ... They rely on the alluring fiction that carefully managed processes can yield an objective consensus. Yet, unofficial accounts, reflecting the messy subjectivity of lived experience, have staying power.' These 'unofficial accounts' moreover have longer roots. Resistance against and truth-telling about repression and violence, in daily life, through stories, music, paintings and so on does not start after the repression.[5]

Cynthia Milton (2007: 4) has also argued that truth commissions 'are not the only paths to the past'. She postulates that the 'social opening' that gives rise to truth commissions, also opens 'spaces for public discussion and "speaking truth to power" that were previously unavailable'. This 'social opening' is, in part, forged through social action and demands for truth, justice and reparations by organizations of family members and victim-survivors and human rights organizations.

Several authors emphasize the importance of truth commissions as official arenas that offer voice to those who were silenced and to express what was silenced. According to Joseph Slaughter, 'Human rights violations target the voice, and therefore, the voice should be the focus of international human rights instruments' (1997: 407). Lisa Laplante underlines the importance of both voice and agency when she draws attention to the *act* of truth-telling in the context of the Peruvian truth commission:

> Importantly, this desire *to tell* is accompanied by a need to be protagonists *in telling*. Victim-survivors are beginning to reject passive telling to third-party authors and instead are appropriating their own agency in disseminating memory ... it is the change in personal and political status as truth-tellers, and not just the

Sociedad y Equidad, Historias, Memorias y Derechos Humanos of the University of Chile; see also Da Silva Catela (2010).

5 See, for example, the work of James Scott (1990: xii) on everyday resistance and 'hidden transcripts' that represent a critique of power spoken behind the back of the dominant.

> content of this truth, that makes memory projects important endeavours. (2007: 435; italics in the original)

This is a crucial point, which brings the focus onto what people do, how they organize and engage in the act of speaking truth to power.

In the following two sections I will analyse the Chilean truth commissions and the local memory initiative Londres 38, Espacio de Memorias, and show how each has emerged from its own particular dynamics – dynamics that are both independent and interrelated and profoundly contest each other, but can also converge and enhance each other at a certain time. The creation of the Chilean truth commissions were in part the result of the demands for truth and justice of a wide variety of social organizations. However, the master narratives of their reports were contested by those organizations. It was (and is) this incessant *act of truth-telling to power* that strengthened the grassroots organizations, which created new social spaces. However, it is important to keep in mind that the local processes were already there. Grassroots organizations have surrounded Londres 38 for a long time; their efforts to make of the house a place of memory and social action was shaped by the need to commemorate the detained-disappeared, to vindicate the political and social agency of the victims and to engage in present-day political and social issues.

The Chilean truth commissions

The issue of human rights violations was central to the campaign of the Concertación de Partidos por la Democracia, a coalition of centre and left-wing political parties that eventually defeated the military dictatorship at the ballot box in 1988. In March 1990 the democratically elected President Patricio Aylwin assumed office. A political and legal reality still dominated by actors and laws of the dictatorship made a thorough investigation of the crimes difficult. The Concertación government presented 'truth' and 'national reconciliation', not criminal justice, as the central stepping stones from violent past to new democracy. Balancing political pressure to leave the past alone, and the legitimate demands from the human rights and family member organizations for truth and justice, President Patricio Aylwin created the Chilean National Truth and Reconciliation Commission (CNVR, Rettig Commission) in April 1990.[6]

The commission's mandate was to establish the most complete picture possible of 'the grave human rights violations' committed under the military regime from

---

6 The Comisión Nacional de Verdad y Reconciliación (CNVR), also known as the Rettig Commission after its president lawyer Raúl Rettig, was created on 25 April 1990 (DS 335). Its report was published in March 1991. Reparation Law 19.123 (8 February 1992) grants reparation to the family members of the victims. For detailed analysis of the politics of reparation, see Lira and Loveman (2005).

11 September 1973 until 11 March 1990. These grave human rights violations were defined as 'the situations of detained disappearance, execution and torture leading to death in which the moral responsibility of the state by acts of its agents or persons in its service is involved, as well as the kidnappings and attempts on the lives of persons committed by private citizens under political pretexts' (CNVR 1991: viii).

For the antecedents of the individual cases, the Rettig Commission relied heavily on the extensive archives of the Chilean human rights organizations which, during the dictatorship, had assisted family members, survivors of torture and other victims of the repression, with legal, social and medical help.[7] According to the report, 3,073 family members requested a personal interview (CNVR 1991: 6) and were heard by the commission and its staff of lawyers and social workers. The Rettig Report described the legal and political context of the dictatorship and the development of the regime's repressive tactics, reconstructing the modus operandi of the secret services. The individual cases of victims were presented throughout the chronological description of the period of dictatorship and alphabetically in a short, factual summary in the last part of the report. In total, 2,025 persons were registered as either disappeared (957) or dead (1,068) at the hands of state agents or people in its service.[8]

The Rettig Report was published in March 1991.[9] For the family members, the report and the reparation law were an official acknowledgement of the repressive practices, the human rights violations, the disappearance of their loved ones which had been denied during the dictatorship, and their suffering. However, the family members of the detained-disappeared and others found the 'truth' of the Rettig Commission deficient as there was still no answer to their main question: 'Where are they?' Moreover the perpetrators of the crimes were not named and were not brought to justice. Other victims, the survivors of political imprisonment and torture, the exiled, the exonerated, were not officially recognized as victims by the Rettig Report.

Family members, survivors, human rights organizations and others pressed on for justice and more truth. They kept the memory of the detained-disappeared alive in countless acts, meetings, commemorations and long-stagnated court

---

7 The Rettig Commission had no subpoena power and received little cooperation from the armed forces (Hayner 2011: 48).

8 The Rettig Commission considered individual victims on 'both sides', 90 persons who had died at the hands of 'individuals acting under political pretexts' were also recognized. Another 164 persons were qualified as victims of political violence. The total of victims recognized was 2,279 (CNVR 1991: 883). The officially recognized total of detained-disappeared and executed in Chile in 2010 was 3,196 persons (Collins 2010: 72).

9 Commander in Chief General Pinochet presented the reaction of the Army before the National Security Council on 27 March 1991 and disqualified the Rettig Report as not objective, violating its explicit judicial limits and inciting violence and hostility (CEP 1991). See also Bakiner (2010).

cases. In the wake of the detention of Pinochet in 1998, their demands gained new momentum, finding their way to the streets and the courts. The accusations against Pinochet also included several cases of torture, an element of the repression that was mentioned in the Rettig Report but otherwise had received little attention in terms of either official recognition or reparation. Former prisoners started to gather antecedents and evidence of their predicaments in preparation for potential court cases against Pinochet and others. In the heat of the renewed activity of human rights organizations and the nascent organizations of former prisoners (although riddled with political tensions and conflict), a new initiative across the organizations arose: the Ethical Commission against Torture.[10] Taking international law on torture as its point of reference, the Ethical Commission against Torture demanded truth, justice and integral reparation of the Chilean state. In 2001, this group started to publish reports on torture, presenting them directly to the president. As the 30th commemoration of the coup in 2003 drew near, the government started to take their incessant demands and those of other organizations into account.

Only weeks before the 30th commemoration of the coup, President Ricardo Lagos announced the creation of the National Commission on Political Imprisonment and Torture (Valech Commission) with a view to reparation for the victims.[11] Its mandate was 'to determine, based on the antecedents presented, who suffered deprivation of liberty and who were tortured for political reasons by agents of the state or persons in the service of the state, in the period between 11 September 1973 and 11 March 1990' (CNPPT 2004: 21).[12] Like the Rettig Commission, the Valech Commission could not make any pronouncements on individual criminal liability..

Over 35,000 victim-survivors went on to testify. In order to qualify the cases brought before it, the commission constructed an information system which included the testimonies of those who approached the commission, the documents they handed in to attest to the fact they had been a prisoner, the archive of the Rettig Commission and once again the archives of the human rights organizations. The testimonies allowed the Commission to identify 1,132 detention precincts throughout the country. Integral testimonies were not reproduced but anonymous

10 The Comisión Ética contra la Tortura (CECT) was created in March 2001 by different human rights organizations, religious, social and political personalities and former political prisoners. The CECT produced reports on torture with testimonies, lists of prisoners, places of torture and detention, and articles of different (international) specialists on the consequences of torture. See also Stern (2010: 280-281).Today it is still an active organization that continues to publish reports and promotes awareness, eradication and prevention of torture in Chile (see www.contralatortura.cl).

11 The Comisión Nacional sobre Prisón Politica y Tortura (CNPPT), also known as the Valech Commission after its president Monsignor Sergio Valech, was created on 11 November 2003 (DS 1.040). Its report was published in November 2004.

12 Three weeks before the Valech Report was published Commander in Chief General Emilio Cheyre officially declared that the Army would assume its contents and conclusions 'with … serenity and responsibility' (CEP 2005: 507). See also Bakiner (2010).

quotes and excerpts of testimonies were published, especially in the chapters on the methods of torture used and the consequences of political imprisonment and torture.

The Valech Report broadened the master narrative of the Rettig Report by recognizing 27,255 persons as victims of political imprisonment and torture during the dictatorship, throughout Chile. Their names are all recorded in the long list in the annex of the report.[13] When the reparation law was passed in December 2004, the organizations of former political prisoners were angry not only about the meagre (economic) reparations offered, but also about the provision that all 'documents, testimonies and antecedents' brought to the commission by the victims are to be kept secret for 50 years. No person, group of persons, authority or magistrate will have access to these documents, testimonies and antecedents, although individuals are still entitled to their own documents, declarations and testimonies and can make these known or hand them over to third parties (Article 15, Reparation Law 19.992). No one – not even the judges in human rights cases – has access to the Valech archive. This has generated renewed actions against impunity.[14]

From 2003 (the 30th anniversary of the coup) onwards, the Concertación government's discourse on the dictatorship focused more on memory and on memorialization, and a modest fund for works of symbolic reparation was created for commemoration of the victims. Moreover, the Valech Report explicitly recommended measures for the 'recognition of memory', among which was to declare 'the main torture centres national monuments' (CNPPT 2004: 528). Many grassroots organizations seized the opportunity and applied for funds, which led to a small boom in monuments and memorials in Chile.[15]

Several former detention and torture houses, such as Londres 38, can be visited today. These initiatives are (partly) government funded but the activities and development of these sites are in the hands of grassroots organizations. As we shall see, this has led to intensive debates between the different actors involved on how to remember the past, and how to relate to pressing political and social issues in the present.

---

13 Reparation Law 19.992 (24 December 2004) and Law 20.405 (10 December 2009) grants reparations to the victims. In August 2010 another 30 cases of disappearance and execution (622 applicants) and 9,795 cases of political prison and torture (31831 applicants) were recognized (see www.comisionvalech.gov.cl).

14 On the criminal prosecution of human rights violations committed under the dictatorship, see Collins (2010).

15 The website of the Program of Human Rights, which administered the funds, has a list of the monuments and memorials built (see www.ddhh.gov.cl). The Concertación government also initiated its own memory project: the Museum of Memory and Human Rights, inaugurated by President Michelle Bachelet in January 2010. The brand new building boasts a permanent exhibition on the 1973-1990 dictatorship and a documentation centre, and offers a series of activities related to human rights topics (see www.museodelamemoria.cl). See also Hite and Collins (2009).

Both commissions and their reports were of crucial importance in officially and publicly acknowledging the predicament of the victims of the dictatorship in Chilean society. The master narratives of the reports, however, have been contested. The reports did not offer answers to imperative questions: where are they, what happened to the detained-disappeared, why did it happen, who are responsible? Moreover the strict mandates, legal language and focus on victimhood contrasted with the lived realities. Victim-survivors and others continued to emphasize a different kind of memory of the dictatorship, based on living memory, which is not only about victimhood but also about political and social agency.

Londres 38, Espacio de Memorias: participative memory and social action

The Valech Report registered 221 detention precincts in the metropolitan region (CNPPT 2004: 430), 12 of which were registered as 'clandestine' (CNPPT 2004: 442-449).[16] After an initial broad wave of repression following the coup on 11 September 1973, the military dictatorship set out to disarticulate the left-wing movements. The secret service Dirección de Inteligencia Nacional (DINA) used houses that had belonged to the, by then, prohibited political parties or private individuals to create secret detention and torture centres. Among the most notorious in Santiago were Villa Grimaldi, Londres 38 and José Domingo Cañas 1367. All three have been saved from oblivion by grassroots organizations and other social actors who have engaged with the sites at the local level and with the government in order to obtain the right to use these spaces.

Villa Grimaldi, once a private estate in the periphery of Santiago de Chile, was used by the secret service DINA from the end of 1973 until 1978 as a detention and torture centre. It is estimated that some 5,000 political prisoners passed through its gates and torture rooms, 229 of whom disappeared. In 1997, the memorial park Peace Park – Villa Grimaldi was inaugurated, and in 2004 it was declared a National Monument. Today, Villa Grimaldi is an (inter)nationally recognized place of memory that can be visited with or without a guide. It has a publicly accessible oral archive with testimonies of survivors, and an education programme on memory and human rights.[17] A place for commemoration of the victims, Villa Grimaldi has also developed into an active space with cultural performances in its open air theatre and seminars and other activities related to memory and human rights topics. The house at José Domingo Cañas 1367 was used by the DINA from August 1974 until November 1974. An estimated 54 political prisoners were disappeared. In 2001, a memorial with the names of the detained-disappeared was inaugurated on the pavement in front of the house. The house itself was destroyed

16 The Valech Report registered 221 detention precincts in the metropolitan region, 12 as 'clandestine' (CNPPT 2004: 430). For a detailed analysis of the 'disappearance' and 're-appearance' of detention and torture sites, see Rojas and Silva (2005).

17 The Peace Park – Villa Grimaldi website can be found at www.villagrimaldi.cl.

before the grassroots organizations could protect the building, but in 2002 the empty site was declared a National Monument. In 2010, after years of struggle, cultural centre Casa de la Memoria was inaugurated on the site of José Domingo Cañas 1367.

Already during the dictatorship, the existence of an underground network of secret detention and torture centres had become '*a secreto a voces*', a public secret. Many of those who survived the houses of terror gave testimony to (inter) national human rights organizations. Londres 38 is related to the 'case of the 119'. Most of these 119 persons were members of the Movimiento de Izquierda Revolucionaria (MIR), some were members of the Socialist Party, Communist Party or the Movimiento de Acción Popular Unitaria (MAPU), while the political affiliation of a few persons is unknown. In July 1975, articles about the deaths of 119 Chilean men and women appeared in the foreign press and later in the Chilean press. According to the articles, they had been killed in fights among themselves. The articles were unmasked as a misinformation scheme of the secret service of the dictatorship in an attempt to cover up the disappearance of these 119 persons, many of whom were last seen either in Londres 38 or in José Domingo Cañas.[18]

In 1975, the secret service DINA left Londres 38. In November 1978, the regime handed the house over to the O'Higgins Institute, a historical research institute related to the military, which was to keep its offices there until December 2007. During the 1980s, when national protests against the Pinochet regime started to take shape, protests were sometimes held in front of the house.[19] Although officially identified as a secret detention and torture centre in the 1991 Rettig Report and under scrutiny in various court cases, the house at Londres 38 (under the guise of a new house number, 40, assigned to it at some point under the dictatorship) sat quietly for many years, occasionally the scene of vigils or protests by grassroots organizations at symbolic dates related to the detained-disappeared or the dictatorship.

The efforts related to Londres 38 gained strength around 2005.[20] In July 2005, grassroots organization Colectivo 119, together with other social organizations, commemorated the 30th anniversary of the so-called list of 119 detained-disappeared with three days of artistic interventions on the Plaza de la Constitución right in front of the presidential palace La Moneda in the heart of Santiago. They brought the detained-disappeared to the Plaza: 119 life-size wooden silhouettes, young people in shades of grey and brown holding a little card with their name, their age and job; the reverse sides of the silhouettes were painted black with

18 For the press clippings of 1975 and related documents, see www.londres38.cl.

19 See Linea de tiempo, www.londres38.cl.

20 Two grassroots organizations initiated the struggle for the recuperation of the house. Colectivo Londres 38, a small group of family members, survivors and others related to Londres 38 and the Colectivo 119, a broad group of family members, friends and others related to the case of the 119. In 2007 the Colectivo 119 split into the Colectivo Familiares y Compañeros de los 119 and Colectivo Memoria 119.

the numbers 1 to 119 in red paint. In an interview, one of the leaders of the Colectivo 119 told me that they had made them life-size to batter at the perception of the ordinary citizen, who tended to understand 'the detained-disappeared' as something very abstract. He emphasized the importance of commemoration and also the importance of vindicating their political militancy, the fact that they, and many others, represented a project of social and political change that 'embodied a whole generation'.[21]

In the same month, the Colectivo Londres 38 filed a petition with the Council of National Monuments to have the house at Londres 38 declared a national historical monument.[22] The projects of the Colectivo 119 and the Colectivo Londres 38 started to come together as the idea took hold to reclaim Londres 38 in order to use the house as a public 'house of memory'. While the Colectivo Londres 38 initiated an intricate bureaucratic-administrative journey to obtain the legal rights to use the house, the Colectivo 119 began to organize a weekly *velatón*, a candle vigil, in front of Londres 38 every Thursday at 7 pm, making the street their stage and the façade of Londres 38 their banner.

Their efforts were successful and, in October 2005 Londres 38, was declared a National Monument because of the historical value derived from its destination as a detention, torture and extermination centre of the secret service up until September 1974.[23] However, in the years that followed, the ownership of the house at Londres 38 was vigorously contested. In August 2007, the Ministry of Public Goods suggested via the media that Londres 38 could become the seat of the future Institute of Human Rights.[24] The grassroots organizations acted immediately, seeking platforms and media attention to prevent a public office from installing its offices in Londres 38. The *Colectivos* underlined that the proposal had been to open Londres 38 to the community and to involve them in a participative exercise so that these citizens could exercise their right to memory and become part of the debate on how to represent and transmit that memory. Colectivo Londres 38 initiated the campaign 'The Persistence of Memory' and denounced what they referred to as an attempt to erase Londres 38 once more. Moreover, they denounced the use of the discourse of human rights to displace the memories, the social and political identities of the victims and the actions of the individuals and grassroots organizations that had made Londres 38 visible and saved it from being destroyed or sold.[25] It was not until 10 December 2007

21 Interview, Santiago de Chile, 11 October 2006.

22 Presentación al Consejo de Monumentos Nacionales para la Declaratoria como monumento histórico del inmueble (Julio 2005), www.londres38.cl.

23 Decree 1413, 4 October 2005, Council of National Monuments.

24 *Radio Cooperativa*, 14 August 2007, 'Ex centro de tortura sera desde fin de año sede del Instituto de DDHH'. *La Nación Domingo*, 15 August 2007, 'Londres 38 será sede del futuro Instituto de DDHH'.

25 *El Mostrador*, 23 August 2007, 'La Persistencia de la Memoria'. For press archives, documents and declarations, see www.londres38.cl. See also Richard (2010:

that the grassroots organizations gained access to the now empty house for the first time. Eventually the government withdrew the plan to use Londres 38 as the seat of the Institute of Human Rights, and in October 2008 President Michelle Bachelet accepted the proposal by grassroots organizations to establish a working group on the future administration, use and funding of the house at Londres 38. In the working group, the grassroots organizations sat down with representatives of governmental institutions related to human rights and memorialization policy: the Program of Human Rights, the Presidential Commission for Human Rights, the Council of National Monuments and the Ministry of Public Goods (who chaired the working group).[26]

In general, the overall position of the government representatives was that the use of the house should connect to the officially established narrative of the dictatorship, framed in terms of individual human rights violations during the period of dictatorship as laid down in the Rettig and Valech reports, both of which referred explicitly to Londres 38 as a secret detention and torture centre of the secret service in the first year of the military dictatorship, as did the decree by which Londres 38 was declared a National Monument. In contrast, the members of the grassroots organizations endorsed a broader view on 'memory'. Londres 38 should not become a sort of museum for the past. The memory of the dictatorship should be used as a starting point to open up a broader, participative debate – both in order to come to an understanding of the past and in relation to the political and social issues of the present such as the situation of the indigenous *Mapuches* in the south of Chile and the protests by the country's high school students.

In the working group, the different positions on how memory of the dictatorship should be understood and how the house should be used were directly contested and negotiated. Eventually, the broad vision endorsed by the grassroots organizations was laid down in the final document of the working group:

> To ask questions about why, how and which circumstances made possible what happened; to ask questions about the responsibilities of society as a whole … and to understand the associated processes of social and political struggles against repression. … [and] their relationship with the present time. From *Londres 38*, house of memory, we want to contribute to and stimulate this debate.[27]

Today Londres 38 is a thriving social space administered by the Corporación Londres 38, Espacio de Memorias composed of the grassroots organizations. The site engages many persons, groups and organizations, and offers debates, performances and guided visits through its rooms. When you visit Londres 38

244-251) and Stern (2010: 314-323).

26 *Proyecto: Un espacio de memoria en construcción Londres 38, casa de la memoria* (June 2009), p. 7, www.londres38.cl.

27 *Proyecto: Un espacio de memoria en construcción Londres 38, casa de la memoria* (June 2009), p. 3, www.londres38.cl.

today not only will your guide tell you the history of the house and what has happened in it rooms, he or she will engage you in a dialogue on the house and Chilean society, on the past and the present. The visitor is considered a participant in constructing understandings of the past and the present, and invited to give his or her opinion on political and social relations in Chilean society and to share personal stories.

Londres 38 expresses both the commemoration of the victims of the dictatorship as social and political agents of societal change and a profound engagement in present social issues. Its website presents the names of the victims, testimonies on the detention and torture centre and the latest news on court cases against the perpetrators, and also the latest news on pressing social issues. When protesting university students called a national plebiscite for fair access to education in October 2011, former detention and torture centre Londres 38, Espacio de Memorias was one of the localities were people could go to vote and make their voice heard.[28]

Final reflections

Imageries of (transitional) justice may be understood as processes by means of which people create meaning and give significance to (past) violations of their individual and collective rights, the acts committed against their bodies, their persons, their families, their organizations and their societies. These 'imageries' are dynamic processes on multiple levels in a society that change through time. In this chapter I have argued that transitional justice initiatives of governments, such as truth commissions, tend to be focused on narratives of victimhood and attempt to create a coherent master narrative to give meaning to the past. Local imageries of justice on the other hand may precede these transitional justice initiatives. They are rooted in mourning and commemoration of the victims, and in narratives of social and political agency and resistance.

Both transitional justice initiatives and grassroots memorial initiatives have their own dynamics, they take place both independently of each other and are related, contest each other and at times may converge and enhance each other. Transitional justice initiatives are often in part created because of the demands of human rights and victim-survivor organizations and in an attempt at nation-building. These initiatives give voice to the victims, and the public acknowledgement of the past violations and its victims may empower them. However, these organizations and others may very well find such initiatives lacking in truth and justice and contest this in public space, and further engage in the act of truth-telling to power which, in its turn, may lead to the opening of new political and social spaces and produce a shift in the imageries of (transitional) justice.

28 'Londres 38 es sede del Plebiscito Educacional' at http://www.londres38.cl/1937/w3-article-92740.html.

Analysing the dynamics at the local level, the push towards the house at Londres 38 was there from the beginning of its use as a secret detention and torture centre in 1973. The detained-disappeared were like invisible but at the same time indelible fingerprints on its façade. During the 1990s, the focus was on the detained-disappeared as victims of individual human rights violations, acknowledged by the Rettig Report. This left little space for the living memory of the survivors, who were reserved and restrained in telling their own story of suffering and of political action. In the wake of the detention of Pinochet, which rekindled hopes for criminal justice and brought torture into the picture as a punishable act, former prisoners started to organize and to demand justice and integral reparation. The Valech Commission was created after pressure from human rights and other organizations and in the heat of the approaching, symbolically charged moment of the 30th anniversary of the coup. Its report broadened the publicly recognized master narrative of the dictatorship to include the victims of imprisonment and torture. The master narratives of the truth commissions were based on strict mandates and written in a legal language with a focus on individual victims of human rights violations, leaving out the perpetrators. However, grassroots organizations and other social actors striving for more truth and justice have tirelessly engaged and challenged the official discourse on the past, and continue to do so. This process of contestation and negotiation opens new spaces for people to voice their memories and to take action, broadening the perspectives on the dictatorship in public space.

One of these social spaces forged by the grassroots organizations was Londres 38. The process of contestation and negotiation, the broadening of the narrative of the dictatorship in society and the unceasing efforts by grassroots organizations at the local level provided an opening at a particular moment in time that allowed the working group of grassroots organizations and government representatives to come together to decide on a project for Londres 38. As we have seen, the use of the house and with that the meaning of the house for the collective memory of the dictatorship was contested. While the government representatives emphasized the master narratives of the truth commissions, the grassroots organizations wanted a more open, broad, participative approach to commemoration and collective memory with a focus on political and social agency. The dynamics at the local level have made Londres 38 an active, participative, social space of commemoration and memory, with demands for more truth and justice, and engagement in pressing present-day social issues. The grassroots organizations have created a new social space from which they assert that social organization and action are democratic rights.

When we think about transitional justice and how it promotes justice, we should look carefully at what kind of justice it is promoting and for whom. What are the imageries of transitional justice? And how do these relate to the imageries of justice at the local level? Transitional justice processes and local memory processes then must be understood both from their own particular, independent dynamics and as co-constituted and interrelated. The *act of truth-telling to power* either as everyday resistance in the context of a truth commission or in contestation of it is crucial to grasping the imageries of justice at the local level.

References

Arthur, P. 2009. How 'Transitions' Reshaped Human Rights: A Conceptual History of Transitional Justice. *Human Rights Quarterly*, 31(2), 321-367.

Ashplant, T.G., Dawson, G. and Roper, M. eds. 2000. *The Politics of War Memory and Commemoration*. London: Routledge.

Bakiner, O. 2010. From Denial to Reluctant Dialogue: The Chilean Military's Confrontation with Human Rights (1990–2006). *International Journal of Transitional Justice*, 4(1), 47-66.

Bilbija, K., Fair J., Milton C.E. and Payne, L.A. eds. 2005. *The Art of Truth-Telling about Authoritarian Rule*. Madison: University of Wisconsin Press.

(CEP) Centro de Estudios Públicos. 1991. Respuestas de las Fuerzas Armadas y de Orden al Informe de la Comisión Nacional de Verdad y Reconciliación, 27 de Marzo 1991. *Estudios Públicos*, 41, 449-504.

(CEP) Centro de Estudios Públicos. 2005. Ejército de Chile: el fin de una visión, 3 noviembre 2004. *Estudios Públicos*, 97, 505-508.

Collins, C. 2008. State Terror and the Law: The (Re)judicialization of Human Rights Accountability in Chile and El Salvador. *Latin American Perspectives*, 35(5), 20-37.

Collins, C. 2010. Human Rights Trials in Chile During and After the 'Pinochet Years'. *International Journal of Transitional Justice*, 4(1), 67-86.

CNPPT. 2004. *Informe de la Comisión Nacional sobre Prisión Política y Tortura*. Santiago de Chile: Ministerio de Interior.

CNVR. 1991. *Informe de la Comisión Nacional de Verdad y Reconciliación*. Santiago de Chile: La Nación.

Da Silva Catela, L. 2010. Exponer lo invisible: una etnografía sobre la transformación de centros clandestinos de detención en sitios de memoria en Córdoba-Argentina. In *Recordar para Pensar. Memoria para la Democracia. La Elaboración del Pasado Reciente en el Cono Sur de América Latina*, edited by T. Medalla *et al*., 44-56. Santiago de Chile: Heinrich Böll Stiftung.

Grandin, G. 2005. The Instruction of Great Catastrophe: Truth Commissions, National History, and State Formation in Argentina, Chile, and Guatemala. *American Historical Review*, 110(1), 46-67.

Hackett, C. and Rolston, R. 2009. The Burden of Memory: Victims, Storytelling and Resistance in Northern Ireland. *Memory Studies*, 2 (3), 355-376.

Hayner, P.B. 2011. *Unspeakable Truths: Transitional Justice and the Challenge of Truth Commissions*. New York: Routledge.

Hite, K. and Collins, C. 2009. Memorial Fragments, Monumental Silences and Reawakenings in 21st-century Chile. *Millennium: Journal of International Studies*, 38(2), 379-401.

Ibreck, R. 2010. The Politics of Mourning: Survivor Contributions to Memorials in Post-genocide Rwanda. *Memory Studies*, 3(4), 330-343.

Laplante, L.J. 2007. The Peruvian Truth Commission's Historical Memory Project: Empowering Truth-tellers to Confront Truth Deniers. *Journal of Human Rights*, 6(4), 433-452.

Lira, E. and Loveman, B. 2005. *Políticas de Reparación: Chile 1990-2004*. Santiago de Chile: Ediciones LOM.

Milton, C.E. 2007. At the Edge of the Peruvian Truth Commission: Alternative Paths to Recounting the Past. *Radical History Review*, 98, 3-31.

Phelps, T. 2004. *Shattered Voices: Language, Violence and the Work of Truth Commissions*. Philadelphia: University of Pennsylvania Press.

Richard, N. 2010. *Crítica de la Memoria (1990-2010)*. Santiago de Chile: Ediciones Universidad Diego Portales.

Rojas Vallejos, M.F. and Silva Bustón, M.P. 2005. *Sufrimiento y Desapariciones. El Manejo Urbano-Arquitectonico de la Memoria Urbana Traumatizada*. Santiago de Chile: Foundation Documentation and Archive of the Vicariate of Solidarity.

Scott, J.C. 1990. *Domination and the Arts of Resistance: Hidden Transcripts*. New Haven: Yale University.

Slaughter, J. 1997. A Question of Narration: The Voice in International Human Rights Law. *Human Rights Quarterly*, 19, 406-430.

Stern, S.J. 2010. *Reckoning with Pinochet: The Memory Question in Democratic Chile, 1989-2006*. Durham, NC: Duke University Press.

Young, J.E. 1993. *The Texture of Memory: Holocaust Memorials and Meaning*. New Haven: Yale University Press.

Chapter 7
The Role of Ritual is Shifting Collective Dispositions

Danielle Celermajer

The two part argument I would like to propose and interrogate in this chapter is first, that collective ritual can be efficacious in addressing significant acts of wrongdoing, and second, that it does so by shifting the collective dispositions that orient individual action. This two part approach is particularly apposite in the context of transitional justice insofar as one of the main tasks of transitional justice mechanisms is to alter the normative framework of the society in question such as to ground laws, policies and practices that respect human rights and the rule of law.

If one is to successfully argue these two propositions, however, one will have to provide a convincing response to two types of what I will call here 'modernist objections'. The first objection is that ritual is 'pure mechanistic externality' and as such fails to engage authentic intentionality or agency in such a way as to penetrate the 'deep drivers' of action. The second is that because only individuals have agency, collectives can never be more than aggregations of individual agents and as such, the very notion of collective ethical orientations or ethical dispositions (which are here identified as the object of ritual action) is a category mistake. The first burden of this chapter, then, will be to respond to these objections, which I will do principally by addressing the set of assumptions about the relationship between authenticity, agency, internality, thought and action that underpins them. In so doing, I will seek to re-present ritual as one of the mechanisms available for shifting the sources and orientations of action in a manner appropriate to the challenges presented in transitional justice contexts.

The first part of the chapter will provide a brief contextual overview of how ritual is being engaged in contemporary transitional justice processes. Here, I will mention several types of transitional justice mechanisms with a view to indicating the broad applicability of a ritual frame to this field, but will take as an exemplary ritual form the political apology, in which a political representative apologizes on behalf of a collective for grave wrongs in its past. The second section of the chapter will turn to interrogating the operation of ritual. Here I will briefly consider some classical theories about the way in which ritual works and the modernist rejection of ritual's efficacy due to its failure to appreciate the primary ontological status of the individual and of his or her beliefs or epistemic commitments as the essential source of action. Contra this modernist critique, I will suggest a theory of ritual based on an appreciation of the ways in which action repertoires can in fact inform the orientations (including the ethical orientations) that underpin individual action. In doing so, I will draw on classical debates within Judaism on the question of ritual efficacy and intentionality as well as social anthropological work on ritual theory.

Building on this argument, in the third part of the chapter I will explicitly turn to questions about the relationship between individual action and morality and collective ethical orientations, specifically addressing ontological worries about propositions that seem to suggest that collectives can have the type of agency required both for responsibility for wrongdoing and for shifts towards more ethical behaviour. In the concluding section, I will turn back to the context of transitional justice more generally to consider the role that ritual might play in effecting the principal objective of transitional mechanisms and the limits of ritual in so doing.

The dimension of ritual in contemporary transitional justice

Transitional justice, as understood in contemporary theory and practice, generally refers to the range of mechanisms adopted by societies seeking to deal with significant wrongdoing in the past as part of the process of moving forward to a situation characterized by respect for the rule of law and human rights. The range of mechanisms placed under the rubric of transitional justice spans domestic and international criminal trials, truth and truth and reconciliation commissions, memorial projects of various types, compensation and reparation schemes, and political apologies (see Minow 1998; Teitel 2000).

While many of these mechanisms represent variations on traditional approaches to justice, for example punishing wrongdoers or compensating those who have suffered wrong, their objectives go beyond attending to setting things right with respect to a distinct and isolated violation, or redressing the balance in relation to the individual perpetrator or victim. Recognizing that the wrongful acts that they seek to address form part of a broader pattern of societal and political injustice, part of their work must necessarily be to shift the conditions, broadly understood, that gave rise to wrongdoing. Thus, although necessarily adopting particular interventions, each intervention is also directed towards the broader structural objective of laying the foundations for a different future. Let us take three cases to flesh this claim out and to get at the sense in which one can say that ritual is at play in transitional justice processes.

The Truth and Reconciliation Commission in South Africa, now exemplary of the truth commission model, sought, through public and publicly broadcast hearings, to have individual perpetrators give voice to the facts and wrongfulness of their act, thereby affording an otherwise inaccessible narrative of what actually happened and, in those cases where they expressed remorse, also giving voice to the new moral framework of an egalitarian South Africa. In this sense, their truth-telling was not simply a form of moral punishment that simultaneously provided a form of moral compensation for victims or their families. The narratives that emerged from such truth-telling across a large number of perpetrators, along with the responses from those who had been harmed, served to establish a type of morality tale about the nation. Moreover, insofar as it was framed by the highly public and socially and politically authorized condemnation of acts that had previously worn the mantle of political legitimacy, this morality tale served to shift the normative compass of the nation. In simple terms, if the apartheid state had, through both its legal regulations and its symbolic actions, established the legitimacy of the view that black South Africans were less than fully human and not worthy of being treated as citizens, the post-apartheid state employed the performance of truth-telling and the highly performative public sanction of racial discrimination to establish the principle of racial equality and the dignity of black South Africans.

While showing contextual variations, this now established modality of the public performance of truth-telling and moral sanction has come to take on a fairly standardized form that, as we shall see, has some of the characteristics of ritual. Moreover, it is in this ritualized dimension that some of the criticisms of truth commissions fall, insofar as they are accused of being purely performative.

Second, let us take the prosecution by the International Criminal Court (ICC) of the militia leader from the Democratic Republic of the Congo Thomas Lubanga Dyilo. Already in 2006, when the ICC prosecutor laid charges against Lubanga for enlisting and conscripting children under the age of 15 and using them to actively participate in hostilities, he referred not only to the specific charges against the specific individual but stated that:

> Regardless of the outcome of the proceedings, this case represents a huge step in the struggle against these serious crimes against children. Child conscription destroys the lives and futures of thousands of children around the world. This case will contribute to exposing the problem and in stopping these criminal practices. (International Criminal Court 2006)

Insofar as the case has been framed as the international community's condemning of the use of child soldiers, those dimensions of criminal trials that Joel Feinberg (1965) had already distinguished as the 'expressive function' of punishment or that Mark Osiel (1997) distinguished as law's 'pedagogic function' are highly evident here. As Osiel writes of criminal trials in transitional justice trials in general, 'when effective as public spectacle', such trials 'stimulate public discussion in ways that foster liberal virtues of toleration, moderation and civil respect' (1997: 2). Importantly for the context of our discussion, one of the key distinguishing marks that anthropologists have used to distinguish ritual activity is precisely this expressive quality (Lukes 1975; Turner 1969). Indeed, and as we shall see problematically, the conflation of rationality with instrumental rationality (or, as Weber coined it, *Zweckrationalität*) has often led to the conclusion that it is precisely this expressive quality that renders ritual actions irrational. As

Mary Douglas observed, however, 'instrumental efficacy (means/ends) is not the only kind to be derived through their symbolic actions. The other kind is to be achieved in the action itself' (1966: 84). Part of our work, then, will be to elucidate the ways in which ritual or symbolic actions can be non-instrumental and yet efficacious.

Third, let us look briefly at the political apology, to which I will return throughout this chapter. By political apology, I mean here apologies for significant collective wrongs of the past, spoken by political representatives on behalf of a nation or people. The political apology, little known until the early 1980s, has now become part of the standard toolbox of political transition as well as of historical justice, being used across a broad range of violations and types of transitional or historical processes. Importantly, despite significant differences in the contexts in which political apologies are given, there are certain formal and predictable characteristics of most political apologies. One might even say that all political apologies more or less adopt a formal script (the apologetic words and a narrative setting out the nature of the wrong), take place in a standardized setting (a formal occasion with representative actors present) and involve a set of dramatis personae (including the representative speaker and the representative of the wronged community). One becomes aware of the sense in which this is true to the extent that we are beginning to have a sense of whether any particular political apology constitutes a correct form or, correlatively, whether it fails in certain critical respects. Certainly, there is significant disagreement over whether such political apologies achieve anything of value for the perpetrator or victim communities, and if so, how outcomes might be achieved. Nevertheless, all parties would likely agree that the apology is seeking to achieve something that goes beyond the impact of the actual words spoken between those parties present at the occasion.

Before proceeding to interrogate both the sense in which these transitional mechanisms can be characterized as having ritual qualities and the issues this raises in terms of how we assess them, we need to establish at least a very basic definition of ritual. Tambiah's formal definition of ritual provides a fairly theoretically indeterminate starting point. He defines ritual as 'patterned and ordered sequences of words and acts, often expressed in multiple media, whose content and arrangement are characterised in varying degree by formality (conventionality), stereotypy (rigidity), condensation (fusion), and redundancy (repetition)' (Tambiah 1979: 119). This definition fairly satisfactorily captures something of what formally distinguishes ritual; it fails, however, to capture our intuitive sense that what distinguishes ritual from other forms of repetitive action (say stopping at a red traffic light) is that the ritual performance goes beyond the utility of the purely instrumental objectives of the action. To capture this sense of ritual's 'supplementary work', I borrow from and paraphrase Moore and Meyerhoff's notion of ritual as *a dramatic occasion, a form of symbolic action that alludes to more than it says* (1977: 5).

Already we can begin to see the sense in which the three forms of transitional justice discussed above can be understood as having a ritual quality in both a formal and a more substantive sense. Formally, they are characterized by more or less formalized sets of words and actions and, more importantly, substantively, we recognize in them a quality of symbolic action that goes beyond the mere achievement of instrumental objectives. Indeed, in the very formality and repetitive nature of their performance, they point to the achievement of something that lies beyond what is immediately apparent.

What is of greater interest to us, however, is the question of the significance of this ritual dimension in terms of such mechanisms achieving the types of objectives noted earlier. The question one might ask is whether, in their ritual dimension, these mechanisms are efficacious in overcoming past patterns of injustice and establishing the social and political conditions for respect for the rule of law and human rights. Or, in even more basic terms, does the ritual aspect of these mechanisms contribute in some way to the achievement of transitional justice, broadly understood? For an initial take on this question, let us turn back briefly to the political apology.

While political apologies have become increasingly popular as responses to significant past injustices, they have also been heavily criticized and indeed the major criticisms bring into relief both the ritualistic dimension of transitional justice mechanisms and the principal ways in which their ritualized quality is seen as having dubious value. For apologies critics, the first significant problem is the alleged insufficiency of 'mere words' to compensate for or otherwise appropriately respond to the grave violations of human rights that are usually at issue. Moreover, the apologetic words, however weighty they may be in themselves, provide no guarantee of authenticity on the part of the speaker who may well, so the criticism runs, be expediently employing words in order to feign *the genuine regret* that alone would provide some form of moral redress. This problem of authenticity or sincerity is further exacerbated by the representative nature of the apology, in which the singular representative speaker is standing in for an entire group (the perpetrator community). Thus, even if one might argue that the speaker herself experiences the genuine regret that would signal that the apology was not inauthentic or pure externality, our modernist commitment to an individualist ontology calls into serious question the legitimacy of attributing emotions or authentic feelings to a group.

Seen in this light, as mere externality without the requisite internality that would signal authentic regret or authentic intention (which could in any case only be attributes of an individual), classifying the apology as a ritual appropriately points to why it fails a series of what we might here call 'modernist tests of efficacy'. In a similar manner, the other two processes noted here, the South African Truth and Reconciliation Commission and the ICC prosecution of an individual responsible for gross violations of human rights, might well have certain ritual qualities, but by similar modernist lights, in this ritual dimension, they do not get at the actual motors of change. To determine what it is about our understanding of rituals that renders them ineffective in our eyes in effecting transitions from patterns of injustice to patterns of justice, we need to turn now to interrogate ritual itself and modernist understandings of causality.

Interrogating ritual and the causes of human action

In his introduction to a recent collection of papers on the problem of ritual efficacy, William Sax (2010: 5-8) makes the bold observation that by virtue of the modernist 'representational theory' of ritual, ineffectiveness or irrationality has become part of what, for us moderns *defines* ritual. To unpack this a little, the argument Sax is making, one now fairly common in social anthropological literature on ritual, begins with the observation that one of the key effects of the modernist turn, clearly evident in Protestant theology, but also more generally in conceptions of the self and agency, is that we moderns, as Talal Asad argued, place a 'priority on belief as a state of mind, rather than as a constituting activity in the world' (1993: 47). Ritual, insofar as it comprises words and acts, is thus viewed, within this schema, as always and only standing in for the 'real' process, which is taking place elsewhere, below the surface and presumably inside the minds (or even souls) of individuals. To believe otherwise is to indulge in some form of magical thinking, whereby change could be affected by some type of invisible external forces and to fail to see that the motor of action lies in human agency, just as the source of responsibility is human intentionality. Words or acts can point us towards the existence of such intentionality or agency, but *in themselves* lack significance or efficacy.

Despite the prevalence and indeed the 'taken for granted' nature of this interpretive frame, it has not, however, gone uncontested. In the context of the ritual dimensions of religious practice, there is an extensive literature both exposing and critiquing this modernist understanding of the limits of so-called external action. Given my focus in this chapter on the apology as one of the mechanisms of transitional justice, let us look briefly at the way in which the work of apologetic words has been understood in Judaism. By way of very brief background, in Jewish practice, speaking the words of apology forms a critical part of the ritual of repentance or *teshuvah*, which takes place at the time of the New Year and is seen as critical for overcoming the past and entering into relations no longer stymied by past infractions. Moreover, in Jewish practices, apologies are to be spoken not only by individuals for specific infractions that they have brought about, but also by communities for the wrongs that they have collectively committed. In this sense, they are particularly apposite for our reflections.

The significance of these practices has long been the subject of theological reflection, and in particular probing as to the significance of the speech act of the apology. Thus, for example, in answer to the question, what is complete repentance, the authoritative twelfth-century Jewish thinker Moses Maimonides (1927: book 1, V, ch. 1) systematized teachings regarding the necessary conditions or components in terms of six necessary components. These were: (1) abandonment of sin, (2) removal of the sin from thoughts, (3) resolution, (4) regret, (5) expression of sincerity before God and (6) oral confession. Throughout these teachings, *teshuvah* is understood simultaneously as attitude, action and, most importantly here, speech. Critically, even if all the other conditions necessary to achieve *teshuvah* are fulfilled, they will not be sufficient, save the spoken words of apology: the sinner must 'confess in words, with his lips and give voice to those matters he has resolved in his heart' (Maimonides 1927: ch. 2). The sine qua non of *teshuvah* is verbal confession – words offered to the other. One must address oneself to the other and with spoken words identify oneself as a wrongdoer, confess the specific sin, expose one's shame and promise not to repeat the sinful act.[1] Indeed, in Jewish law, if the injured party has died, the perpetrator must still *speak the words of apology*, not to the victim's face but at the side of his or her grave.

This emphasis on the spoken word is remarkable when compared with the common conception that apology is a mere representation, the signifier of an elsewhere signified. But clearly, what is being gestured at here is an interdependence of language and relationship that our habitual schema fails to encode. As the twentieth-century Jewish philosopher Emanuel Levinas (1994) observes, in Jewish thought, the material form of expression is not arbitrary, a trapping which might be shed so as to get to the essence that it contains, but is rather itself a site of significance. Speech has real weight.[2] More specifically, Levinas sees in Judaic teachings on repentance an implicit understanding of the interdependence of inside and outside. He too places himself in the line of Maimonides, arguing, 'all that is said of God in Judaism signifies through human *praxis*' (Levinas 1994: 14). Repentance cannot be correctly understood as essentially disembodied, and then 'named'; it is in the naming that it exists.

The philosophy that Levinas here attributes to Judaism is a particularly valuable tool for making sense of the apologetic act because it does not simply champion the value of the performative, but presents a more profound challenge to the modernist dichotomy and hierarchization of inside/outside.[3] Ritual, the *mitzvoth* (blessings or ritual acts of observance) and specifically those brought down in the tradition for

---

1 'How is the verbal confession made? The sinner says thus: "I beseech Thee, O great Name! I have sinned; I have been obstinate; I have committed profanity against Thee. Particularly in doing such and such. Now behold! I have repented and am ashamed of my actions; forever will I not relapse into this thing again"' (Maimonides, 1927: bk 1, V, ch. 1.1).

2 'Ideas do not become fixed by a process of conceptualization which would extinguish many of the sparks dancing beneath the gaze riveted upon the real. I have already had occasion here to speak of another process which consists in respecting these possibilities … Ideas are never separated from the example which both suggests and delimits them' (Levinas 1994: 21).

3 Levinas was no doubt also influenced by Nietszche's scathing critique of the assumed distinction between surface and depth, seeing it as an artefact of modernity: 'The

seeking forgiveness do not stand outside a sealed consciousness, which might or might not authentically repent. Rather, 'originating communally, in collective law and commandment, ritual is not at all external to conscience. It conditions it and permits it to enter into itself and stay awake. It preserves it, prepares it for healing' (Levinas 1994: 17).

More generally in Jewish thought, including in modernist Jewish thought, there is an explicit debate on the relative role of ritual acts in themselves (*keva*) on the one hand and intention or authenticity (*kavanah*) on the other. The twentieth-century theologian and philosopher Abraham Joshua Heschel provides perhaps the most insightful discussion of the tension between these two 'poles' in Jewish thought and practice. Particularly given his powerful commitment to the role of religious practice in effecting social justice, Heschel is distinctly alive to the dangers of what he calls 'religious behaviourism', that is, a view of Judaism as mere and mindless compliance with ritual precepts (1955: 320-332). Heschel observes, nevertheless, that in relation to, say, the act of prayer, the pole of regularity or lawful observance of ritual rules (*keva*) is stronger than the pole of spontaneity or intention of the heart (*kavanah*), raising the 'perpetual danger of our observance and worship becoming mere habit, a ritual performance' (1955: 343). Why then, Heschel asks, would we not simply obviate this danger by extinguishing the pole of law-like ritual performance, leaving only acts that are spontaneously generated? Responding to his own suggestion, Heschel warns that such a move represents a failure to appreciate that in ritual, the dynamic of causality does not, as we might assume, move simply from individual intentionality to act, but rather, and importantly, from act to intentionality. Thus, it is not simply a matter of external acts conforming to inner intention, but rather of intention coming to be shaped by the forms of ritual action that are embraced through practice. In Heschel's terms, we are not called upon to do as we 'naturally' or 'spontaneously' intend, but rather, for the ritual acts of prayer to shape our intention. As he puts it:

> While love is hibernating, our loyal deeds speak. It is right that the good actions should become a habit, that the performance of justice should become second nature; even though it is not native to the self. A good person is not he who does the right thing, but he who is in the habit of doing the right thing. (Heschel 1955: 345)

Seligman *et al.* (2008) mount a similar argument in their essay on ritual and the limits of sincerity. Their argument, summarily put, is that any view of ritual that casts it as representative action pointing us down to an authentic self or intention not only misses the distinct logic of ritual but fails to understand the complex relationship between the formation of selves and practice. Thus, quoting Jonathon Smith, they suggest that 'ritual is a means of performing the way things ought

"apparent" world is the only one. The "real" world has only been lyingly added' (Nietzsche 1968: 36).

to be in conscious tension to the way things are in such a way that this ritualised perfection is recollected in the ordinary, uncontrolled course of things' (Seligman *et al.* 2008: 27). Ritual, on this understanding, creates a practised repertoire of appropriate responses or dispositions, from which individuals can thence, when the world presents novel situations, generate appropriate responses.

Reminiscent of Douglas' argument noted earlier, they suggest that ritual cannot be properly analysed as 'a coherent system of beliefs', because the meaning of ritual is the meaning 'produced through the ritual action itself' (Seligman *et al.* 2008: 26). Importantly, in mounting this argument they systematically deconstruct the dichotomy between pre-modern or magical world views and modern or rational world views and practices, drawing not only on Confucian and Talmudic understandings, which might well be cast as themselves indicative of a pre-modern and outmoded understanding of the world, but also on psychoanalytic, social psychological and anthropological literature.

Taking an example that is both banal and appropriately removed from the metaphysical context of religious analyses, they point out that in the repetitive requests we make that our children say 'please' or 'thank you', our understanding is that by assuming such ritualized actions, eventually the child will be disposed towards the expression of gratitude, not simply by rote, but as a subject who has acquired the disposition of appropriate gratitude. What is critical to understand here is that the reorganization being suggested is not simply a reversal of the usual modernist preference for the inner, whereby external or constraining rules would shape the self, thus rendering the argument vulnerable to accusations of failing to appreciate the autonomy of the subject. It is rather a more radical recasting of our notions of social rules of practices and the acting or believing self, whereby the latter is not seen as having a fragile authenticity that must be sheltered from rules, but rather as an ongoing project that acquires *its own* dispositions in part through social practices.

What is particularly valuable about Seligman and his colleagues' argument in the context of thinking about transitional justice is that they understand this type of work of ritual as a response to a proper recognition of the fragmented and tragic nature of the social and indeed natural world. True enough, ritual creates a subjunctive or 'as if' space, where we enact the world as we would have it be; in the case of the rituals of transitional justice, such would be a world that is just, that accords appropriate recognition to the rights of all parties and that redresses the structural imbalances of power that habitually marginalize certain parties. In so creating this ritual world, we are not naively or magically assuming that it thereby recreates reality, overcoming the fragmentation and injustice in a way that will then hold across time and in the world as it is. We are rather systematically and formally placing ourselves in the subjunctive space, such that we might acquire the habits or dispositions from which to respond to the world in its unavoidable brokenness and fragmentation.

One of the major questions that this theory of ritual raises, however, and which takes us back to the problem of efficacy raised earlier, is how can we explain the link between the performance of an 'as if' world and our assuming the disposition towards this type of world? Seligman *et al.* point us in this regard to psychoanalytic understandings of the development of a social world. Here, they appositely quote Modell's summary of Winnicott's understanding of illusion:

> Winnicott recognised that illusions are an essential part of living and not something to be depreciated as unreal. Illusions create a psychological space in which cultural experience occurs. It is a space that belongs neither to the subject nor the object: it is a potential space, a third area of being that belongs neither to the self nor the other, it is a space in which we experience the illusion of shared imaginations. (Modell in Seligman *et al.* 2008: 50)

The particular value of Winnicott's insight for our purposes is that it begins to suggest a way in which we can understand how it is that the ritualized establishment of the subjunctive or 'as if' space does its work. That is, one might ask, if the alternative space in which the 'as if' world appears does not emerge from the authentic self 'on the inside' as it were, where does it exist and how does it work to make a difference to the ways in which we will act in the future? To answer this question in a way directly relevant to our context, we might turn to a group of theoretical approaches from social anthropology that seek to understand the distinct role of *practice* in the construction of social relations and social order. Particularly apposite here is Bordieu's notion of the *habitus*. Much like Winnicott's third space, the habitus is neither purely inside the individual (as a property of agency), nor purely outside in the objective structures of the world. It consists rather of 'structured principles of the generation and structuring of practices and representations' (Bordieu 2002: 72). Habitus resides as this 'dialectic of objectification and incorporation', of the structured environment, as held in agents' practical interpretation of the world and 'the structured dispositions engendered in people which lead them to reproduce the environment even in transformed form' (Bell 1992: 78). Most importantly for our purposes, it is through *practice* understood as informed by and informing habitus that dispositions and actions are shaped, and not the other way around. Drawing on both Bordieu and Ortner, Bell suggests that 'habitus is the principle by which individual and collective practices are produced and the matrix in which objective structures are realised within the (subjective) dispositions that produce practices' (1992: 79).

Ritual, as understood within this framework is then one of the ways in which human beings seek to shape not particular structures, actions or dispositions, but the habitus or web of enacted meanings in which such structures, actions and dispositions emerge. Its modality of symbolic action or words is thus not representative of a deeper internal meaning, but is itself a mode of meaning-making. As Roy Rappaport (1979: 173-221) suggested, ritual is not a reflection of individuals' commitment to certain forms of social space or social order, but rather the manner in which such commitment is produced.

Linking this back to our principal concern, that is, the question of the ritual dimension of transitional justice mechanisms, this type of theoretical approach has some very important implications for our understanding of the ways in which individual dispositions are shaped, and in particular for the way in which we organize our conceptualization of individuals and collectives. At the same time, it brings into relief the second major problem that collective rituals raise from the modernist perspective, that is, the problem of how we can conceptualize collective actions or orientations in a manner consistent with our commitments to ethical individualism. It is to this then that I now turn.

Ethical individualism and the challenge of conceptualizing collective norms

Coming back to my exemplary case of the political apology, we recall that the second type of objection to such apologies being afforded as viable responses to wrongs of the past related to their assumptions about collective action, collective responsibility and collective norms. According to such objections, insofar as a representative speaker presumes to speak in the name of a collective and through such speech to influence collective norms or dispositions, the political apology rests on the propositions that 'a collective' can act or that one can seek to alter 'collective norms', propositions that, according to this line of criticism, make no sense. Underlying this objection is a series of ontological, epistemological and ethical commitments to the primacy of the individual agent and the derivative status of groups or collectives.

Before responding to this objection, let us flesh out a little exactly what is at issue, as the problem of the collective is implicated in several ways in the context of ritual and of transitional justice. One of the frequently cited objections to a number of transitional justice approaches, including public memorials, state-based compensation schemes and political apologies, is that they hold collectives responsible for wrongs committed by individuals, thereby violating the important principle of ethical individualism and indeed, as Karl Jaspers pointed out in his analysis of German guilt in the wake of the Holocaust, perhaps falling victim to the very collectivist thinking that underpinned the wrongs at issue.[4] This objection becomes still stronger in cases of historical justice, where persons no longer even alive committed the crimes in question, raising the 'sins of the fathers' objection. This type of objection was, for example, one of the major lines of defence that the

4 Jaspers writes: 'Morally one can judge the individual only, never a group. The mentality which considers, characterizes and judges people collectively is very widespread. Such characterizations … never fit generic conceptions under which the individual human beings might be classified, but are the type of conceptions to which they may more or less correspond. This confusion, of the generic with the typological conception, marks the thinking in collective groups … For centuries this mentality has fostered hatred among nations and communities' (1961: 40-41).

Australian Prime Minister John Howard took during the 10 years that he refused to offer an apology for the forced removal of Indigenous children from their families.[5]

A second type of objection to collectivism, and one more directly related to our interrogation, is that transitional mechanisms, to the extent that they are concerned with collective norms or that they engage with arguments about collective responsibility, fall prey to a logical error, insofar as the very idea of collective norms or collective responsibility involves a type of ontological category mistake. The intentionality, agency and reflexivity required for responsibility, or normative orientation, so this argument runs, can only ever be properties of individuals.[6] Connected with this analytic objection to collectivist approaches is a more practical objection that such approaches, insofar as they operate at the collective or performative level, will fail to actually alter the intentions or action of individuals, and that ultimately, it is always and only individuals who act (for right or wrong).

Linking this back more explicitly to the types of transitional justice mechanisms we have been speaking about, the objection would thus be that even if the sanctioned performance of condemnation of wrongful acts through truth commissions or the international criminal prosecution of exemplary perpetrators or political apologies do express a certain type of collective norm, this symbolic expression in itself cannot be efficacious in actually altering individual belief, intention or action. Once again, we see at work here the same set of assumptions as I discussed in the previous section about what it is that causes individuals to act as they do. As understood here, individual action is a product of individual belief or intention, and the idea that individual action might be shaped through symbolic action at a collective level rests on an outmoded form of magical thinking.

To respond to this line of criticism, we must thus develop an alternative schema that maps the relationship between norms that are expressed symbolically or through what we are here identifying as ritual forms and individual action. To comprehensively articulate such an argument exceeds the limits of the current chapter, but building on the line of argumentation developed in the previous section, we can begin to sketch the direction of the argument.

To move in this direction, the first principle we must establish is that our commitments to ethical individualism, or the principle that individuals are responsible for their own actions for the purposes of, say, criminal law, need not blind us to the complex and co-constitutional nature of social or collective norms and individual orientations and actions. That is, the modernist turn to the individual, including its important ethical achievements, need not entail a rejection of the social constitution of selves. As I argued above, for example, Bordieu's notion of *habitus* exemplifies a group of theories that seek to deconstruct the dichotomy

5 For example, 'To say to them that they are personally responsible and that they should feel a sense of shame about those events is to visit upon them an unreasonable penalty and an injustice' (Australia, House of Representatives 1999: 9206-9207).

6 In the context of apologies, this argument has been most forcefully articulated by Michel-Rolph Trouillot (2000).

between analyses that privilege agency (inside) *or* structure (outside), allowing us to reconceptualize collective norms, individual intentions and schemas, and objective social structures as moments of a broader pattern, rather than as causes or effects.

Usefully for our purposes, this theoretical approach finds resonances in the work of a number of theorists who have specifically addressed the question of collective responsibility. Coming at the problem via analyses of collective responsibility will in turn provide a theoretical framework for thinking about the role that shifting collective norms can play in reorienting individual action.

With clear resonances with Durkheim's notion of the 'collective conscience' (1982) and the idea of social facts that mediate between external influence and subjective agency, Joel Feinberg (1970: 247) identified what he called the *cultural context* of specific violations as the effective link between collectives and individual actors for the purposes of broadening our understanding of responsibility. Following Feinburg, Larry May refers to a group's *dispositions*, which 'create a climate of attitudes in which harm is more likely to occur' (1996: 46).[7] Like Feinberg, May identifies the pertinent collective characteristic in this zone of *disposition*, as distinct from decision, action or even authorization. Building on this notion, David Miller suggests the 'like-minded group' model as a way of capturing in its net all those who, even without *acting* or formally assenting, implicitly supported the manifest wrongful acts through their shared 'general attitude' (2004: 253). Iris Marion Young's term 'social connection' (2004) does similar work in casting the net of responsibility over a group of people standing in the background or off to the side of the actual wrongdoing, but who share a social or cultural space that one senses is the ground for the actual wrongdoing.

Insofar as they point to the space of the cultural field and network of hard and soft institutions that provide individuals with the normative map against which they judge and act, these accounts conform well to our intuitions about the relevance of normative contexts for individual decisions, judgements and actions. They do not yet, however, explicitly set out the links between this shared disposition and the actions that individuals take. Correlatively, and for our purposes, they do not explain how an altered 'shared disposition', as expressed through ritual actions, would shift individual intention or action.

For this purpose, once again, we might return first to Jaspers and thence to more recent interpretive theorists. In trying to explicate a form of collective responsibility that did not violate his own tenets of individual agency, Jaspers used the term *dasein* – that in which – *Ich mein Dasein habe* – I have my being/place of being. *Dasein* is of course not simply the physical dimensions of the shared space, but also comprehends its cultural and political dimensions; it is the medium from which individuals emerge. Jaspers thus conceptualized *dasein* as

7 May stresses that the attitudes relevant for a story about responsibility are not theoretical or '*mere* thoughts', but rather affective states in which people are moved to *act* in certain ways.

a field of meaning, an ongoing process of political cultural production, through which context is folded into the identity of individual members of the group, at the same time as the judgements, actions and aspirations of individuals form the context in which the political institutions of the nation take shape.[8] In place of the metaphor of the being in space, one might think of *dasein* as a melody that organizes those playing the instruments, but only has its existence in so far as they play it, and is transformed as they interpret it within the horizon of their own lives.

In a similar move, interpretive or process theorists sought to resolve the dilemma raised by the dichotomy between agency and structure-based analyses of society and politics by recasting the term 'political culture' as something that adheres neither in objective structures nor inside individuals' heads, but rather as the grammar that patterns political action at an individual and institutional level.[9] Thus, posited neither as free floating first cause nor as ideological reflection, evaluative schemes, actions, systems of belief and assumptions about rightful behaviour are sites at which actual people make their judgements and take their actions, and in so doing perpetuate or reform political culture or morality.[10] National culture, the nation and the individuals who take actions are thus not three distinct entities that stand in a causal relationship, but dimensions that mutually construct and constrain each other, and *dasein* emerges in this movement. Importantly, widening the lens to take in the context in which actions occur does not negate the fact that ultimately there must always be an individual actor who brings about the wrongful act.

This still leaves open the question of how it is that such general norms inform individuals' choices and actions. For these purposes, George Mead's model of subject formation (1934), which attends both to the acquisition of pre-existing patterns of action and identity and the subject's agency in the enactment of those norms, proves particularly fertile. As a basic framework, Mead uses the metaphor of the movement between play and games to explain how individuals acquire a general set of conventions or norms of action and identity that extend well beyond the specific rules or meanings conveyed in their immediate relations and direct interactions. In play the child organizes her activity according to the behaviour of the concrete other with whom she is playing; in the game, she orients her actions according to a generalized set of rules that she understands orient the actions and

8 Drawing on Jaspers, Larry May characterizes moral values as 'action guiding and compelling in that they define initial (or prima facie) reasons for behaving in a certain way' and cultures as 'both the products of individuals actions and attitudes and the producers of new actions and attitudes in the world' (1996: 77, 153).

9 Reconceptualizations of political culture fall within a broader turn to process orientations principally articulated by Elias (1987) and Bordieu (2002).

10 'All these routines and scenarios are predicated upon and embody within themselves, the fundamental notions of temporal, spatial and social ordering that underlie and organize the system as a whole. In enacting these routines, actors not only continue to be shaped by the underlying organizational principles involved, but continually re-endorse those principles in the world of public observation and discourse' (Ortner 1984: 154).

expectations of the other players in the game. This shift links her sense of herself (and others), what is expected of her (and others) and what she (and others) can do to an abstract set of norms which organize the social field and which flow, not from a particular other, but from the generalized Other, even as they are only ever manifest in particular interactions. This generalized Other, like the written rules of a board game, only takes positive form in an after-the-fact act of articulation. Only in the cardboard cut-out version do players read the rules and then play; in the lived version that it mimics, the rules are embedded in actions they join and then take themselves.

The advantage of the game metaphor is that unlike some forms of social structuralism, it is dynamic and always already located in relational action; the 'I' that is formed through social interactions is not a type of static being, but a self oriented to act in certain ways, according to certain rules about what is permissible, who can (and is expected to) do what, who deserves what and so on.

Concluding thoughts

Where then does this leave us with respect to our original questions about the possibility of recognizing the efficacy of ritual in addressing significant societal wrongs in a manner that contributes to the objectives of transitional justice? Recalling the two major objections to the proposition that the ritual dimensions of transitional justice could be efficacious, this chapter has sought to recast ritual in a manner that resisted accusations concerning ritual's externality and problematic collectivist understanding of wrongdoing and normativity. In particular, I have sought to rethink the underpinnings of both wrongdoing and 'setting action right' themselves so as to point to the critical role that generalized social norms play in orienting individual actions. Moreover, I have sought to call into question taken-for-granted assumptions that we have about the relationship between action or performance (as externality) and thought or intention (as internality) with a view to illuminating the co-constitutional relationship of practice and intention or agency. Drawing on now well-accepted understandings of the development of individual's own normative orientation, I have also argued that the type of mimetic practices that ritualized performances of justice represent may play a critical role in shifting the normative orientations of individuals.

Even if, however, we have established an analytic case for the possible efficacy of ritual in a manner that convincingly counters some of the modernist impediments to such an appreciation, a number of questions remain. In particular, we might ask whether the rituals that we have so far developed in relation to transitional justice are in fact efficacious. There are two principal types of reasons that may lead us to conclude in the negative. First, and more superficially, it may be that we moderns lack what Bell calls 'the ritual sense'. By this I mean that the modernist objections that I have outlined here are not simply the objections of the theorist but are also part of the phenomenology of the modern subject. Were this the case, it may be that our notions about what really brings about our actions and about the nature of the self are such as to impede our being open to the effects of ritual. Whether we judge this to be the case will depend in part on how we come to understand the conditions of efficacy. One needs to ask, for example, whether we can be affected by ritual despite our cynicism, or whether a certain willingness to be engaged is a prerequisite of efficacy.

The second reason that the rituals of transitional justice may remain inefficacious may be that they are simply the wrong rituals. Thus, it may be that our alienation from the business of ritual-making has undermined our ability to design rituals that powerfully resonate or simply that we have not yet come up with broadly resonant rituals. If this is the case, then part of the work of those concerned in efficacious transitional justice mechanisms ought to be attention to ritual-making and ritual-testing. We are likely to find that some types of rituals are more resonant than others, and such data might assist us in sharpening our own ritual-making tools and sensibilities. Such work may in turn interact with the first problem, the lack of a ritual sense, insofar as the very experience of being affected by ritual may in itself re-open the ritual sense of those thus exposed.

My tentative conclusion would be that we have reason for believing, first, that rituals of transition do have potentially transformative effects and, second, that there remains significant work to be done in achieving efficacious rituals of transition, not least because our cynicism about such work has undercut our attention to developing the necessary knowledge and sensibilities. One need only, for example, look at the disproportionate number of people working in the field of transitional justice trained in the highly analytic disciplines of law and even political science, as distinct from those trained in, say, theatre or performance studies or the arts. Were we to take seriously the prospect of powerful ritual efficacy, we would need to turn our attention to those disciplines and practices for whom the power of the performative is not a claim that requires extensive argumentation but is itself a taken-for-granted practice.

References

Asad, T. 1993. *Genealogies of Religion: Discipline and Reasons of Power in Christianity and Islam*. Baltimore: Johns Hopkins University Press.

Australia, House of Representatives. 1999. *Parliamentary Debates*, 26 August, pp. 9206-9207 (The Hon. John Howard MP).

Bell, C. 1992. *Ritual Theory, Ritual Practice*. New York and Oxford: Oxford University Press.

Bordieu, P. 2002. *An Outline of a Theory of Practice*. Trans. R. Nice. Cambridge: Cambridge University Press.

Douglas, M. 1966. *Purity and Danger*. Harmondsworth: Penguin.

Durkheim, E. 1982. *The Rules of Sociological Method*. Trans. W.D. Halls. New York: Free Press.

Elias, N. 1987. *What is Sociology?* Trans. Stephen Mennell and Grace Morrissey. New York: Columbia University Press.

Feinberg, J. 1965. The Expressive Function of Punishment. *The Monist*, 49, 397-423.

Feinberg, J. 1970. *Doing and Deserving: Essays in the Theory of Responsibility*. Princeton: Princeton University Press.

Heschel, H. 1955. *God in Search of Man*. New York: Farrar, Strauss and Giroux.

International Criminal Court. 2006. Child Soldier Charges in the First International Criminal Court Case. Press release, ICC-OTP-20060828-157.

Jaspers, K. 1961. *The Question of German Guilt*. Trans. E.B. Ashton. New York: Capricorn.

Levinas, E. 1994. *Nine Talmudic Readings*. Ed. and trans. Annette Aronowicz. Bloomington and Indianapolis: Indiana University Press.

Lukes, S. 1975. Political Ritual and Social Integration. *Sociology*, 9, 289-308.

Maimonides. 1927. *Mishnah Torah*. Trans. Simon Glazer. New York: Maimonides.

May, M. 1996. *Sharing Responsibility*. Chicago: University of Chicago Press.

Mead, G.H. 1934. *Mind, Self and Society: From the Standpoint of a Social Behaviorist*. Ed. Charles W. Morris. Chicago: University of Chicago Press.

Miller, D. 2004. Holding Nations Responsible. *Ethics*, 114(2), 240-268.

Minow, M. 1998. *Between Vengeance and Forgiveness; Facing History after Genocide and Mass Violence*. Boston: Beacon Press.

Moore, S. and Meyerhoff, B. eds. 1977. *Secular Ritual*. Assen and Amsterdam: Van Gorcum.

Nietzsche, F. 1968. *Twilight of the Idols*. Trans. R.J. Hollingdale. Harmondsworth: Penguin.

Ortner, S. 1984. Theory in Anthropology since the Sixties. *Comparative Studies in Society and History*, 26(1), 126-166.

Osiel, M. 1997. *Mass Atrocity, Collective Memory and the Law*. New Brunswick, NJ and London: Transaction.

Rappaport, R. 1979. *Ecology, Meaning and Religion*. Berkeley, CA: Northern Atlantic Books.

Sax, W. 2010. Introduction to *The Problem of Ritual Efficacy*. Ed. William Sax, Johannes Quack and Jan Weinhold. New York: Oxford University Press.

Seligman, A., Weller R., Puett, M. and Simon, B. 2008. *Ritual and Its Consequences: An Essay on the Limits of Sincerity*. New York: Oxford University Press.

Tambiah, S. 1979. A Performative Approach to Ritual. *Proceedings of the British Academy*, 65, 113-169.

Teitel, R. 2000. *Transitional Justice*. New York: Oxford University Press.

Trouillot, M. 2000. Abortive Rituals: Historical Apologies in the Global Era. *Interventions*, 2(2), 171-186.

Turner, V. 1969. *The Ritual Process: Structure and Anti-Structure*. London: Routledge and Kegan Paul.

Young, I. 2004. Responsibility and Global Labor Justice. *Journal of Political Philosophy*, 12(4), 365-388.

PART III
Contradictory Perceptions of Conflict and Justice

Chapter 8
Communicating the ICC: Imagery and Image-Building in Uganda

Chrisje Brants, Kees Brants and Lauren Gould

The adoption of the Rome Statute in 1998 and subsequent establishment of the International Criminal Court (ICC) in 2002 form the apotheosis (for the time being) of the 'new paradigm of the rule of law' that is international criminal justice (Teitel 2002: 355). In the euphoric discourse of international politicians and the legal establishment, its aims have proliferated beyond ending the impunity of perpetrators of mass atrocity to which the Preamble to the Statute refers.[1] They are now said to include reconciliation, conflict resolution, rehabilitation, deterrence and retribution, promoting democracy and providing victims satisfaction (Brants 2011). The domestication of violence by law through the establishment of a just peace (Hazan 2010) reflects just how idealistic but also political is this unique venture in cosmopolitan liberalism and human rights (Roach 2009; Teitel 2002).

From the start, critical voices were raised against overblown promises (Turner 2005: 1) and expectations flowing from a surfeit of aims 'as ambitious as they are contradictory' (Alvarez 2004: 321). An international criminal trial, it is said, cannot bring satisfaction to victims, reduces and demeans their experience of atrocity, provides neither proportional punishment nor just retribution, overrides traditional means of conflict resolution and is therefore unlikely to do much for reconciliation (for example Drumbl 2005). Others question whether this focus on victims is reconcilable with the requirements of a fair trial (Haslam 2004). And promoting democracy is an idea with so many political ramifications that Alvarez (2004: 322) warns of the point at which international trials become the tools of power politics.

The politics of international criminal justice led to some of the most powerful players on the international stage withholding or withdrawing their support for the ICC. In 2002, Israel and the USA announced they had no intention of becoming a party to the treaty and accordingly had no legal obligations arising from its signature. The American position is fuelled to a large degree by self-interest. Like Israel, which signed with an explicit rejection of 'any attempt to interpret provisions ... in a politically motivated manner against Israel and its citizens',[2] Americans fear that the ICC could be used as a political tool against the

1 www.icc-cpi.int/Menus/ICC/Legal+Texts+and+Tools (accessed 4 December 2011).

2 http://treaties.un.org/Pages/ViewDetails.aspx?src=INDandmtdsg_no=XVIII-10andchapter=18andlang=en#10 (accessed 4 December 2011).

USA. More thoughtful critiques question the democratic deficit of the Court and in particular the powerful position of the Prosecutor (see Morris 2001).

Academic criticism, political doubts, the very public démarche of the United States and subsequent attempts by that country to undermine the Court among other states left the ICC with something of a credibility problem, which exacerbates a more fundamental issue. The core identity of the ICC rests per definition on the global moral disapprobation of the crimes under its jurisdiction, and on its ability to make good the delivery of universal justice. In the abstract, few, if any, would challenge the legitimacy that derives from this. But at the same time, that identity is normatively constructed and, unlike that of national criminal justice systems, is not embedded in traditional constitutional structures and legal culture. Moreover, the circumstances in which an intervention is regarded as necessary to achieve what the international community defines as 'universal justice' need not correspond to the perceived social reality in the conflict-ridden community where the intervention takes place: acceptance of the ICC's legitimacy in the societies where it is expected to intervene is not a given.

In the dirty, confused business of armed conflict, atrocities are rarely committed by one side only and perceptions of what constitutes a crime, and who are defined as perpetrators and who as victims, are far from straightforward. Likewise, definitions of what constitutes the 'just' reaction, 'fairness' and 'victim satisfaction' that international justice promises may be contested. Like all crime and criminal justice, core international crimes and international criminal justice are social constructions. That is not to deny that mass atrocities occur, nor is it to negate the suffering of those involved. It is merely to point out that the concretization of the aims of international criminal justice is part of a socially constructed, contested reality of contradictory images, definitions and expectations. The acceptance of ICC interventions as legitimate thus begins with the ability to successfully communicate its core identity to relevant audiences and to counter any contestation.

In this chapter, we propose to unravel such communication and counter-communication in the specific case of Uganda, the first to be considered by the ICC. Seeing this ICC case as a social construction is to regard it as the outcome of a process of implicit and unwitting negotiation between different actors and groups, each with their own perceptions, expectations, authority, discursive tools and positions of power, and with different agendas, frames and priorities. Together, in collaboration and/or opposition, they create the Ugandan realities of international criminal justice.

The ICC as corporate communicator

Getting the 'normative' and 'lived' realities of international criminal justice to correspond as much as possible is a prerequisite to establishing legitimacy and requires the ICC to convince different audiences with different interests of the integrity of its aims and the quality, necessity and usefulness of the justice it dispenses. In that sense, the ICC is a corporate entity with an immaterial product to 'sell' and, like all corporate entities, it engages in corporate communication in which image-building plays an important part. The ICC, however, is not just any corporate entity and it does not sell toothpaste. It is one of the most important organs of international law, its communication framed by its core identity of dispenser of global justice and maintainer of the international rule of law, which gives its communications status by definition and creates high expectations. At the same time, its messages are, a priori, governed by principles such as independence, impartiality and fairness, and are determined specifically by the Rome Statute and corresponding rules and regulations. The ICC's core – corporate – identity therefore provides a powerful yet restricted framework for communicating what may be expected of it.

The Court's jurisdiction is limited to war crimes, crimes against humanity and genocide, committed after the Rome Statute entered into force, that is, after 1 July 2002, and is focused on political and military leaders who bear the greatest responsibility. As the Preamble to the Statute emphasizes, these core international crimes are the concern of all of humanity, so the community of states as such is entitled, indeed required to prosecute the perpetrators (Schabas 2001: 22). However, deciding what, who and how to prosecute is a typical prerogative of sovereign states. For that reason, the principle of complementarity in the Rome Statute allows the Prosecutor to investigate, and the ICC to declare admissible, only those cases that the state concerned is unwilling or unable to prosecute fairly and impartially.

The Rome Statute gives the Prosecutor much pre-trial power. Although he or she can neither issue arrest warrants nor decide definitively that a suspect should come to trial (these being powers of the Court's Pre-trial chamber), only the Prosecutor can decide to start an investigation. This may occur *proprio motu* if the Security Council asks that a situation be investigated (or that investigation be deferred) or after a situation has been referred by a State Party (referral by State – or even Security Council – is not binding). The Prosecutor (giving serious consideration to victims' interests) conducts the preliminary investigation and decides whether to apply for an arrest warrant and against whom. However, the Statute provides no enforcement mechanism: the Prosecutor is dependent on the cooperation of States Parties in arresting those against whom an ICC warrant has been issued.

Communication activities at the ICC are complicated, not least because the Office of the Prosecutor (OTP) is independent of the Court and has its own communications department – the Public Information Unit of the Office of the Prosecutor (PIU). The ICC's Outreach programme is part of the Registry's Public Information and Documentation Section (PIDS), which also coordinates court-wide public information, including 'where appropriate' OTP messages (ICC 2010: 4). Both the OTP and the Court include victims in their communications but there is also a Victims Participation and Reparation Section with 'wide discretion to use all possible means to give adequate publicity to the proceedings before the Court'.[3] All of these organs, sections and units are bound to disseminate the same core values of global justice, but each may well have a slightly different take given their different focus, which could somewhat muddy the communicative waters. In any event, before the Court has any official role, it is the Prosecutor who communicates to the affected communities and the outside world what steps he or she has taken, plans to take and why.

Bearing the above in mind, we shall deconstruct the preferred or ideal image – corporate identity – the ICC communicates to different audiences – and the images or perceptions that different audiences have of that identity. Successful corporate communication requires, ideally, that the two coincide, but in practice this is rarely the case, if only because all communication involves misunderstanding and distortion – 'noise' – that may come from internal factors (for example the audience's pre-conceptions or inability to access what is being communicated) or may be caused (intentionally or unintentionally) by external factors such as the communication of competing imagery (Van Riel 1995). Communication strategies aim at bolstering corporate identity by removing discrepancies with audience image(s) and countering competing imagery. One of the most important of such strategies is framing: 'select[ing] some aspects of a perceived reality and mak[ing] them more salient in a communicating text, in such a way as to promote a particular problem definition, causal interpretation, moral evaluation, and/or treatment recommendation' (Entman 1993: 52).

The resulting message can be communicated (or, more persuasively, 'spinned') in several ways and its content may differ, depending on the intended audience. Actors may address the audience directly (reports, meetings, websites). They may communicate through the traditional mass media (press, radio, television, film) in press releases and at press conferences, and/or by answering a journalist's questions, giving interviews or allowing representatives of the media access to their activities. The now mediated message may not be framed exactly as the communicator intended. While media may use or reinforce the original frame, they are not simply a hatch through which information passes for consumption by audiences. In their production of news, journalists select, emphasize, interpret and define, and thus engage in framing. Audiences have their own interpretative frame(s) built on personal experience and shared memories, within which people 'translate' what is communicated to them.

We intend to use these insights from (corporate) communication theory to examine what image-building strategies were employed in Uganda and by whom, what role the inherent legally principled nature of the ICC's core identity played and whether the resulting strategies could compete with interpretations and imagery of local and other actors. But first we must make clear both what triggered

3 www.icc-cpi.int/Menus/ICC/Structure+of+the+Court/Victims/Participation (accessed 5 January 2012).

ICC intervention in Uganda and which methods we used to address the subsequent mêlée of conflicting interpretations.

Researching Uganda

In 1986, a military coup brought the Southern Ugandan Yoweri Museveni the presidency, marking a shift in military power from north to south, alienating and traumatizing the northern Ugandan Acholi people and leading to the emergence of several rebel groups, the last remaining of which is the Lord's Resistance Army (LRA). According to its leader Joseph Kony, it fights to regain political autonomy and to retain the culture and tradition of the Acholi (Finnström 2010). It is generally agreed that the LRA has been involved in mass atrocities and in the abduction and forced recruitment of its own people, including children, as soldiers and sex-slaves. The Ugandan government forces (UPDF) have also been accused of committing grave atrocities against the population, particularly before 2002. As a result of the government's anti-insurgency policy, from 1996 onwards an estimated 90 per cent of the population in Acholi-land, many abused by either the LRA or the UPDF, were displaced to internally displaced person (IDP) camps with severe shortages of food and abysmal sanitary facilities, health care and security (Human Rights Watch 2005).

On 14 June 2002, Uganda became a State Party to the Rome Statute. In December 2003, President Museveni surprised many observers by referring 'the situation of the LRA' to the ICC, following encouragement by the Prosecutor, Luis Moreno Ocampo, who announced the opening of the investigation on 8 July 2004 during a joint press conference with Museveni in London. The requested arrest warrants were issued against five senior LRA commanders in October 2005 (including Joseph Kony; two of the others are now presumed dead) in connection with war crimes and crimes against humanity. As the ICC's temporal jurisdiction stretches back no further than 2002, the majority of atrocities committed since 1986 cannot be taken into account so the Prosecutor feels he has no case against the government military. To date, no state agents have been indicted because, since 2002, 'crimes committed by the LRA were much more numerous and of much higher gravity' than those of state forces (Office of the Prosecutor 2005: 2-3). Nor have any LRA leaders been arrested.

Uganda's self-referral seemed to present the Prosecutor a straightforward, uncontested first case on a plate:

> From the beginning it was the idea to start with the right case. The fear in those days was to start with the frivolous cases. What I did was to choose the worst crimes and started inviting and welcoming referrals from the territorial states. I knew I had to show, I had to run, I had to show some outcomes, some results. (Luis Moreno Ocampo in *The Reckoning* 2008)

Indeed, in depicting the LRA as particularly brutal, the Prosecutor was effortlessly in line with the dominant international understanding of the conflict that sees Joseph Kony as an evil maniac and LRA violence as bizarre and irrational. For the Ugandan government, the referral engaged the international community and held it to its promise of global justice (Akhavan 2005: 404). But the President and Ministry of Defence also saw it as a way of breaking the military stalemate of the civil war and enlisting international help in arresting the rebels. 'The ICC's legal and the Ministry's military approaches thus shared the avowed aim of catching the LRA, the former with a view to legal proceedings, the latter in order to defeat the enemy' (Nouwen and Werner 2010: 949).

From the beginning then, the case of Uganda was at least ambiguous and it is only to be expected that communications by different actors reflect such ambiguity. To deconstruct the communication process and evolving narratives and frames, we analysed ICC annual reports, official documents and press releases and interviewed representatives of the Outreach offices in The Hague and Kampala. We also spoke to representatives of the (Ugandan) Coalition for the ICC and other NGOs.[4] To discover the imagery prevalent in the affected communities in Uganda, we held in-depth interviews and focus group discussions in northern Uganda (in 2007, 2009 and 2011) with both ordinary members of the public and local elites, were participant observers in outreach activities, analysed official overviews of frequently asked questions at Outreach meetings in Uganda and held interviews with political and social elites. This was supplemented with a secondary analysis of existing community surveys. Finally, we interviewed journalists in Uganda and journalists covering the Court in The Hague about their perception of the role and performance of the ICC. We also analysed the coverage, frames and narratives in two newspapers in Uganda, and compared this with reports in two western newspapers.

Communications and negotiations

The first communications that framed the ICC in relation to the conflict took place when the intervention was just beginning, and were therefore a matter for the Public Information Unit (PIU) of the Prosecutor's Office (OTP), usually not in direct communication with the affected communities but through press conferences and press releases aimed at a wider, more global audience – making the Prosecutor the most visible ICC representative. Yet, in Uganda itself, a 'low profile' was a deliberate OTP strategy to avoid compromising 'confidential and sensitive investigations' and 'witness protection' (Human Rights Watch 2008: 101). This limited any direct communication with the war-affected communities until the

4 We were unable to obtain cooperation from the public information unit of the OTP although we were in contact with them throughout 2011. They finally agreed to answer a number of questions by email, but as of June 2012 have not done so.

Court set up a field office in Kampala in 2005 and later the Public Information and Documentation Section (PIDS) of the Registry started local outreach sessions in northern Uganda. Outreach has also included 'consultative discussions' with local media and support for radio programmes across the northern region to produce documentaries involving 'opinion shapers', prominent members of the (international) community and intellectuals.

Selling the ICC

Although the PIU elected not to inform the Ugandan people directly about the Prosecutor's selection strategy, the OTP's position on who should be investigated and held responsible for the crimes was clearly communicated in other ways. Not only did the Prosecutor encourage Uganda's 'self-referral' and announce it during a joint press conference where he demonstratively shook hands with President Museveni, ICC prosecution investigators were guided by government military in Acholi-land and Ugandan government officials were received and entertained in The Hague (Otim and Wierda 2010). As Nouwen and Werner show persuasively (2011: 951-954), the idea that the Prosecutor was on the government side was enduring and reinforced by his apparently taking over the Ugandan government's discourse, portraying it as a friend of the Court and the LRA as the enemy of the human race. The referral had already named the LRA as the main issue (although after criticism by NGOs this was changed to 'the situation in northern Uganda') and several times the Prosecutor himself has seemed to imply that there is evidence against the LRA only. In any event, he has been explicit in depicting Kony and the LRA as the major obstacle to peace, and successful ICC intervention as the means of attaining it: 'If you arrest Kony, peace and justice will be achieved in one day' (Moreno Ocampo in *The Reckoning* 2008).

But it soon became apparent that, contrary to popular belief, the Prosecutor could make no arrests. The warrants did have the effect of forcing the LRA over the border into Sudan and bringing them to the negotiating table. But they proved a double-edged sword, allowing Kony to use them (or rather their lifting) as a bargaining chip and, when that failed, to portray the ICC as the main obstacle to peace – painfully illustrated in *The Reckoning*, where an LRA contingent is seen to enter an Acholi village with impunity and insist to the gathering of villagers that not they but the 'coalition' of government and ICC is keeping the conflict alive. Kony also managed to bargain for peace in exchange for Ugandan rather than international justice, and 2008 saw the establishment of the International Crimes Division of Uganda's High Court (also known as the War Crimes Division or War Court), thereby raising the question of the role of the ICC in Uganda now, given the principle of complementarity. The OTP is adamant that the War Court will not prevent the Prosecutor going ahead, whatever Kony and the government may have agreed (Nouwen and Werner 2011: 954).

Nevertheless, the image of close ties between the ICC and the Ugandan government and army has not been successfully erased and, to this date, one of the most frequently asked questions during Outreach sessions remains the lack of state accountability. This is at odds both with the core identity of the ICC and with what the OTP actively aims to disseminate. It is also at odds with what the Prosecutor himself has said in numerous press releases, speeches and interviews: he represents truth, law and justice, without preference, and his aim is to end the impunity of international criminals wherever he finds them.

Aware of problems the international tribunals for the former Yugoslavia and Rwanda had faced in establishing understanding and legitimacy among local populations, the Court's outreach programme in Uganda (established in 2006) originally aimed to explain what the ICC can and cannot do, 'fostering realistic expectations about the Court's work', as the head of Outreach Kampala put it, preventing 'myths' and 'misconceptions' from taking root in popular consciousness and undermining the larger goals of an accountability mechanism. Its outreach policy is twofold: to reach as many people as possible through local NGOs, elites and communities, and to inform and provide material to the media.

The 'low profile' role of the Prosecutor, lack of resources, the perceived security situation and the negative discourse that had already developed at the grassroots level rather put Outreach on the back foot at first. Their activities consisted primarily of conducting seminars with local NGOs, journalists, members of parliament and the judiciary in the hope that they would disseminate the information provided to the affected communities. When this did not appear to be happening, the level of outreach steadily increased towards the end of the peace talks in 2008 and was broadened to other stakeholders in Uganda – from specific groups like market women and small-scale farmers, traditional leaders, internally displaced people and local councils, to legal professionals, police, academics and students – through the organization of workshops, panel discussions, roundtables, community information sessions and plays – both in the northern regions and in Kampala. In addition, a number of lawyers were trained and given their own local radio programmes about the ICC in five northern districts during which people could call in with questions. These activities are all similar in structure and content: audiences receive legal information about the court, its origin, mandate, the indictments, the need for state cooperation in enforcing arrest warrants and victim participation. Frequently asked questions such as 'what evidence is there that arresting the top five commanders will end the war?' receive a standardized response: 'Having analysed the situation in northern Uganda, the Prosecutor believes that the arrest of the top five commanders of the LRA is a vital component to a meaningful peace.'

Of the 61 ICC press releases on Uganda, the majority are from the Public Information and Documentation Section (PIDS) of the Registry. They are mostly informational and educational, reporting (intensified) Outreach activities and successes in changing grassroot perceptions. In 2010, the question 'why is the ICC targeting only Africans for prosecution' is mentioned for the first time. Several press releases contain rebuttals by prominent Africans such as former UN Secretary-General Kofi Annan: 'when he meets Africans from all walks of life they demand justice: from their own courts if possible, from international courts if no credible alternative exists' and 'as an African, he is proud of the continent's contribution to the ICC'.[5]

In short, the Court's outreach strategy is reactive and cognitive, evolving to include a more persuasive and attitudinal aim of intensifying ICC engagement with grassroots communities in order to raise awareness of justice and accountability, and enhance continuous support of ICC activities. Following Entman's operationalization of a frame, both the OTP's and Outreach's problem definition is the need to bring impunity to an end, the LRA to justice and peace to northern Uganda. The causal interpretation focuses on the LRA as the perpetrator of the greatest evil and disruptor of the peace talks. The underscoring moral evaluation is one of outrage over the atrocities, and international criminal justice as the best answer to impunity. The treatment recommendation is that, while local justice initiatives are to be respected, the ICC is the organization best equipped to bring justice and peace. The result can be summed up as a peace-through-justice frame. Although it is the same as that of Outreach, the Prosecutor's message personalizes the core identity of the ICC in Luis Moreno Ocampo himself. He is justice personified and gives no quarter: 'I apply the law without political considerations' (quoted in Nouwen and Werner 2010: 942). But both OTP and Outreach officers struggle to convince journalists and community leaders in Uganda of that core identity, given the compelling, competing image that the Prosecutor also helped to establish at the beginning, placing the issue of ICC impartiality firmly on the agenda.

This issue is also reflected in collaboration between the ICC and the Ugandan Coalition for the International Criminal Court (UCICC). As a coalition of 265 NGOs that seek to provide information about the Court, the UCICC generally embraces and disseminates the peace-through-justice frame and supports the ICC intervention. However, increasingly there are tensions in its relationship with the Prosecutor and the Court and not only because of the Prosecutor's press conference with Museveni (often described as a dramatic 'PR disaster'). The head of the UCICC explained the following when discussing 'selective prosecution' in Uganda:

> Sometimes the Prosecutor gets so mad and he says: are you people working with us? We say no, we give you positive criticism … You came to Uganda, carried out investigations, there has been information compiled with good pieces of evidence, so you should start on atrocities committed by the UPDF. And he gets so mad and he gets so annoyed.[6]

5 31 May 2010. Available at http://www.icc\cpi.int/menus/icc/press%20and%20media/press%20releases/press%20releases%20%282010%29/review%20conference%20of%20the%20rome%20statute%20opened%20in%20kampala (accessed 5 October 2012.

6 Interview with Joyce Apio, Kampala, Uganda, 27 October 2011.

Another UCICC concern is the scaling down of Outreach operations in Uganda and the assumption that local partners will take over. Outreach Uganda originally had five and later three staff officers. Because of the world economic crisis and lack of judicial developments, they were reduced to one in 2012 and the focus in East Africa shifted to Kenya after the Prosecutor opened investigations there in 2010. But while the ICC counts on the UCICC to continue to disseminate its message, the head of UCICC fears that staff cuts will trigger a backlash ('the Court is abandoning us') and have a negative impact on the progress made since 2007 and, in the end, on the legitimacy of the ICC.

Reporting the ICC

As we have seen, ICC Outreach officers actively inform, train and carefully direct the media to get their message and desired image across and to counter misconceptions, while both the OTP and the Court regularly provide journalists with press releases. This begs the question whether the images and frames of the ICC are reflected in the attitude of journalists and in media content, both in Uganda and elsewhere.

Media can be neutral informers, critical watchdogs, platform providers, opinion leaders or advocates, and sometimes a mixture of all these. But to perform any of these roles, journalists must be knowledgeable, or at least think they are. The aims and expectations of Outreach efforts notwithstanding, the Ugandan reporters we spoke to do not think they know very much. Unlike the western journalists, who are international criminal justice experts, they admit finding it difficult to report on transitional justice processes. That in itself is problematic, because the Ugandan journalists see themselves first and foremost as neutral informers, educators of an affected but not necessarily well-informed citizenry. They say they lack the expertise to be critical watchdogs, even if they wanted to be.

All of our interviewees agree on what one described as a 'growing fatigue and frustration' about the lack of arrests and judicial developments. 'The war has kind of fizzled out', a journalist of Kampala-based *New Vision* put it. And almost with a sense of relief he and his colleagues point to the War Court and its first case. It has definite news value and has put the war back on the media agenda. At the same time, the complexity of the relationship between the War Court and the ICC puzzles them and makes factual reporting difficult.

The western journalists say they mix factual knowledge with what they call a realistic assessment of what the ICC can do. They are also (to a greater or lesser extent) critical of the high-profile role of the Prosecutor. Ugandan journalists make no distinction between Court, Prosecutor or Outreach. All say that in the beginning they had more knowledge of and interest in the ICC and what it is doing in their country, and sympathized with the claim of ending impunity and creating peace through justice. However, the interviews reveal a gap opening up between sympathy for the ICC and belief in its ability to deliver the goods. The question is how this ambivalent attitude is reflected in the media's content.

In total, the four newspapers we analysed carried 255 items on the ICC and Uganda: 113 in the northern Ugandan *Daily Monitor* (between 2007 and 2012), 69 in the pro-government *New Vision* (due to limited online accessibility only in 2010 and 2011), 48 in the *New York Times* (between 2004 and 2012) and 25 in the Netherlands *de Volkskrant* (between 2005 and 2012). Unsurprisingly, the Ugandan papers published more about the ICC in their country than did the western media. In all four newspapers, around half of the items analysed consisted of factual and neutral news reports, a common feature in journalism. This neutral news revealed no problem definition or moral evaluation. The other half consisted of opinion pieces and editorials (a priori not neutral), and background articles and news reports with 'loaded content'. It is here that we find framing, and the following relates to that 50 per cent only.

With the exception of the *New York Times*, the imagery these items reflect has a positive connotation in only one-third of the reports: 43 per cent are negative, in 9 per cent positive and negative images are mixed and in 15 per cent news criticizing the ICC is followed by a rebuttal, a denial of the negative claim that provided the original frame of the news item. From 2007, especially in the *Daily Monitor* and *New Vision*, there is an increasing amount of news about official rebuttals of claims by local leaders and others concerning the assumed political nature of the ICC, its pro-Museveni approach, its bias in prosecuting Africans and its hindrance to peace by not dropping the arrest warrants.

In its 'loaded reports', the Ugandan pro-government *New Vision* is surprisingly more negative (44 per cent) than the *Daily Monitor* (39 per cent), although the negative slant is probably due to the fact that professional journalistic selection criteria of deviance and conflict tends to lend news items a negative starting point. The two western newspapers differ not only from the Ugandan dailies in the amount of ICC news, but also from each other. The most negative (62 per cent) is the newspaper that published the least: *De Volkskrant* mainly carried background articles from one or two correspondents and foreign news editors, who focused predominantly on the lack of achievements of the ICC, and on who and what is to blame. The *New York Times* was the least negative (28 per cent). However, it should be noted that almost half of its items were opinion articles (42 per cent) written predominantly not by journalists but by opinion leaders such as Prosecutor Moreno Ocampo, Kofi Annan and a whole range of NGO representatives. Given the predominance of positive opinion pieces, the *New York Times* could be said to present a platform for support and debate about the ICC.

The resulting frame in the four media is mixed. They more or less agree that the problem is lack of peace in victimized northern Uganda and limited progress. But there is a difference in causal interpretation, not only between the different publications, but also within the newspapers themselves. At times, more or less everyone and everything seems to be at fault: Kony and the LRA; President Museveni and his political agenda; the ICC and its stubborn refusal to withdraw the arrest warrants; the Prosecutor promising more than he can deliver. The underlying moral evaluation is equally mixed: on the one hand, professional neutrality stands in the way of empathy, but on the other, journalists seem angry and increasingly worried about what is seen as white man's justice, and find the lack of progress incomprehensible. In spite of the negativism about the ICC's role and functioning, the treatment recommendation sees the solution in ICC action, although this is often contradicted by the urgent suggestion that the Prosecutor drop his indictments. The confusing result can best be defined as a help-and-hindrance frame.

After our research period, in March 2012, the appearance on YouTube of *Kony 2012* – a film by the US charity Invisible Children that reflects the ICC's framing of the Ugandan situation – sparked an explosion of western media attention on the atrocities in Uganda, Kony, the LRA and the ICC. The media in the US and Europe showed considerably more interest in this YouTube video than in what had happened in Uganda in the nine years following President Museveni's referral to the ICC. The success of this propaganda film, which went viral, raises some intriguing questions: Did the OTP give Invisible Children permission to use footage of Moreno Ocampo talking about Uganda? Did it play an active part in defining how the conflict was framed in the film? Preliminary analysis of western media implies that the YouTube film has been more successful in establishing a positive ICC frame than the ICC itself. Is this image likely to remain or be contested? The propaganda film advocates 'stopping' Joseph Kony through an increase in international and regional military support for the Ugandan government. Its portrayal of conflict and solution has been met with fierce criticism among northern Ugandans. How will this affect the legitimacy of the ICC there?

Living the ICC

Given the efforts of the ICC's Outreach, the tens of thousands they claim to reach and their use of opinion leaders, local partners and media to inform local populations, it is important to ask whether, and how, this communication strategy has affected the key audiences. If an increase in familiarity with the court is the yardstick, then originally Outreach was successful. In 2005, before the programme was established, a survey by the University of Berkeley in northern Uganda showed that 73 per cent of respondents knew (next to) nothing about the ICC (Pham *et al.* 2005: 36). By 2007, up to 70 per cent had heard of it (Pham *et al.* 2007) and during our interviews in 2009, the majority of people had a basic knowledge of the ICC. By 2011, know-how and interest seemed to be declining and only very few of our respondents had been in contact with the Outreach team (this is reaffirmed by Pham *et al.* 2010; of those who had heard of the ICC only 3 per cent had participated in a meeting that discussed the Court).

These findings hardly imply a positive effect of the Court's outreach strategy. Yet, its impact cannot simply be measured by the number of meetings and people informed, without examining what was said and how it was received. Although Outreach activities have increasingly allowed for dialogue in the form of Q&As, local activists complain that ICC speakers were more interested in their own agendas than in the concerns of the audience. Our respondents also complained that the content was too legal and inaccessible and that tough questions met only standardized answers. At the same time, whatever happens through Outreach, the Prosecutor's selection strategy seems to have had the earliest and most visible impact on how the reality of the ICC intervention is defined on the ground.

The Prosecutor's support for self-referral and public appearances with President Museveni, combined with a lack of outreach, provided space and legitimacy for ICC opponents to create an image of the court as biased and a form of victor's justice. Importantly, the majority of our respondents are not, per definition, against international criminal law and support the ICC focus on 'those most responsible', which corresponds with their perception that the top LRA commanders (not the abducted lower-rank combatants) should be held accountable. But the Prosecutor's single focus on the LRA is regarded by many Acholi as a virtual denial of government violence, which affronts and misinterprets reality (in the 2010 Pham *et al.* survey more than two-thirds of the respondents in the four northern provinces said that the government should also be held accountable). A former LRA combatant, now counsellor, told us:

> It is because of the approach of the ICC that led to the negative opinion of the ICC being formed so strongly. The first time they came people were exited that somebody will whip for us those people who did wrong to us. They are going to whip the LRA and they are also going to whip the government. But on understanding that they cannot whip the government, that is where the problems started coming and why the people were fed up with the ICC straight away.

This negative image was exacerbated during the peace talks (2006-2008), when local stakeholders, including political elites, civil society actors and traditional and religious leaders increasingly argued against the ICC indictments. Not only was the UPDF seen as a major perpetrator, many regarded the ICC intervention as an obstacle to peace (asking the rebels to come to the negotiating table while risking arrest was seen as making the war more difficult to resolve) and argued against the 'one-sided, western style' retributive justice approach that is far removed from Acholi customary law. Civil society and traditional and religious leaders promoted the traditional restorative justice instrument 'Mato Oput' as a preferred alternative to the ICC. This discourse increased the internationally recognized power of the elite Acholi at the negotiation table and political support for their position among their people (Allen 2010). Their language rang true to Acholi reality: peace talks, an end to the rebellion and consideration for the affected communities' desire to return home and rebuild their lives.

After 2008, without the political arena of the peace talks, ICC outreach met with less opposition or counter arguments and, by 2009, a majority of our respondents were in favour of an international trial of top LRA leaders. This, however, seemed to be based on a misconception about the mandate of the ICC. The majority of the respondents believed that the ICC itself could arrest the LRA leaders and bring the conflict to an official end, something the peace talks had been unable to do.

By 2011, our respondents seem disillusioned about the effectiveness of the Court; not only was it seen as obstructing peace, three years after the peace talks failed the LRA top commanders were still at large and no judicial developments had taken place – all of which had seemingly further legitimized government-led military campaigns in the name of enforcing international law. Knowledgeable respondents continued to assert that the 2002 limit was arbitrary and left the bulk of atrocities by both sides beyond justice. This seems to imply that the Outreach response (the law does not permit otherwise and of the violence that falls under the ICC's jurisdiction the most serious has been perpetrated by the LRA) had not had – or at least consolidated – the desired cognitive effect. In light of no final peace accord (although the security situation had improved immensely in northern Uganda) and no justice, and given the ICC's limited temporal jurisdiction and lack of powers to execute arrest warrants, many in the community at large still questioned whether the Court was an appropriate means of achieving justice.

This frustration with the Court and its declining relevance in people's day-to-day lives has been further complicated by the establishment of the War Court. The first trial ended with the accused (Kwoyelo), who was not indicted by the ICC, being granted amnesty.[7] The trial highlights the dilemma of victims being perpetrators: Kwoyelo was a child soldier. The efficacy of the War Court can be questioned on the strength of its first case, but this does not mean that its existence and the confusion about its relationship to the ICC will not undermine the latter's legitimacy; as may the African Union's advice to its member states in 2010 to cease cooperation with the ICC. The latter issue had already appeared as a frequently asked question 'why is the Court only active in African countries; is this a new form of western imperialism?' and is increasingly present in people's narratives on the Court.

The problem definition to be distilled from this complex tangle of competing images has changed over the years and remains mixed. While some still believe in the ICC and its mission, a sizeable group questions this, even redefining the problem as a western model of justice that might result in losing the peace. The causal interpretation focuses on both the LRA and the Ugandan government as responsible for the atrocities, but also on the ICC as an obstacle to the solution. The moral evaluation, while always decrying the violence, does not look to the Rome Statute only, but includes a preference for alternatives over what is sometimes defined as 'white man's justice'. This is reflected in the treatment recommendation which includes national justice, traditional reconciliation rituals, amnesty and negotiation between the government and the LRA. In any event, where the greatest

7 On the basis of equality before the law, the Amnesty Law 2000 granted many LRA members amnesty but Kwoyelo had been refused without reason. The prosecution has appealed to the Supreme Court (International Justice Resource Center http://ihrlaw.org (accessed 7 January 2012)).

desire among the population is for enduring peace, the resulting frame can best be summed up as peace-first-justice-later-but-when-and-how?

Conclusions

While the image Ugandans hold of the role and performance of the Court has fluctuated with the political situation and differs according to geographical location, in the affected communities it is often the reverse of what the ICC wishes to communicate. Both the Court and the Prosecutor frame their message as peace-through-justice: problem and solution are the need to end impunity and to bring the Lord's Resistance Army to justice and thus peace to northern Uganda, with the ICC as the most appropriate form of justice. The affected communities, on the other hand, increasingly hold a peace-first-justice-later frame. They question the role of the ICC, and whether what is seen as western-style justice, with a high profile Prosecutor who seems on good terms with President Museveni and who promises a lot but delivers little, *can* achieve peace and justice. The picture emerging from the media is mixed and, interestingly, there is little difference between the Ugandan and western newspapers we analysed. Criticism of the Prosecutor and the lack of progress and references to 'white man's justice' go hand in hand with support for the ICC and adoption of its framing of the problem.

That the ICC has apparently not succeeded in synchronizing the image held by the population and the local elites in northern Uganda with the core identity that is the heart of the message it must communicate points to a failure in ICC communication strategy, but also to a more serious problem. From the start, the ICC intervention in Uganda was contested by social and political elites in the north. Some of their concerns – the ICC's lack of impartiality, ignoring government army atrocities and local traditions of justice – could be construed as misconceptions and lack of knowledge, but not only has the ICC's communication policy been mostly unsuccessful in countering them, concerns have grown and intensified. The image of effectiveness, efficiency and empathy the ICC was expecting to establish of itself by succeeding in an apparently clear-cut and unproblematic case has not materialized. As a consequence, the legitimacy of the ICC in Uganda was, and continues to be, contested. This has created something of a Catch 22 situation. If Outreach is scaled down or withdrawn – or the case even dropped following the establishment of the War Court – and, more importantly, as the Ugandan situation no longer takes priority given both scarcer funds and a proliferation of cases elsewhere, the ICC will be accused of failure. If its active and high profile role of bringing the LRA to justice is maintained but Kony *et al*. are not captured and brought to The Hague and sentenced, the ICC will also be seen as standing in the way of reconciliation and, ultimately, of peace itself. Either way, the Ugandan image of the ICC will be that of an unsuccessful, wavering and perhaps even unreliable organization.

This failure to successfully 'communicate' the ICC seems to derive from the specificity of the organization itself and that of the Ugandan case. It is difficult to avoid the conclusion that President Museveni used the ICC – and the Prosecutor – to establish legitimacy for himself in a political and military struggle against a rebel faction. Uganda may have seemed a clear-cut case at the time, and the Prosecutor's insistence that the gravity of crimes since 2002 justified using his resources against Kony only may carry some weight, but the self-referral of the Ugandan government served to underline the political nature of ICC operations and cast doubts on its impartiality and independence. The way the ICC is seen to operate is partly a consequence of both statutory prosecutorial powers and the performance of this Prosecutor in particular. Moreno Ocampo is energetic, charismatic and above all high profile. A Prosecutor with a strong personality, unafraid of tackling political situations and up to dealing with United Nations and local governments was a must for the ICC after its shaky start when many, egged on by the United States, doubted its legitimacy and efficacy. At the same time, where the Prosecutor promotes himself as the personification of international justice, this has been an invitation for criticism and ambivalence among NGO supporters and journalists.

The activities and communications of the OTP and Outreach have created expectations of retribution, reconciliation and peace for victims and displaced or otherwise affected communities (whose primary desire is, logically, an end to the situation in which they find themselves). These aims have been criticized in theory as contradictory. In the practice of Uganda, with the LRA able to promote a counter-image of the ICC as an obstacle to peace, the lack of any enforcement capability has rendered the ICC particularly impotent. Where trust and reliability are the cornerstones of legitimacy, not fulfilling expectations creates disappointment and distrust. That is exacerbated by an undermining discourse on the part of Ugandan elites, local and otherwise, and African states. Africa has many unstable states where gross violence is perpetrated against the population, but that holds for many other parts of the world too. Although six of the eight situations under preliminary consideration by the OTP do not concern African states, all of the seven situations brought before the ICC are in Africa. The fact that visible ICC activities are concentrated on the African continent feeds an image of the ICC as 'white man's justice', and that too has been absorbed into Ugandan discourse.

As many have emphasized, international criminal justice is an idealistic but above all international political undertaking and it is well-nigh impossible to escape the consequences. The ICC's communication strategy is based on the belief that any lack of legitimacy derives from a lack of information, which promotes misunderstandings and myths, and can be resolved through increasing factual knowledge. The images and narratives we found in Uganda are not myths or misunderstandings. Rather, they are the social construction of a lived reality that includes the ICC, but reflects its inherently political nature, while ideals figure only if they are realized. It may well be that communication of the ICC's core identity – the embodiment of the ideal – is impossible, precisely because it must always be in denial of the inevitable political image it presents in practice.

References

Akhavan, P. 2005. Developments at the International Criminal Court: The Lord's Resistance Army Case: Uganda's Submission of the First State Referral to the International Criminal Court. *American Journal of International Law*, 99, 403-421.

Allen, T. 2010. Bitter roots: the 'invention' of Acholi traditional justice. In *The Lord's Resistance Army: Myth and Reality*, edited by T. Allen and K. Vlassenroot, 74-89. London: Zed Books.

Alvarez, J. 2004. Trying Hussein: Between Hubris and Hegemony. *Journal of International Criminal Justice*, 2, 319-329.

Brants, C.H. 2011. Universal Crimes, Universal Justice? The Legitimacy of the International Response to Genocide, Crimes against Humanity and War Crimes. In *International and Comparative Criminal Justice and Urban Governance: Convergence and Divergence in Global, National and Local Settings*, edited by A. Crawford, 86-109. Cambridge: Cambridge University Press.

Drumbl, M. 2005. Collective Violence and Individual Punishment: The Criminality of Mass Atrocity. *Northwestern University Law Review*, 99, 539-610.

Entman, D. 1993. Framing: Towards Clarification of a Fractured Paradigm. *Journal of Communication*, 43(4), 51-59.

Finnström, S. 2010. An African Hell of Colonial Imagination? The Lord's Resistance Army in Uganda, Another Story. In *The Lord's Resistance Army: Myth and Reality*, edited by T. Allen and K. Vlassenroot, 74-89. London: Zed Books.

Haslam, E. 2004. Victim Participation at the International Criminal Court: A Triumph of Hope over Experience? In *The Permanent International Criminal Court: Legal and Policy Issues*, edited by D. MacGoldrick, P. Rowe and E. Donnelly, 315-334. Oxford: Hart.

Hazan, P. 2010. *Judging War, Judging History: Behind Truth and Reconciliation.* Stanford, CA: Stanford University Press.

Human Rights Watch. 2005. Uprooted and Forgotten – Impunity and Human Rights Abuses in Northern Uganda. *Human Rights Watch*, 20, 1-76. Available at http://www.hrw.org/en/reports/2005/09/19/uprooted-and-forgotten-0(accessed 5 October 2012).

Human Rights Watch. 2008. *Courting History: The Landmark International Criminal Court's First Years*. New York: Human Rights Watch. Available at http://www.hrw.org/sites/default/files/reports/icc0708webwcover.pdf (accessed 5 October 2012).

International Criminal Court. 2010. *Report of the Court on the Public Information Strategy 2011-2013*. ICC-ASP/9/29. The Hague: ICC. Available at http://www.icc-cpi.int/iccdocs/asp_docs/ASP9/ICC-ASP-9-29-ENG.pdf (accessed 5 October 2012).

Morris, M. ed. 2001. The United States and the International Criminal Court. *Law and Contemporary Problems*, 64. Special issue.

Nouwen, S. and Werner, W. 2010. Doing Justice to the Political: The International Criminal Court in Uganda and Sudan. *European Journal of International Law*, 21(4), 941-965.

Office of the Prosecutor. 2005. Statement by the Chief Prosecutor on the Uganda Arrest Warrants, The Hague, 14 October. Available at http://www.icc-cpi.int/NR/rdonlyres/AF169689-AFC9-41B9-8A3E222F07DA42AD/143834/LMO_20051014_English1.pdf (accessed 22 November 2011).

Otim, M. and Wierda, M. 2010. International Center for Transitional Justice. Briefing for the Rome Statute Review Conference, Kampala, Uganda: Impact of the Rome Statute and the International Criminal Court. Available at www.ictj.org/sites/default/files/ICTJ-Uganda-Impact-ICC-2010-English.pdf (accessed 5 October 2012).

Pham, P., Vinck, P., Wierda, M., Stover, E. and Di Giovanni, A. 2005. *Forgotten Voices: A Population-Based Survey of Attitudes about Peace and Justice in Northern Uganda*. International Center for Transitional Justice and the Human Rights Center, University of California, Berkeley.

Pham, P., Vinck, P, Stover, E., Moss, A. and Wierda M. 2007. *When the War Ends: A Population-Based Survey on Attitudes about Peace, Justice and Social Reconstruction in Northern Uganda*. Human Rights Center, University of California, Berkeley; Payson Center for International Development, Tulane University; International Center for Transitional Justice, New York.

Pham, P, Vinck, P. and Stover, E. 2010. *Transition to Peace: A Population-Based Survey on Attitudes about Social Reconstruction and Justice in Northern Uganda*. International Center for Transitional Justice and the Human Rights Center, University of California, Berkeley.

Roach, S. ed. 2009. *Governance, Order, and the International Criminal Court: Between Realpolitik and a Cosmopolitan Court*. Oxford: Oxford University Press.

Schabas, W. 2001. *An Introduction to the International Criminal Court*. Cambridge: Cambridge University Press.

Teitel, R. 2002. Humanity's Law: Rule of Law for the New Global Politics. *Cornell International Law Journal*, 35, 355-387.

Turner, J. 2005. Nationalizing International Criminal Law. *Stanford Journal of International Law*, 41, 1-15.

Van Riel, C. 1995. *Principles of Corporate Communication*. London: Prentice Hall.

Films

The Reckoning (dir. Pamela Yates, 2008).

Chapter 9

Child Soldiers: Towards a Rights-Based Imagery

Ton Liefaard[1]

Armed conflict has a devastating impact on societies and on the lives of individuals. Again and again, international and internal wars and conflicts disrupt entire communities and harm their members in scarcely imaginable ways. The most vulnerable members of society are hit the hardest. Children belong to this group. Various reports, particularly since the groundbreaking 1996 United Nations (UN) study by Graça Machel (1996), have pointed at the millions of children worldwide affected by armed conflict in one way or the other, directly or indirectly (see, for example, Coalition to Stop the Use of Child Soldiers 2008; Denov 2010; Drumbl 2012; Mels *et al.* 2012; Sarkin 2012; UNICEF 2005; Wessels 2006). It is assumed that there are hundreds of thousands of child soldiers in the world today (*Paris Principles*,[2] para. 1.0 (UNICEF 2007a); Mels *et al.* 2012). Although not a new phenomenon (see, for example, Denov 2010), the recruitment and conscription of child soldiers has received much attention in international discourse (Mezmur 2008; Nyland 2012), particularly after it was reported that children were also involved in heinous forms of warfare and even in war crimes.

This chapter concerns the imagery of child soldiers in international discourse. Child soldiers are portrayed in different ways. A classical distinction of images is that between child soldiers as 'victims' and child soldiers as 'perpetrators'. Drumbl distinguishes, with reference to transnational discourse, four alternative images of child soldiers: 'faultless passive victims', 'irreparable damaged goods', 'heroes' and 'demon and bandits' (2012: 6-8). Denov refers to portrayals by media

1 The author would like to thank the editors and all the other contributors to this volume, in particular Prof. Dr Sanja Kutnjak Ivković, for their valuable comments on an earlier draft of this paper. The author is also very grateful to Prof. Dr Wouter Vandenhole, one of the editors of *Re-Member* (Intersentia, 2012), and Prof. Dr Mark Drumbl, author of *Reimagining Child Soldiers* (Oxford University Press, 2012) for allowing him to consult proof copies of their books.

2 The Paris Principles and Guidelines on children associated with armed forces or armed groups were adopted by 58 states at the 2007 international conference 'Free children from war' in Paris, together with the Paris Commitments to protect children from unlawful recruitment or use by armed forces or armed groups. Both documents were built upon the 1997 Cape Town Principles and best practices on the recruitment of children into the armed forces and on demobilization and social reintegration of child soldiers in Africa.

and policy discourse: the child soldier as 'dangerous and disorderly', as 'hapless victim' or as 'redeemed hero' (2010: 6). She also points to the general absence of interest in girl soldiers 'whose invisibility defines them'. It is impossible to capture child soldiers in one or two snapshots. However, such portrayals are used to cast the extreme differences between children in armed conflict, while denying that in reality they may very well be different sides of the same coin: the complexity of the involvement of children in armed conflict. Denov observes that 'the one-sided, gendered and largely uni-dimensional depictions highlight our uncertainty and ambivalence in dealing with girl and boy soldiers' and – more importantly – that 'they offer no attempt at capturing or understanding what occurred to bring children into the fold of violence and armed conflict, and what may be needed to bring them out again' (2010: 14).

In light of this, it is remarkable that international discourse, *inter alia* manifested in international law and policy, primarily portrays child soldiers as vulnerable, passive and innocent victims who have been pulled, pushed or forced into armed forces or armed groups and subjected to all kinds of violence, abuse and exploitation by adults, who subsequently force them to participate in committing heinous crimes, including war crimes (Drumbl 2012; Hanson 2011).

This chapter analyses the focus on the child soldier as a vulnerable victim in need of protection and special assistance and its implications for the implementation of the human rights of child soldiers, in particular their right to recovery and social reintegration (Art. 39 UN Convention on the Rights of the Child (CRC) 1989).[3] It will be argued that the primary focus on child soldiers as victims in international discourse is understandable, but problematic and potentially contra productive at the same time, not only in light of the complex reality of armed conflict and local perceptions, but also in comparison to the image of the child under international human rights law in general. The ultimate aim is to define the key principles that should be taken into account in a rights-based imagery regarding child soldiers, which serves the best interests of both the children and their families and communities.

Terminology

Much can be said about the accuracy of the term 'child soldiers'. The active involvement of children in armed conflict has different forms and varies from a direct, active role in warfare to a more indirect, less prominent and less visible role (for example Coomaraswamy 2010; Wessels 2006). In light of this variety of activities it arguably is better to speak of 'children associated with an armed force or armed group' (*Paris Principles*, para 2.1 (UNICEF 2007a)), defined in the Paris Principles as 'any person below 18 years of age who is or who has been recruited or used by an armed force or armed group in any capacity, including but

3 UN General Assembly 1989.

not limited to children, boys, and girls used as fighters, cooks, porters, messengers, spies or for sexual purposes'. Nevertheless, I shall continue to use the term 'child soldiers'. More importantly, it is crucial to keep in mind that the wide variety of specific roles affects the way these children should be looked at.

According to paragraphs 2.2 and 2.3 of the Paris Principles, the term 'armed forces' has been defined as 'the military institution of a State with a legal basis, and supporting institutional infrastructure (salaries, benefits, basic services, etc.)' and 'armed groups' as 'groups distinct from armed forces as defined by Article 4 of the Optional Protocol to the Convention on the Rights of the Child on the involvement of children in armed conflict' (that is, non-state entities). I use the term armed forces. If not stated otherwise, this also covers armed groups.

Furthermore, where I refer to the child in the masculine form, this includes the position of girls unless explicitly stated otherwise.

Child soldiers in international law and discourse

The position of child soldiers has been recognized under international humanitarian law, international human rights law, international criminal law and also international labour law, where ILO Convention No. 182 considers forced or compulsory recruitment of children (that is, persons under the age of 18; Art. 2) one of the worst forms of child labour (Art. 3), which should be prohibited and eliminated (Art. 1).

International humanitarian law

The 1949 Geneva Conventions consider children as members of the civilian population requiring protection. Under the Geneva Convention relative to the Protection of Civilian Persons in Time of War (1949, entry into force 21 October 1950), children under the age of 15 are awarded special protection, including, for example, education, maintenance and medical aid (Art. 24). However, children are not considered as (potential) participants in armed conflicts and are therefore not awarded the special protection they need as child soldiers (Mezmur 2008: 200). The position of child soldiers is explicitly addressed in the two Additional Protocols (AP I resp. AP II) to the 1949 Geneva Conventions, drawn up to protect victims of international and non-international armed conflicts, respectively.[4] Children under the age of 15 must not take (direct) part in hostilities and must not be recruited into armed forces or groups (Art. 77 (2) AP I; Art. 4 (3) AP II). In addition, children

4 Protocol Additional to the Geneva Conventions of 12 August 1949, and relating to the Protection of Victims of International Armed Conflicts, 8 June 1977 (entry into force 7 December 1979) and Protocol Additional to the Geneva Conventions of 12 August 1949, and Relating to the Protection of Victims of Non-International Armed Conflicts, 8 June 1977 (entry into force 7 December 1978).

must be granted special protection including protection against indecent assault, care and aid, education and special treatment if arrested or detained. Children younger than 15 who do take part in hostilities and are captured must be awarded the same protection and additional protection if detained or interned (Art. 77 (1), (3)-(4) AP I; Arts 4 and 5 AP II).

In general, the provisions of international humanitarian law focus on prevention of recruitment and protection of child soldiers in the first place and less on aspects such as recovery and reintegration (Doek 2012: x).

International human rights law

The general human rights treaties of the UN, the International Covenant on Economic, Social and Cultural Rights (ICESCR) and the International Covenant on Civil and Political Rights (ICCPR) contain no special provisions regarding armed conflict, but the 1989 Convention on the Rights of the Child (CRC) does. It contains specific provisions regarding the recruitment of children as well as their protection, recovery and reintegration.

As far as recruitment is concerned, the CRC sets the same 15 years old standard as international humanitarian law (Art. 38 CRC), although there have been many efforts to raise it to 18 years of age (Doek 2012: x, with further reference to Detrick 1992, *inter alia*). In addition, Article 38 CRC provides that children are entitled to protection and care if affected by armed conflict, thereby strongly linking up with international humanitarian law (Doek 2012; Mezmur 2008: 201).

The drafters of the CRC did not choose the 'straight 18' position – an absolute prohibition of direct or indirect participation of children in hostilities, implying a prohibition of recruitment or conscription, forcibly or voluntarily, for all children under the age of 18 (cf. Art. 1 CRC). This met with criticism and there were concerns about the inadequacy of Article 38 CRC (Coomaraswamy 2010: 538; Hanson 2011: 41; Mezmur 2008: 203). This resulted in the drafting, and adoption in 2000, of the Optional Protocol to the Convention on the Rights of the Child on the Involvement of Children in Armed Conflict (OPAC) (Vandewiele 2006). The OPAC increased the age for direct participation and compulsory recruitment to 18 (Art. 1). However, it does not represent a real 'straight 18' position. Indirect participation is not included and the age for voluntary recruitment in armed forces of the state has been retained at 15 (Arts 1-3; cf. Art. 4 regarding armed groups). Unlike the CRC and the OPAC, the African Charter on the Rights and the Welfare of the Child (ACRWC) does provide a 'straight-18' approach (Art. 22 jo. 2) and 'sends a clear message that the participation of children in conflict is unacceptable and will not be tolerated on the [African] continent' (Mezmur 2008: 202). Mezmur (2008: 204) and UN Special Representative for Children and Armed Conflict Coomaraswamy (2010: 540) argue that a 'straight 18' position would best serve the protective aims of international human rights law to offer all children the same level of protection and prevent tipping the scale through the use of rather vague terminology such as indirect participation or voluntary recruitment. At the same time, Hanson (2011: 61) highlights that de facto the 'straight 18' position is proclaimed in international human rights discourse, under the influence of intensive lobbying by different advocacy groups. This also applies to the Committee on the Rights of the Child and to states through the adoption of instruments such as the Paris Principles and Guidelines and the Paris Commitments to protect children from unlawful recruitment or use by armed forces and armed groups (for example Paris Commitment No. 11: 'children who are accused of crimes under international law allegedly committed while they were associated with armed forces or armed groups, should be considered primarily as victims and not as perpetrators'), which were endorsed by ministers of 58 states in February 2007. According to Hanson this reveals that human rights discourse is 'trapped in "all-are-victims" discourse championed by humanitarian agencies' (2011: 61). Drumbl is also concerned about the dominancy of the victim-oriented imagery of child soldiers in international discourse. He claims that 'the faultless passive victim image' has been filling the 'international legal imagination' throughout the years, including international law, policy and practice, under the constant direct or indirect influence of 'a broad constellation of actors', including donors, advocacy groups, activists and international and intergovernmental organizations (Drumbl 2012: 9).

The CRC and the OPAC also aim to safeguard the demobilization, physical and psychological recovery and social reintegration of children who have been involved in hostilities (Art. 6 OPAC) or are victims of armed conflicts in a broader sense (Art. 39 CRC; see, for example, Robinson 2012). Social reintegration, which starts with 'release' from the armed force or group, including disarmament and demobilization (*Paris Principles*, para. 2.6 (UNICEF 2007a)), can be understood as 'the process through which children transition into civil society and enter meaningful roles and identities as civilians who are accepted by their families and communities in a context of local and national reconciliation' (*Paris Principles*, para. 3.0 (UNICEF 2007a)). Recovery and reintegration are entitlements of every child in armed conflict, including child soldiers, and must take place 'in an environment which fosters the health, self-respect and dignity of the child'. This reflects a children's rights approach (the Paris Principles refer to the core principles of the CRC at this point; see also Sarkin 2012: 90ff), including social reintegration aimed at fostering the child's development. In this regard, it is also important that children can participate in the process of recovery, reintegration and transition (Art. 12 CRC; Nylund 2012: 38-39; Sarkin 2012).

International criminal law

The OPAC refers in its preamble to the Rome Statute of the International Criminal Court (ICC), under which the conscription or enlisting of children under the age of 15 years or using them in hostilities is considered a war crime (Art. 8 (2)(b)(xxvi) and (2)(e)(vii) of the Rome Statute). It has thus become 'a matter of international concern' and international criminal law to ensure that those who violate international rules regarding children in armed conflict can be held accountable (Happold 2011: 82-83). Consequently, child soldiers – under the age of 15 – are considered victims of a war crime under international criminal law.

The Rome Statute also provides that the ICC does not have jurisdiction over children who have allegedly committed crimes under international law (that is, persons under the age of 18 at the time of the alleged commission of the offence; Art. 26), which indicates that under international criminal law children should not be regarded as perpetrators (Grossman 2007: 342). The Special Court of Sierra Leone, however, does have jurisdiction over children of 15, 16 or 17 years of age (Art. 7 of the Statute), which was directly linked to the context of Sierra Leone's conflict in which many children were used as combatants (Grossman 2007: 342). Happold assumes that this minimum age of criminal responsibility was deliberately set at 15 'to mirror the provisions on recruitment and use of child soldiers in the two APs and the CRC, on the ground that if children under fifteen are too young to be recruited, they must be too young to be held criminally accountable for their actions' (2008: 80). Thus far, no child soldier has been brought before the court (Coomaraswamy 2010; Nylund 2012: 45), which fits in with the recognition of 'the victimhood of all child soldiers' that accompanied the establishment of the Special Court (Grossman 2007: 342). As Grossmann points out, '[t]he Rome Statute and the [OPAC] arguably demonstrate an emerging consensus that children aged fifteen to eighteen should also be shielded from criminal liability' (2007: 342; see also Coomaraswamy 2010: 544).

In conclusion, under international law child soldiers are primarily seen as victims of armed conflict who should be protected, recovered and reintegrated. Additionally, international law does not stipulate that children who have been actively involved in committing atrocities and (war) crimes, should be held accountable and subsequently prosecuted. The main assumption underlying international discourse is that children who (are about to) participate in armed conflict require special protection and assistance due to their particular vulnerability and immaturity (Coomaraswamy 2010; Vandenhole *et al.* 2011: 9). It is interesting to note that a children's rights approach is proclaimed when it comes to recovery and reintegration, which assumes a different approach towards the competences of (former) child soldiers.

The victim image under consideration

This primary focus on the vulnerability and the victim status of the child soldier, resulting in a desire to provide adequate protection against recruitment, is justifiable given the atrocities child soldiers encounter and the gross violation of their human rights. At the same time, the primacy of this imagery is problematic for a number of reasons, two of which will be addressed below. First, it is questionable whether the 'victim image', like any other of the above mentioned images as such, fully captures the reality or local perceptions of communities and the children themselves. Empirical research indicates that it does not and that this is detrimental to the interests of both the children and the communities longing for a successful transition.

A second problem concerns the justification of the 'victim image' under international human rights law. The human rights framework seems inconsistent as far as the imagery of children in general and child soldiers in particular are concerned. This could jeopardize the achievements of the CRC and pave the way for a paternalistic approach (Denov 2010: 9; Hanson 2011) that distinguishes between groups of children as far as their legal status is concerned and – arguably even more important – may not adequately serve the right of child soldiers to recovery and reintegration (Art. 39 CRC).

The child victim image and empirical research

Like the role of child soldiers during armed conflict, how they are recruited, conscripted or enlisted in armed forces or armed groups (here generally referred to as recruitment of children in armed forces) varies significantly. Both the different ways of recruiting children as well the actual participation of child soldiers during armed conflict are relevant for how these children should be understood and dealt with as far as their recovery and reintegration is concerned. In addition, the process of recovery and reintegration itself can benefit from a more nuanced imagery.

Recruitment

The recruitment of children in armed forces has many manifestations and backgrounds. They may be drawn into armed forces at different ages, ranging from children younger than 10 (in the Democratic Republic of Congo, child soldiers of age 7 have been reported; Wessels 2006: 8) up to adolescents who are older and more mature. They may very well be forcibly recruited or abducted; abduction was one of the recruitment strategies, particularly in Sierra Leone, Uganda and to some extent the Democratic Republic of Congo (Drumbl 2012). However, many children come from poor families or marginalized backgrounds. While they join 'voluntarily', they may de facto be pushed or pulled by 'economic hardship, lack of opportunities, sense of belonging, ideological attraction, feelings of revenge or mere survival' (Coomaraswamy 2010; 536; Machel 1996). Some children 'are sent by their families to join armed forces in order to defend their communities or to find a basic source of income' (Coomaraswamy 2010: 536). Sometimes the armed force or group provides the child with a new family (Mezmur 2008: 206). Recruitment should be seen in the specific context of armed conflicts; even when children are not forcibly recruited or abducted, one can question whether voluntary recruitment really is a matter of free choice and informed consent (Coomaraswamy: 541-542; Machel 1996). In addition, structural forces, such as demographic developments, an increased number of civil conflicts and the proliferation and availability of small and lightweight weapons have been connected with the use of children in armed conflict, although these have been contested as well as clarifying factors (Denov 2010: 37-39; Drumbl 2010: 223).

It is questionable whether this forced or quasi-voluntary recruitment implies that the child did not participate in the recruitment process at all, or make any informed and/or strategic decisions in this regard. It would be too simplistic to assume that children cannot and do not influence their recruitment and subsequent participation and that they are merely subjected to external incidental and/or structural forces, including the influence of adults who (ab)use and exploit children for the purpose of warfare. Research indicates that some children choose to join armed forces because they want to fight for justice or for socio-economic reasons, 'to take advantage of benefits of military recruitment in circumstances of war' (Hanson 2011: 58 with reference to Lee 2009). Wessels observes that 'children's choices to join armed groups seldom reflect only one motive' and that '[s]oldiering is often attractive to children because it provides meaning, identity and options civilian life does not afford' (2006: 55, 4). Drumbl suggests 'the child as a social navigator endeavouring to advance within extremely difficult circumstances [and] the child as interstitially trying to make the best of a bad situation through tactical decisions and some forethought' (2010: 223-224 with reference to the research of Shepler 2004). These research-based observations provide quite a nuanced picture of children as far as their involvement in the recruitment process is concerned, including an image of agents making deliberate and strategic choices.

Participation

Anthropological research shows a variety of forms of participation after recruitment (Wessels 2006: 57ff). Some children actually fight and can be considered as direct combatants. Many children never fight, but fulfil supportive or other roles as cooks, messengers, spies, porters, sexual slaves or bodyguards. 'Children's roles vary according to the context and the children's characteristics such as their gender, age, size, and skill levels.' Moreover, '[c]hildren's roles within armed groups are highly fluid and contextual, as children may perform multiple roles in the same day' (Wessels 2006: 71-72).

Not infrequently, children are subjected to significant force, violence and brutality: girls are raped, sexually assaulted or exploited and boys beaten up and made dependent upon drugs. According to the UN Secretary-General's Special Representative for Children and Armed Conflict Radhika Coomaraswamy, child soldiers 'are being used by their commanders in many ways' and '[t]heir inexperience and lack of training leave them extremely vulnerable in the heat of battle' (2010: 536). She underscores the vulnerability of many, if not all of these children and portrays them as tools of their commanders. Particularly as far as child combatants are concerned, Wessels observes that, although their lives 'exhibit significant diversity', 'all child combatant have been forged by exposure to combat' (2006: 74).

At the same time, research indicates that child soldiers are not only passive objects, but may develop a certain strategy and autonomy while they are part of an armed force or group, seeming to behave differently after conscription. Some turn into sadists who torture and kill; others try to escape or run away, which requires determination and courage, or make themselves useful in a way that prevents them from becoming involved in human rights violations or heinous crimes (Drumbl 2010: 226). According to Wessels, '[a] child's entry into an armed group marks a profound life transition'. A child is confronted with multiple hardships, including being separated from parents and family, military rules and discipline, exposure to warfare and death. 'It is a world full of risks – attack, exploitation, disease – and the child's survival is very much at risk.' '[C]hild soldiers undergo self-guided, internal changes in adaptation to their new situation.' As a result, 'they may commit unspeakable acts that their morals and values would have prohibited in civilian life' (Wessels 2006: 57-58). This process of 'resocialization' is not accepted by all children. Many children resist and try to find ways to escape. Many other academic studies support these findings and underline that 'even when profoundly distressed and troubled, the young frequently exercise remarkable resilience' (Boyden and De Berry 2004: xvii).

These general observations and conclusions based on empirical research justify a nuanced image of the capacities of child soldiers. They confirm the extreme hardship these children encounter and underscore the need for special protection and assistance. However, they also point to the ability of these children to cope with the situation and to adjust their lives in order to survive. This assumes a certain level of agency and autonomy in their strategies. In this regard, it is also important to realize that *the* child does not exist, but that there is a wide variety of children along the continuum of age and developing maturity. These differences should be taken into account when portraying these children.

Recovery and reintegration

International human rights law stipulates that children affected by armed conflict, including child soldiers, are entitled to physical and psychological recovery and social reintegration. This refers to the recovery of the individual child, requiring that his individual needs are addressed, including means to deal with the trauma resulting from participation in armed conflict, to foster physical recovery or to address drug addiction (for example through medical and psychological assistance). Second, it concerns social reintegration, which focuses on the role of the individual child within his (extended) family and the local community. On the one hand, this requires special assistance furthering the individual development of the child and enabling him to play a constructive role in society in the future. Education or job opportunities are important among many other things. On the other hand, reintegration aims at integration of the child within the local community, including his family, which comes down to the interplay between child and community and may require the restoration of relationships between the community and family members and the individual child (Sarkin 2012).

The reintegration of child soldiers may be frustrated due to communities' reactions of 'revenge, stigmatization and even rejection' (Derluyn 2011: 4). Child soldiers are often regarded as 'perpetrators', regardless of the reason for their involvement in armed conflict, and the humanitarian support child soldiers receive may contribute to frustration within communities (Derluyn 2011: 4). It is also argued that the children themselves fear returning home, since they may be confronted with revenge or rejection by the community or their families (Schotmans 2012). Successful reintegration of child soldiers therefore requires special attention to the children's communities through 'specific awareness-raising or trust-building activities, as they may have carried out crime against their own communities'. In addition, there is a need for an 'inclusive approach to reintegration' (Nylund 2012: 45, with reference to the Paris Principles) which aims to provide no services to child soldiers that are not available to the other members of the community. Moreover, the accountability of former child soldiers is said to play a significant role in their social reintegration, in particular that of child combatants, and is regarded as 'one of the key values of transitional justice' (Mels *et al.* 2012: 28; see also Drumbl 2012).

Projecting (former) child soldiers as victims furthermore runs the risk of neglecting the feelings of guilt child soldiers often encounter, which may jeopardize full reintegration. According to Weyns '[t]he question coming to the fore is once again whether the silence hanging around children's perpetrator side or even the structural neglect thereof is in their best interest' (2012: 497). And with reference to the statement by an NGO worker with 10 years experience working with child soldiers, he reflects: 'Throughout these years, he found that the most recurring complaint of these children was their constant victimisation by the programs, being soothed, instead of being understood and acknowledged in the guilt they are confronted with' (Weyns 2012: 549).

Another problem of the one-sided portrayal of child soldiers is that it may result in denying the children a specific role in the transitional process. Or as Drumbl has put it: 'when child soldiers are constructed as completely lacking in agency during conflict, a risk arises that they are believed to lack ability to play a vigorous or independent role in post-conflict reconstruction, thereby relegating them to the perimeter of the transformative project' (2010: 218). This is linked to the second issue that will be addressed in this chapter, the accuracy and justification of the 'victim image' in light of the image of the child under international human rights law, particularly under the CRC.

The child victim image and the image of children under the CRC

The general image of the child under the CRC is based on the assumption that a child should no longer solely be seen as a human being in need of special measures of protection (cf., for example, Art. 24 ICCPR). Instead, the CRC acknowledges children (that is, human beings below the age of 18 years of age, unless domestic law provides otherwise; Art. 1 CRC) 'as being fully-fledged beneficiaries of human rights' (Cantwell 1992: 27). The adoption of the CRC in 1989 marked a change in how children are perceived from an international human rights perspective (Doek 2007) and the almost universal ratification of the CRC indicates that the international community has taken this human rights image of the child seriously. Although one should keep in mind that this imagery is a legal construct which may differ from perceptions at the local level (Cipriani 2009), it can be argued that the image of the child based on the CRC has increasingly affected its portrayal at the regional and domestic level (see, for example, Art. 1 ACRWC and Sloth-Nielsen 2012).

The CRC attributes civil, political, economic, social and cultural rights to children and places states parties under the obligation to protect their human rights and to ensure that they can enjoy and exercise their rights effectively, either directly or indirectly through the support of parents (or, for example, family members; Arts 18 and 5 CRC). According to the Committee on the Rights of the Child (2003), guiding principles in this regard are the principle of non-discrimination (Art. 2), the best interests of the child principle (Art. 3 (1)), the child's right to life, survival and development (Art. 6), and the child's right to be heard (Art. 12 CRC), also referred to as the broader right to participate in all matters affecting the child (Krappmann 2010).

Article 5 of the CRC acknowledges that children should be regarded as capable of exercising their rights 'in a manner consistent with the evolving capacities of the child'. The dynamic concept of the child's evolving capacities has made the recognition of the child capable of exercising his human rights contingent on the developmental phase he is in (Landsdown 2005). It emphasizes that children should be seen as human beings in development towards full autonomy, who are considered capable of acting independently and of making autonomous decisions in accordance with their age and maturity. Article 12 (1) CRC provides a fine example by stipulating that 'States Parties shall assure to the child who is capable of forming his or her own views the right to express those views freely in all matters affecting the child, the views of the child being given due weight in accordance with the age and maturity of the child.' This provision represents, arguably in the clearest form, 'the concept of the child underlying the entire Convention' (Krappmann 2010: 501) and it therefore can be regarded as one of 'the most notable improvement and innovations' of the CRC (Cantwell 1992: 28).

The general image of the child under the CRC has a number of implications for the position of child soldiers. The state has a special responsibility for the well-being of children, which includes that it should safeguard, without discrimination, that children's best interests are a primary consideration in all actions concerning them and that their rights are fully respected, including the right to life, survival and development, and the right to participate. As far as the position of child soldiers is concerned, this state responsibility primarily aims at preventing children from becoming involved in armed conflict. It needs no explanation that child soldiering has a negative impact on the child's chances for a successful and harmonious development, let alone a carefree childhood. A protective approach towards child soldiers is certainly justifiable in light of the general principles of the CRC, and the emphasis on the particular vulnerability of children in the specific context of armed conflict fits well with the CRC's general image of children. At the same time, it is questionable whether it should be excluded that in this particular context children can also be regarded as agents, capable of participating actively in the recruitment process, during their presence in the armed force and during the process of recovery and reintegration. It seems inappropriate to deny children agency, solely because of their status as a child, a human being under the age of 18. A nuanced and tailored approach is required with regard to the legal capacities of a child, which should result in a flexible and dynamic application and interpretation of the CRC provisions, while taking into account a child's evolving capacities. For example, an 8 year old may require a higher level of support and protection during armed conflict than a 15 year old. In addition, regarding an older child soldier, one could arguably assume a higher level of agency and autonomy than regarding a younger child soldier. At the same time, age alone may be insufficient to determine competence (Committee on the Rights of the Child 2009; Landsdown 2005; see also Boyden and De Berry 2004).

This sheds a different – and a more nuanced – light on the prominent victim orientation towards child soldiers in international discourse and points to an inconsistency in the framework of the CRC. This may not only disregard the perceptions of child soldiers themselves, but also neglect children's right to participation and children's accountability as prerequisites for a successful reintegration and the process of transition as a whole.

Children's participation

If the recovery and reintegration of child soldiers should include a children's rights approach, *inter alia* the participation of children, this has policy implications. The Committee on the Rights of the Child (2009) has provided detailed recommendations regarding the implementation of Article 12 CRC in general, which comes down to the safeguarding of child-sensitive and child-friendly proceedings in which former child soldiers can participate freely and effectively (see, for example, Beijer and Liefaard 2011). *Inter alia*, this means that a child should be provided with adequate information and assistance, in accordance with his age and maturity, and that the consultation of children should take place in a safe environment far away from conflict (Mels *et al.* 2012: 27).

According to the Committee on the Rights of the Child, children affected by emergencies 'should be encouraged and enabled to participate in analysing their situation and future prospects', which could help them 'to regain control over their lives, contributes to rehabilitation, develops organizational skills and strengthens a sense of identity' (2009: para. 125 with reference to UNICEF 2007b), although one has to be careful not to expose children again to situations that can be harmful or traumatic (Committee on the Rights of the Child 2009: para. 21; Derluyn 2011: 3).

Unfortunately, too often children are not involved in these processes (Vandenhole *et al.* 2011: 10).

Children's accountability

A child's accountability for his behaviour and decisions is also directly linked to the general image of the child under international human rights law. It can be assumed that a child's accountability develops along the line of the development of a child's capabilities to exercise his rights independently (Cipriani 2009). The only explicit reference to children's accountability under international human rights law can be found in Article 40 CRC, concerning criminal accountability. Article 40 (3)(a) CRC provides that 'States Parties shall seek to promote ... [t]he establishment of a minimum age below which children shall be presumed not to have the capacity to infringe the penal law.' This minimum age of criminal responsibility (MACR) defines at which point a child can be assumed accountable for behaviour constituting a criminal offence under penal law. The CRC does not provide for a specific age limit, but Rule 4.1 of the UN Standard Minimum Rules for the Administration of Juvenile Justice (Beijing Rules) (UN General Assembly 1985) provides that the MACR 'shall not be fixed at too low an age level, bearing in mind the facts of emotional, mental and intellectual maturity'. In 2007, the Committee on the Rights of the Child recommended setting the 'age of criminal responsibility' at the 'absolute minimum' of 12; a lower age limit would not be 'internationally acceptable', a higher age of 14 or 16, recommendable (Committee on the Rights of the Child 2007: para. 32). Despite the risks and downsides of criminal justice interventions, the CRC Committee has not recommended the minimum age of criminal responsibility be set at 18. This would deny children's accountability and thus agency as far as their criminal behaviour is concerned and does not fit in the general image of the child under the CRC (for more on the MACR, see Cipriani 2009).

The individual accountability of child soldiers could be assessed along the same lines, but, as clarified earlier, international law, in particular international criminal law, tends to exclude the criminal accountability of child soldiers. There is much against the use of international criminal justice interventions against child soldiers and the best interests of the child may very well require that children are excluded from international jurisdiction concerning war crimes and other atrocities (Coomaraswamy 2010: 544). However, a categorical exclusion of child soldiers from criminal liability represents a legal fiction that neglects children's accountability and, as a consequence, their evolving capacities. It does not correspond with the CRC, which has called for the minimum age of criminal responsibility to be set at age 12 or somewhat higher (Committee on the Rights of the Child 2007), and with the assumption in many domestic jurisdictions throughout the world that children can be held criminally accountable from a certain age (Cipriani 2009; cf. Coomaraswamy 2010: 545, who falsely claims that 18 is the 'widely accepted' and preferred minimum age of criminal responsibility, since it would reflect the 'widely accepted ... threshold for society after which adolescents can be legally accountable for their acts'). It is unclear why a different approach regarding children's accountability is justified in the specific context of armed conflict. Although criminal accountability at the domestic level is not excluded, these international assumptions may have an impact on domestic justice mechanisms. Drumbl warns that they might even 'hollow the rigor of transitional accountability mechanisms from outside the criminal law – such as truth commissions, welcoming ceremonies, cleansing rituals, or community service requirements – in their application to former child soldiers in post-conflict societies' (2012: 133).

Instead of categorically denying child soldiers (criminal) accountability, it is better to query how to deal with their role in armed conflict in order to serve the interests of both the children and the societies concerned. This requires a search for the most effective approach towards the recovery and reintegration of the children involved, which may well include protection but should not exclude accountability, since the latter is regarded as one of the key factors in the process of reintegration, reconciliation and transition. Subsequently, it is important for the process of psychological recovery of child soldiers. It goes beyond the scope of this chapter to elaborate extensively on the mechanisms that could be used to facilitate both the recovery and reintegration of child soldiers and the transition of the societies concerned (see, for example, Sarkin 2012 and Drumbl 2012). However, a few observations will be made regarding the main human rights principles that should be taken into account with regard to the role children play in these mechanisms, assuming a recognition of their accountability, in accordance with their age and maturity.

Although prosecution of children at the domestic level for crimes committed during armed conflict is not excluded, human rights instruments call upon states to award children treatment that acknowledges the special status of children as human beings in development, requiring special attention for the needs and interests of children, while taking into account the age of the child (Art. 40 (1) CRC). This call for a separate juvenile justice system with specialized institutions aims to further children's development and reintegration in society in which they can play a constructive role (Committee on the Rights of the Child 2007). In this regard, it is important to underline that addressing the accountability of children should not result in responses that are primarily repressive or used for general deterrence. The human rights framework also proclaims that children should preferably not be dealt with through judicial proceedings. Instead, they should be diverted to alternative mechanisms outside the juvenile justice arena (Art. 40 (3)(b) CRC). This is where transitional justice mechanisms or local, informal or traditional procedures can be of significance (Drumbl 2012; Parmar *et al.* 2010; Sarkin 2012; Schotsmans 2012). One could, for example, think of restorative justice mechanisms that foster reconciliation (Sarkin 2012; see also Drumbl 2012). When using alternative dispositions, it is important that they are embedded in human rights (Sarkin 2012) with implications for both the community and the children involved. The CRC particularly stresses that the human rights and legal safeguards of children should be fully respected when diverted (Art. 40 (3)(b) CRC). This should be seen in light of the second principle applicable when considering state or community responses to child soldiers, assuming their accountability: children are entitled to be treated in a fair manner, in a lawful and non-arbitrary way. *Inter alia*, children should be awarded a fair trial, if prosecuted (Art. 40 (2) CRC) and are entitled to participate effectively in proceedings aimed at addressing their (criminal) accountability (see Art. 40; see also Art. 12 CRC). This calls for child-friendly proceedings (see, for example, Liefaard *et al.* 2011; see also Council of Europe 2010). Furthermore, deprivation of liberty (that is, 'any form of detention or imprisonment or the placement of a person in a public or private custodial setting, from which this person is not permitted to leave at will, by order of any judicial, administrative or other public authority'; rule 11 (b) Havana Rules; UN General Assembly 1990b) should be used with the utmost restraint, only for the shortest appropriate period of time and only if the child is provided with relevant legal safeguards (Art. 37 (b), (c) and (d) CRC; Liefaard 2008; see also Art. 7 the Statute of the Special Court for Sierra Leone). In this regard, Article 40 (4) CRC provides that '[a] variety of dispositions, such as care, guidance, and supervision orders; counselling; probation; foster care; education and vocational training programmes and other alternatives to institutional care shall be available to ensure that children are dealt with in a manner appropriate to their well-being and proportionate both to their circumstances and the offence.'

This combination of fair and child-specific treatment has many implications, which have been elaborated upon in soft legal instruments at the global and regional level. These include the 1985 Beijing Rules, the 1990 UN Rules for the Treatment of Juveniles Deprived of their Liberty (Havana Rules) and the 1990 UN Guidelines for the Prevention of Juvenile Delinquency (Riyadh Guidelines; UN General Assembly 1990a). Recently, the Committee of Ministers of the Council of Europe adopted the 2008 European Rules for juvenile offenders subject to sanctions or measures (Council of Europe 2008) and the 2010 Guidelines for Child-Friendly Justice (Council of Europe 2010). In addition, the Committee on the Rights of the Child has provided detailed recommendations regarding the implementation of children's rights in the context of juvenile justice in its 10th general comment (Committee on the Rights of the Child 2007).

Conclusions

This chapter has addressed the most prominent portrayal of child soldiers in international discourse: as vulnerable, passive victims. It can be argued that, although understandable and justifiable to a large extent, this imagery is too limited. It does not fit with the complex reality of children's participation in armed conflict and perceptions of local communities and children themselves, and it can jeopardize the children's right to recovery and reintegration into society, as well as the process of transition. The 'victim image' of child soldiers is, furthermore, on strained terms with the general image of the child under international human rights law, which attributes to children an increasing amount of autonomy and independence in accordance with their developmental level and evolving capacities. Without denying the important fact that children in armed conflict are also victims and without proclaiming international or domestic prosecution of child soldiers, I have tried to highlight a nuanced imagery of child soldiers that is more conducive with the rights of these children and can arguably be more beneficial to the future perspectives of the communities in which they live and in which they can play a constructive role.

References

Beijer, A. and Liefaard, T. 2011. A Bermuda Triangle? Balancing Protection, Participation and Proof in Criminal Proceedings Affecting Child Victims and Witnesses. *Utrecht Law Review*, 7(3), 70-106.

Boyden, J. and De Berry, J. eds. 2004. *Children and Youth on the Front Line: Ethnography, Armed Conflict and Displacement*. New York and Oxford: Berghahn.

Cantwell, N. 1992. The Origins, Development and Significance of the United Nations Convention on the Rights of the Child, in *The United Nations Convention on the Rights of the Child: A Guide to the 'Travaux Preparatoires'*, edited by S. Detrick, 19-30. Dordrecht: Martinus Nijhoff.

Cipriani, D. 2009. *Children's Rights and the Minimum Age of Criminal Responsibility: A Global Perspective*. Aldershot: Ashgate.

Coalition to Stop the Use of Child Soldiers. 2008. *Child Soldiers Global Report*. Available at http://www.childsoldiersglobalreport.org (accessed 28 December 2011).

Committee on the Rights of the Child. 2003. *General Comment No. 5: General Measures of Implementation of the Convention on the Rights of the Child* (arts. 4, 42 and 44, para. 6), CRC/GC/2003/5, 27. Available at http://www.unhcr.org/refworld/docid/4538834f11.html (accessed 10 October 2012).

Committee on the Rights of the Child. 2007. *General Comment No. 10: Children's Rights in Juvenile Justice*, CRC/C/GC/10. Available at http://www.unhcr.org/refworld/docid/4670fca12.html (accessed 10 October 2012).

Committee on the Rights of the Child. 2009. *General Comment No. 12: The Right of the Child to be Heard*, CRC/C/GC/12. Available at http://www.unhcr.org/refworld/docid/4ae562c52.html (accessed 10 October 2012).

Coomaraswamy, R. 2010. The Optional Protocol to the Convention on the Rights of the Child on the Involvement of Children in Armed Conflict – Towards

Universal Ratification. *International Journal of Children's Rights*, 2010(4), 535-549.

Council of Europe. 2008. *Recommendation CM/Rec(2008)11 of the Committee of Ministers to Member States on the European Rules for Juvenile Offenders Subject to Sanctions or Measures*. Adopted 5 November 2008. Available at wcd.coe.int/ViewDoc.jsp?id=1367113&Site=CM (accessed 10 October 2012).

Council of Europe. 2010. *Guidelines of the Committee of the Council of Ministers of the Council of Europe on Child-Friendly Justice*. Adopted 17 November 2010. Available at wcd.coe.int/ViewDoc.jsp?id=1705197&Site=CM (accessed 10 October 2012).

Denov, M. 2010. *Child Soldiers: Sierra Leone's Revolutionary United Front*. Cambridge: Cambridge University Press.

Derluyn, I. 2011. Towards a New Agenda for Rehabilitation and Reintegration Processes for Child Soldiers. *Journal of Adolescent Health*, 49, 3-4.

Derluyn, I., Mels, C., Parmentier, S. and Vandenhole, W. eds. 2012. *Re-Member: Rehabilitation, Reintegration and Reconciliation of War-Affected Children*. Cambridge: Intersentia.

Detrick, S. ed. 1992. *The United Nations Convention on the Rights of the Child: A Guide to the 'Travaux Preparatoires'*. Dordrecht: Martinus Nijhoff.

Doek, J.E. 2007. The Eighteenth Birthday of the Convention on the Rights of the Child: Achievements and Challenges. *University of Michigan Journal of Law Reform*, 41(1), 61-76.

Doek, J.E. 2012. Foreword. In *Re-Member: Rehabilitation, Reintegration and Reconciliation of War-Affected Children*, edited by I. Derluyn, C. Mels, S. Parmentier and W. Vandenhole, ix-xxiii. Cambridge: Intersentia.

Drumbl, M.A. 2010. Child Soldiers. In *Collective Violence and International Criminal Justice*, edited by A. Smeulers, 207-231. Antwerp, Oxford and Portland, OR: Intersentia.

Drumbl, M.A. 2012. *Reimagining Child Soldiers in International Law and Policy*. Oxford: Oxford University Press.

Grossman, N. 2007. Rehabilitation or Revenge: Prosecuting Child Soldiers for Human Rights Violations. *Georgetown Journal of International Law*, 38, 323-361.

Hanson, K. 2011. International Children's Rights and Armed Conflict, International Law on Children and Armed Conflict: The Interface between Various Normative Frameworks. *Human Rights & International Legal Discourse*, 5(1), 40-62.

Happold, M. 2008. Child Soldiers: Victims or Perpetrators? *University of La Verne Law Review*, 29, 56-87.

Happold, M. 2011. Children Participating in Armed Conflict and International Criminal Law. *Human Rights & International Legal Discourse*, 5(1), 82-100.

Krappmann, L. 2010. The Weight of the Child's View (Article 12 of the Convention on the Rights of the Child). *International Journal of Children's Rights*, 2010(4), 501-513.

Landsdown, G. 2005. *The Evolving Capacities of the Child*. Florence: UNICEF.

Lee, A.J. 2009. *Understanding and Addressing the Phenomenon of 'Child Soldiers': The Gap between the Global Humanitarian Discourse and the Local Understandings and Experiences of Young People's Military Recruitment*. RSC Working Paper 52. Oxford: Refugee Studies Centre, University of Oxford.

Liefaard, T. 2008. *Deprivation of Liberty of Children in Light of International Human Rights Law and Standards*. Antwerp, Oxford and Portland, OR: Intersentia.

Liefaard, T., Rap, S.E. and Weijers, I. 2011. Procedural Rights for Juveniles: A Human Rights and Developmental Psychology Perspective. *Chronicle of the International Association of Youth and Family Judges and Magistrates*, 47-52.

Machel, Graça/UN General Assembly. 1996. *Impact of Armed Conflict on Children*. UN Doc. A/51/306. Available at http://www.unhcr.org/refworld/docid/3b00f2d30.html (accessed 10 October 2012).

Mels, C., Derluyn, I., Parmentier, S. and Vandenhole, W. 2012. Introduction: Children Affected by Armed Conflict at the Intersection of Three Fields of Study. In *Re-Member: Rehabilitation, Reintegration and Reconciliation of War-Affected Children*, edited by I. Derluyn, C. Mels, S. Parmentier and W. Vandenhole, 1-31. Cambridge: Intersentia.

Mezmur, B.D. 2008. Children at Both Ends of the Gun: Child Soldiers in Africa. In *Children's Rights in Africa: A Legal Perspective*, edited by J. Sloth-Nielsen, 199-217. Aldershot: Ashgate.

Nylund, B.V. 2012. International Legal Protection for the Recovery and Reintegration of War-Affected Children. In *Re-Member: Rehabilitation, Reintegration and Reconciliation of War-Affected Children*, edited by I. Derluyn, C. Mels, S. Parmentier and W. Vandenhole, 35-56. Cambridge: Intersentia.

Parmar, S., Roseman, M.J., Siegrist, S and Sowa, Th. eds. 2010. *Children and Transitional Justice: Truth-Telling, Accountability and Reconciliation*. Cambridge, MA: Harvard University Press.

Robinson, J.A. 2012. The Right of Child Victims of Armed Conflict to Reintegration and Recovery. *Potchefstroom Electronic Law Journal*, 15(1), 46-101.

Sarkin, J. 2012. Integrating Transitional Justice and Disarmament, Demobilisation and Reintegration: The Need to Achieve Rehabilitation, Reintegration and Reconciliation for Child Soldiers and Child Victims of Enforced Disappearances. In *Re-Member: Rehabilitation, Reintegration and Reconciliation of War-Affected Children*, edited by I. Derluyn, C. Mels, S. Parmentier and W. Vandenhole, 77-101. Cambridge: Intersentia.

Schotsmans, M. 2012. No Return Home: The (Non-)Reintegration of Youth Ex-Combatants in Sierra Leone as a Challenge to the Contextualisation of DDR and Transitional Justice. In *Re-Member: Rehabilitation, Reintegration and Reconciliation of War-Affected Children*, edited by I. Derluyn, C. Mels, S. Parmentier and W. Vandenhole, 197-224. Cambridge: Intersentia.

Shepler, S. 2004. The Social and Cultural Context of Child Soldiering in Sierra Leone. Manuscript on file with the author, 12-13.

Sloth-Nielsen, J. 2012. Modern African Childhoods: Does Law Matter? In *Law and Childhood Studies*, edited by M. Freeman, 117-132. Oxford: Oxford University Press.

UN General Assembly. 1985. *United Nations Standard Minimum Rules for the Administration of Juvenile Justice ("The Beijing Rules")*. Adopted 29 November 1985, A/RES/40/33. Available at http://www.unhcr.org/refworld/docid/3b00f2203c.html (accessed 10 October 2012).

UN General Assembly. 1989. *Convention on the Rights of the Child*. 20 November 1989, United Nations, Treaty Series, vol. 1577, p. 3. Available at http://www.unhcr.org/refworld/docid/3ae6b38f0.html (accessed 10 October 2012).

UN General Assembly. 1990a. *United Nations Guidelines for the Prevention of Juvenile Delinquency ("The Riyadh Guidelines"): resolution adopted by the General Assembly*, 14 December 1990, A/RES/45/112. Available at http://www.unhcr.org/refworld/docid/3b00f21d1c.html (accessed 10 October 2012).

UN General Assembly. 1990b. *United Nations Rules for the Protection of Juveniles Deprived of Their Liberty: resolution adopted by the General Assembly*, 14 December 1990, A/RES/45/113 [Havana Rules]. Available at http://www.unhcr.org/refworld/docid/3b00f18628.html (accessed 10 October 2012).

UNICEF. 2005. *The State of the World's Children 2006: Excluded and Invisible*. New York: UNICEF.

UNICEF. 2007a. *The Paris Principles: Principles and Guidelines on Children Associated With Armed Forces or Armed Groups*, February 2007. Available at http://www.unhcr.org/refworld/docid/465198442.html (accessed 10 October 2012).

UNICEF. 2007b. *The Participation of Children and Young People in Emergencies: A Guide for Relief Agencies Based Largely on Experiences in the Asian Tsunami Response*. Bangkok: UNICEF East Asia and Pacific Regional Office.

Vandenhole, W., Parmentier, S. and Derluyn, I. 2011. International Law on Children and Armed Conflict: The Interface between Various Normative Frameworks. *Human Rights & International Legal Discourse*, 5(1), 2-13.

Vandewiele, T. 2006. Optional Protocol: The Involvement of Children in Armed Conflicts. In *A Commentary on the United Nations Convention on the Rights of the Child*, edited by A. Alen, J. Vande Lanotte, E. Verhellen, F. Ang, E. Berghmans and M. Verheyde. Leiden: Martinus Nijhoff.

Wessells, M.G. 2006. *Child Soldiers: From Violence to Protection*. Cambridge, MA: Harvard University Press.

Weyns, Y. 2012. On Children's Rights and Wrongs. In *Re-Member: Rehabilitation, Reintegration and Reconciliation of War-Affected Children*, edited by I. Derluyn, C. Mels, S. Parmentier and W. Vandenhole, 481-503. Cambridge: Intersentia.

Chapter 10
Images of International Criminal Justice in the Former Yugoslavia

Sanja Kutnjak Ivković and John Hagan

The war in the former Yugoslavia created thousands of victims of war crimes and crimes against humanity; the 1994 Commission of Experts report estimated more than three million refugees, 200,000 to 250,000 people killed, another 50,000 tortured, and 20,000 raped (UN Security Council 1994).

In 1993, UN Security Council Resolution 827 established the International Criminal Tribunal for the former Yugoslavia (ICTY). At the time, war was raging throughout parts of the former Yugoslavia, and most of the local courts in Bosnia and Herzegovina (BiH) and Croatia were either unable or unwilling to try war crime cases, particularly those committed by the members of 'their own' ethnic group. The ICTY was established with several purposes in mind (such as to punish the offenders or contribute towards the restoration of peace). One of the key purposes of the ICTY is to render justice to the victims of war crimes and crimes against humanity committed on the territory of the former Yugoslavia (ICTY 2012a).

The victims who testified had an opportunity to have their story heard by the judges and recorded for posterity. However, the reality is that most of the victims will never see the inside of a courtroom at the ICTY in this capacity. At best, they could watch the ICTY trials online, read the media reports about the ongoing cases and listen to the politicians interpret the events and decisions in the ICTY cases. Their evaluations of the ICTY will be based on both objective information (for example, the actual sentence in a specific case) and interpretations of the ICTY decisions and procedures provided by journalists and politicians.

Existing literature on public perceptions of the ICTY in general, and on the victims' views of the ICTY in particular, is quite limited. This chapter contributes towards the literature by exploring empirically who the victims of war crimes and crimes against humanity – some of whom have testified before the ICTY and local courts – think the appropriate decision-makers in the aftermath of a violent conflict should be. It also explores the factors associated with their views. In addition, it provides the victims' views about the ICTY and the justice it delivers.

Public support for the ICTY in the former Yugoslavia and the imagery of the ICTY

Public support for the ICTY among its constituency in the former Yugoslavia can be framed from the perspective of four different imageries. We explore each of them and analyse the related extant research.

Perception of treatment of ethnic groups

The first imagery focuses on perceptions of the way the ICTY has been treating various ethnic groups. The war in Bosnia and Herzegovina (BiH) ended without declared victors. Instead, the ICTY has been providing a legal framework to decide the 'defeated' and the 'defended' by conducting trials and meting out sentences (see, for example, Kutnjak Ivković and Hagan 2011). Perceptions of the justice that the ICTY is delivering are affected by the degree to which each ethnic group is treated and viewed as 'defended' as opposed to 'defeated'. In accordance with the basic principles of distributive justice, the ethnic groups labelled as 'defeated' – those whom the ICTY mostly views as the aggressors, convicting their members of war crimes and crimes against humanity – should have a less positive opinion about the tribunal than the ethnic groups labelled as 'defended'. Thus, evaluations of the ICTY undoubtedly vary across countries of the former Yugoslavia and depend on how the ICTY is perceived to be treating the dominant and minority ethnic groups.

Kutnjak Ivković and Hagan have analysed the ICTY cases completed by 2005 and conclude that 'the Serbs typically are seen as offenders or the "defeated", Muslims/Bosniaks as victims or the "defended," and Croats somewhere in between: about two-thirds of the ICTY defendants have been Serbs, a quarter have been Croats, and less than one-tenth have been Muslims/Bosniaks' (2011: 53). Consequently, the Serbs should exhibit attitudes least supportive of the ICTY, whereas Muslims/Bosnians should exhibit attitudes most supportive of the ICTY.

Indeed, prior research concerning levels of public support for the ICTY in the former Yugoslavia (for example, Arzt 2006; Human Rights Center 2000; Kutnjak Ivković and Hagan 2011; Stover 2005; Stover and Weinstein 2004) indicates that the support that the ICTY enjoys varies greatly across successor countries and in accordance with the division into the 'defeated' and 'defended' categories. For example, the 2002 International Institute for Democracy and Electoral Assistance survey of public opinion revealed that, while about a quarter of the respondents in Croatia (21 per cent) and less than 10 per cent in Serbia (8 per cent in Serbia and 4 per cent in Republika Srpska) showed moderate levels of trust in the ICTY, the fraction of the respondents who expressed trust in the ICTY in the Bosnian Federation was about half (51 per cent). Similarly, Kutnjak Ivković and Hagan (2011) report that the ICTY enjoyed some support among the respondents surveyed in Vukovar, Croatia, in 2004 and in Sarajevo, BiH. By contrast, the level of support among the Belgrade, Serbia respondents (surveyed in 2004 and 2005) seems to have been rather low (Kutnjak Ivković and Hagan 2011).

Cognitive landscapes

The second imagery focuses on the ethnic groups' perceptions of the how the ICTY is treating them and the level of influence they feel that they have on ICTY decisions. Sampson and Bartusch's fundamental hypothesis of 'cognitive landscapes' holds that structural settings 'where inability to influence the structures of power that constrain lives is greatest, also breed cynicism and perceptions of legal injustice' (1998: 783). Linking their work to earlier research by Kapsis (1978), Sampson and Bartusch argue (1998: 783) that individual and group perceptions of appropriate conduct are grounded in structural landscapes that define 'defeated' and 'defended' peoples and settings. When applied to the context of international law and the ICTY, the concept of 'cognitive landscapes' suggests that the structural landscape of the country's current national circumstances determines its localized attitudes towards the ICTY. As political structures in each country determine what the popular view of the ICTY is going to be, it is quite possible that members of the same ethnic group would have different views depending on where they live. For example, we expect that Serbs removed from the localized structural circumstances of defeat in Serbia – for example, by living among the 'defended' in BiH or Croatia – may not be as embittered as Serbs residing in Serbia.

Kutnjak Ivković and Hagan (2011) show that Serbs' and Croats' assessments of the ICTY's fairness depend both on their ethnicity and on their place of residence, reporting substantial variation in the Serbs' and Croats' level of support for the ICTY, depending on where they resided. Furthermore, they report that the diversity of views expressed by members of the same ethnic group often corresponds closely to the views expressed by members of other ethnic groups from the same site; the views within the same ethnic group were thus shaped differently depending on whether the respondents resided in the 'defeated' or 'defended' areas. For example, the results showed that Serbs in Belgrade were most affected by the 'defeated' set of views, while the effect of being Serb and defeated is culturally diffused and mitigated in Sarajevo and Vukovar by countervailing cultural beliefs shared with the local, non-Serb groups (Kutnjak Ivković and Hagan 2011).

Internal and external images

The third imagery focuses on the potential mismatch between an ethnic group's own perceptions of themselves as aggressors, victims or both (that is, internal images) and the way in which they perceive that the ICTY is treating their own ethnic group (that is, external images). The mismatch between the internal and external images is likely the smallest for Muslims/Bosnians and the largest for Serbs. The larger the gap, the more the ethnic group will feel that the ICTY is unjust towards them and the more they will lack support for the ICTY.

Biro and colleagues (2004: 193) reported that almost half of their respondents – Croats in Mostar and Serbs in Prijedor, both of whom constituted the dominant ethnic majority in their respective communities – did not accept the fact that their group participated in the commission of war crimes. In contrast, about three-quarters of the Bosnians in Mostar, Bosnians in Prijedor and Serbs in Vukovar, all of whom constituted the minority in these communities, were willing to accept the possibility that members of their ethnic group participated in the commission of war crimes.

The group identity, formed around the concept of ethnicity, further prevents the realization that members of the same group can be both victims *and* aggressors (see, for example, Stover 2005: 143). The ICTY's trials of defendants of a certain ethnicity may signal that the ICTY is biased against that ethnic group and that it does not understand the roles performed during the war. Indeed, the results of limited prior research indicate the presence of this notion of victimhood; the respondents expressed negative views of the ICTY primarily because they 'were convinced that the court was biased against their national group' (Biro *et al.* 2004: 200; Stover 2005: 144). Local judges and prosecutors were also influenced by the views of collective victimhood of their ethnic group; the 1999 Berkeley survey of judges and prosecutors in Bosnia indicates that the ICTY is viewed as 'a political institution', one that is 'biased and incapable of providing fair trials' (Stover 2005: 38). The same sentiments were echoed by the residents from Mostar, Prijedor (BiH) and Vukovar (Croatia) in the study by Čorkalo and colleagues (2004: 147); the respondents challenged the ICTY's impartiality and argued that it is a political court.

Public opinion polls conducted in Croatia and Serbia detected the presence of very similar attitudes. About 60 per cent of the Croatian respondents in a 2000 survey (*Jutarnji List* 2000: 13) believed that the ICTY is unfair and about half (52 per cent) believed that 'The Hague wants to criminalize the Homeland War'. A July 2003 opinion poll of the Serbian population revealed that it overwhelmingly distrusts the ICTY. The reason for this high level of distrust lies in widespread perceptions of the ICTY as politically motivated and biased against the defeated, that is, Serbs; more than 70 per cent of the respondents believed that the ICTY will act partially with respect to Serb defendants (Arzt 2006: 233-234). However, the respondents may have been quite ignorant of the ICTY cases and, fuelled by anti-ICTY media propaganda, may have assumed that the ICTY is selecting only Serb defendants and completely avoiding trying any non-Serb defendants (McMahon and Miller 2009: 19). Indeed, 2004 and 2005 polls conducted by the Belgrade Centre for Human Rights confirm these hypotheses and suggest that three-quarters of the respondents did not know what the ICTY does (Humanitarian Law Center 2006: 29). In fact, some 'moderate Serbs' participating in the survey were not even aware that several non-Serbs had been indicted and tried by the ICTY. Wilson suggests that, in particular, low approval in Serb areas should hardly be surprising, arguing that 'any historical account which punctures nationalist mythologies is likely to be rejected as long as a region is dominated by nationalist politicians who have regularly denied responsibility for mass atrocities' (2005: 941-942). As recently as the fall of 2002, the Republika Srpska government was in deep denial of its responsibility, insisting, for example, that only about a thousand Bosnian Muslim soldiers, rather than seven to eight thousand Bosnian Muslim civilians, had been killed at Srebrenica.

Passage of time

The fourth imagery focuses on the passage of time. It is quite possible that the initial enthusiasm surrounding the establishment of the ICTY is gradually weakening as the reality of the ICTY operation (that is, the difficulties of executing an arrest warrant on the political and military leaders, the slow pace of the ICTY trials, the inability to impose the death sentence) sinks in. Indeed, research conducted by Kutnjak Ivković and Hagan (2011) suggests that Muslims/Bosnians and Croats surveyed before 2000 showed more positive attitudes towards the ICTY than did the respondents surveyed later.

Victims and the ICTY

Scientific research regarding the ways victims perceive international tribunals in general and how victims from the former Yugoslavia perceive the ICTY in particular is quite limited (Stover 2005: 17). Eric Stover's *The Witnesses* (2005) is the only extant empirical study that provides in-depth exploration of victims and their views of an international criminal tribunal. However, the study primarily focused on the respondents' actual experiences at the ICTY, an atypical circumstance for the vast majority of war victims in the former Yugoslavia.

Stover's study of the ICTY is based on his interviews with 87 victims or witnesses who testified in seven trials at the ICTY. The overwhelming majority of the witnesses (72 per cent) were Bosnian Muslims who testified in the five Lašva Valley cases, in which Bosnian Croats were accused of committing war crimes. About a quarter of the respondents (23 per cent) were Croats who testified in the trial of Slavko Dokmanović, former mayor of Vukovar, Croatia, and 5 per cent were Bosnian Serbs who testified in the Čelebići prison camp case (Stover 2005: xi).

The respondents' interaction with the ICTY, including the prosecutor's office and the office for the protection of witnesses and victims, was generally evaluated in positive terms (Stover 2005: 91). Three-quarters of Stover's respondents (77 per cent; Stover 2005: 103) evaluated their experience as positive, and most said that they would testify again. The prosecutors' treatment of the witnesses turned out to be directly related to the respondents' satisfaction with the experience (Stover 2005: 90).

Although Stover's study provides a valuable insight into victims' perspectives of the ICTY and its trials, the reality is that the most of the victims will never testify before the ICTY, and their impression of ICTY justice will come only from indirect sources. Kutnjak Ivković and Hagan (2011) concluded that the respondents' overall evaluations of the ICTY's fairness were primarily influenced by the assessments of outcome fairness, procedural fairness and judges' political independence. Whereas issues of both procedural and distributive fairness mattered, the latter carried more weight (Kutnjak Ivković and Hagan 2011). The respondents in the study, particularly in the post-2001 surveys – those who tend to be more critical of the ICTY – had no problem approving of many defendants' rights (such as the right to have an attorney, to present a defence, to propose witnesses, to an impartial judge, to a jury trial, to an appeal) and, with the exception of Belgrade respondents, mostly evaluated the procedures as fair. Yet, with the exception of the Priština respondents, respondents in post-2001 surveys mostly viewed ICTY decisions as unfair. In a nutshell, the respondents cared more about whether someone was convicted and whether the punishment was appropriate than about whether the procedure used to evaluate someone's guilt was fair.

Methodology

We approached a victims' association from Bosnia and Herzegovina whose members are primarily victims of sexual violence. The association has several hundred members. The head of the association granted us permission to survey its current and prospective members.[1] However, to protect their privacy (several members have experienced, or were threatened with, reprisal from the offenders), the head of the association gave only very sparse details about its members. We surveyed more than 1,100 individuals through the association, including their current and potential members, with the response rate of 80 per cent (N=932). The questionnaire was anonymous.

Out of 932 respondents, about two-thirds are women (69.8 per cent, Table 10.1). Most respondents were aged between 21 and 50 at the end of the war (Table 10.1). They are mostly high-school graduates (61.4 per cent, Table 10.1). Muslims/Bosniaks comprise the majority among the respondents (69.8 per cent, Table 10.1), whereas Croats and Serbs each accounted for 15 per cent of the sample (see Table 10.1).[2]

1 To protect the association and its members, we promised to disclose only very limited information about the association and its members.

2 Our sample is not a representative, but a convenience sample obtained through the victims' association. Prior research indicates that ethnicity was one of the important variables related to the level of support for the ICTY. To minimize the effect of our sampling techniques and in particular the ethnicity composition on the results, we present bi-variable analyses, followed by multivariate models in which we control for ethnicity.

Table 10.1 Respondents' demographic characteristics

	Percentage of respondents (N = 932)
Gender	
Women	69.8
Age at the end of war (1995)	
20 or below	10.0
21-35	46.7
36-50	38.8
Above 50	4.5
Education	
Below high school	15.5
High school	61.4
Some college	15.5
College	7.7
Ethnicity	
Bosniaks/Muslims	69.8
Croats	15.1
Serbs	15.1
Victimization status	
Personally victimized[a]	88.8
Witnessed[b]	71.2
Family victimized[c]	93.3
Neighbours victimized[d]	97.0
Number of family members killed	
0	22.9
1	27.2
2-3	26.5
4-10	15.9
Over 10	7.4
Respondent testified	
ICTY	4.2
Court of BiH	18.8
Court in the Federation	2.0
Court in RS	0.2

	Percentage of respondents (N = 932)
Court in Croatia	0.3
Court in Serbia	0.2
Did not testify	74.2

[a] The question was worded as follows: 'Do you consider yourself a victim of war crimes or crimes against humanity?' The possible answers were: 'yes' and 'no'.

[b] The question was worded as follows: 'Have you witnessed a war crime or a crime against humanity?' The possible answers were: 'yes' and 'no'.

[c] The question was worded as follows: 'Has a member of your family or a close friend been a victim of war crimes or crimes against humanity?' The possible answers were: 'yes' and 'no'.

[d] The question was worded as follows: 'Has an acquaintance or a fellow citizen been a victim of a war crime or a crime against humanity?' The possible answers were: 'yes' and 'no'.

Almost all respondents perceived being personally victimized (88.8 per cent, Table 10.1), reported witnessing a war crime or a crime against humanity (71.2 per cent) and stated that their family members (93.3 per cent) and/or their neighbours were victimized (97.0 per cent). In fact, fewer than one in four respondents (22.9 per cent, Table 10.1) had no family members killed during the war, with the majority of the respondents having between one and three family members killed.

Lastly, the overwhelming majority of the respondents (74.2 per cent) did not testify at any court. Testifying at the ICTY was a rare experience, reported by only 4.2 per cent of respondents. A few respondents (typically below 1 per cent) testified at various local courts throughout the former Yugoslavia. The most frequent experience of testifying before a local court was doing so before the Court of Bosnia and Herzegovina (Court of BiH), an experience shared by about one in five respondents (18.8 per cent).

Views about the appropriate decision-maker

The ICTY was established in 1993, when the wars were still ongoing in the territory of the former Yugoslavia. At the time, local courts were not in a position to conduct the trials in cases of war crimes and crimes against humanity effectively and fairly. To address this issue ('to take effective measures to bring to justice the persons who are responsible' Resolution 808, 1993) and to provide an avenue for such trials, the ICTY was not only established, but also provided with the right to have primacy over national courts (ICTY 2012b). Although the ICTY and the local courts have concurrent jurisdiction, the ICTY has the right to request a case to be deferred from a local court to the ICTY.

As part of our survey, we asked the respondents to select the *primary* decision-maker they would prefer for trials involving war crimes and crimes against humanity.[3] Following this general question, the respondents were asked a series of preferred decision-maker questions for the specific eleven defendants (Slobodan Milošević, Radovan Karadžić, Ratko Mladić, Tihomir Blaškić, Esad Landžo, Stanislav Galić, Miodrag Jokić, Mile Mrkšić, Miroslav Radić, Veselin Šljivančanin and Radovan Stanković) (Table 10.2). Our questions included the defendants of various ethnic backgrounds (for example Esad Landžo is a Muslim/Bosniak, Tihomir Blaškić is a Croat, Slobodan Milošević was a Serb).

Table 10.2 Respondent designations of appropriate jurisdiction

	Percentage of respondents
Jurisdiction in general[a]	
ICTY	63.8
Local courts (BiH & CRO)	19.0
Courts in offender's country	4.8
Victims' families	12.4
For Milošević[b]	
ICTY	71.7
Local courts (BiH & CRO)	14.6
Courts in offender's country	1.7
Victims' families	12.0
For Karadžić and Mladić[c]	
ICTY	70.9
Local courts (BiH)	13.4
Courts in offender's country	2.6
Victims' families	13.1

3 The question was worded as follows: 'Who should primarily try the persons accused of war crimes committed in the territory of the former Yugoslavia?' Possible answers included 'the courts on the territory of Croatia and Bosnia and Herzegovina where the crimes have been committed', 'the courts of the offender's country or country whose army force he was a member of', 'the International Tribunal in The Hague', 'the families of the victims' and other options for respondents to fill in.

	Percentage of respondents
For Blaškić[d]	
ICTY	69.0
Local courts (BiH)	5.8
Courts in offender's country	14.9
Victims' families	10.3
For Landžo[e]	
ICTY	69.7
Local courts (BiH)	18.5
Courts in offender's country	3.8
Victims' families	8.1
For Galić[f]	
ICTY	69.7
Local courts (BiH)	18.5
Courts in offender's country	3.8
Victims' families	8.1
For Jokić[g]	
ICTY	69.0
Local courts (CRO)	20.1
Courts in offender's country	3.9
Victims' families	7.0
For Mrkšić, Radić, and Šljivančanin[h]	
ICTY	66.9
Local courts (BiH)	16.7
Courts in offender's country	4.1
Victims' families	12.3
For Stanković[i]	
ICTY	62.9
Local courts (BiH)	16.2
Courts in offender's country	5.1
Victims' families	15.9

[a] The question was worded as follows: 'Who should try the persons accused of war crimes committed in the territory of the former Yugoslavia?' The possible answers were: 'a) the courts on the territory of Croatia and Bosnia and Herzegovina where the crimes have been

committed; b) the courts of the offender's country or country whose army force he was a member of; c) the International Tribunal in The Hague; d) the families of the victims; e) other ______'.

[b] The question was worded as follows: 'In your opinion, who should try Slobodan Milošević?' The possible answers were: 'a) courts in Bosnia and Herzegovina/Croatia; b) courts in Serbia/the Serb Republic; c) the International Tribunal in The Hague; d) the families of the victims; e) other ______'.

[c] The question was worded as follows: 'In your opinion, who should try Radovan Karadžić and Ratko Mladić?' The possible answers were: 'a) courts in Bosnia and Herzegovina; b) courts in Serbia/the Serb Republic; c) the International Tribunal in The Hague; d) the families of the victims; e) other ______'. Because only a few respondents selected answers 'families of victims' and 'courts in Serbia/the Serb Republic', they were omitted from the 2000 cross-ethnicity analysis.

[d] The question was worded as follows: 'In your opinion, who should have tried Tihomir Blaškić?' In the 2003 version we added the explanation: 'In your opinion, who should have tried Tihomir Blaškić (the Commander of the Regional Headquarters of the HVO Armed Forces in central Bosnia as of June 1992)?' The possible answers were the same: 'a) courts in Croatia; b) courts in Bosnia and Herzegovina; c) the International Tribunal in The Hague; d) the families of the victims; and e) other ______'. Because only a few respondents selected answers 'families of victims' and 'courts in Croatia', they were omitted from the 2000 cross-ethnicity analysis.

[e] The question was worded as follows: 'In your opinion, who should have tried Esad Landžo?' In the 2003 version we added the explanation: 'In your opinion, who should have tried Esad Landžo (a guard at the Čelebići concentration camp)?' The possible answers were the same: 'a) courts in Croatia; b) courts in Bosnia and Herzegovina; c) the International Tribunal in The Hague; d) the families of the victims; and e) other ______'.

[f] The question was worded as follows: 'In your opinion, who should have tried Stanislav Galić (the major general who lead the Romanija Corps and maintained the siege of Sarajevo from 1992 to 1994)?' The possible answers were: 'a) courts in Bosnia and Herzegovina; b) courts in Serbia/the Serb Republic; c) the International Tribunal in The Hague; d) the families of the victims; e) other ______'.

[g] The question was worded as follows: 'In your opinion, who should have tried Miodrag Jokić (the admiral who led the shelling of Dubrovnik in 1991)?' The possible answers were: 'a) courts in Croatia; b) courts in Serbia/the Serb Republic; c) the International Tribunal in The Hague; d) the families of the victims; e) other ______'.

[h] The question was worded as follows: 'In your opinion, who should try Mile Mrkšić, Miroslav Radić, and Veselin Šljivančanin (accused of participating in the criminal enterprise in which the Serb forces after the fall of Vukovar mistreated and killed non-Serbs from the Vukovar Hospital)?' The possible answers were: 'a) courts in Croatia; b) courts in Serbia/the Serb Republic; c) the International Tribunal in The Hague; d) the families of the victims; e) other ______'.

[i] The question was worded as follows: 'In your opinion, who should have tried Radovan Stanković (accused of being a soldier in charge of a house in Foča in which Muslim women and girls were repeatedly raped and sexually assaulted)?' The possible answers were: 'a) courts in Bosnia and Herzegovina; b) courts in Serbia/the Serb Republic; c) the International Tribunal in The Hague; d) the families of the victims; e) other ______'.

The results show very clearly that the majority of respondents – about two-thirds – preferred the ICTY as the primary decision-maker in these types of cases. While in a minority, about one out of five respondents would prefer the local courts in Bosnia and Herzegovina or Croatia instead as the primary decision-makers. In addition, a small proportion of the respondents preferred either the victims' families or the courts in the offender's country as the primary decision-makers.

Dominant views about the primary decision-maker in cases involving war crimes and crimes against humanity did not change substantially when we followed up with the questions about specific defendants. Although the potential defendants varied across ethnicities, a strong majority of the respondents (above 60 per cent) supported the ICTY as the primary decision-maker for each and every one of these cases. The support seems to be somewhat weaker for Radovan Stanković (member of the Miljevina battalion, a Bosnian Serb paramilitary unit in Foča), whose case the ICTY had transferred to the Court of BiH.

Views on appropriate decision-maker and ethnicity

The war in the former Yugoslavia was fought along ethnicity lines and, as opinion polls and research studies show (for example Arzt 2006; Human Rights Center 2000; Kutnjak Ivković and Hagan 2011; Stover 2005; Stover and Weinstein 2004), the level of support for the ICTY varies substantially across the former republics and provinces. Accordingly, we also explore whether the respondents' choice of the primary decision-maker is related to their ethnicity.

The results, presented in Table 10.3, show that ethnicity and support for the ICTY are related. On the one hand, the overwhelming majority of the Bosniak/Muslim respondents preferred the ICTY as the primary decision-maker for all eight cases. On the other hand, the Croat respondents preferred the ICTY only for the key leaders, such as Slobodan Milošević (former President of Serbia), Radovan Karadžić (former President of the Serbian part of Bosnia, Republika Srpska) and Ratko Mladić (former Commander of the Bosnian Serb Army), and the Serb respondents did so only for Tihomir Blaškić (former Commander of the Regional Headquarters of the Bosnian Croat Army in central Bosnia).

Table 10.3 Respondent designations of appropriate jurisdiction by ethnicity

	Croats (%)	Bosiaks/ Muslims (%)	Serbs (%)	χ^2	*Phi*
Jurisdiction in general[a]					
ICTY	39.8	77.8	27.9	350.0***	.647***
Local courts (BiH & CRO)	51.6	12.1	16.3		
Courts in offender's country	0.1	0.3	27.9		
Victims' families	7.8	9.8	27.9		
For Milošević[b]					
ICTY	51.1	80.8	48.1	199.7***	.487***
Local courts (BiH & CRO)	39.1	9.8	8.7		
Courts in offender's country (Serbia/RS)	0.8	0.2	11.5		
Victims' families	9.0	9.3	31.7		
For Karadžić and Mladić[c]					
ICTY	54.2	78.7	48.5	206.0***	.496***
Local courts (BiH)	35.9	8.8	8.9		
Courts in offender's country (Serbia/RS)	1.5	0.2	18.8		
Victims' families	8.4	12.4	23.8		
For Blaškić[d]					
ICTY	40.6	79.8	50.0	192.3***	.469***
Local courts (BiH)	10.5	1.8	19.7		
Courts in offender's country (Croatia)	42.1	9.2	11.4		
Victims' families	6.8	9.2	18.9		
For Landžo[e]					
ICTY	36.6	66.9	43.9	106.4***	.350***
Local courts (Croatia)	1.5	0.8	1.5		
Courts in offender's country (BiH)	53.7	24.3	24.2		
Victims' families	8.2	8.0	30.3		
For Galić[f]					
ICTY	48.1	80.3	41.7	299.5***	.591***
Local courts (BiH)	45.1	13.8	8.7		

	Croats (%)	Bosiaks/ Muslims (%)	Serbs (%)	χ^2	*Phi*
Courts in offender's country (Serbia/RS)	1.5	0.3	25.2		
Victims' families	5.3	5.6	24.3		
For Jokić[g]					
ICTY	38.3	82.9	36.9	337.3***	.625***
Local courts (CRO)	54.9	10.4	27.0		
Courts in offender's country (Serbia/RS)	1.5	0.2	25.4		
Victims' families	5.3	6.6	10.7		
For Mrkšić, Radić, and Šljivančanin[h]					
ICTY	43.2	79.5	31.7	363.4***	.648***
Local courts (Croatia)	50.0	9.7	13.8		
Courts in offender's country (Serbia/RS)	0.8	0.3	26.8		
Victims' families	6.1	10.5	27.6		
For Stanković[i]					
ICTY	41.4	75.2	29.0	423.6***	.699***
Local courts (BiH)	49.6	10.0	6.5		
Courts in offender's country (Serbia/RS)	0.8	0.2	33.9		
Victims' families	8.3	14.6	30.6		

[a] The question was worded as follows: 'Who should try the persons accused of war crimes committed in the territory of the former Yugoslavia?' The possible answers were: 'a) the courts on the territory of Croatia and Bosnia and Herzegovina where the crimes have been committed; b) the courts of the offender's country or country whose army force he was a member of; c) the International Tribunal in The Hague; d) the families of the victims; e) other ______'.

[b] The question was worded as follows: 'In your opinion, who should try Slobodan Milošević?' The possible answers were: 'a) courts in Bosnia and Herzegovina/Croatia; b) courts in Serbia/the Serb Republic; c) the International Tribunal in The Hague; d) the families of the victims; e) other ______'.

[c] The question was worded as follows: 'In your opinion, who should try Radovan Karadžić and Ratko Mladić?' The possible answers were: 'a) courts in Bosnia and Herzegovina; b) courts in Serbia/the Serb Republic; c) the International Tribunal in The Hague; d) the families of the victims; e) other ______'. Because only a few respondents selected answers 'families of victims' and 'courts in Serbia/the Serb Republic', they were omitted from the

2000 cross-ethnicity analysis.

[d] The question was worded as follows: 'In your opinion, who should have tried Tihomir Blaškić?' In the 2003 version we added the explanation: 'In your opinion, who should have tried Tihomir Blaškić (the Commander of the Regional Headquarters of the HVO Armed Forces in central Bosnia as of June 1992)?' The possible answers were the same: 'a) courts in Croatia; b) courts in Bosnia and Herzegovina; c) the International Tribunal in The Hague; d) the families of the victims; and e) other ______'. Because only a few respondents selected answers 'families of victims' and 'courts in Croatia', they were omitted from the 2000 cross-ethnicity analysis.

[e] The question was worded as follows: 'In your opinion, who should have tried Esad Landžo?' In the 2003 version we added the explanation: 'In your opinion, who should have tried Esad Landžo (a guard at the Čelebići concentration camp)?' The possible answers were the same: 'a) courts in Croatia; b) courts in Bosnia and Herzegovina; c) the International Tribunal in The Hague; d) the families of the victims; and e) other ______'.

[f] The question was worded as follows: 'In your opinion, who should have tried Stanislav Galić (the major general who lead the Romanija Corps and maintained the siege of Sarajevo from 1992 to 1994)?' The possible answers were: 'a) courts in Bosnia and Herzegovina; b) courts in Serbia/the Serb Republic; c) the International Tribunal in The Hague; d) the families of the victims; e) other ______'.

[g] The question was worded as follows: 'In your opinion, who should have tried Miodrag Jokić (the admiral who led the shelling of Dubrovnik in 1991)?' The possible answers were: 'a) courts in Croatia; b) courts in Serbia/the Serb Republic; c) the International Tribunal in The Hague; d) the families of the victims; e) other ______'.

[h] The question was worded as follows: 'In your opinion, who should try Mile Mrkšić, Miroslav Radić, and Veselin Šljivančanin (accused of participating in the criminal enterprise in which the Serb forces after the fall of Vukovar mistreated and killed non-Serbs from the Vukovar Hospital)?' The possible answers were: 'a) courts in Croatia; b) courts in Serbia/the Serb Republic; c) the International Tribunal in The Hague; d) the families of the victims; e) other ______'.

[i] The question was worded as follows: 'In your opinion, who should have tried Radovan Stanković (accused of being a soldier in charge of a house in Foča in which Muslim women and girls were repeatedly raped and sexually assaulted)?' The possible answers were: 'a) courts in Bosnia and Herzegovina; b) courts in Serbia/the Serb Republic; c) the International Tribunal in The Hague; d) the families of the victims; e) other ______'.

Not selecting the ICTY implied that the respondents preferred other courts and there was rarely a strong, unified preference. On the other hand, there are certain patterns. With two exceptions (Tihomir Blaškić and Esad Landžo), the Croat respondents tended to be more likely to select the local courts in Bosnia and Herzegovina and Croatia as the alternatives, and less likely to select either the courts in the offender's country or victims' families. Our Serb respondents tended to be the strongest advocates of the courts in the offender's country and victims' families as the alternative decision-makers (particularly for Milošević, Karadžić and Mladić, Blaškić, Landžo, Galić, Mrkšić, Radić and Šljivančanin, and Stanković). Lastly, the Bosniak/Muslim respondents had the most homogeneous voice among the three ethnic groups. Typically, more than two-thirds of the Bosniak/Muslim respondents selected the ICTY. Among the Bosniak/Muslim respondents who did not select the ICTY, the answers were spread out across the other options (that is, local courts in BiH, victims' families), with a very small percentage (typically below 1 per cent) selecting the courts in Serbia/Republika Srpska.

Perceptions of the ICTY and ethnicity

Aside from asking the respondents to select the preferred decision-maker, we also explored the respondents' views of the ICTY and incorporated questions tapping into their perceptions of the ICTY fairness and its potential bias (Table 10.4).

Table 10.4 Perceptions of the ICTY by ethnicity

	Percentage of respondents	Croats (%)	Bosniaks/ Muslims (%)	Serbs (%)	χ^2	*Phi*
ICTY fairness[a]						
Fair	67.3	43.1	81.5	29.5	170.5***	.448***
ICTY independence achieved[b]						
Yes	70.2	51.5	82.7	36.8	140.7***	.400***

[a] The question was worded as follows: 'Do you think that the ICTY conducts the trials correctly and fairly and makes just decisions?' Possible answers range on a four-point Likert scale from a) 'definitely yes' to d) 'definitely no'. The variable has been dichotomized with 'definitely yes' and 'yes' coded as 1 and 'no' and 'definitely no' coded as 2.

[b] The question was worded as follows: 'Do you think that the International Tribunal in The Hague resists political pressure?' Possible answers range on a four-point Likert scale from a) 'definitely yes' to d) 'definitely no'. The variable has been dichotomized with 'definitely yes' and 'yes' coded as 1 and 'no' and 'definitely no' coded as 2.

The majority of respondents agreed that the ICTY makes fair decisions and conducts trials fairly. This finding, however, masks considerable heterogeneity of opinion related to respondent ethnicity. In particular, the majority of our respondents are Bosnian/Muslim and, at the same time, the overwhelming majority of Bosnian/ Muslim respondents evaluated the ICTY as fair (82 per cent). By contrast, the majority of our Croat and Serb respondents did not perceive the ICTY as fair (only about a quarter of the Serb respondents evaluated the ICTY as fair).

Most of the respondents thought that political independence of the ICTY has been achieved. Once again, though, the results are strongly related to the respondents' ethnicity. While the overwhelming majority of Bosnian/Muslim respondents (83 per cent) and about half of the Croat respondents (52 per cent) agreed that political independence has been achieved, only about one-third of the Serb respondents (37 per cent) agreed.

Multivariate models of the preferred decision-maker

We further explore the choice of the preferred decision-maker[4] with a logistic regression analysis in which selection of the decision-maker is the dependent variable, and the independent variables are the respondents' demographic characteristics (age, education, ethnicity and gender) and their views about the ICTY and its fairness.[5] The results of the logistic regression are summarized in Table 10.5.

Table 10.5 Logistic coefficients from the regression of the preferred decision-maker on respondents' attitudes and background characteristics

	Model 1			**Model 2**		
	B	s.e.	odds	B	s.e.	odds
Age in 1995[a]						
20 or younger	-.488	.479	.614	-.939	.774	.391
21-35	-.230	.410	.795	-.131	.693	.877
36-50	.161	.408	1.175	.297	.697	1.346

4 The question was worded as follows: 'Who should primarily try the persons accused of war crimes committed in the territory of the former Yugoslavia?' Possible answers included: 'the courts on the territory of Croatia and Bosnia and Herzegovina where the crimes have been committed', 'the courts of the offender's country or country whose army force he was a member of', 'the International Tribunal in The Hague', 'the families of the victims' and other options for respondents to fill in.

5 In addition to including measures of the respondents' perceptions of the ICTY overall fairness and the punishment purposes (for example retribution, special deterrence, general deterrence), we created a scale of 'political neutrality' to measure perceived political bias of the ICTY. The four items comprising the ICTY political neutrality scale capture the judges' ability to resist political pressure, judicial independence, national bias and the role played by political factors in judicial decisions.

	Model 1				Model 2			
	B		s.e.	odds	B		s.e.	odds
Education[b]								
Less than HS	-.420		.380	.657	.018		.564	1.018
HS	.278		.315	1.320	.140		.457	1.151
Some college	-.437		.364	.646	-.943		.526	.389
Ethnicity[c]								
Croat	.492		.289	1.636	-.289		.457	.749
Bosniak/ Muslim	2.355	***	.248	10.537	1.030	*	.401	2.801
Gender[d]	.406	*	.190	1.501	.277		.286	1.320
Political scale					-.172	*	.081	.842
ICTY fairness[e]					3.456	***	.327	31.696
Punishment purpose[f]								
Deterrence					-.867	**	.289	.420
Constant	-1.212		.538	.298	-.408		1.233	.665
Model Nagelkerke R Square	.261				.641			

* p < .05; ** p< .01; *** p< .001.

[a] Reference category is the oldest (above 50 years of age).

[b] Reference category is 'college'.

[c] Reference category is 'Serb'.

[d] Reference category is 'male'.

[e] Reference category is 'unfair'.

[f] Reference category is 'retribution'.

Compared to the views about the ICTY, demographic characteristics overall carry little weight as predictors of the preferred decision-maker in the full specification. The only demographic variable in the full specification that enters with statistical significance is ethnicity. Namely, the odds that the Muslim/Bosnian respondents would select the ICTY as the preferred decision-maker are 2.8 times as high as those of the Serb respondents.[6] Views about the ICTY's overall fairness

6 The odds effects are obtained by exponentiation of the logistic coefficients.

are *the* strongest predictor of the preferred decision-maker. The odds that the respondents who evaluated the ICTY overall as fair would select the ICTY as their preferred decision-maker are estimated to be 31.7 times as high as those of the respondents who evaluated the ICTY overall as unfair, all other covariates being equal. The respondents' views about ICTY judges' political independence were also relevant for the respondents' preferred decision-maker. In particular, a one-unit increase on the scale of perceived political influence decreases the odds that the respondents would evaluate the ICTY as fair overall by 0.8 times. Lastly, the respondents' view of the purpose of punishment for war crimes and crimes against humanity is related to their preferred decision-maker. The odds that the respondents who advocated retribution would select the ICTY as the preferred decision-maker decrease 0.4 times compared to the odds for the respondents who advocated deterrence.

Conclusions

The results of our study, based on the data from the 2007 survey of victims of war crimes and crimes against humanity, indicate that the respondents' choice of the preferred decision-maker in cases of war crimes and crimes against humanity is related to their ethnicity. Our results show support for different imageries of the ICTY, depending on whether the ethnic groups perceived that they were evaluated as 'defended' or 'defeated'. Bosnian/Muslim respondents (typically perceived by the ICTY as the 'defended') were more likely to the select the ICTY as the preferred decision-maker than were either Croat respondents (perceived by the ICTY as either the 'defeated' or the 'defended') or Serb respondents (perceived by the ICTY as primarily 'defeated'). These findings are stable regardless of whether we asked the question in general or targeted a particular defendant.

Our results emphasize that the respondents' ethnicity remains the most critical demographic characteristic. Controlling for other covariates in our models, Bosnian/Muslim respondents were more likely to select the ICTY as the preferred decision-maker and view it as fair than Serb respondents did, whereas there are no statistically significant differences between the Croat and Bosnian/Muslim views. That ethnicity matters should not be surprising in light of the fact that the war in the former Yugoslavia was fought along ethnicity lines and, as prior research indicates, public confidence in the ICTY typically is found to be substantially lower in Serbia than it is in Bosnia and Herzegovina. Our results fit well with the results of the 2002 International Institute for Democracy and Electoral Assistance survey, in which only a miniscule minority of Serb respondents (8 per cent in Serbia and 4 per cent in *Republika Srpska*) and a small proportion of Croat respondents (21 per cent) showed trust in the ICTY, compared to about half of the respondents from the Bosnian Federation (51 per cent; International Institute for Democracy and Electoral Assistance 2002).

On the other hand, the finding that there were no statistically significant differences between the views about the primary decision-maker expressed by Croat and Serb respondents once additional control variables are entered into the model suggests that ethnicity is an approximation of different sets of values, potentially influenced by the political climate in the country or 'cognitive landscapes', the term coined by Sampson and Bartusch (1998) and applied by Kutnjak Ivković and Hagan (2011) to the context of international law. It emphasizes the influence of the environment on the formation of attitudes towards the ICTY. Indeed, our results are in accordance with Sampson and Bartusch's notion of 'cognitive landscapes', indicating that 'defeated' ethnic groups – such as Serbs – generate more negative views of justice delivered than do 'defended' ethnic groups – such as Bosnians/Muslims. Thus, the political environments in which these ethnic groups live are of critical importance to their understanding of the ICTY and its justice. Being viewed as members of a 'defeated' ethnic group, regardless of whether this notion is sometimes interchanged with the perception of the 'defended' group (as is the case for Croats), has very strong connotations for the overall level of support for the ICTY.

A potentially larger mismatch between the ethnic group's own perceptions and the ICTY's perceptions of the ethnic group – another imagery explored – could generate stronger perceptions of ICTY's bias and less satisfaction with the ICTY. Clearly, as the mismatch is larger for Croats and Serbs than it is for Muslims/Bosnians, the level of support for the ICTY is lower among Croats and Serbs than it is among Muslims/Bosnians. Perceptions of ICTY fairness – fairness of its decisions and its procedures – are *the* key in explaining the respondents' choice of the primary decision-maker. If the respondents had believed that the ICTY was not fair, they were much less likely to have advocated the ICTY as the preferred decision-maker. Thus, in accordance with justice theories, be the justice distributive or procedural, confidence in the ICTY was related to how fair or unbiased the respondents perceived the ICTY to be. Whereas these are respondents' evaluations of the ICTY fairness, lacking direct experience with the ICTY, their views likely have been shaped primarily by the media and politicians' comments about the ICTY. This finding further reinforces the role of 'cognitive landscapes' (see Kutnjak Ivković and Hagan 2011) in understanding the evaluations of the ICTY and its justice, and it contributes towards understanding the key to the differences in the levels of support for the ICTY among 'defended' and 'defeated' ethnic groups. To put it plainly, although justice may be international, its interpretation is highly contextual and local.

References

Arzt, D. 2006. Views on the Ground: The Local Perception of International Criminal Tribunals in the Former Yugoslavia and Sierra Leone. *Annals of the American Academy of Political and Social Science*, 601(1), 226-239.

Biro, M., Ajduković, D., Čorkalo, D., Dijpa, D., Milin, P. and Weinstein, H.M. 2004. Attitudes towards Justice and Social Reconstruction in Bosnia and Herzegovina and Croatia. In *My Neighbor, My Enemy: Justice and Community after Mass Atrocity*, edited by E. Stover and H.M. Weinstein, 183-205. Cambridge: Cambridge University Press.

Čorkalo, D., Ajduković, D., Weinstein, Harvey M., Stover, E., Djipa, D. and Biro, M. 2004. Neighbors Again? Intercommunity Relations after Ethnic Cleansing. In *My Neighbor, My Enemy: Justice and Community after Mass Atrocity*, edited by E. Stover and H.M. Weinstein, 143-161. Cambridge: Cambridge University Press.

Ellis, M.S. 1999. Bringing Justice to an Embattled Region – Creating and Implementing the 'Rules of the Road' for Bosnia-Herzegovina. *Berkeley Journal of International Law*, 17, 1-25.

Humanitarian Law Center. 2006. *Transitional Justice Report Serbia, Montenegro and Kosovo, 1999–2005*. Available at http://www.b92.net/eng/download.phtml?35394,0,0 (accessed 2 October 2012).

Human Rights Center and the International Human Rights Law Clinic 2000. Report: Justice Accountability and Social Reconstruction: An Interview Study of Bosnian Judges and Prosecutors. *Berkeley Journal of International Law*, 18, 102-164.

Husejnović, M. 2007. Waiting for a Strategy. Balkans Investigative Reporting Network. Available at http://www.bim.ba/en/95/10/7165/?tpl=30 (accessed 10 May 2010).

International Institute for Democracy and Electoral Assistance. 2002. *South East Europe Public Agenda Survey.* Stockholm, Sweden. Available at http://www.idea.int/europe_cis/balkans/see_survey.cfm (accessed 5 January 2010).

ICTY. 2012a. *About the ICTY*. Available at http://www.icty.org/sections/AbouttheICTY (accessed 2 October 2012).

ICTY. 2012b. *Statute of the Tribunal*. Available at http://www.icty.org/sections/LegalLibrary/StatuteoftheTribunal (accessed 2 October 2012).

Jutarnji List. 2000. Survey shows 'Anti-Hague atmosphere' increasing in Croatia. *FBIS Doc. EUP20000823000244*, 19 August (trans. of *Jutarnji List* (Zagreb)).

Kapsis, R.E. 1978. Black Ghetto Diversity and Anomie: A Sociopolitical View. *American Journal of Sociology*, 83(5), 1132-1153.

Kutnjak Ivković, S. and Hagan, J. 2011. *Reclaiming Justice*. New York: Oxford University Press.

McMahon, P. and Miller, J. 2009. On a Wing and a Prayer: The Effect of the ICTY on the Balkans. Paper presented at the annual meeting of the Midwest Political Association 67th Annual National Conference, The Palmer House Hilton, Chicago, IL, 2 April.

Sampson, R.J. and Bartusch, D.J. 1998. Legal Cynicism and Subcultural Tolerance of Deviance: The Neighborhood Context of Racial Differences. *Law and Society Review*, 32, 777-804.

Stover, E. 2005. *The Witnesses: War Crimes and the Promise of Justice in The Hague*. Philadelphia: University of Pennsylvania Press.

Stover, E. and Weinstein, H.M. 2004. *My Neighbor, My Enemy: Justice and Community in the Aftermath of Mass Atrocity*. Cambridge: Cambridge University Press.

UN Security Council. 1993. *Resolution 827, adopted 25 May 1993* S/RES/827, 1993. UN, A/59/215-S/2004/627. Available at http://www.unhcr.org/refworld/docid/3b00f21b1c.html (accessed 10 May 2010).

UN Security Council. 1994. *Final Report of the Commission of Experts Established Pursuant to Security Council Resolution 780 (1982)*, UN Doc. S/1994/674 (27 May 1994). Available at http://www.icty.org/x/file/About/OTP/un_commission_of_experts_report1994_en.pdf (accessed 2 October 2012).

Wilson, R. (2005). Judging History: The Historical Record of the International Criminal Tribunal for the Former Yugoslavia. *Human Rights Quarterly*, 27(3), 908-942.

PART IV
Discourse and Artistic Expression

Chapter 11

Wagner in Israel: The Mixture of Politics and Music

Dina Siegel[1]

There are countless publications on Richard Wagner (1813-1883): Wagner the composer, Wagner the philosopher, Wagner the storyteller, Wagner the genius and Wagner the anti-Semite. The last one is the crucial element, which places him in an ongoing social debate on whether the composer as a person with his beliefs and ideas can be separated from the composer as a musician whose brilliant creations have had an enormous impact on the hearts and minds of millions of admirers around the world.

In his lifetime, Wagner created 13 musical dramas, many instrumental works and vocal compositions. He was one of the inventors of a new musical language, which some consider the beginning of modern classical music, while others view it as a sophisticated variant of Romanticism. He introduced a new multi-dimensional opera, which combined music, poetry (legends), drama, scenery and even architecture and design (referring to the Bayreuth building, which had an acoustic significance). He enlarged the orchestra by including a greater number of instruments, thereby enhancing the volume of the sound, and made frequent use of 'off-stage instruments' for special effects (Cares 1964). Other novelties in musical techniques included increased chromaticism and the first attempts at 'atonality', which was later developed by Arnold Schoenberg and his followers. Wagner's musical ideas were further developed and refined by many composers in the twentieth century.

But Wagner was not only a musician; he also wrote and published hundreds of essays, stories, libretti for his own operas, plays and pamphlets. Wagner immersed himself in philosophy, theology, sociology and political science. His turbulent personal and professional life was marked by scandalous love affairs, political exile and extreme poverty (which later turned into enormous wealth). He was a controversial person during his lifetime, but even more so after his death.

Richard Wagner created operas about dwarves, witches, giants and heroes, about the struggle between light and darkness and about the power of beautiful women and courageous men whose pure blood and uncorrupted souls could defeat all the evils in the world. These fairy tales he put to wonderful music, full of emotions, from tender love to endless hatred, music played in sophisticated

1 I would like to thank Lodewijk Brunt and Willem de Haan for their useful comments.

counterpoints, chromatic phrases and unexpected sounds and effects. Nobody could remain indifferent to these 'musical dramas', whether they admired or hated the stories, messages and music in Wagner's own times, but even more after his death, in his own country and elsewhere in the world. The most extreme form of emotional reaction to his music came almost a century later from a country that did not even exist in Wagner's time, namely Israel.

This chapter is about one of the greatest myths in the social history of music, the so-called 'Wagner myth', as it has been created and preserved in Israel since the Second World War. And my purpose is twofold: first, to analyse the expression of Wagner's anti-Semitism in his operas and other music, and second, to discuss the political reasons for preserving the 'Wagner myth' in Israel as part of the collective memory of the Holocaust.

The questions in themselves are not new: a great number of scholars have tried to analyse Wagner's ideas from his own writings, or to interpret the messages of his mainly verbal musical work. In this chapter, I will analyse Wagner's music in the historical context in which it was created and in the context of his own social world, including his contacts, the presentation of his ideas in oral and written form and the reaction of his environment. But, in my own contribution to our understanding of the 'Wagner myth', I will also place his music in a context where the social position of the composer himself plays no role at all, since he is no longer alive. The focus here is on how and by whom his music, its symbols, messages and emotions have been presented, interpreted and manipulated in Israel in the second half of the twentieth and the beginning of the twenty-first century.

The 'Wagner myth' in Israel is based on the belief that the composer's extreme anti-Semitism has inspired, and even became part of, Nazi ideology; that at the sounds of his music Jews were led to the gas chambers, and that he therefore is a personification of all the evils committed against Jews. As a result, his music, which is viewed in Israel as the 'music of death', should not be played in the Jewish state – out of compassion for the victims of the Holocaust and as an effort towards social solidarity. I will argue here that by creating this taboo about Wagner and his work, by forcing his music to be forgotten, the opposite has been achieved: we are forced to remember.

From 2008 to 2010 I conducted research on the impact of Wagner's music. In addition to a content analysis of Wagner's work (that is, all his operas, including both musical and verbal expressions), I also employed other ethnographic research methods, such as observations of how people (varying from Holocaust survivors to young Israelis) react to his music. I conducted long conversations with respondents and carried out musical experiments, which I will describe in more detail later in this chapter. I also analysed various internet blogs and the reactions of listeners and readers to news and other information about Wagner in Israel. Ethnographic research makes it possible to collect material not only on the specific situation with regard to Wagner's music, but also on the whole socio-political context in which Israeli views and perceptions are formed.

Anti-Semitism in nineteenth-century Germany: Wagner and Herzl

Wagner was one of the most notorious anti-Semites of the nineteenth century. His anti-Jewish ideas should be understood in the socio-political context of Europe in his time. Anti-Semitism was embedded in society and the Jews were always blamed for a myriad of political, economic and even environmental problems.

The ninth child of a police official and a baker's daughter, Richard Wagner was born on 22 May 1813 in Leipzig, where he spent his early childhood in the Jewish quarter of the city. His father died when he was only six months old and nine months later his mother married the actor and poet Ludwig Geyer, and the family moved to Dresden. All his life Wagner suspected that Geyer was his biological father, but he also feared that Geyer was Jewish, which meant that he himself might also be (partially) Jewish. This preoccupation with his alleged Jewishness from a very early age greatly influenced his own life, and much later the lives of many other people. His obsession with his (step)father's alleged Jewish roots was not based on real evidence. Derek Watson (1979: 22) has argued that, first of all, Ludwig Geyer was not Jewish at all, that his family was Protestant on both sides, and second, that there is no strong evidence that Geyer was Wagner's biological father. The mystery surrounding Geyer's parenthood comes from the letters Geyer sent to the widow Wagner, referring to Richard by the nickname 'the Cossack', which allegedly showed some intimate affection, sometimes interpreted by Wagner's biographers as father–son sentiment (Watson 1979: 21). Geyer's paternity, however, was never proved, and it remains one of the mysteries of Wagner's life.

Nineteenth-century Germany was characterized by so-called Germanomania, the glorification of the German people as 'chosen' (Poliakov 2003), and the terms 'Blut und Boden' (blood and soil), 'race' and 'ancestry' were regularly used in the language of certain circles. In 1850, Wagner anonymously published an essay entitled 'Das Judenthum in der Musik' (Jewishness in Music) in the *Neue Zeitschrift für Musik*, in which he attacked Jewish composers, particularly his contemporaries Felix Mendelssohn and Giacomo Meyerbeer, and claimed that Jews were a harmful element in German culture in general and in music in particular. According to Wagner these two composers could imitate western music, but were unable to understand, feel and express its complexity and depth (Poliakov 2003: 118). Looking back on Wagner's biography we see, however, that he had several good friends who were Jewish, including Herman Levi, the brilliant conductor of the opera *Parsifal*, Joseph Rubinstein and particularly Samuel Lehr, the relationship with whom Wagner described in his memoires *Mein Leben* as one of the best in his life (Watson 1979: 61).

Perhaps it was the essay 'Das Judenthum in der Musik', inspired by his difficult relationship with Giacomo Meyerbeer, perhaps Wagner was strongly influenced by his second wife Cosima (the daughter of Franz Liszt), who openly expressed her hatred for Jews,[2] but in any case his image as one of the most notorious anti-Semites of his epoch was already formed during his lifetime. One hypothesis is that he wrote the essay because of his rivalry with Mendelssohn, who was enormously popular, and whose music Wagner himself sometimes admired and sometimes despised (Deathridge 2008: 182). In any case, Wagner's anti-Semitism was not welcomed and following the publication of 'Das Judenthum in der Musik', the editor of the journal, Franz Brendel, professor of musical history at the Conservatory of Leipzig, was called to resign (Watson 1979: 119).

Even among German anti-Semites of his period, Wagner stood out for his malicious ranting. His first anti-Semitic essay was later followed by a number of other articles in his *Bayreuther Blatter*, full of even more extreme anti-Jewish sentiments. With the years, Wagner's ideas became more radical. In the 1880s, the relationship between the Germans and the Jews deteriorated even further because of the stock-market crash of 1873, for which Jews were blamed (Buruma 1999: 197). In 1881 Wagner wrote to Ludwig II, the King of Bavaria: 'I regard the Jewish race as the born enemy of pure humanity and everything that is noble in it' (quoted in Poliakov 2003: 447). It is also clear from numerous other letters and documents that Wagner was an anti-Semite who openly expressed his hatred for Jews, and attempts made by some authors to play this down are unconvincing. There is no consensus, however, on the explanation for Wagner's anti-Semitism. Poliakov (2003: 452) considered it a form of neurosis, the inner suffering of the artist. His 'disease' allegedly came from his childhood conflict regarding the dual and uncertain paternity of his alleged Jewish stepfather. 'Wagner's conversion to anti-Semitism can be thought to have put some balsam on the wound' (Poliakov 2003: 452).

On the other hand, it is also viewed as a sign of the times in which he lived, a *mal du siècle*. In the course of the nineteenth century, anti-Semitism in Europe had grown from relatively insignificant incidents into a vibrant phenomenon, which culminated in France during and after the Dreyfus affair, when anti-Semitism divided French society, famous writers, composers, actors and philosophers into two hostile ideological camps.

The prevalent ideology in most European countries was romantic nationalism, characterized by tribal loyalty and rooted in language, the significance of local customs and traditions, expressions and meanings. Nationalist romantic music came *inter alia* from Bohemia, Scandinavia and Russia. Bedřich Smetana and Antonin Dvořák in Czechia, Pyotr Ilyich Tchaikovsky and the members of

2 It is remarkable that Cosima's anti-Semitism, too, is connected to her family roots. However, unlike Wagner, who only suspected his (step)father of being Jewish, Cosima's maternal grandmother did have a Jewish father (Watson 1979: 151).

moguchaya kuchka (Mighty Handful)[3] in Russia, and Edvard Grieg and Jean Sibelius in Norway and Finland respectively are just some examples of composers whose music was inspired by folk songs and ancient melodies.

In Germany and Austria, much research in various academic disciplines was dedicated at the time to the search for the origins of the German language, and to Nordic folklore, songs and legends. This research was geared to a historical justification of nationalistic ideas, and the superiority of the German nation, whereas all other peoples were considered to be culturally, and later also biologically, inferior. Anti-Semitism was a part of this general tendency to categorize and identify races and peoples. In 1815, the brothers Wilhelm and Jacob Grimm published two volumes of *Fairy Tales*, some of which openly expressed anti-Jewish sentiments and portrayed Jews as villains. Various intellectuals also expressed anti-Semitic views, including Ludwig Feuerbach, Friedrich Hegel, Bruno Bauer and Karl Gutzkow. According to Adorno, Wagner's anti-Semitic ideas were shared by 'representatives of what Marx called the German Socialism of 1848' (1952: 13). Adorno himself criticized Wagner's music as the reinforcement of ethno-nationalism, or in his words 'collective narcissism'.

One of the many paradoxes reflecting the 'Wagner myth' and the responses to his music is that Theodor Herzl, the founder of modern Zionism, was an admirer of Wagner's music, regardless of what he may have felt about the composer's anti-Semitism. According to some authors, Herzl wrote his famous *Der Judenstaat* after attending the opera *Tannhäuser* and at his request the Second Zionist Congress was opened to the sound of the opera's overture (Beller 1994; Garrett 2011). In his novel *Altneuland*, Miriam, the symbol of a modern Jew living in a new Jewish state sings: 'Wagner, Verdi, Gounod, the music of all the nations' (Herzl 1941: 263). In his detailed analysis of the different interpretations of the opera's ideas and symbols, Steven Beller compares Wagner and Herzl, arguing that while Wagner claimed that for Jews 'to become human-beings' they should cease being Jews, Herzl proposed to separate and preserve Jewish identity, since the emancipation in Europe had failed, and to solve the problem of anti-Semitism by an exodus (Beller 1994: 142). Both ideas are present, according to researchers, in the symbolism of *Tannhäuser* and specifically in its two main themes, self-sacrifice and redemption: when Tannhäuser leaves the grotto of Venus (reminiscent of the Jewish ghetto), when Elisabeth sacrifices herself for true love (true identity) and when Tannhäuser chooses death (redemption) over being repressed in the grotto again (that is, living in a society with embedded anti-Semitic sentiments). Herzl allegedly saw this redemption as the main reason for European Jews to establish their own Jewish state somewhere else, and he dreamed of a new type of strong Jewish Knight (an Israeli) (Beller 1994; Garrett 2011). Herzl admired Wagner's opera perhaps

3 This group of composers included Mily Balakirev, Alexander Borodin, Modest Mussorgsky, Nikolai Rimsky-Korsakov and César Cui. They aimed to create a pure Russian music, based on Cossack songs and melodies, which also included the sound of Russian Orthodox Church bells and chants.

because he could identify with the ideas of European liberalism and nationalism by applying them to the Jewish identity and by emphasizing the importance of historical roots, blood, race and the land of Israel as the ancient homeland of the Jewish people. 'And if Hitler's Third Reich was set to Wagnerian music, so was Herzl's vision of Zion' (Buruma 1999: 198). Herzl was inspired by the strength of the emotional expressions and musical effects of Wagner's music.

There is a variety of studies on Wagner's anti-Semitism in his life and work. Some authors try to prove that Wagner was a fanatical anti-Semite in his ideas and in his operas (Millington 1999; Rose 1996; Weiner 1995), but there are also Wagner apologists, who distinguish between Wagner the thinker and Wagner the musician and play down the anti-Jewish sentiments expressed in his art (Dahlhaus 1979; Deathridge 2008; Skelton 1994; Van Amerongen 1984; Watson 1979). The main purpose of the latter group is to preserve Wagner's musical legacy.

Anti-Semitism in Wagner's operas

Did Wagner express his anti-Semitism in his musical dramas? Writing libretti for his operas Wagner turned to ancient Germanic myths as the essence of Folk, in which the verbal message appeared to be even more powerful than the music. Actually, Wagner himself believed that music can only interpret, reflect and strengthen the message of the text (Poliakov 2003: 121). Following Simmel's argument, a composer creates his work as an expression of the essence of the society in which he lives and therefore music also expressed the anti-Jewish sentiments prevailing in nineteenth-century Germany.

In some of Wagner's operas, there is a clear distinction between heroic German music, full of dramatic and victorious sounds, and Teutonic heroes with deep voices on the one hand, and the (Jewish) anti-heroes characterized by high, broken, almost squeaking sounds on the other. The German heroes, accompanied by 'loud noises made by trumpets, shrill sounding oboes, and drums so that everyone hears the approach of the powerful monarch' (Honigsheim 1989: 58), stand in contrast to the ridiculous and inferior hunchbacks, witches, magicians and jabbering dwarves such as Alberich and Mime in *Das Rheingold*, Klingsor in *Parsifal* and Beckmesser in *Die Meistersinger* (Ross 2007: 336). The image of Kundry from *Parsifal* in particular is often associated with Wagner's ideas about Judaism and its destruction. Wagner himself compared Kundry to the 'Wandering Jew', who can never die and is therefore dangerous (Deathridge 2008: 175). The character of Alberich in *Das Rheingold* is a greedy creature who thinks only about gold. The stereotypical Jew in medieval Europe was strongly associated with money and gold: many Jewish names began with 'Gelt' ('Gold') and the main Jewish occupations included tax collecting and money-lending. The symbol of the Rhine as Germanic territory invaded by Jews represents another alleged anti-Semitic intention of Wagner's operas. Alberich's brother Mime (*Die Walküre*) lives in a dark cave and looks like a toad, another symbolic image of the Jew in medieval Europe which, in this context, represents the darkness and lowness of Jews as opposed to the brightness and might of the Aryan race.[4] Even though these characters are not directly and explicitly mentioned as representing Jews, small nuances, such as the way in which Mime and Kundry complain, may give hints that they are Jewish. Slavoj Žižek wrote in his foreword to Adorno's analysis of Wagner: 'it is not enough to "decode" Alberich, Mime, Hagen and so on as Jews, making the point that the *Ring* is one big anti-Semitic tract … the more basic fact is that the anti-Semitic figure of the Jew itself is not a direct ultimate referent, but is already "encoded", a cipher of ideological and social antagonism' (Žižek 1952: xiv).

Wagner assigned musical themes (*Leitmotifs*) to his characters, whether human or divine. The clear contrast between music attributed to the inferior Nibelungs and the heroic Volsungs can also be viewed as an anti-Semitic message, which shows the contrasting images of contemptible Jews versus powerful Germans. Hartmut Zelinsky linked *Parsifal* with Wagner's racial approach, with the pure Aryan race supposedly being cleansed from any mixture, particularly with the Jewish race (Weiner 1995: 366). According to Deathridge (2008: 177), *Parsifal* is a myth about humankind, often interpreted as related to Wagner's ideas of race and misunderstood ideas about identity.

It is doubtful whether a listener in the nineteenth century would have been able to recognize the anti-Jewish sentiments in the music or the stories of Wagner's operas. But even if Wagner's operas include symbols and language that could only be understood by 'insiders', people who shared the nationalistic ideas and codes hidden in Wagner's scenes and music, and even if it is not easy to establish a clear link between music, fairy tale and ideology, the numerous drafts, notes and letters written by the composer explain his ideas quite clearly and leave no doubt about his anti-Semitic intentions. A question rarely addressed in the vast literature on Wagner's anti-Jewish messages in his music is to what extent they propagated violence or the destruction of Jews as inferior folk. A quick search of the content of the operas shows that they include plenty of crimes, such as murder, various forms of violence, theft and more. In addition, the dominant message, although not directly targeted specifically against Jews as such, is the propaganda of racial superiority based on high moral values and physical strength, which was popular in the age of national romanticism. Wagner's messages can be logically interpreted in the framework of his extreme anti-Semitism.

Other authors have tried to introduce alternative interpretations of the ideas and messages of Wagner's operas, such as Theodor Adorno (1952), who viewed Wagner's operas in terms of a rejection of capitalism and commodity fetishism. Wagner perhaps used myth, which he himself considered as something universal, not connected to one specific nation or land, to present contemporary ideas and

4 According to Adorno, Wagner himself looked like a dwarf: 'his own physical appearance, disproportionately small, with over-large head and protruding chin, bordered on the abnormal and only fame preserved him from ridicule' (1952: 14).

symbols of European society in the nineteenth century. He indeed did not hide his ideas in his writings, therefore the question is why should he hide them in his music? The obsession with Wagner's anti-Semitism is perhaps born of revulsion, ideas attributed to him may never have entered his mind and the interpretation of his musical and literary messages is not grounded (see also Sheffi 2001). The question, therefore, is not whether people can understand his symbols, but how and by whom the main issue of Wagner's anti-Semitism was emphasized and put on the political agenda, particularly in Israel.

Wagner and Hitler

Wagner died in 1889, six years before another great anti-Semite was born. Hitler loved Wagner. He also liked other German composers, such as Ludwig van Beethoven and Anton Bruckner, a disciple of Wagner, but he worshipped Richard Wagner. As a soldier in the First World War he had carried Wagner's music from *Tristan* in his knapsack. 'In 1934, when he appeared at a Wagner commemoration in Leipzig, observers noted that he spoke with "tears in his voice"' (Ross 2007: 333). A performance of Wagner's opera *Rienzi* had inspired him, in his own words, to enter politics (Ross 2007: 340). Hitler's obsession with the opera *Parsifal* was so strong that, when Goebbels and Himmler wanted it removed from German stages because of its message of mystical Christianity (which did not fit the Nazi spirit), Hitler ordered in response: 'Design a timeless Grail temple', thereby going against his own party and ideology (Ross 2007: 359). Hitler did not want to banish *Parsifal* because of its Christianity, but tried to interpret it in a new non-religious spirit, using Wagner's own approach that, despite its doctrine borrowed from the Church, it is a denial of 'the whole phenomenon of Christianity in history' (Deathridge 2008: 174). As a result, more than 23 performances of the opera were staged between 1939 and 1942 in Vienna alone (Deathridge 2008: 174).

Hitler often wanted Wagner's music to be performed at party rallies. He also maintained a close relationship with the Wagner family and regularly participated in Wagner festivals in Bayreuth. After the death of her husband, Cosima Wagner devoted her life to creating a Wagner cult, a kind of religious sect, which she called 'the Knights of the Grail', by preserving the anti-Semitic slogans of the Bayreuth Circle (Der Bayreuther Kreis) and what the members of the Circle considered Wagner's philosophical operas (Kohler 2000: 111-113). Hitler became a close friend of the Wagner family. The re-birth of the Nazi movement has sometimes been considered to have resulted from the performances of Wagner's music at the *Festspielhaus* in Bayreuth (Kohler 2000: 191).

Hitler obviously admired Wagner's music, but it is unclear whether or not he had read his anti-Semitic essay, as it was not reprinted before the Nazi period, and it is unlikely that it influenced Hitler's anti-Semitism.

The fact that Richard Wagner was Hitler's favourite composer had an impact all around the world. The Nazis embraced Wagner as their national composer, while in the Soviet Union and several other countries Wagner was totally excluded from the repertoire of orchestras and educational programmes. Because he was idolized by Hitler, Wagner came to be seen as a proto-Nazi.[5]

Wagner in Israel – the historical background and the construction of the problem

Before 1938, Wagner's music was very popular in the Hebrew *Yeshuv* (settlement) in pre-Israel Palestine. During its first two years, the Palestine Orchestra, founded in 1936 by Bronisław Huberman (which later became the Israeli Philharmonic Orchestra), played different works by Richard Wagner, whom it considered one of the great western composers, despite his anti-Semitism. This all changed with *Kristallnacht* (9 November 1938), after which the Palestine Symphonic Orchestra cancelled a performance of the prelude to *Die Meistersinger von Nürnberg* at the last minute and swore never to play Wagner in Palestine again (Sheffi 2001).

After the Second World War, the Israeli government tried to normalize its relations with West Germany, while the survivors of the Nazi concentration camps who had moved to Israel protested against any contact with the Germans. Memories of the Holocaust determined the official restrictions regarding the import of German products and the use of the German language in Israel in public (Hirshberg and Ramot 2006: 512; Sheffi 1999: 622-627). Famous German arias and songs were translated into Hebrew, which made it almost impossible for non-Hebrew singers to perform them in a proper way.

The collective memory also included Wagner. Holocaust survivors remembered that his music was played in the concentration camps, often forcibly performed by Jewish musicians. How the Nazis, who treated their prisoners with such brutality in the concentration camps, could at the same time show such admiration for classical music would be a fascinating criminological subject. Survivors of the Shoah testified on different occasions that Wagner's music was performed at their arrival in Terezín and Auschwitz and when the prisoners were led to the gas chambers. Almost all Nazi camps had their own orchestra (Gilbert 2005). On the other hand, there were also survivors, including Jewish musicians who had played in the orchestras, who did not remember Wagner being played. As Anita Lasker-Wallfisch said in an interview with Stephen Fry, the orchestras in the camps were neither large enough nor good enough to play Wagner: 'We certainly did not play Wagner.'[6] In addition, Wagner was not played in camps, where 'subhumans' – Jews, Roma, Sinti – were interned, because Germans would not allow the

5 In his book *The Rest is Noise*, Alex Ross (2007) asks whether there was such a thing as the 'Nazi sound' and the question arises as to whether Wagner was indeed the foremost representative or maybe even the inventor of the 'Nazi sound'.

6 Interview with Anita Lasker-Wallfisch by Stephen Fry, 1996, *Wagner and Me*, documentary film, Wavelength Films production in Association with the BBC.

music of their idol to be played by or for these 'creatures' out of respect to him. However, the truth of whether or not Wagner was played in the camps was no longer relevant. 'The possibility that his music had been played in the camps and the dark connotation his name had for Holocaust survivors, made any concession unthinkable' (Sheffi 2001: 51). The collective memory is based in this case on the possibility and not on the facts.

Between the 1950s and 1970s, several German composers were transformed into the embodiment of the Nazi evils and injustice towards the Jews and associated with the music of the concentration camps, 'the music of death'. These 'forbidden composers' included Liszt, Lehár, Orff and Wagner.[7] Playing this music in Israel was considered highly insensitive and immoral. In 1953, on his fourth tour of Israel, the famous violinist Jascha Heifetz played a violin sonata by Richard Strauss in a recital. Attempts by the Israeli Minister of Education to stop him from playing the 'Nazi composer' were unsuccessful. The incident took place only eight years after the Holocaust and the memory was still fresh. Heifetz's decision to play music by Strauss to a (as it turned out) mostly hostile audience was based on his conviction that music must stand above history and that every musician has the right to choose his own repertoire. As one of my respondents remembers the concert: 'When he finished playing nobody applauded, there was a dead silence in the concert hall. We looked at each other in disbelief: I liked Heifetz, everybody of my generation did, but I did not expect a Jew to be so indifferent, cold, apathetic. I never again bought his records.'

The incident caused uproar in the Israeli media. Heifetz continued to play Strauss in other Israeli cities during the tour. In Jerusalem, the police blocked off access to the concert hall. Heifetz received anonymous letters and threatening phone calls in his hotel. During the concert, the fuses from the electrical box were removed and the lights in the concert hall went out, irritating the violinist and interfering with his performance. After the concert in Jerusalem, Heifetz was attacked in the street by a man with an iron bar and hit on his right arm. The Municipal Council of Jerusalem later apologized to Heifetz for the 'rude attack' on him (Jerusalem Municipal Council 1953). The assailant was never found, but the attack was attributed to an extremist from the Jewish terrorist group Malchut Israel (Kingdom of Israel), which was opposed to the Israeli-German 'reparation agreement' and involved in carrying out attacks on diplomats and other representatives from countries it considered to be 'anti-Semitic' (Pedahzur and Perliger 2009: 176).

The music of Richard Strauss, Carl Orff, Franz Lehár and other collaborators with the Nazi regime, however, has been performed in Israel since the 1970s. Straus was 'forgiven for two main reasons: he was a good friend of the Jewish writer Stefan Zweig, and his daughter-in-law was Jewish, which meant that he was the grandfather of two Jewish children according to Jewish law' (Sheffi 2001: 126,

7 Remarkably, Beethoven, who was not living but was adored by the Nazis just as much as Wagner, did not become a 'forbidden composer' in Israel.

127). Lehár too was included in the repertoire of the Israeli orchestras: his wife Sophie was Jewish before her conversion to Christianity. Even the music of Carl Orff was back in Israel, although his claims that he was one of the founders of the resistance movement in Germany were never proven.

In the 1990s, Wagner remained the only composer to whom there was strong opposition. The boycott of Wagner's music is still ongoing. Since he became the symbol of the Holocaust, 'the Wagner phenomenon' has started to lead a life of its own.

Although never officially legalized, the ban on Wagner's music has been discussed several times in the Israeli Knesset, and some politicians have promised that, as long as the last Holocaust survivor was still alive in Israel, no Wagner music would be played in public.

There were several attempts to perform Wagner's music in Israel, especially by Zubin Mehta, the musical director of the Israeli Philharmonic Orchestra. Almost all these attempts failed, but Zubin Mehta was excused as a foreigner who was allegedly unable to understand the sensitivities of the Israeli public and in no position to solve Israel's cultural dilemmas.

The turning point came in 2001. On 5 May 2001, the planned performance of Wagner's *Die Walküre* by the Berlin Staatskapelle, conducted by Daniel Barenboim and featuring Placido Domingo as first tenor, was excluded from the programme of the Israeli Festival. Later Barenboim agreed to change the programme: pieces by Schumann and Stravinsky were supposed to replace Wagner. But on the day of the performance, after the second encore, Barenboim asked the public if they would like to hear Wagner. After half an hour of debate, with some shouting 'fascist', and after about 30 people had left the auditorium, slamming the doors behind them, it turned out that the majority of the audience had stayed, including many Holocaust survivors, and the performance was received with a standing ovation. This was perhaps the first social protest against the political ban on Wagner's music in Israel. But the incident had immediate consequences: Barenboim was proclaimed *persona non grata* by the Israeli Knesset and was asked to publicly apologize for his 'terrible action', which he never did.

Why or why not Wagner in Israel in the twenty-first century?

In 2009-2010, I conducted interviews with seven survivors of the Holocaust about the Wagner myth in Israel. I played Wagner's music to them (prelude to *Die Meistersinger* and overture to *Parsifal*). None of the respondents recognized the music as Wagner's, although one of them identified the prelude as 'music of war'.

When I later discussed with them the disapproval of Wagner's music in Israel, I got responses varying from strong opposition to Wagner as a 'Nazi composer' and absolute rejection of his music to full acceptance and enjoyment. One of the most remarkable observations is that the discussion about Wagner's music was almost immediately associated by all respondents with political questions either connected to the Second World War or to the current Israeli-Palestinian conflict.

On the internet I also collected a great variety of reactions and attitudes: 'Wagner should be banned'; 'Wagner hurts, it is a real physical pain what I experience, when I am forced to listen to him'; 'No doubt he must be banned' to 'toothpaste was invented in Dresden and surely Hitler loved it too', 'Wagner was himself a half Jew', 'If you ban Wagner you should ban Pink Floyd as well', 'Henry Ford was an anti-Semite as well, don't ride his cars, this is ridiculous, and Volkswagen also not…', 'Ban them all!' and 'Playing Wagner in Bayreuth is a Jewish victory'.[8] One respondent told me:

> Watching movies such as *Schindler's List* and *Hashoah* [sic] was much more traumatic for me than Wagner's operas. But in all cases I have a choice: to go to the cinema, to change the TV channel or to turn off the radio. I would not bother other people about their decision to see these films or listen to this music. It is my own responsibility; I will not force it on others.

That Wagner's music has political connotations among contemporary Israelis is understandable in the context of the ongoing discourse on Wagner, anti-Semitism, Jewishness and Israel. From the beginning of the state of Israel in 1948, a new Jew, a strong, independent Israeli who has nothing to do with the image of a diaspora Jew, was propagated. The Law of Return passed by the Israeli Knesset in 1949 recognized the right of all Jews to settle in Israel and the Zionist leaders of the new state emphasized their desire for a normal state. During the first years following the founding of Israel, every first Jewish soldier, every first Jewish champion, every first Jewish musician was celebrated. The Zionist commitment to the rescue of diaspora Jews evolved into an obligation on the part of Jews to sustain the Jewish homeland. Each side, the Israeli authorities and the Jewish immigrants, depended on the other in forming the ideological principles and influencing the identity of the new Israeli citizen (Siegel 1998: 9, 10). This identity was that of a strong, powerful, independent Israeli in contrast to the 'exile Jew'. For many years the prevalent stereotype of the diaspora Jew was that of a weak victim of the Nazis who led the Jewish 'cattle' to the gas chambers. Those who survived the concentration camps and managed to arrive on Israeli shores during the British Mandate were considered inferior, 'exile Jews', an image at variance with the newly created stereotype of the brave and strong Israeli *kibbutznik* or soldier. The Holocaust was viewed as a weak episode in Jewish history and was partly ignored in educational programmes. Immigrants of the post-war period were encouraged to 'rebuild' themselves and get away from their past in the 'shameful exile'. This was one of the many Israeli myths, which prevailed for more than 40 years, that

---

8 These are comments posted in response to the article 'Wagner should be banned' by Guilio Meotti, 26 July 2011, at http://www.ynetnews.com/articles/0,7340,L-4100497,00.html (accessed 14 December 2011).

only by living in Israel can one be liberated from the psychological and even physical complexes of the exile and become independent, healthy and happy (Siegel 1998: 175).[9] According to Anthony Cohen 'It is a selective construction of the past, which resonates with contemporary influences' (1985: 99). Such a myth justifies a specific course of action and its symbolic discourse.

While on the one hand the survivors of the Holocaust were viewed as 'shameful victims', who covered their tattooed concentration camps numbers by always wearing long sleeves and who for many years avoided questions about their sufferings, on the other hand the collective suffering was widely aired by politicians, even those who did not experience the Shoah or were born much later. Following the Eichmann trial the memory of the Holocaust was internalized in Israeli society, and 'Wagner's myth' was opened even to Israelis who had no personal background in European life, especially immigrants from North Africa (Sephardim). People who never visited concerts halls, who had no affection with classical music, felt they had the right to join the process of shaping Israeli identity and collective memory (Sheffi 2001: 88).

In 2011, more than two-thirds of Israel's Jewish population who are Israeli-born claimed that the Holocaust today has little impact on society. However, the post-Holocaust collective trauma is still there – preserved and triggered not only by Wagner's music but also by every new military attack, terrorist suicide bombing, shooting incident or hate crime involving Jews abroad.

The Holocaust is utilized and manipulated today for political purposes in different ways. The symbolic meaning of the Holocaust seems to have lost its original significance and is pulled out of its historical context. Today, the Holocaust is a symbol of the division between the two ideological camps: conservative and progressive. It is used either as a warning or as a threat for a new *Intifada*, usually by right-wing hard-line politicians, or as a comparison of the Israeli occupation and the treatment of Palestinians to Nazi behaviour by left-wing activists. The whole debate about playing Wagner in Israel today has nothing to do with the quality of his music or even with his ideas. It is not about Wagner's anti-Semitism (Frederic Chopin and Johan Sebastian Bach are also perceived as anti-Semites), but it is about Wagner as a symbol of German nationalism. The conservative politicians insist on keeping the ban on Wagner's music, claiming that those who forgive and forget their enemies, symbolic or real, become enemies of the Jewish people themselves. The refusal of the Palestinians to recognize the state of Israel, for example, is often considered as historically continuous with European anti-Semitism. The signing of a peace agreement by Itzhak Rabin with the Palestinian authorities in 1993 was viewed by militant ultra right politicians as a betrayal of the collective memory, namely of the suffering of Jews from the hatred of

9 Only with the mass immigration of post-Soviet Jews, among whom were hundreds of Jewish veterans who had fought against the Nazis in the Soviet Army and contributed to the liberation of Europe, was the image of the 'weak Jewish victim' challenged (Siegel, 1998: 175, 176).

Goyim.[10] Ultra orthodox and extreme right parties sometimes depicted Rabin in an SS uniform to bolster their argument.[11]

On the other hand, left-wing politicians always talk about moving forward by accepting and performing Wagner in public. The proponents of Wagner performances often remind their audience that Wagner lived long before the Nazi era and that he was not responsible for the Nazi horrors.

By the 1990s and 2000s the Wagner controversy had reached such a level that Wagner had been completely disconnected from his historical background. Consequently, knowledge about the real Richard Wagner is very limited. One young respondent asked me: 'Wagner ... Isn't he a composer who wrote Nazi songs during the war?' Where there is no knowledge, stereotypes and myths usually gain the upper hand. This can easily lead to manipulation and misinterpretation, which only strengthen the existing problems and taboos. Young people should study Wagner if only to be able to make their own judgement. Watson warns in his book not to judge Wagner's music 'in terms of the man' (1979: 316). Nietzsche, who attacked Wagner's ideas as immoral, praised his music (Watson 1979: 317). There are Israelis who like his operas and listen to his work in private settings.

To other Israelis Wagner's music, especially his operas, remains linked to Nazism, with *Die Meistersinger* symbolizing power, *Walküre*, war and destruction, *Siegfried*, Nazi youth, and *Parsifal*, racism. To elderly Jewish survivors of the Nazi concentration camps Wagner still reminds them of the horrors of Nazism, of 'the music of death' and this is what matters. 'It is only with the cultural context of that age in mind that the anti-Semitic implications of music can be demonstrated – indeed, only through consideration of such a context can a discussion make sense at all' (Weiner 1995: 21).

The debate about Wagner in Israel is an important aspect in the mixture of politics and art which resulted in the banning and criminalization of classical music. Freedom of expression and performance and the freedom to listen to music were never openly discussed in Israel. Politicians manipulated the emotions of the Israelis by banning Wagner and controlling and influencing the leaders of the Israeli musical world. The banning of Wagner's music became part of the national agenda (Sheffi 1999). In this regard, the Israeli authorities placed themselves in a dangerous position, as they engaged in political interference and cultural censorship. Since *Kristallnacht*, the music of Richard Wagner has come to be considered *Entartete Musik* in Israel, similar to what the Nazis did. Sheffi rightly summarized the problem of Wagner in Israel: 'The Nazis' aim was to revive the glory of Teutonic legend by apotheosizing Wagner's artistic work and political thought; the Israelis sought to condemn them. Ironically, they ended up by creating their own set of myths about Wagner and German culture' (Sheffi 2001: viii).

10 Literally: non-Jews, but often with a hostile connotation.

11 Rabin's death still provokes allegations in Israel; see *CNN*, 7 November 1997 at http://edition.cnn.com/WORLD/9711/07/israel.rabin.row/ (accessed 21 December 2011).

The revival of Wagner's music in Israel today and the demand to separate the music from the Nazi context and return it to the people are symbols of resistance to the violation of the right of freedom of expression and against censorship and control by the authorities. Perhaps, playing Wagner in Israel again will force Israelis to reconsider the Wagner myth. But the question remains: does the music itself express specific (in this case anti-Semitic) emotions or does prior knowledge of the history and background of the composer determine our interpretation of his music? Should Wagner forever be considered a 'Nazi possession', as composer Ernest Bloch once asked, or if Wagner continues to be forbidden in Israel today, does it mean, as Daniel Barenboim has stated, that 'we let Hitler have the last word' (2009).

In 2012, the debate is still as hot as immediately after the Holocaust. Uri Hanoch, a member of the Central Organization of Holocaust Survivors and a member of the Israel Opera Council, continues to claim that 'Wagner was an anti-Semite on the same level as Hitler and I promise: Wagner won't be played here' (quoted in O'Sullivan 2010). On the other hand, a new Israeli Wagner association was established to promote the works of the controversial composer, based on the argument that the right of the Israeli public to hear Wagner's music does not mean that it has to listen to his political views. According to the head of the association, Yonatan Livni, himself the son of Holocaust survivors, 'If we were to boycott every composer who was anti-Semitic then there would be very few composers we would be able to hear in Israel' (quoted in O'Sullivan 2010).

In the summer of 2011, another event shocked the opponents of Wagner in Israel. The Israeli Chamber Orchestra and the members of the Israeli Symphony Orchestra, conducted by Roberto Paternostro, performed Wagner's symphonic poem the *Siegfried Idyll* at the Bayreuth Festival, this 'nest of anti-Semitism'. Several angry Israeli politicians announced that funding would be cut. Reportedly, this was the first time that an Israeli orchestra had played Wagner in Germany (and received a standing ovation).

The danger of Wagner's music lies in the interpretation and manipulation of images and symbols in many parts of the world, especially in Israel. What if Wagner were to return to the Israeli concert halls and his art slowly be brought back into Israel's musical life? What symbols would then emerge to preserve the collective memory of the Nazi horrors? Given that one of the major arguments for the foundation of the Jewish state was the extreme anti-Semitism of the Nazis, Israeli ideologists need symbols and examples of evil enemies. Allowing the music of Wagner to be performed would amount to forgiving at least one of these enemies and thereby, in an indirect way, forgiving the Nazis. With some imagination it could even be argued that forgiving Wagner is tantamount to forgetting why Israel exists in the first place, which would give some extremists a justification to deny the legality of Israel as a state. A recent interpretation of the importance of the ban on Wagner is founded on the idea that Europe and the Arab world, both allegedly anti-Semitic and anti-Zionist, should always be reminded of the fact that evil ideas, books and even music can have consequences.

On the other hand, the Wagner myth is a social construct. There is no denying that our individual understanding and perception of Wagner's music depend on our personal experience, histories and values. To some, Wagner as a person continues to be a symbol of evil and his creations cannot be separated from his personality, ideas and messages. To others, performing Wagner's music in public is a symbol of resistance to the establishment and the repression of freedom of expression.

Concluding remarks

Israel is a western democracy where people are denied the right to choose which works of art and music should be introduced to the stages of their cultural institutions. Is it that Israelis are not aware of their rights and privileges, since few of them seem to question the logic and persistence of certain myths and taboos? The politicization of Israeli life and the intense daily struggle in the Israeli political arena between the right and the left, each armed with their own symbols and myths, have shaped Israeli attitudes, including those regarding art and music.

For the last 65 years, Israel has been going through a process of transition, striving to become a strong and independent state that is recognized and respected by the international community. This demands that specific memories that contribute to solidarity and social identity are kept alive, including the collective memory of the Holocaust with its imageries of extreme anti-Semitism, concentration camps and the suffering of millions. In this context, the ban on Wagner's 'music of death' is a way of doing justice to the survivors of the Nazi horrors. The contested imagery of the 'Wagner myth', whether or not it is based on real facts, contributes to the ongoing political and public discourse on the character of the state of Israel both in the present and in the future.

Wagner's music provides everyone with their own individual experience. The Wagner myth is still alive in Israel, but the meaning is changing from Wagner as a symbol of Nazism to Wagner as a symbol of a social discrepancy, and even conflict between various Israeli camps. On the other hand, Israelis are tired of the controversy about Wagner. The associations connected to Wagner's operas in the nineteenth century are not the same as those of the twenty-first century; in our times we have different stereotypes and images, or in the words of Marc Weiner: 'the fact that our culture is not Wagner's may constitute our redemption … from the Wagnerian agenda' (1995: 29). We can enjoy and interpret Wagner's music guided by our own imagination.

References

Adorno, Theodor. 1952. *In Search of Wagner*. London: Verso.

Barenboim, Daniel. 2009. *Wagner, Israel and the Palestinians*. Available at http://www.danielbarenboim.com/index.php?lid=72 (accessed 30 January 2012).

Beller, Steven. 1994. Herzl, Wagner, and the Ironies of 'True Emancipation'. In *Tainted Greatness: Antisemitism and Cultural Heroes*, edited by N. Harrowitz, 127-156. Philadelphia: Temple University Press.

Buruma, Ian. 1999. *Voltaire's Coconuts or Anglomania in Europe*. London: Weidenfeld & Nicolson.

Cares, Adam. 1964. *The History of Orchestration*. New York: Dover.

Cohen, Anthony. 1985. *The Symbolic Construction of Community*. London and New York: Tavistock.

Dahlhaus, Carl. 1979. *Richard Wagner's Music Drama*. Translated by M. Whittall. Cambridge and New York: Cambridge University Press.

Deathridge, John. 2008. *Wagner Beyond Good and Evil*. Berkeley: University of California Press.

Garrett, Leah. 2011. *A Knight of the Opera: Heine, Wagner, Herzl, Peretz, and the Legacy of Der Tannhäuser*. West Lafayette, IN: Purdue University Press.

Gilbert, Shirli. 2005. *Music in the Holocaust: Confronting Life in the Nazi Ghettos and Camps*. Oxford: Clarendon Press.

Herzl, Theodor. 1941. *Old-New Land*. Translated by L. Levensohn. New York: Bloch.

Hirshberg, Jehoash and Ramot, Na'ama. 2006. The Tangled Road to Legalization: The Admission of the German Language in Musical Performances in Israel. *Jewish Quarterly Review*, 96(4), 510-521.

Honigsheim, Paul. 1989. *Sociologists and Music*. New Brunswick, NJ and London: Transaction.

Jerusalem Municipal Council Decides to Apologize to Jascha Heifetz. 1953. *Jewish Telegraphic Agency*, 24 April.

Kohler, Joachim. 2000. *Wagner's Hitler*. Translated by R. Taylor. Cambridge: Polity Press.

Millington, Barry. 1999. *Wagner*. Oxford and New York: Oxford University Press.

O'Sullivan, Arieh. 2010. Wagner gets His First Israeli Fan Club. *Jerusalem Post*, 16 November. Available at http://www.jpost.com/Israel/Article.aspx?id=195522.

Pedahzur, Ami and Perliger, Arie 2009. *Jewish Terrorism in Israel*. New York: Columbia University Press.

Poliakov, L. 2003. *The History of Anti-Semitism: From Voltaire to Wagner*, vol. III. Philadelphia: University of Pennsylvania Press.

Rose, Paul. 1996. *Wagner: Race and Revolution*. New Haven: Yale University Press.

Ross, Alex. 2007. *The Rest is Noise: Listening to the Twentieth Century*. New York: Picador.

Sheffi, Na'ama. 1999. Cultural Manipulation: Richard Wagner and Richard Strauss in Israel in the 1950s. *Journal of Contemporary History*, 34(4), 619-639.

Sheffi, Na'ama. 2001. *The Ring of Myths: The Israelis, Wagner and the Nazis*. Brighton and Portland, OR: Sussex Academic Press.

Siegel, Dina. 1998. *The Great Immigration: Russian Jews in Israel*. New York and Oxford: Berghahn.

Skelton, Geoffrey. 1994. *Cosima Wagner's Diaries: An Abridgement*. Mississauga, Ont.: Random House.
Van Amerongen, Martin. 1984. *Wagner: A Case History*. New York: G. Braziller.
Watson, Derek. 1979. *Richard Wagner: A Biography*. London: J.M. Dent & Sons.
Weiner, Marc. 1995. *Richard Wagner and the Anti-Semitic Imagination*. Lincoln and London: University of Nebraska Press.
Žižek, Slavoj. 1952. Foreword: Why is Wagner Worth Saving? In T. Adorno. *In Search of Wagner*. London: Verso.

Chapter 12

'Maybe if the world had paid more attention'.[1] Western Cinematic Perspectives on the Rwandan Genocide and the Role of the West: *Hotel Rwanda*, *Shooting Dogs* and *Sometimes in April*

Bernadette Kester

In 2014 it will be 20 years since the Rwandan genocide took place. In its aftermath the country was left in deep shock and mourning, and in many ways the state of Rwanda and its population of Hutu (84 per cent), Tutsi (15 per cent) and Twa (1 per cent) can still be called a country in transition. In Rwanda the human disaster is commemorated annually and decennially with a national week of mourning in April. Memorials and gravesites are scattered across the country. Even in the most remote spots of Rwanda, one can read banners with 'Remember', 'Never forget' and 'Never again' (Brandstetter 2010: 3). Outside Rwanda, the memory of the genocide has been more or less preserved by the international media, through literature and in films. In 2001, *New York Times* reporter and at the time Nairobi Bureau chief Marc Lacey wrote 'The land of a thousand hills, as Rwanda is known, has become the land of a thousand memorials, a thousand trials, a thousand bad memories that linger.' In her book on the representation of suffering and human catastrophes from a holocaust frame, Angi Buettner writes that there are two dominant themes running through the international media coverage of the Rwandan genocide: 'While the genocide was unfolding, the piled up bodies in the streets, hills and rivers of Rwanda captured the international imagination. After the genocide it was the memorials and trials, and over time both the dead bodies and the originating memorial sites have become integrated into the various discourses about Rwanda, and, in the course of this process, have become part of Rwanda's image' (2011: 64).

In this chapter I will argue that another theme also became dominant in what we could call the 'global mediated memory' of the genocide, and that is the West's negation of the genocide (see Cohen 2001; Mirzoeff 2005). The western powers are here represented by the United Nations, Europe, the United States

1 Augustin in *Sometimes in April*. See concluding paragraph of this chapter.

and the international media. In various media formats, such as feature films or docudramas, documentaries, history and memorial websites, literary accounts and journalistic articles, the West is mainly portrayed as a negative force. It is more or less accepted knowledge, or it is at least assumed, that western powers could have prevented the genocide or could have brought it to a halt. But they chose to do the opposite and to play it down or deny it and finally they withdrew altogether at a very early stage of the massacres. The role of the international media in this respect has been generally and severely condemned although we will never know if (more) media exposure would have activated the world (Melvern 2004: 221-244). In these media saturated times, in which audiences are often considered to suffer from compassion fatigue, it has become an illusion to expect a 'CNN-effect' – news media as stimulating forces for governments to take preventive action in regard to humanitarian disasters (Moeller 1999). After Rwanda there was Darfur… However, the idea that media exposure and western intervention really could have prevented (and would prevent) human disasters like the Rwandan genocide is still persistent and a dominant theme in many narratives about the genocide.

In 2004, while Rwanda remembered its victims through the opening of the Kigali Genocide Memorial Centre, international audiences outside Africa could become acquainted (again) with media representations of the disaster that had taken place in 1994. This time, audiences could hear about the past genocide not only through fragments in the news, but also via 'fictionalized' characters and coherent cinematic narratives. Several films about the Rwandan genocide premiered in that same or the following year. *Hotel Rwanda*, *Shooting Dogs* and *Sometimes in April* have become landmarks in the mainstream cinematic representation of the genocide. The films, which according to Xan Rice of *The Guardian* (2006) are much too painful and traumatizing for Rwandans to watch, are mainly produced for western audiences. As historical narratives are constructions highlighting certain elements above others, the question from which this study starts is whether and how these films – particularly *Sometimes in April* which tried to include as many facets of the genocide as possible – could be considered successful attempts in making audiences aware of the role the West played in this human disaster.

Summarizing history

In the summer of 1994, Rwanda, a small country in the African Great Lakes region, became the location of a genocide in which an estimated 800,000 Tutsi and moderate Hutu (Hutu opposing extremist politics regarding the Tutsi) were killed, mutilated, maimed, raped and otherwise abused or tortured. It was a disaster from which the country still hasn't recovered and maybe never will. There is no one who denies that it happened: the massacres took place in the open, everybody was involved, whether as victim or as perpetrator. Almost every Rwandan family has its victims to commemorate or perpetrators to be ashamed of; some families have both. Although, historically, the causes of the violent outburst can be related to a large degree to the construction (or fabrication) and institutionalization of ethnic 'differences' by colonial powers, the actors and instigators at the time of the genocide were the Rwandan government, a Hutu majority led by Hutu president Juvénal Habyarimama. From an early stage, the killings were premeditated and designed, black lists were compiled and for a long time an influential propagandistic radio station – Radio Télévision Libre de Mille Collines (RTLM) – disseminated hateful messages about the Rwandan minority, the Tutsi, calling them cockroaches (*Inyenzi*), snakes or dogs. What finally triggered the actual genocide was the shooting down of a plane carrying Habyarimama and his colleague from Burundi Cyprien Ntaryamira on their way to Kigali International Airport. It is still disputed who could be held responsible for the shooting, although at the time the Tutsi were accused of killing both (Hutu) presidents. Immediately after the plane crashed, the news spread like a wildfire. Hutu extremist mobs took to the streets and started a large-scale massacre of Tutsis and Hutu moderates.

When the massacres started, a United Nations Observation Mission was monitoring the Arusha Accord (Tanzania), a peace agreement between the Rwandan (Hutu) government and the Tutsi-led Rwandan Patriotic Front (RPF), who, under the command of Paul Kagame, invaded Rwanda in 1990. Because the UN mission was purely observational, the rules of engagement did not legally allow it to protect potential and actual victims when the killings started. The UN commanders indeed did not exceed their mandate. They would only have received permission to take military action upon the massacres being officially defined as genocide. An official declaration of genocide only happened after the fact. At a certain stage, the UN mission received orders, from their international superiors, to leave the country as soon as possible and to take only western civilians – press, aid workers, diplomats and others – with them (Sitkowski 2006: 111-124).

The massacres continued and lasted for about one hundred days, from 6 April until the end of June, without any outsiders or foreign witnesses present who could have testified about them. Although initially some news reports, and a video film, reached western media outlets, they did not give the news story the weight and spin it deserved. Other occurrences, with apparently more news value (for example Kurt Cobain's suicide, the O.J. Simpson trial) garnered all public attention.

While western media representatives were accused of ignoring a major news story about an unprecedented human disaster, both the United Nations and the United States were equally accused of turning their backs on mass killings that could have been prevented by international intervention. All three power institutions were assumed to be able to stop or prevent further killings. However, other similar cases of the UN peacekeeping missions (in Lebanon and Bosnia for instance) have shown that this idea is based on an illusion. Ignored by foreign powers, the Rwandan massacres went on until the rebellious Tutsi army, the RPF, had regained power and the Hutu population had fled the country towards Tanzania and the Congo. Hundreds of thousands of refugees were given shelter in camps just across the border. This location was safe enough for aid workers to build camps and take care of the refugees, who largely consisted of the former perpetrators of the genocide, the (extremist) Hutu. It was also safe again for western journalists to report about the large-scale refugee problem and about what had taken place in Rwanda.

Since the 1994 genocide, Rwandan society has become a society in transition. Heavily traumatized, the Rwandan people had to regain their psychological and social balance. They had to come to terms with their private emotions on the one hand and restore peace and rebuild the country on the other. In addition, the judicial system in Rwanda had been completely decapitated by the massive killings, although impunity was the rule rather than the exception (Berry and Berry 1999: 12). One of the means to heal the wounds and restore internal peace was to implement a judicial system that would monitor the indictment, prosecution and punishment of the perpetrators and most of the instigators of the genocide. This group consisted of people who themselves had not killed, but could be held politically or otherwise responsible for instigating massacres. In order to be able to bring the culprits to trial in a legally sound way, a (new) institutional system of law and order had to be implemented. This process of transitional justice was in fact a two-track policy that took place on a macro level by way of a transnationally governed tribunal, the International Criminal Tribunal for Rwanda (ICTR), which sat in Arusha (Tanzania). On a micro level, community justice took place through the *gacaca* courts, 'justice adapted to societies transforming themselves after a period of pervasive human rights abuse' (ICTJ 2009). In 1996 the first Rwandan tribunals took place; the *gacaca*s started in 2001. Together with the International Tribunal for the Former Yugoslavia (ICTY), the ICTR was a forerunner of the International Criminal Court which was established in 2002.

Each type of court, the local and the international, represents different ways of dealing with crimes on this scale and therefore proceeds from different principles. The official international criminal tribunal is principally an invention of the West. Because of its many complicated judicial rules and procedures, it can sometimes be years before a judgement is made. This legal institution is particularly fit for bringing former government and military representatives to court. As long as justice is done and as long as it is done according to the established criminal law, it does not matter how long it takes. On a community level, however, many and perhaps most Rwandans tried to move on with their lives and to leave the past behind them. For many, listening to the publicly expressed confessions of the perpetrators themselves is the most constructive and healing part of the process of coming to terms with what happened (Molenaar 2005; Westberg 2011: 332). This perspective on justice, making peace and coming to terms, is deeply rooted in African society. It is one part of a process of reconciliation that contains different aspects, from confession, forgiveness and the uncovering of truth, to justice and good government (Molenaar 2005). The first three are at the heart of the *gacaca*s.

How complicated the uncovering of truth is, as being one aspect of the communal way of reconciliation, is revealed by Helena Cobban (2004), international relations expert and author of books on legacies of violence, who compared the ICTR with the Nuremberg processes:

> What is different in comparing the ICTR and Nuremberg is that the Nazis had left extensive records and documentation of everything that they had done, whereas Rwanda doesn't have that kind of documentation. The ICTR prosecutors have been trying to establish the historical record, but they have had to rely overwhelmingly on witness testimony. That is a big problem for the court and it also doesn't have the same kind of incontrovertible, indisputable kind of evidence that the Nazi documents bring.

Coherence where there is none: narrative strategies

Describing the Rwandan genocide and its aftermath in only one or two pages does not do justice to the immense complexities of the past and present of Rwandan society. However, in whatever discourse or narrative form this historical event is represented, it is always based on a selection of facts and fragments, it is structured and framed in a certain way, and different terms and concepts are used, bearing different connotations. Narratives of past events are therefore always 'true' and 'false' at the same time. They are 'true' in the sense that they refer to an actual event that took place at a certain moment with certain people. They are 'false' in the sense that narrations of an event – when, how and where it started, by what or whom it was caused, in what chronological order it took place, how it was ended and by whom – are always more or less based on selection and remain, in many cases, the subject of continuous debate.

Moreover, where a highly contested past is concerned, as is the case in regard to Rwanda, selection in the construction process of memory and history can be highly political and symbolic, favouring one position over another and leaving out some elements at the cost of others. 'Hence, any collective and political mediation of the past constitutes a carefully crafted version of what should be remembered and forgotten, of what is significant and insignificant' (Dauge-Roth 2010: 6). As in the case of the Armenian genocide and the Holocaust, historians construct master narratives which become dominant discursive interpretations of the past, until new ones take over. In the end a master narrative sometimes becomes more or less consensual, often being a narrative that includes various perspectives on different aspects of an event. The discourse on the genocide in Rwanda has not reached that stage yet (Adelman 2003; Berry and Berry 1999; Gourevitch 1999).

Both historical narratives and narrative accounts in general comprise more than just bare facts or indicators like names, locations, years and numbers. Even witnessing the same incidents can lead to different accounts. When we experience or witness something that happens in front of our eyes and it fits in an already existing cognitive scheme (we recognize something as a car accident), when we want to make sense of it and subsequently share it with someone else, we tend to structure it according to certain basic narrative rules, for example starting with how something began, who was involved, how it evolved and finally if, how, when and by whom it was concluded. Inherent to this narration process is the selection and highlighting of certain aspects over others, drawing of inferences and use of particular words bearing certain connotations. It resembles what in communication studies is called framing (see Chapter 8 in this volume and, for example, Entman 1993).

Considering an event as a construct does not mean that the (f)actual (or past) existence is denied. Narrated events are constructs and embedded in a particular textual and generic discourse. It also matters in what context the narrative is received, in court, on television, in the theatre or in an educational environment. Moreover, the social status of an oral eyewitness account or a history text that uses the account as a source differs from a literary text, a work of art, a press photo, a television news item or a feature film or documentary in an ontological and epistemological way.

Every type of discourse has its own characteristics and its own social, political and cultural status in society. Only through narratives are people able to give an event *existence*, to share it with others and to (try to) make others understand what happened. Media are paramount channels in this respect. Nowadays, people are able to share through social media every tiny bit of thought and feeling that was long considered to belong exclusively to the realm of the private sphere. More importantly, social media have become channels for disseminating information and images that previously were barely accessible to regular journalists or correspondents. Currently, these are accepted sources in journalistic practices, as is demonstrated in the recent Middle Eastern uprisings. The thought of what social media could have meant during the Rwandan genocide … particularly considering the role of western media at the time.

One of the first visual accounts that reached the international audience was the scene shot by the British freelance camera reporter (and filmmaker) Nick Hughes. He was the only journalist to capture the moment of a genocidal act with his camera. On the 11 April 1994, Hughes happened to be one of the few foreign reporters who had not yet fled the country. It was five days after the Rwandan president's plane had been shot down and the actual genocide launched. From a building, a French school that served as a gathering point for foreigners awaiting evacuation and that looked over a valley, Hughes witnessed a horrendous scene. On the road down the valley, he watched how a father and his daughter were brutally killed.

This rare piece of film has been used as evidence before the ICTR. Moreover, every filmmaker who has directed a film or documentary about the genocide has watched it or used it as footage, as a real scene or as a re-enactment.

Western perspectives and perspectives on the West

As has been mentioned, the year 2004 was the year of the decennial commemoration of the genocide. Around the same time several films about the Rwandan genocide were released. The year 2004 also marked a specific moment in the judicial process instigated by the ICTR. By the end of that year, the investigations called for by the UN Security Council had to be completed in order to let the tribunal proceed to its next phase.

The occasions had enough news value to gain the attention of the international press. However, after a period of about eight years during which Rwanda seldom received media exposure except perhaps for irregular short reports on the proceedings of the tribunal, (international) public memory about the facts of April 1994 had to be refreshed. In other words, more explanation and clarification was needed of what exactly had taken place. For that reason, several broadsheets and websites published timelines and factual and background articles highlighting the benchmarks of the genocide and its history (for example Frontline 2004). At around the same time, several documentaries were produced, addressing the devastating role of western powers and the UN, such as *Shake Hands with the Devil: The Journey of Roméo Dallaire* (dir. Peter Raymont, 2004) and the PBS production: *Ghosts of Rwanda* (no dir., 2005).

However, addressing the massacre and its aftermath in this way did not necessarily imply that people were now able to construct a more or less coherent picture of this past occurrence, if that were even possible. In order to gain more insight into the genocide, the media should have paid more attention to the historical and socio-political circumstances from the very beginning (Philo *et al.* 1999: 213-223). Unfortunately, mainstream news organizations do not consider it their function to make the public aware of the historical and cultural roots of an event, nor do they consider it their duty specifically to address people or countries that are of no political or economic interest to western countries. However cynical this may sound, mainstream news media adhere predominantly to their traditional news values (Galtung and Ruge 1965; Williams 2011: 151-153). This is at the expense of offering enough context to the news to make the public understand the background to an event. The same is true of reporting about Third World countries in general and countries from the African continent in particular (Beattie *et al.* 1999: 229-267; Franks 2005, 2006, 2010).

Most strikingly, in 2004, the international western media were (indeed one could say 'again') in a sense predominantly focused on their own position. In April 1994, journalists fled the country and/or were recalled by their editors out of fear for their lives. As a result, news about the genocide was scarce and scattered during the hundred days of the genocide. Even the scene shot by Nick Hughes was more or less ignored by the main international news organizations. Most of the pictures or news reels that were disseminated through the media were made after the fact, showing piles of dead, dismembered bodies scattered around the streets of Kigali and the villages and roads of Rwanda. Ten years later, despite some attempts to give more insight into the historical context of the massacre, for the most part news media again focused on how 'the' western world had handled and dealt with the disaster. In addition, ample attention was given to the negative role of the media at the time.

Again the story was not primarily about the Rwandan people and their history and tragedy, but most of all, to various extents, about the roles of the West: as former colonists (Germany, Belgium); as members of the Security Council; as a UN Observer Mission Uganda-Rwanda (UNOMUR, June 1993–September 1996); as a Belgium-led peacekeeping force, UN Assistance Mission for Rwanda (UNAMIR, October 1993–March 1996) under the Canadian command of General Roméo Dallaire; as arms supplier (France); as US administration; and last, but not least, as international press corps.

In most discourses the role of the West is reduced to two main positions: the press and the United Nations. This is certainly the case for perhaps the two most famous mainstream feature films about the genocide: *Hotel Rwanda* (dir. Terry George, 2004) and *Shooting Dogs* (dir. Michael Caton-Jones, 2004). To a lesser extent this also applies to *Sometimes in April* (dir. Raoul Peck, 2005), except that this film was produced by the American cable television network HBO and thus primarily intended for an American audience. It is therefore not surprising that this film addresses, more specifically than the other two films, the political role of US officials at the time. What is particularly interesting in all three films is the way in which the moral dilemma between staying in Rwanda and leaving the country is represented. To show how this is cinematographically represented would include a close analysis of the staging and shot design, camera movement and angle, editing and so forth. The focus in this chapter, however, is on a selection of meaningful parts of the dialogues instead, in particular where moral dilemmas or the position of the West is concerned.

The most well-known, widely acclaimed and widely distributed film of the three is *Hotel Rwanda*. It received three Oscar nominations and won several prizes at film festivals. The film is based on real life events and shot partly on location in Kigali and partly in South Africa. The main character, Paul Rusesabagina (played by Don Cheadle), is a real person and Hôtel des Mille Collines, which at the time of the genocide functioned as a place of refuge, also exists. There is some debate, however, about how heroic the role of Rusesabagina really was at the time of the genocide (Dauge-Roth 2010: 201-202; Ndahiro and Rutazibwa 2008). He was nevertheless consulted for the film. The character representing the UN peacekeeping officer Colonel Oliver, played by Nick Nolte, was inspired by the UNAMIR force commander Roméo Dallaire.

The two other films are less well known than *Hotel Rwanda*, although both came out at approximately the same time. *Shooting Dogs* was released in the US as *Beyond the Gates*, so audiences would not associate the title wrongly with Rwandan people or with maltreatment of animals (Thomson, 2007). Like *Hotel Rwanda*, *Shooting Dogs* is a fictionalized account; it centres around and was shot at an actual site, which was the École Technique Officielle of Kicukiro, in

Kigali. Some survivors of the genocide played minor roles and/or were part of the production crew. The story is based on the experiences of BBC producer and reporter David Belton.

Both *Shooting Dogs* and *Sometimes in April* are less famous than *Hotel Rwanda* but still regularly shown on television. Contrary to *Shooting Dogs* and *Hotel Rwanda*, which are mainly focused on the period of the genocide itself, *Sometimes in April* takes a broader perspective in time (1994-2004) as well as with regard to the issues that are chronicled. It not only includes some of the incidents that are the main narrative issues in the other films (for example Hôtel des Mille Collines as a place of refuge), but is also the only film that takes the present, which at the time was 2004, as its main narrative starting point (see below). The film was shot on location and, like *Hotel Rwanda*, has mainly Rwandan characters as protagonists.

Hotel Rwanda

In *Hotel Rwanda* the plot revolves around the Hôtel des Milles Collines, situated in the capital city Kigali, and its manager Paul Rusesabagina (PR) and his family. In the film, Rusesabagina's marriage causes much tension because he is a Hutu and his wife a Tutsi, which makes them both a target for the extremist Hutu. The extremist Hutu are organized in the *Interahamwe*, civilian death squads, whose main goal is to exterminate the Tutsi. After being threatened by the extremists, the manager and his family (and neighbours) take refuge in the hotel together with many others. Among the refugees is also a group of foreign, white westerners. After a while, Rusesabagina, who is trying to keep his hotel running, has to take care of no less than 1,200 refugees. Most of them are Tutsi or non-extremist Hutu. At a certain point, a select group of hotel 'guests' tries to escape with a UN truck. However, after having been violently threatened by the *Interahamwe* they are forced to return to the hotel. Finally, after a devastating period almost all of them are saved by the RPF and brought behind the Tutsi rebel lines and finally into the UN refugee camps. A Red Cross aid worker finally reunites the family with their two daughters, from whom they were separated earlier in the film.

The first scene that refers to a non-intervention by the UN is when a team of two foreign reporters (of whom one is a cameraman) interviews the UN peacekeeping officer, Colonel Oliver. The reporter tells him they have received reports about massacres that are going on and asks if the UN will intervene. The commander answers that he is here to keep peace not to make peace, 'My orders are not to intervene.'

In one of the next scenes, the hope for intervention is further refuted, this time by the cameraman talking to Paul Rusesabagina (PR). The hotel manager believes a western intervention is imminent. In this scene, the same foreign reporter (Rep), who is staying at the hotel, apologizes to Rusesabagina, who accidently saw the gruesome footage of massacres the reporter had shot earlier that day. The hotel manager tells him that there is no need to apologize.

> PR: I am glad you shot this footage and that the world will see it. It's the only way we have a chance that people might intervene.
>
> Rep: And if there will be no interventions?
>
> PR: How can they not intervene, when they witness such atrocities?
>
> Rep: I think if people see this footage, they'll say 'Oh my God, that's horrible' and then go on eating their dinners.

The following scene shows how a group of wounded Rwandan people chased by the *Interahamwe* seeks refuge in the hotel. The UN soldiers (UNAMIR) protecting the hotel and offering help to the newly arrived refugees are then confronted with a jeep full of threatening extremist Hutus of the *Interahamwe*, yelling and blowing whistles, who show the soldiers their trophies: blue helmets. Colonel Oliver tells the hotel manager that he has lost ten of his men, Belgian UN soldiers, but that 'the Europeans are putting together an intervention force. They will be here in a few days.'

A short while later in the film, a UN convoy of several jeeps with French soldiers approaches the hotel in order to pick up a few selected (French and other European) refugees. We see (but do not hear) Colonel Oliver talk to the other commander and suddenly become very angry. He walks back to the hotel and goes straight to the bar where the manager offers him a drink and congratulates him. The commander responds: 'You should spit in my face.' Showing further disillusion, the conversation continues:

> UN Oliver: We think you are dirt, Paul.
>
> PR: Who is we?
>
> UN Oliver: The West, all the superpowers, everything you believed in, Paul. [...] You are the smartest man here [...] you can own this freaking hotel, except for one thing: you're BLACK, you're not even a nigger, you're an AFRICAN. We are not gonna stay Paul, we are not going to stop the slaughter.

The scene that finally portrays the departure of the western people from the hotel, including the two reporters, shows the despair of one of the journalists when asked by a Rwandan friend to take her with him. Instead he offers her money. When a Rwandan hotel servant holds an umbrella for him, he expresses his shame and embarrassment.

Later on in the film, we see the hotel refugees listening to the radio, hearing the US deputy assistant secretary of state for African Affairs, Prudence Bushnell, at a press conference (4 April 1994), in which she more or less admits that officially she is not allowed to call what is going on in Rwanda 'genocide'.

Shooting Dogs

The main characters in *Shooting Dogs* are a fearless Catholic priest, Father Christopher (John Hurt), and a young idealistic English teacher, Joe (Hugh Dancy), both working at the École Technique Officielle in Kigali. Because part of the school grounds also functions as a UN compound (UNAMIR), the campus becomes a refuge for the Tutsi. Outside the fences, the *Interahamwe* are vociferously and impatiently waiting for a chance to get in and kill the Tutsi. The UN troops are under the command of Captain Charles Delon, who is repeatedly asked to stay and protect the refugees and to shoot the Hutu mob, instead of the dogs that eat the dead bodies. When the UN peacekeepers receive orders to leave the country and thus to leave the school grounds and abandon the children and other refugees, a physical and moral struggle unfolds. Ultimately, Father Christopher decides to stay and together with the Tutsi await their imminent death. But the formerly idealistic English teacher chooses, however desperate he feels, to leave with the UN convoy which only helps westerners to escape the country, including two BBC reporters. In leaving he also abandons a Tutsi student, Marie, with whom he had become friends and whom he had earlier promised to protect. After the UN soldiers have left, the extremist Hutu slaughter all the people left in the compound. But, just before this happens, Father Christopher succeeds in smuggling a small group of children outside the compound with his pick-up truck, including Marie. Late at night, when they arrive at a road block, the children secretly escape while Christopher distracts the drunken Hutu. When they see through his deceit he is killed on the spot. In the end, Marie has managed to escape her ruined country and make it to the western world. Five years later she finds Joe again at a university college in England. When she asks him 'Why did you leave us', he simply answers 'I was afraid to die.' This is where the film ends.

In this film, both the UN and the press are repeatedly put in morally devastating positions. When the first Tutsi have sought refuge in the school compound, a conversation between Father Christopher and a UN officer takes place.

> UN officer: My orders are not to let this school become a safe haven.
>
> Christopher: But you are UN peacekeepers, Charles. Surely you are here to prevent bloodshed.
>
> […]
>
> UN: No, our mandate is not to enforce the peace, but to monitor it.
>
> Christopher: I must confess if I can't understand the difference, certainly these people [the Tutsi refugees] won't.

In one of the following scenes, the UN commander explains to a former minister of the Rwandan government (who presumably as a moderate Hutu also seeks refuge at the school) what the UN's position is in exactly the same words. The Rwandan politician states in turn that the slaughter that is going on is 'all planned [...] You MUST intervene.' He continues: 'Captain, you without doubt know what the Nazis attempted to do with the Jews [...] This is what we are facing here.' No response follows, but a cut to the next scene.

The representation of the foreign press is even more condemning than in *Hotel Rwanda*. The female BBC reporter in particular displays a shocking cynicism, comparable to that of the UN commander Oliver in *Hotel Rwanda*. First, Joe decides to bring the two British journalists, with whom he is acquainted, to the school grounds stating that 'nothing exists when it is not on TV'. At first, the reporters are reluctant to come with Joe, until they hear 40 Europeans are also hiding in the school. When they arrive, Joe reassures Marie: 'they are going to film us and then no one can touch us.'

A little while later, Joe and the female reporter have a conversation. Hesitantly she tells him about Bosnia where she was the year before: 'I cried every day, strangely enough, over here, not a tear [...] Any time I saw a dead Bosnian woman, a white woman, I thought: That could have been my mum. Over here they are just dead Africans.' And then sighing: 'What a thing to say. We are all selfish pieces of muck, in the end.'

Sometimes in April

The story of *Sometimes in April* does not start, as the other films do, at the beginning of April 1994, but ten years later. The main character, Augustin (Idris Elba), a moderate Hutu, ex-officer and in the time of the narrative a widower and a school teacher, receives a letter from his brother Honoré (Oris Erhuero) who is in prison and awaiting trial at the Rwanda tribunal in Arusha (Tanzania). In 1994, Honoré belonged to the extremist Hutu and worked as a propagandist for the RTLM – hate radio, also called Hutu Power radio. This made him an accomplice to the genocide, but despite his political position at the time, he tried to save his brother's wife (a Tutsi) and his two (Hutu) sons. Augustin's daughter stayed at a missionary school. In his letter, Honoré asks Augustin to visit him in prison, so that he can tell him what happened to his wife and sons during their attempt to escape. Apparently, Augustin still does not know exactly what happened to his family. Through flashbacks the film narrative tells the viewer what happened to Augustin himself (as a moderate Hutu he found refuge in the Hôtel des Mille Collines) and to the members of his family, who were all brutally killed. Finally, Augustin finds the courage to visit his brother and face the past. The film shows how Augustin hears his brother's account and how he admits the guilty role he played in the genocide, but at the same time claims that he was unaware of implications of his actions at the time. Augustin also witnesses the testimony of a Tutsi woman who was raped by several men during the genocide. Something similar had happened to his wife, who, according to his brother, finally killed herself and her rapists with a hand grenade. Despite the gruesome images and stories, the film ends when Augustin flies back to Rwanda. The last scene, however, shows his (pregnant) girlfriend, Martine (Pamela Nomvete), who is testifying at one of the open air *gacaca*s about the massacre she witnessed. She had been Augustin's daughter's teacher and had tried to save her life after the girl was wounded by the *Interahamwe* who had killed all the other students in the school.

In contrast to the other two films, *Sometimes in April* does not display any kind of heroism, either from the Rwandan side, as portrayed by Paul Rusesabagina in *Hotel Rwanda*, or from the western side, as shown by Father Christopher in *Shooting Dogs*. All characters, more or less, demonstrate the different states of mind and emotions – from fear to complicity and courage. In order to move on with their lives, the main characters, especially the two brothers, both show courage to acknowledge and courage to forgive. *Sometimes in April* can also be distinguished from the other two films by the fact that it reaches beyond the genocide itself to a Rwandan future of remembrance and reconciliation. Besides, it also delves deeper into the past. Most notably it demonstrates the complicity of the US.

The film starts with its motto 'In the end, we will remember not the words of our enemies but the silence of our friends' by Martin Luther King, Jr., which clearly alludes to the role of the West. In its accusation of the West *Sometimes* takes a different position than the other two films. There the frustration about western non-intervention is mainly demonstrated through, and verbally expressed by, the characters, whereas in *Sometimes* the narrative itself is much less focused on the role of the western powers or the western press and more on the process of mourning and coming to terms with the past of the Rwandan people themselves. However, where the West is represented in this film, it is mainly limited to the US.

Six relatively short intermittent scenes show Prudence Bushnell (Debra Winger) discussing the situation in Rwanda with other US officials. Their main concern is how to save the US citizens who have remained in Rwanda. Moreover, the US wants to avoid another Mogadishu; during a US intervention in Somalia, in 1993, dead US soldiers were dragged through the street, an incident that was filmed and broadcast. Chronologically, almost every scene displays the number of days the genocide is ongoing, followed by showing the number of people killed in the massacres. This is juxtaposed with the US refusal to call the ongoing massacre genocide. The scenes differ from the other scenes by their almost documentary, television-like style. Together, they represent a parallel plot, a different narrative universe, in which the characters do not (seem to) bear any relation to the characters of the main plot. This estranging effect corresponds with the attitude of non-attachment the US displayed towards the Rwandan people in reality (see Dauge-Roth 2010: 186).

All three films represent more or less the same master narrative about the Rwandan genocide and display similar dramatic and narrative ingredients. The history of the ethnic struggle between the Hutu and the Tutsi is told through dialogues between the characters (*Hotel Rwanda*, *Shooting Dogs*), through a textual representation or a voice-over (*Shooting Dogs*, *Sometimes in April*) or by showing actual footage (*Sometimes in April*). In order to enhance the authenticity of their narratives, the films make use of historical sources in various forms: facts and images. The opening scenes summon up some of the historical facts about Rwanda in previous eras and all three 'show' radio hate speeches as disseminated by the propaganda broadcaster Radio-Télévision Libre des Mille Collines (RTLM). These speeches relentlessly called for the extermination of the Tutsi. Use is also made of TV news clips with President Clinton and other US officials, particularly the scenes in which Bushnell, a US official, hesitates to call the atrocities 'genocide'. All three films show (or mention) the deadly attack on the plane carrying the (Hutu) Rwandan president as setting off the violent reactions.

Sometimes in April starts by just showing the main factual dates or periods that were crucial in the coming into being of the ethnic conflict. This short historical introduction highlights the role of the West in the process of growing enmity. After showing the first lines that say 'For centuries, the Hutu, Tutsi and Twa of Rwanda shared the same culture, language and religion', *Sometimes* continues by retrieving the following dates and the events that took place during the years 1916, 1959, 1988, 1990 and 1993. The film's text mentions how Belgian colonizers took control from Germany in 1916 and introduced a rigid racial system by constructing and institutionalizing the two identities. In 1959 Rwanda gained independence and Belgium put power in the hands of the Hutu majority. Formerly, colonial power had been more or less shared with the Tutsi minority, for which they became deeply hated by the humiliated Hutu community. When the Hutu came into power, many Tutsi were forced into exile for fear of revenge. In 1988, radical Tutsi refugees formed the Rwandan Patriotic Front (RPF) to reclaim their homeland; two years later in 1990, the RPF launched an offensive against the Hutu regime, which was stopped with Belgian and French military support. From then until 1993, the two groups slaughtered each other. In that same year, the UN negotiated a power-sharing agreement between the two groups. The extremist Hutu were against sharing their power and started to plan the genocide of 1994.

This textual résumé of Rwanda's modern history is followed by Rwanda's mythical history. A soft male voice (belonging to Augustin) tells us about the mythical origin of the country with the thousand hills. Together with the dreamlike images of the Rwandan landscape and the atmospheric music, this tale of the national myth sets the melancholic mood of the film. It will be the last dreamlike images the audience will see in the coming two hours. While the voice-over and music continue, the scene is disrupted by archival footage showing the colonial invader shaking hands with a very reluctant Rwandan king, and doing skull measurements in order to base the ethnical separation on biological proof. The voice says: 'it was never about civilization, never about tribe and race; it was always about greed, arrogance and power.'

From the historical footage the film moves slowly, still guided by the voice-over, to more recent times. This historical sequence starts with an American (the quotation by King) and 'ends' with an American. We see Bill Clinton giving a speech during his visit to Kigali in 1996. His last few sentences were as follows: 'It is not an African phenomenon and must never be viewed as such. We have seen it in industrialized Europe. We have seen it in Asia. We must have global vigilance and never again must we be shy in the face of the evidence' (Bill Clinton cited in *Sometimes in April*).

In the last sequence that revolves around the US position (which is not the last scene of the film), the circle is closed again. It shows Bushnell and other officials having a video conference and expressing their positive feelings about the new US relief programme 'Support Hope', aimed at the Rwandan Hutu refugees. After the conference Bushnell informally talks a little longer with the US officer with whom she collaborated during the Rwandan crisis.

> Bushnell: Well, I guess that's it.
>
> US officer: Prudence, our mission was not to intervene. Well, the system functioned perfectly. In a few years down the road, the President will ask for forgiveness, he'll make the promise of 'never again'. But in terms of national interest we did everything right.
>
> Bushnell: We were loyal to a policy that allowed hundreds of thousands of people to be killed. As far as moral imperative is concerned, we did not do the right thing
>
> US officer: We're bureaucrats, not the political leadership.
>
> Bushnell: Is it because they are Africans?
>
> US officer: Let's not do that, Pru. It was Rwandans killing Rwandans.

To conclude

An obvious conclusion one can draw from the selected scenes and the complete films is that they are indeed condemning towards the West and the international press. It is more interesting, however, to consider how these films address the underlying reasons for the passive attitude. On an individual level, it is about leaving out of fear and pure self-preservation; on a military level, it is about obeying orders; on a governmental level it is about national interests and bureaucracy. However, all these rationalizations amount to what I would call a dominant 'cynicism frame'. More than once do the western characters themselves explain the western attitude in terms of racism, western centrism and even Nazism. Conspicuously, this 'west-bashing' is mostly done by the western characters themselves. A UN officer, war reporters and a priest, they are the champions of cynicism or self-criticism, almost as an act of repentance, which is also considered the first step on the way to redemption. To take the cynicism frame a step further, one could also argue that these western characters represent a position of 'seeing through' the western ideal of humanitarianism, while most of the Rwandan characters are portrayed as naive.

But one film goes beyond the conventional route: *Sometimes in April*. Besides displaying all the 'ingredients' of a regular genocide film, it also presents a narrative from a predominantly Rwandan perspective, which more or less follows the underlying ideas of *gacaca*. This judicial process is also a way of coming to terms with (and at the same time acknowledging) a never-ending past. Augustin is the only character who 'sees through', but in a different way, who includes a human uncertainty, a not-knowing (which is not the same as naivety). As one of his students asks him: 'Could it have been stopped?' He answers: 'Maybe if some of us were more courageous. Maybe if the world had paid more attention, I don't know.'

References

Adelman, H. 2003. Bystanders to Genocide in Rwanda: A Review Article. *International History Review*, 25(2), 357-374.

Beattie, L., Miller, D., Miller, E. and Philo, G. 1999. The Media and Africa: Images of Disaster and Rebellion. In *Message Received: Glasgow Media Group Research 1993-1998*, edited by G. Philo, 229-267. Harlow: Longman.

Berry, J.A. and Berry, C.P. 1999. *Genocide in Rwanda: A Collective Memory*. Washington, DC: Howard University Press.

Brandstetter, A.-M. 2010. *Contested Pasts: The Politics of Remembrance in Post Genocide Rwanda*, Ortelius Lectures 6. Wassenaar: NIAS.

Buettner, A. 2011. *Holocaust Images and Picturing Catastrophe: The Cultural Politics of Seeing*. Farnham and Burlington, VT: Ashgate.

Cobban, H. 2004. *Rwanda Today: The International Criminal Tribunal and the Prospects for Peace and Reconciliation*. Online *Frontline* interview with Helena Cobban. Available at http://www.pbs.org/wgbh/pages/frontline/shows/ghosts/today/ (accessed 15 April 2012).

Cohen, S. 2001. *States of Denial: Knowing about Atrocities and Suffering*. Cambridge, Oxford and Malden, MA: Polity.

Dauge-Roth, A. 2010. *Writing and Filming the Genocide of the Tutsis in Rwanda: Dismembering and Remembering Traumatic History*. Plymouth: Lexington.

Dowden, R. 2004. Comment: The Rwandan Genocide: How the Press Missed the Story. *African Affairs*, 103, 283-290.

Entman, R.M. 1993. Framing: Toward Clarification of a Fractured Paradigm. *Journal of Communication*, 43(4), 51-58.

Franks, S. 2005. Lacking a Clear Narrative: Foreign Reporting after the Cold War. *Political Quarterly*, 76(51), 91-101.

Franks, S. 2006. The CARMA Report: Western Media Coverage of Humanitarian Disasters. *Political Quarterly*, 77(2), 281-284.

Franks, S. 2010. The Neglect of Africa and the Power of Aid. *International Communication Gazette*, 72(1), 71-84.

Frontline. 2004. *Ghosts of Rwanda*. Available at http://www.pbs.org/wgbh/pages/frontline/shows/ghosts/ (accessed 15 April 2012).

Galtung, J. and Ruge, M.H. 1965. The Structure of Foreign News. *Journal of International Peace Research*, 1, 64-90.

Gourevitch, P. 1999. *We Wish to Inform You That Tomorrow We Will be Killed With Our Families: Stories from Rwanda*. London: Picador.

ICTJ (International Center for Transitional Justice). 2009. Online: International Criminal Tribunal for Rwanda. Available at http://ictj.org/sites/default/files/ICTJ-Global-Transitional-Justice-2009 English.pdf (accessed 14 May 2012).

Lacey, M. 2001. Memorials Dot Rwanda, Recalling '94 Carnage. *New York Times*, 17 September.

Melvern, L. 2004. *Conspiracy to Murder: The Rwandan Genocide*. London and New York: Verso.

Moeller, S.D. 1999. *Compassion Fatigue: How the Media sell Disease, Famine, War and Death*. London: Routledge.

Mirzoeff, N. 2005. Invisible Again: Rwanda and Representation after Genocide. *African Arts*, Autumn, 36-91.

Molenaar, Arthur. 2005. *Gacaca: Grassroots Justice after Genocide. The Key to Reconciliation in Rwanda*. Leiden: African Studies Centre.

Ndahiro, A. and Rutazibwa, P. 2008. *Hotel Rwanda or the Tutsi Genocide as seen by Hollywood*. Paris: L'Harmattan.

Philo, G., Hilsum, L., Beattie, L. and Holliman, R. 1999. The Media and the Rwanda Crisis: Effects on Audiences and Public Policy. In *Message Received: Glasgow Media Group Research 1993-1998*, edited by G. Philo, 213-228. Harlow: Longman.

Rice, X. 2006. Rwandans to see Genocide on Big Screen: Premiere of Shooting Dogs held in Kigali Stadium: Making of Film Triggered Panic and Flashbacks. *The Guardian* (London), 27 March.

Sitkowski, A. 2006. *UN Peacekeeping: Myth and Reality*. Westport, CT: Praeger Security International.

Thompson, A. ed. 2007. *The Media and the Rwanda Genocide*. London: Pluto Press.

Thomson, D. 2007. Desperation, Fear on Both Sides of 'Gates'; Moral Ambiguities Haunt Rwanda Story. *Washington Post*, 16 March.

Westberg, M.M. 2011. Rwanda's Use of Transitional Justice after Genocide: The Gacaca Courts and the ICTR. *Kansas Law Review*, 59, 331-67. Available at http://www.law.ku.edu/publications/lawreview/pdf/04-Westberg_Final.pdf (accessed 14 May 2012).

Williams, K. 2011. *International Journalism*. Los Angeles: Sage.

Films

Hotel Rwanda (dir. Terry George, 2004).
Shooting Dogs (dir. Michael Caton-Jones, 2004).
Sometimes in April (dir. Raoul Peck, 2005).

Chapter 13
An Eye for an Eye: The Imagery of the 1947 Partition (India, Pakistan)

Lodewijk Brunt

> What a horrible nightmare this Partition has turned out to be!
>
> (Yashpal, 2010: 741)

In his recent 'intimate biography' of India, French (2011: 28) writes that the 1947 partition of India and Pakistan still shocks us. How true, but what exactly did happen? It is difficult, if not impossible to recreate the dazzling scale and intensity of the violence that accompanied the creation of these two states, formerly being the undivided Indian subcontinent, ruled by colonial Britain. Searching for inside knowledge about what actually took place I made extensive use of novels, short stories, diaries and other literary expressions. It is practically the only way to go back in time and observe what contemporaries saw, thought and felt, and what it meant in the course of time. The best way to start is to make a journey into the heart of the Indian subcontinent, the world of the small village where in the 1940s more than 70 per cent of the population was living.

Punjab

Mano Majra is a hamlet near the Sutlej River, Punjab. The rhythm of daily life is punctuated by the trains which pass close by on the line between Delhi and Lahore. The passenger train in the morning urges people to get up and the one in the evening tells them to go to sleep. Only a few trains actually stop at the local station and few passengers get off. The village has three brick buildings, the mosque, the Sikh temple and the mansion of moneylender Lala Ram Lal. He is the only Hindu among the 70 Muslim and Sikh families who live in traditional mud huts. The Sikhs own the land on which the majority of the Muslims work as tenants or hired hands – other Muslims are small shopkeepers or artisans. Not many people are interested in the religious background of the sweepers and garbage collectors living on the outskirts of Mano Majra.

Although it is the summer of 1947, just after Pakistan and India have become independent nations, the villagers don't know much about what has been going on. Most of them don't even know that the British colonial authorities have left. When Iqbal Singh visits the village, coming all the way from Delhi, he is asked to provide the necessary information. 'Tell us something. What is happening in the world?' people ask him. 'What is all this about Pakistan and Hindustan?' The *lambardar* (municipal secretary) remarks: 'We live in this little village and know nothing. Babuji, tell us, why did the English leave?' (K. Singh 1981: 27).

Later it becomes clear that elsewhere in the Punjab region 'communal trouble' has erupted, Sikhs and Muslims are fighting each other. In Mano Majra, a village meeting is organized where representatives of both religious groups discuss whether the Muslims should leave for refugee camps or possibly for Pakistan – just for reasons of safety. Imam Baksh confronts his Sikh co-villagers with the dilemma: 'All the neighbouring villages have been evacuated. Only we are left. If you want us to go too, we will go.' But a bright young man from the Sikh community stands up and addresses the audience:

> 'It is like this, Uncle Imam Baksh. As long as we are here nobody will dare to touch you. We die first and then you can look after yourselves'. 'Yes', adds another enthusiastically, 'we first, then you. If anyone raises his eyebrows at you we will rape his mother'. 'Mother, sister and daughter', added the others. (K. Singh 1981: 125-126)

Pari Darvaza

More to the North, between the Indus and Jhelum rivers, near the Pothwar Plateau, we find another tiny village – Pari Darvaza. Roop is the daughter of the local *lambardar* and she has been brought up a Sikh, although part of her family is Hindu. She was born in the early 1930s and has learned that the British have been trying to install some kind of democratic government with different groups represented on the basis of their numbers. 'So, now Hindus need more Hindus, and we Sikhs need more Sikhs. Mahatma Gandhi is a Hindu – he just needs more Sikhs to cut their hair and say that they are Hindus next time the census people ask' (Singh Baldwin 1999: 58). Despite her young age she is wise about the world – about little things like the separate water taps for Hindus and Muslims on train stations, but also about big, important things. Mahatma Gandhi devised a national flag of a free India, but it didn't have a strip of deep Sikh blue as he had promised. 'Across Punjab, Sikhs mutter the reason – the Mahatma doesn't care for meat-eaters' (Singh Baldwin 1999: 92).

In the years before the Second World War there had been much discussion about the secular nature of the independent nation of India desired by the Indian National Congress, the political movement of Mahatma Gandhi and Jawaharlal Nehru. But once Hindus forget to remember the word 'secular' – Roop realizes – Muslim men throughout India know they will be forced – along with Sikh men, Christians, Buddhists, Jains, Jews, Parsis, tribals and animists – to accept the whims of many gods not of their own choosing. Muslims especially know deep down that Hindus have not forgotten the cruel Moghul dynasty. 'And so Muslims scattered far away through the subcontinent began first to whisper, then to shout pleas to brother-

Muslims: "Do not forget us, you must protect us, protect all Muslims, against the coming Hindu raj"' (Singh Baldwin 1999: 136-137).

In Pari Darvaza most people are aware of communal tensions. As the local *lambardar* Roop's father has to be careful. '"The number of Muslims here!", he thinks as the hairs on the back of his neck begin to rise. All about him, round-capped men say "Salaam Aleikum" quite loudly as he passes. There is not one voice that greets him, in deference to his faith, with "Sat Sri Akal".' And he realizes who is to blame for this: 'It's all Jinnah's fault. He is everywhere, rabble-rousing, repeating his freshly minted word, Pakistan, letting the least-qualified Muslims, like these men here, assign it whatever meaning they desire. Jinnah with his two-nation theory, as if Hindus and Muslims were the only rulers India had ever known before the British raj' (Singh Baldwin 1999: 287).

Fiction and reality

Both Mano Majra and Pari Darvaza are fictionalized villages, but they have much in common. Both were created by authors with a Sikh background, Khushwant Singh and Shauna Singh Baldwin respectively, and both are situated in Punjab at the time of Indian and Pakistan independence in 1947. In both villages one finds the same kind of social constellation: Sikhs and Muslims form the bulk of the population, the Sikhs being landowners, the Muslims artisans and labourers. But there are also striking differences. In Khushwant Singh's novel *Train to Pakistan*, published ten years after Independence, the villagers are depicted as an innocent lot, considering each other as brothers and sisters and trying to make a front against the outside world. In Pari Darvaza, the village in Shauna Singh Baldwin's novel *What the Body Remembers*, published in 1999, religious tensions are prevalent, even within families. The political developments leading to Independence cause fear and anxious speculation and Indian history, from times before the British colonial government, makes people aware of what might be expected: glory for some, doom for others.

The independence of India and Pakistan on 15 August 1947 embodied the breaking up of the Indian subcontinent; Pakistan, to the West and the East (the part that became Bangladesh in 1971), and India, in between. The Partition, as it is called, is one of the most tragic and dramatic incidents of twentieth-century world history and still haunts the memories of millions. Only a few weeks before the festivities of Independence were to take place, the British government decided that it would give up the ideal of an undivided India and, instead, give in to Muhammad Ali Jinnah's Muslim League's demand for a separate Muslim state, Pakistan ('The Land of the Pure'). Sir Cyril Radcliffe, who had never before been to India, was burdened with the task of dividing the subcontinent; an impossible task, dramatically commemorated by W.H. Auden in his poem "Partition" (2007: 803). In it, he tells of Radcliffe arriving in India to deal with the problem of hostilities between the Muslim and Hindu populations, and of his instructions from London:

not to waste time on reconciliation efforts, but to separate these 'incompatible' peoples as quickly as possible and partition the sub-continent.

Premier Nehru gave his Independence speech at midnight on 14 August; Jinnah's speech was to be broadcasted the next day. But even as their famous words were spoken, the precise boundaries between India and Pakistan had still not been decided upon. Against the background of optimistic expectations and solemn promises, masses of fugitives were desperately looking for safety – the streets and alleys ran red with blood. Hundreds of thousands were brutally killed, temples and mosques were ravaged, houses and neighbourhoods were put to fire. Muslims fled from India to Pakistan and Hindus, Sikhs and others moved in the opposite direction. For many months after August 1947 this drama was continued, every move leading to further tragedies. An estimated 14 million people migrated – leaving the homes and land where they had lived and worked for as long as could be remembered. Nobody knows exactly how many people were wounded or killed, but some think the number of deaths alone must have been at least two million or more (French 1997: 348).

According to French the 'horror' of the Partition 'hit deeply into the memories of the inhabitants' (1997: 349). In India this memory is expressed in numerous ways, politically in the first place: Pakistan is considered as the 'arch enemy' and three wars were fought between the two countries after 1947. Every act of terrorism is blamed on Pakistan and its much feared Secret Service. But the memory of Partition is articulated in other ways too – film, art, poetry, dance, music. Not only are the memories kept alive through artistic expression, they are also emotionally coloured and qualified in accordance with shifting judgements and evaluations. The above mentioned novels by Khushwant Singh and Shauna Singh Baldwin are a case in point. I suspect that the outburst of violence that accompanied Independence did appear much more sudden and unexpected – and was perhaps much harder to understand – to a contemporary writer who was himself an eyewitness (Khushwant Singh; see also Singh 2005) than to a writer who has had more than fifty years to contemplate what happened and who could take the necessary distance to study, analyse and explain (Singh Baldwin).

Memory

In his introduction to the translation of Sahni's novel about Partition, *Tamas* (Sahni 1988), Govind Nihalani remarks that literary memories can be considered of two kinds: the personal and emotional of the eyewitness and the more objective and analytical of the writer who considers historical developments from further away. This seems obvious, although Dresden (1991) has shown that the differences in genres of the so-called 'ghetto literature' about the persecution of Jews in the Second World War are not always clear-cut. Public opinion can also play a role. When *Tamas* was first published in Hindi in 1974, the book was received well, Partition obviously being a legitimate subject for a novel. In 1988, the book was again published, now translated into English, and made into a television series and a film. This time *Tamas* appeared to be highly controversial and several pressure groups attempted to have the series banned from Indian television. Since the 1970s, the Hindu nationalist movement had become a strong force in Indian politics and representatives of this movement protested against the 'soft' attitude towards Pakistan and the Muslims in *Tamas*.

Literature – novels, poetry and short stories – is a guide to exploring both sides of Indian independence. First, the glorious side of successfully driving away the British colonial power after a long and difficult struggle – strongly associated with the non-violent heroism of Mahatma Gandhi and the secular Congress Party – and second, the subject of this chapter, the dark side of unspeakable crimes in the wake of this struggle – not crimes against the colonizer, but crimes against fellow citizens, members of 'other' communities. The most serious reproach one could probably make of the British authorities is their departure at the very moment the Indian subcontinent seemed to collapse. Time and time again, people prayed for protection and interference, but the British looked the other way. Their reaction seemed to be: 'You people found it so important to rule your own country ... just go ahead and rule it! If there are any problems, ask your Mr Gandhi or Mr Nehru to find a solution!' As in many other similar situations in the world after such an uproar, there has been a precarious balance among the survivors. Hitchens (2003) discusses several examples of British preference for dividing up people, including India and Pakistan. Not (nearly) every Muslim fled to Pakistan – on the basis of population statistics India is, after Indonesia, the second largest Muslim nation in the world. And so, Indian Hindus and Indian Muslims have had to find some kind of balance and as we know from numerous religious riots, this has not always been successful. During the latest 'riots' in Gujarat, in 2002, thousands of Muslims were brutally killed. The killers have not been prosecuted, with one or two exceptions, and many more thousands of survivors are still suffering in desolate refugee camps. The memory of Partition is still a raw nerve in India (and probably in Pakistan as well).

The emotional colouring of memory is also an important underlying theme in Partition literature. Some books are explicitly written or presented as 'moral tales': they are meant to be a warning to the reader. In the introduction to *Tamas*, for instance, Nihalani remarks that the book is more than just literature. 'It is a grim reminder of the intense tragedy that results whenever the religious sentiments of communities are manipulated to achieve political objectives. It is a prophetic warning against the use of religion as a weapon to gain and perpetuate political power' (Sahni 1988: 8). But novels and short stories may have yet other functions. Verma (2004: lxvi) remarks that explanations of atrocities and other violent outbursts are often based on 'hard' social facts like economic competition, class differences, migration, ethnicity or – in the case of India – caste. But we also need of a kind of 'social forensics' she argues, we must know who the killers were, who were the supporters, their modi operandi, why things took place on that spot and at that time, who the parties in the background were. And then there are the victims:

how could people survive as moral beings in situations of intense terror? Is it true, as many have told Verma, that they acted impulsively in a moral vacuum?

Imagery

In order to get a little closer to such important questions I have found it useful to read novels and short stories about Partition, although I realize that there are some obvious difficulties implied in such an undertaking, one of the most important being the unknown quantity (and quality) of books which have been written on this subject.

In India, there are many languages that are hardly known, except of course by native speakers and writers (quite a number of languages, however, have no written tradition). Despite my familiarity with Hindi and Urdu, I am mainly dependent on books in English (written or translated into English) and I have no coherent idea to what extent they are 'representative' of Indian literature in general (if that would be a useful concept at all). Some authors write 'high literature' and would be of eminent interest irrespective of the Partition theme: Manto is an example, as is Chughtai – both authors wrote in Urdu. Literary praise is also due to Parsi author Sidhwa who has used pre-Partition Lahore (now Pakistan) as the background to her novel *Ice-Candy-Man*, and Singh Baldwin whom we have already met. A case in itself is Yashpal, creator of the epic classic *Jhoota Sach* (translated from Hindi as *This is Not That Dawn*) in which both pre-Partition and post-Partition histories of several families are extensively described, comprising more than 1,100 pages. In their minute observations of intimate situations, the authors of these books have far more to offer than writers who stick to flat generalizations and perhaps somewhat stereotypical characters. Moreover, there are books by representatives of different communities – Hindus, Muslims, Parsis, Sikhs. Last but not least: writers have vastly different geographical orientations. For instance, most of the literature I have been reading deals with North India and/or West India, especially Punjab (now split into Indian and Pakistani parts).

In view of these shortcomings it would be impossible to pretend that I'm able to give any kind of systematic answer to the above mentioned questions and problems; what I do hope to accomplish is to sensitize the reader to the Partition. I have been reading novels and short stories against the background of some essential historical studies of Partition – in which a certain over-representation of Punjab is also present. Some of these studies have been conducted by eyewitnesses. The English official Moon is a case in point. He travelled right through Punjab on his way to Simla at the very time the violence was exploding. His observations were as shocking as some of the fictionalized representations by novelists (Moon and also Khosla, Page and Inder Singh in Hasan 2004). Nobody needed to make things up, the reality of Partition was much worse than anybody could have imagined.

Friends and neighbours

While reading my novels and short stories, I seemed to get a definite feel for the way Partition was depicted by novelists and short story writers, and sometimes professional historians too. Roughly speaking, one could say that Partition is like lightning and thunder in a clear sky, a profound shock in a seemingly harmonious arrangement, an earthquake or tsunami. At one moment a village is living peacefully, even if the population belongs to different religious communities; the next moment the peace is disturbed and people have started chasing each other and behaving like murderous madmen.

Historian Khosla offers an excellent example. In his classical study *Stern Reckoning*, written in 1949 and reproduced in Hasan's *Partition Omnibus* (2004), he states that the different groups had lived together 'in peace and amity'. There were Hindu majority areas and Muslim majority areas, but no area was exclusively inhabited by any one single community.

> Everywhere, Hindus, Muslims and Sikhs lived together as neighbours. In the urban areas the various communities could not, in the very nature of things, live in separate, airtight compartments. There were, no doubt, Hindu *mohallas*, Sikh *mohallas* and Muslims *mohallas*, but these were situated side by side and it could not be said of any town in India that it was owned or inhabited by one community or that a particular area of the town belonged exclusively to the Hindus, Muslims or Sikhs. (Hasan 2004: 3)

The author goes on to underline the fact that members of different groups met not only at home but also at work. Muslim landlords had Hindu tenants and Hindu industrialists employed Sikh and Muslim workers. 'The unifying force of geographical entity, historical and cultural influences, extending over a period of ten centuries, had welded the various elements into a homogeneous whole' (Hasan 2004: 4). Khosla goes so far as to say that 'minor differences in custom and outlook' never stood in the way of 'most amicable and friendly' forms of living together. But, in view of the Indian caste divisions, sanctioned by strict rules of purity and impurity, it is almost shocking to read that the different communities even 'dined at each other's houses and seldom allowed their religious persuasions to interfere with their social and friendly intercourse' (Hasan 2004: 5). This is a vast exaggeration and even to this day grossly misleading.

Not even Singh is willing to present such harmony in his Mano Majra, but generally speaking some of the core elements of Khosla's idealization can be found in other images as well. In her short story 'Roots' Chughtai (1997) tells us that in the state of Marwar Hindus and Muslims had so much in common that it was impossible to tell them apart on the basis of names, features or dress. Her story is about two families who are closely related and we see things developing from the viewpoint of a daughter of a Muslim household. After the Partition her family is tempted to move to Pakistan, mainly because the eldest son is pushing them. But grandmother refuses to go. The thought of going to Sindh makes her sick. 'Do you think I'll go to die among those Sindhis. God's curse on them! They wander about in flowing *burqas* and *pyjamas*.' She doesn't want to live with a younger son in Dhaka (East Pakistan) either. '*Aye,* why should I go to Dhaka? Those head-hunting Bengalis knead rice in their hands and then slurp it down.' Rawalpindi, in Punjab, is equally out of the question: '*Tobah* ! May *Allah* save us from the Punjabis. They speak like the denizens of hell' (Chughtai 1997: 284). She wants to stay where she is, very close to her (Hindu) family doctor. A similar refusal to leave for a 'strange' country is described in Badiuzzaman's 'The Last Wish' (1997). Notwithstanding the widening gap between Hindus and Muslims in a political sense, their social nature hasn't changed. 'But was there any difference in the daily lives of the two communities? None. They were plodding along in much the same way … Their squabbles went on, but there wasn't a point of estrangement.' Here too an elder son is urging the other members of his family to leave for Pakistan. 'You come along. Otherwise, you'll regret.' But his mother answered: 'We will be the last to do so. How can we leave our home to live in a country of which we know so little?' (Badiuzzaman 1997: 137-138).

These stories underline the internal differences in the Muslim population: Muslims from Bengal, Punjab or Sindh are strangers to each other. In other words, Muslims and Hindus from one region have more in common and are closer to each other. Yet, apparent 'friends' and 'neighbours' murdered each other relentlessly, as if violence is more intense among people who are more alike in outlook and culture. Hitchens (2010) employs the Freudian concept 'narcissism of the small difference' to highlight this phenomenon: minor differences between equals lead to intense feelings of hostility. In his view, this has been amply demonstrated in the very situation we are dealing with in this chapter.

> The partition of India and Pakistan, which gives us one of the longest-standing and most toxic confrontations extant, involved most of all the partition of the Punjab. Visit Punjab and see if you can detect the remotest difference in people on either side of the border. Language, literature, ethnic heritage, physical appearance – virtually indistinguishable. Here it is mainly religion that symbolizes the narcissism and makes the most of the least discrepancy. (Hitchens 2010: para. 3).

The Hindu doctor in 'Roots' is grandmother's long-standing friend. 'His sons were my brothers' friends and his daughters-in-law were friends of my sisters-in-law. This close friendship extended to the children. The two families were so close to each other over three generations that no one had the slightest suspicion that the country's partition would rupture their relationship' (Chughtai 1997: 281). The fierce discussions between family members, who stood on opposing sides in their adherence to the Congress Party or the Muslim League, were more like a football or cricket match. One party wrote *Pakistan Zindabad* on the walls, the other answered with *Akhand Hindustan* – but at heart it was a question of 'jokes' and 'jibes'. All the while the grandmother and her friend would listen to all this and smile. 'They would make plans for a united Asia' (Chughtai 1997: 282).

Not only neighbourly and friendly families were split, of course; separate families as such were also partitioned. Salman Rushdie, who wrote perhaps the most impressive novel about Indian independence – *Midnight's Children* (1981) – remarks that his own family 'was cut in half by Partition'. 'My parents', he says, 'opted to stay in Bombay, and so did my two uncles and their families, but my aunts and their families went to West Pakistan, as it was called until 1971, when East Pakistan seceded and became Bangladesh.' 'We were lucky', Rushdie concludes, 'escaping the worst of the bloodletting, but our lives were defined and shaped by the frontier separating us' (2002: 176).

Lahore

Sidhwa's *Ice-Candy-Man* (1988) centres on Lenny and her ayah – Lenny being the daughter of a well-to-do Parsi family in Lahore, and her ayah an 18-year-old Hindu girl. Lenny grows up in the late 1930s and early 1940s in the centre of a close-knit network of nephews, aunts, cousins, neighbours (in Lenny's case, Sikhs), household staff, hawkers and even some street-people. The Parsis are a tiny, but important minority on the Indian subcontinent; in Lahore their community was so small that they even had no cemetery of their own. The ice-candy-man is a Muslim vendor of ice cream, always flirting with the ayah; he sells parrots, sparrows and other birds in the winter. The man who sharpens the kitchen knives is a Pathan from Afghanistan, the cook is a Muslim and the garden boy is Hindu. The Parsis find themselves in an awkward position in view of the future plans for partition. To which country will the city of Lahore belong? As one aunt puts it: 'If we're stuck with the Hindus they'll swipe our businesses from under our noses and sell our grandfathers in the bargain; if we're stuck with the Muslims they'll convert us by the sword! And God help us if we're stuck with the Sikhs' (Sidhwa 1988: 37). Some suggest that all the Parsis should move to Bombay in case Lahore becomes Muslim, but in general their attitude is confident and constructive: 'Let whoever wishes rule! Hindu, Muslim, Sikh, Christian! We will abide by the rules of their land!' (Sidhwa 1988: 39).

In the villages around Lahore there is much speculation about the 'troubles' between different communities. Lenny witnesses a discussion in Pir Pindo, the village of the family cook. A Sikh leader says: 'Muslim or Sikh, we are basically the same stock. We are brothers. How can we fight each other?' The Muslim landlord answers:

> I'm alert to what is happening … I have a radio. But our relationships with the Hindus are bound by strong ties. The city folk can afford to fight … we can't. We are dependent on each other: bound by our toil … To us villagers, what does it matter if a peasant is a Hindu or a Muslim or a Sikh? (Sidhwa 1988: 56-57)

The 'brothers' promise to protect one another. All this talking about religious communities and troubles makes Lenny realize the importance of religion and the religious group one belongs to. 'One day everybody is themselves – and the next day they are Hindu, Muslims, Sikh, Christian. People shrink, dwindling into symbols. Ayah is no longer just my all-encompassing Ayah – she is also a token: a Hindu' (Sidhwa 1988: 93). The heterogeneous network around Lenny is gradually divided into homogeneous groups. Even if one would rather not acquiesce, one is forced by others: 'Now I know surely', Lenny tells herself, 'one man's religion is another man's poison.' She thinks of her own family: 'Godmother, Slavesister, Electric-aunt and my nuclear family are reduced to irrelevant nomenclatures – we are Parsee. What is God?' (Sidhwa 1988: 94). The only person who is able to maintain a colourful group of followers is ayah with her bunch of eager admirers – her Pathan knife sharpener, her masseur, her garden boy and her ice-candy-man. Elsewhere (Sidhwa 2005), the author discloses her sources of inspiration. To a large extent, Yashpal's awesome book is also situated in Lahore – albeit not in Lenny's posh neighbourhood: in both books, identical incidents are described and the historical correctness of both tales can easily be deducted from Singh's memoir (Singh 2005) – the author spent a good many years in Lahore as a young lawyer and was a keen observer of the events which took place in the city during Partition.

Musical instrument

In Sahni's 1988 novel *Tamas*, the population of the little town in which the story unfolds is compared to a musical instrument. The Hindus take care of textile and grain, the Muslims are responsible for transportation and make shoes, and both groups are evenly represented among shopkeepers and street vendors. 'The entire range of activities was orchestrated to a certain rhythm – the rhythm of the city' (Sahni 1988: 88). In other words, if one single string were to break, city life would be interrupted. Sometimes the underlying peace and order was threatened, for instance when the Sikhs had their annual festivities for the anniversary of the Guru; then they marched through the streets and passed the mosque. Will they be quiet? Will there be people throwing stones? At other times, Muslims roamed the streets shouting '*Ya Hussain*'. 'On such occasions the fear of communal clashes became real. But soon after, the tension would ease and people would lapse into their normal routine' (Sahni 1988: 88). At the time of Partition, however, normal routine seems to be broken forever. Repeated attempts by the local elite, the leaders of the different religious communities, to keep the peace are to no avail. And the same effect as we have seen in Lahore occurs in this locality (somewhere in the north-east of India) too.

> The limits of Hindu and Muslim mohallas had suddenly been clearly demarcated. The Hindus and the Sikhs dared not trespass into Muslim mohallas, nor the Muslims into Hindu and Sikh lanes. Holding *lathis* and spears, people guarded

> the entrances to their lanes. Where Hindus and Muslims happened to live together, only one sentence was heard, uttered again and again. 'It's too bad! It's too bad!' (Sahni 1988: 117)

Lightning

Although some writers are rather subtle in their observations of the beginning of the conflicts – Singh Baldwin is a case in point with her carefully built up tensions and controversies, as is Yashpal, part of whose story takes place in the milieu of students and activists with communist leanings – in most books and stories the situation is clearly marked: a more or less harmonious village, town or urban district is suddenly and unexpectedly struck by disaster, as if by lightning. This cannot be a literary effect only. Of course, the more peaceful your portrayal of the situation before Partition, the harder your (literary) punch will be at the moment when you introduce the fighting. There must be more to it. As we have seen, the imagery of brotherhood/sisterhood and neighbourliness and amity is also to be found in the studies of professional historians. Despite a long history of invasions and struggles, enmity and fierce communal strife on the subcontinent, it seems that the idea of a peaceful Indian nation is an obligatory background to the tales of horror in order to provide profile. Indian history is obviously conceived or even experienced as a linear process, with Partition as a nasty break or crash – and after Partition it took its (normal) course again. However dramatic and painful the incidents were for many millions of people, such a conception allows us to consider Partition as an isolated 'black page' in history. Better to forget it as soon as possible. Also better not to talk about it. In Europe there is something similar in the almost autistic attitude of Jews who survived the concentration camps – in the circle of their friends and even their children the experiences of the war have always been a taboo subject. Organized silence.

Not every writer has been willing to elaborate the 'punch' which followed the undermining of the communal harmony. As far as the high literature is concerned, I have already mentioned Sidhwa and Singh Baldwin but this certainly applies to Yashpal as well, where the description of the violence is more or less 'functional'. In *Ice-Candy-Man* everything is seen from the standpoint of a young and rather innocent Parsi girl: Lenny – and that goes for the horror too. The same is true for *What the Body Remembers*, although Roop is no longer a young girl in August 1947 – she is a mother of two who tries to save herself and her children by fleeing Punjab and travelling to Delhi. Roop gets stranded – like so many other fugitives – on the Grand Trunk Road and during the night the danger comes near from 10 different directions. She hears war cries everywhere: '*Allah ho Akbar! Allah ho Akbar!*' Her heart is pounding but she hears a voice urging her to live and to survive. A small band of soldiers attacks wherever they see people in hiding.

> They forgot all Koranic admonitions as they drank the contents of a bhang still in the last Sikh village they raided. Finding themselves free of officers, Indian

> or English, they felt themselves descending into disorder, a state more fear-filled than hell. And to stop that fear, though not their descent, they have named themselves teachers of lessons to unbelievers, the only pure followers of an only God. (Singh Baldwin 1999: 421-422)

They have learned that a man who kills, maims, hurts or rapes somebody from another religion finds his second and his third offences become ever easier. They drive along the columns of refugees, looking for victims and 'to amuse themselves, dragging struggling Sikh and Hindu women into the lorry, shooting or maiming Sikhs and Hindus plodding to India, or at whim, converting men to Islam, simply, by tearing off salwars or dhotis, and slashing off foreskins' (Singh Baldwin 1999: 422).

In Yashpal's book, the violence takes place mostly after Partition, a period of many months without law and order. One of his main characters, Tara, is raped and is sold by her rapist to shady businessmen who consider women like her as commodities to be dealt with as sex slaves. Later she ends up in a Delhi fugitive camp where corruption and fraud is rife. Her brother, Purim, is robbed during his attempts to save his family from the fierce Lahore riots and has to beg on the streets among many thousands of confused fugitives who don't know where they are and where they are going. The situation he finds himself in seems like an inferno: 'On the roadside, as far as his eyes could see, was the evidence of devastation and plunder – broken, upturned bullock carts, dead bodies, vultures and dogs fighting over the carcasses of oxen. A heavy, nauseating, choking stench hung in the air' (Yashpal 2010: 473-474).

Forced conversion is a common theme in Partition literature and also in *Tamas*. A young Sikh is chased by a group of Muslims. He is in hiding but the gang knows where. 'Oh, Sikh', they shout, 'if you agree to accept Islam we shall let you off ... Are you willing to accept Islam? ... If Islam is acceptable to you, come out of hiding. We'll do you no harm. Otherwise we shall stone you to death!' (Sahni 1988: 188). The Sikh comes out of hiding and is thoroughly humiliated – eventually they cut his hair and shave him and he is undressed. While his torturers put beef into his mouth and force him to eat, they give him a new name: Iqbal Ahmed. Then he is circumcised. 'Before nightfall all the signs of Iqbal Singh's Sikhism had been carefully obliterated; in their place were all the external Muslim signs. From an enemy he had been transformed into a friend, not an infidel, but a believer – a Mussalman. The doors of all Muslim houses were now open to him.' And then the sorry scene ends: 'Lying on a cot Iqbal Ahmed passed the night in torment' (Sahni 1988: 192). In the same novel a rape is described, committed by a bunch of Muslim hooligans on a young Hindu girl. The rapists are boasting about their victory. One of them tells his friends: 'When my turn came, she said neither "no" nor "yes" as she lay under me. She didn't even stir. And then I found that she was dead. I had been doing it with a corpse' (Sahni 1988: 196-197). He laughed, twisted his mouth and spat on the ground. In Yashpal's novel, rape also receives much attention, especially the fact that the victims are rejected by their husbands and families. During Tara's stay in fugitive camps, she realizes that she is not the only rape victim. The women in the camps know quite well that in times of war it is they who will take the hardest blows, from all sides. Tara sighs: 'Men fight with other men and kill each other, but they don't strip one another naked and disgrace their bodies.' Whereupon one of her companions remarks: 'What sins must we have committed in our past lives to be born as women' (Yashpal 2010: 483). As well as rape, shooting and killing, abduction, humiliation and forced conversion, the literature abounds with every conceivable crime.

Supporters

Often, committing crimes is encouraged, as we can see both in *Ice-Candy-Man* and in *This is Not That Dawn* when a mass meeting is organized. In the case of Lahore, Master Tara Singh – the great leader of the Sikh community – is mentioned time and again. He is regularly invited to speak in public and invariably this leads to violence and arson. Like Singh for the Sikhs and Jinnah for the Muslims, political leaders felt compelled to use strong language to keep their followers satisfied. In India, Nehru and Gandhi were repeatedly abused by their Hindu supporters when they tried to coach them into non-violent behaviour – this was considered as pampering the Muslims and suppressing the Hindus (many examples are to be found in Ganda Singh's diary of the Partition days (G. Singh 1997) and in Yashpal's epic this is a central theme).

In Sidhwa's novel, Lenny witnesses what Singh is saying. 'We will see how the Muslim swine get Pakistan! We will fight to the last man! We will show them *who* will leave Lahore! *Raj karega khalsa, aki rahi na koi*!' The spectators are jubilant and many people start swinging hockey sticks and swords around. '*Pakistan murdabad! Sat Sri Akaal! Bolay se nihaal!*', thunders across the square (Sidhwa 1988: 133-134). And during the Hindu festivities of Holi soon after this meeting, the fighting starts all over Lahore. 'The terror the mob generates is palpable – like an evil, paralysing spell.' From above Lenny sees a procession, 'flowing like a sluggish river', where every so often small groups of men stall, leaving in its centre 'the pulpy red flotsam of a mangled body' (Sidhwa 1988: 135). Later Lenny sees another incident:

> My eyes focus on a emaciated Banya wearing a white Gandhi cap. The man is knocked down. His lips are drawn away from rotting, *paan*-stained teeth in a scream. The men move back and in the small clearing I see his legs sticking out of his dhoti right up to the groin – each thin, brown leg tied to a jeep. There is a roar of a hundred throats: "*Allah-o-Akbar*!" and beneath it the growl of revving motors. (Sidhwa 1988: 153)

Lenny's journey through the city is a tour of torture. Her head is spinning when she watches the attack on a Hindu neighbourhood.

> I stare at the *tamasha*, mesmerized by the spectacle. It is like a gigantic fireworks display in which stiff figures looking like spread-eagled stick-dolls leap into the air, black against the magenta furnace. Trapped by the spreading flames, the panicked Hindus rush in droves from one end of the street to the other. Many disappear down the smoking lanes. Some collapse in the street. Charred limbs and burnt logs are falling from the sky … The whole world is burning. (Sidhwa 1988: 153)

In her 'Roots', Chughtai points out that it took some time for people to realize that the British had left and that their departure had caused a deadly wound. 'India was operated upon by such clumsy hands and blunt knives that thousands of arteries were left open. Rivers of blood flowed and no one had the strength left to stitch the wounds' (Chughtai 1997: 279).

Cynics

Only a few authors have been able to arrive at enough distance to cynically comment on the ongoing violence. Naqvi (1997) writes a short story about two watchmen at a Parsi cemetery, Bhatina and Hormoz. They get corpses from the Parsi community and are supposed to expose these in the open air – on top of the Tower of Silence – in order to allow the vultures and crows to eat the human remains. During the riots, they are overloaded with corpses, but there are no vultures in sight. It takes some time before they realize the reason for the continued absence of the birds.

> Oh these idiot Hindus and Muslims are at each other's throats again. There's been a riot. The bastards, they've torched everything: houses, shops, even ambulances and hearses, the whole lot. The street is littered with corpses. One right on top of the other. Piled high. Our vultures – well, they're having a field day there. (Naqvi 1997: 295)

Some policeman tells them that the vultures will come back once the fighting is over, but they are not convinced. 'What makes you think the vultures will return? This fucking India … there is a riot every day here, every day a fire, every day people die. The vultures'll come back? The hell they will' (Naqvi 1997: 295).

Naqvi was born in Bombay in 1945, so he did not experience any part of Partition consciously – his language gives him away as well – but a writer like Manto lived through it indeed. He is a master of the very short story and has left many similar impressions – quite a few about the violence he experienced personally. In 'Black Margins' (Manto 2005), he writes about national politics, looting and plundering, refugees, murder, rape, rioting, burning. After publishing his work, Manto was prosecuted repeatedly and critics have accused him of desecrating the dead and making money at the cost of tragic victims. Disillusioned, he left Bombay after

Partition, where he worked for the film industry, and emigrated to Pakistan. Some of his stories are no longer than a few sentences. 'A Mishtake', for instance:

> The knife slid down his groin. His *pyjama* cord was cut into two. '*Chi, chi, chi, chi*, I've made a *mishtake*', the assassin said with a sense of remorse. (Manto 1997: 99)

Or 'A Respite Needed', in which people have become physically tired of killing.

> 'He isn't dead yet. See, see, he is still gasping for breath'. 'Let it go, *yaar*. I'm already exhausted'. (Manto 1997: 99)

And in 'What's the Difference' one finds a similar theme.

> I placed my knife across his windpipe and, slowly, very slowly, I slaughtered him. 'What have you done?' 'Why?' 'Why kill him like that?' 'I love it that way'. 'You idiot, you should have hacked his neck off with a single blow. Like this'. And the kosher-killer's neck was chopped off accordingly. (Manto 1997: 99, 100)

What is it we see?

A remarkable feature of Partition literature is the apparent difficulty many writers have in deciding what they are actually writing about. I experienced the same problem in my own reproduction of this literature. I have used words like 'fighting' and 'violence' and 'crimes', but I realize that these are weak terms in view of the enormity of what really took place. I suddenly understood that certain historical dramas create their own terminology – existing language no longer suffices. 'Civil war', for instance, is strongly associated with the American Civil War, just as 'holocaust' seems to be practically reserved for the Second World War. In concluding this chapter I shall elaborate on this phenomenon further.

While studying Partition literature, historical, journalistic as well as literary, I noticed the great variety of concepts that were used and at a certain moment I started writing them down – just for curiosity's sake. I suspected that such a procedure might lead to an interesting topic of further research – provided of course that the counting would be somewhat more systematic and analytic than mine. I found words like 'rioting', 'catastrophe', 'communal warfare', 'fury', 'trouble', 'breaches of peace', 'uprising', 'massacres', 'civil war', 'ethnic cleansing', 'slaughter', 'bloodlust', 'revenge', 'mutual genocide', 'holocaust', 'horror'. As far as I could see, one might create some order by dividing the words into emic terms and etic terms, those used by insiders and those used by outsiders. Insiders meaning eyewitnesses, novelists and short story writers, outsiders meaning students of Partition looking back from a greater distance in time or in point of view, analysing reports and secondary materials. Yashpal, for instance, is a typical insider; a large part of his book is clearly autobiographical. French, on the other hand, is an outsider, using etic concepts like 'holocaust' and 'genocide' (1997: 346-349). Each term implies an abstracted way of looking at the world and these more or less analytical concepts are attempts at a comparative perspective, that is to say, the things that took place in 1947 were of the same kind of seriousness or cruelty as the things that took place in Germany (holocaust) and Bosnia (ethnic cleansing) or the United States (civil war) for that matter. In a certain sense, the use of such terms might even be interpreted as a kind of 'decolonizing' the Indian (and Pakistani) past. The atrocities that took place were not primitive random killings in some backwater region by barbaric natives, but actions and incidents that have had the same significance for humanity as western, European, 'civilized' forms of civil warfare (or whatever term would be appropriate). And what is more: even the crimes committed fall into a pattern and can be analysed scientifically.

The imagery one finds in novels and short stories is much more emotional: 'fury', 'catastrophe', 'massacres', 'slaughter'. It's about another kind of violence: not abstract, organized or state-sponsored but direct, personal and confrontational. This is in close correspondence with what actually took place. The crimes committed during Partition had a 'human face', so to speak; there were no bombs thrown from unmanned airplanes, but the weapons used were common, everyday objects. Killings were conducted with knives, swords, sticks, stones and bare hands; killer and victim could look each other in the eye and could see hate, fear, pride, rage, astonishment or any other sort of expression. It's understandable that people who have been bombed from high flying machines feel powerless and impotent, whereas such direct confrontations as took place during Partition normally cried out for revenge: an eye for an eye. Violence experienced in terms of a sporting contest is also what Verma found in her interviews with survivors of Partition: 'they will surely win if we don't strike back' (2004: 26, 27).

I presume that the imagery of 'friendly families' who suddenly turn into killing beasts also has something to do with this direct violence. Even without being friends, many people had developed a sort of routine in living in each other's immediate surroundings – people were neighbours, worked together, attended the same meetings, all the while supposing some kind of common (cultural) ground. And then the masks fell … or at least so it felt. The enemy did not come from afar, but had always lived next door ('they seemed to be such nice people').

We know that, despite the joy and pride of Independence, Partition cut deep into the soul of Indian (and Pakistani) society. How deep we still don't know, but we can safely assume that it will remain an open wound for a long time to come. With the Urdu poet Faiz we must realize that Partition brought much more sinister things than just independence and political freedom. The morning after independence appeared to him like a hangover: 'This daybreak, pockmarked – this morning, night-bitten/Surely it is not the morning we'd longed for' (Faiz 1997: 86-87).

References

Fiction

Auden, W.H. 2007. Partition. In *Collected Poems*, edited by E. Mendelson, Modern Library edition, 803. New York: Random House.

Badiuzzaman. 1997. The Last Wish. In *India Partitioned: The Other Face of Freedom*, Vol. I, edited by M. Hasan, 136-146. New Delhi: The Lotus Collection.

Chughtai, Ismat. 1997. Roots. In *India Partitioned: The Other Face of Freedom*, Vol. I, edited by M. Hasan, 279-289. New Delhi: The Lotus Collection.

Faiz, Ahmad. 1997. The Morning of Freedom. In *India Partitioned: The Other Face of Freedom*, Vol. I, edited by M. Hasan, 86-88. New Delhi: The Lotus Collection.

Manto, Saadat Hasan. 1997. Black Margins. In *India Partitioned: The Other Face of Freedom*, Vol. I, edited by M. Hasan, 88-102. New Delhi: The Lotus Collection.

Naqvi, Ali Imam. 1997. The Vultures of the Parsi Cemetry. In *India Partitioned: The Other Face of Freedom*, Vol. I, edited by M. Hasan, 290-295. New Delhi: The Lotus Collection.

Rushdie, S. 1981. *Midnight's Children*. London: Jonathan Cape.

Sahni, B. 1988. *Tamas*. New Delhi etc.: Penguin.

Sidhwa, B. 1988. *Ice-Candy-Man*. London: William Heinemann.

Singh, K. 1981. *Train to Pakistan*. New York: Grove Press.

Singh Baldwin, S. 1999. *What the Body Remembers*. London etc.: Doubleday.

Yashpal. 2010. *This is Not That Dawn*. New Delhi etc.: Penguin.

Non-fiction

Dresden, S. 1991. *Vervolging, vernietiging, literatuur*. Amsterdam: Meulenhoff.

French, P. 1997. *Liberty or Death: India's Journey to Independence and Division*. London: HarperCollins.

French, P. 2011. *India: An Intimate Biography of 1, 2 Billion People*. London: Allen Lane.

Hasan, M. ed. 1997. *India Partitioned: The Other Face of Freedom*, 2 vols. New Delhi: The Lotus Collection.

Hasan, M. ed. 2004. *The Partition Omnibus*. New Delhi etc.: Oxford India.

Hitchens, C. 2003. The Perils of Partition. *Atlantic Monthly*, 291(20), 99-107.

Hitchens, C. 2010. The Narcissism of the Small Difference. *Slate Magazine*, 28(June). Available at http://www.slate.com/articles/news_and_politics/fighting_words/2010/06/the_narcissism_of_the_small_difference.html (accessed August 2012).

Rushdie, S. 2002. *Step Across This Line: Collected Non-Fiction 1992-2002*. London: Jonathan Cape.

Sidhwa, B. ed. 2005. *City of Sin and Splendour: Writings on Lahore*. New Delhi etc.: Penguin.
Singh, G. 1997. A Diary of Partition Days. In *India Partitioned: The Other Face of Freedom*, Vol. II, edited by M. Hasan, 27-87. New Delhi: The Lotus Collection.
Singh, K. 2005. Lahore, Partition and Independence. In *City of Sin and Splendour: Writings on Lahore*, edited by B. Sidhwa, 189-205. New Delhi etc.: Penguin.
Verma, M. 2004. *Aftermath: An Oral History of Violence*. New Delhi etc.: Penguin.

Index

Advances in Criminology

Full series list

The Arts of Imprisonment:
Control, Resistance and Empowerment
Edited by Leonidas K. Cheliotis

The Hidden Order of Corruption:
An Institutional Approach
*Donatella della Porta and
Alberto Vannucci*

Comparative Criminal Justice and
Globalization
Edited by David Nelken

Racial Criminalization of Migrants
in the 21st Century
Edited by Salvatore Palidda

Pervasive Prevention:
A Feminist Reading of the Rise of
the Security Society
Tamar Pitch

Children's Rights and the Minimum
Age of Criminal Responsibility:
A Global Perspective
Don Cipriani

Hate on the Net:
Extremist Sites, Neo-fascism On-line,
Electronic Jihad
Antonio Roversi

Decisions to Imprison:
Court Decision-Making Inside
and Outside the Law
Rasmus H. Wandall

The Policing of Transnational Protest
*Edited by Donatella della Porta,
Abby Peterson and Herbert Reiter*

Migration, Culture Conflict, Crime
and Terrorism
*Edited by Joshua D. Freilich and
Rob T. Guerette*

Re-Thinking the Political Economy
of Punishment:
Perspectives on Post-Fordism
and Penal Politics
Alessandro De Giorgi

Deleuze and Environmental Damage:
Violence of the Text
Mark Halsey

Globalization and Regulatory Character:
Regulatory Reform after the Kader Toy
Factory Fire
Fiona Haines

Family Violence and Police Response:
Learning From Research, Policy and
Practice in European Countries
*Edited by Wilma Smeenk and
Marijke Malsch*

Crime and Culture:
An Historical Perspective
*Edited by Amy Gilman Srebnick and
René Lévy*

Power, Discourse and Resistance:
A Genealogy of the Strangeways Prison
Riot
Eamonn Carrabine

Hard Lessons:
Reflections on Governance and Crime
Control in Late Modernity
Edited by Richard Hil and Gordon Tait

Becoming Delinquent: British and European Youth, 1650–1950
Edited by Pamela Cox and Heather Shore

Migration, Culture Conflict and Crime
Edited by Joshua D. Freilich, Graeme Newman, S. Giora Shoham and Moshe Addad

Critique and Radical Discourses on Crime
George Pavlich

Integrating a Victim Perspective within Criminal Justice: International Debates
Edited by Adam Crawford and Jo Goodey

Blood in the Bank: Social and Legal Aspects of Death at Work
Gary Slapper

Engendering Resistance: Agency and Power in Women's Prisons
Mary Bosworth

Governable Places: Readings on Governmentality and Crime Control
Edited by Russell Smandych